Systems for Change in Literacy Education

A Guide to Professional Development

Carol A. Lyons and Gay Su Pinnell

HEINEMANN
Portsmouth, NH

Heinemann
A division of Reed Elsevier Inc.
361 Hanover Street
Portsmouth, NH 03801–3912
www.heinemann.com

Offices and agents throughout the world

The author and publisher wish to thank those who have generously given permission to reprint borrowed material:

Excerpts from "High Standards for Whom?" by D. B. Gratz from *Phi Delta Kappan* 81 (9). Copyright © 2000 by Phi Delta Kappan. Reprinted by permission.

Excerpts from "Thinking About Standards" by N. Nodding from *Phi Delta Kappan* 79 (3). Copyright © 1997 by Phi Delta Kappan. Reprinted by permission.

Library of Congress Cataloging-in-Publication Data
Lyons, Carol A.
    Systems for change in literacy education : a guide to professional development / Carol A. Lyons and Gay Su Pinnell.
        p.   cm.
    Includes bibliographical references and index.
    ISBN 0-325-00282-7
    1. English teachers—Training of. 2. Language arts teachers—
Training of. 3. Language arts (Elementary). 4. Literacy. I. Pinnell,
Gay Su. II. Title.

PE1066 .L96 2001
372.6—dc21   00-053616

Acquisitions Editor: Lois Bridges
Manuscript Editor: Alan Huisman
Production Editor: Elizabeth Valway
Interior Design: UpperCase Production & Design, Inc.
Cover Design: Robin Herr
Author photos on cover by Ed Zirkle
Cover and interior photos: Tom Dubanowich
A Day of Learning photos by Barbara Joan Wiley, Literacy
    Collaboration, Ohio State University
Manufacturing: Louise Richardson

Printed in the United States of America on acid-free paper
05 04 03 02 01 ML 2 3 4 5

To my husband Fran, for thirty-five years of
unconditional love, commitment, and support,
and my son Ken, who continues to help me better
understand and appreciate the complexities,
wonders, and joys of learning.

To Ron, for encouragement and constant support.

Contents

Acknowledgements

This book is about learning and teaching. Through the research and talk that surrounded it's writing, we have learned much. We wish to thank all the individuals who have been so important to us throughout the process.

First, we wish to thank the teachers and literacy coordinators in the Literacy Collaborative, who continue to provide dynamic demonstrations of ongoing learning and excellent teaching—of both children and adult educators. We are especially grateful to Ann Bigelow, Rosalydia Diaz, Mary McElroy, Wendy Naughton, Delia Rico, and Renee Schneiderman, who have generously shared with us their work with teachers. And we thank Angela Andreas, Barbara Arnold, Peg Becvar, Ruth Canji, Sarah Duiven, Terry Gonzales, Kathy Moore, Mary Fran Nolan, Edith Ortigoza, Kathy Riley, Ronelle Robinson, Tianna Witschy, and Natasha Witschy, who invited us into their classrooms again and again. We have learned so much from their work.

The principal, literacy coordinator, and teachers at Fairwood Elementary School were willing to open their school to provide photographic images for this book. We are especially grateful to the principal, Dr. Wilbert Jones, Lisa Chappel, Literacy Coordinator, and the following classroom teachers: Alicia C. Carpenter, Teyon Florence, Myrta Fuertes, Lee Harris, Mary P. Held, Lindsey Jensen, Holly M. Kane, Christina Lang, Cynthia Meister, Shirley Meyer, Candance Moore, Elizabeth Ralph, Amy Robinson, and Chalita A. Sadler.

We acknowledge the outstanding contributions of following members of The 1999–2000 Literacy Collaborative university and district level course: Max Brand, Lori Fanello, Suki Glasser, Robin Griffith, Kathy Harrell, Kathryn Haun, Kecia Hicks, Ann Ketch, Sandra Lowry, Anna Lyon, Sharon Piazza, Deb Rock, Patti Starnes, Joan Stone, and Norma Zermano. We are also indebted to Max Brand, Mary Fried, Paige Furgerson, Peg Gwyther, Sharon Gibson, Tina Henry, Tony Keefer, Andy Knight, Lynda Mudre, Shelly Schaub, Jean Weston, Linda Wold and Joan Wiley, who provided feedback that was most useful in refining the instruments incorporated into this text and who spent many hours analyzing data that has informed our research efforts.

For the last twelve years, we have had the privilege of working with colleagues at Ohio State and other universities who have helped us clarify our thinking about the nature of teaching. From them, we have also learned the complexity and the challenge that we must meet if we are to educate teachers effectively. We especially thank Diane E. DeFord who has been our partner in many ventures over the years. We also express appreciation to Mary Fried, Peg Gwyther, Justina Henry, Andrea McCarrier, Linda Mudre, Pat Scharer and Joan Wiley, wonderful colleagues that we enjoy daily.

We thank Sharon Freeman for providing so much help in so many ways throughout the process of writing this book. We are most appreciative to Becky Kitchen and Polly Taylor for assisting in all phases of the final preparation of the manuscript as well as in communication that was so necessary for preparing this book.

The research reported in this book would not have been possible without the rewarding and most appreciated partnership we have enjoyed over the years with Anthony Bryk and the Center for School Improvement at the University of Chicago. We thank Sharon Greenberg, David Kerbow, Carmen Manning, Virginia Watson, and Linda Wold for their commitment to improving education, their vision, and their impeccable work.

The exciting and visionary work of Ken Wilson has guided our thinking as we worked to conceptualize the problems and design of school change. We also express appreciation to Constance Barsky as well as to George Smith for informative and creative conversations about important ideas.

Our publisher, Heinemann, has provided the support of exceedingly skilled and visionary editorial staff. We thank our editor, Lois Bridges, for her always-exceptional work. Her advice and counsel in organizing the text and clarifying her vision has been invaluable. We also express appreciation to Alan Huisman for his attention to detail and editorial skills, and we thank our Production editor, Elizabeth Valway for her attention to detail and artistic quality. We thank Michael Cirone for his guidance in the process of production and we also express appreciation to Lisa Fowler for her suggestions, both practical and creative. As always, we are grateful for the leadership of Leigh Peake and Mike Gibbons.

We also wish to express appreciation to scholars and researchers who have helped us think more deeply about our work as well as helped us to think in new ways about teaching and learning. Our thinking about children and teachers' learning has been profoundly influenced by Marie Clay, both for her dynamic theory of literacy learning and for the brilliant design of the Reading Recovery program, from which we have learned so much about professional development.

Other scholars who have given us many gifts of learning are Martha L. King, who challenges our thinking constantly and Charlotte Huck, who keeps us centered on generating a love of reading in students. We thank Moira McKenzie for her work in shared writing, which underlies the interactive writing lessons that we describe in this book.

In addition to the researchers in literacy, from whom we have learned so much, we have also learned from our extensive reading of the literature in teacher education. We thank all of the scholars whose work is referenced here.

We express appreciation to Billie Askew and Trika Smith-Burke, for the many conversations about learning and learning to teach that we have enjoyed and learned from over the years. They have stretched our thinking.

We are grateful to Irene Fountas for reading this book and providing valuable feedback as well as for all we have learned from her over the years. Her collegiality has provided an environment for discussing ideas and she has moved our thinking forward.

As always, we express our love and appreciation to our families and thank them for their support and diverse perspectives, especially Fran and Ken Lyons, Elizabeth Mueller, and Elfrieda Pinnell.

Finally, we salute those teachers who continue, in the face of public criticism and sometimes arbitrary and oppressive directives toward prescriptive approaches to education, to reflect deeply, learn more, make careful and informed decisions about all of their instruction, and advocate for the rights of their students to enjoy competent, joyful literacy. Thank you for learning so that your students can become lifelong readers and writers.

Carol A. Lyons
Gay Su Pinnell

Introduction

Teacher education in the United States becomes ever more important as we continue to recognize and acknowledge the particular and challenging skills teaching requires. Our students deserve the very best literacy instruction: whatever challenges they will meet in their future, literacy will be an essential tool. Our teachers must be skilled enough to turn *all* children into competent readers and writers.

Instruction that makes a difference is delivered through thousands of moment-to-moment decisions. You do not learn to be a good teacher of reading and writing in a few months, in a year, or even over a period of several years. Teaching skills develop over a lifetime and are connected to many kinds of learning—what reading and writing entail and how these processes develop, how to adjust instruction to particular students, how to use a range of effective pedagogical approaches and techniques.

The literature of education is filled with information on learning to teach, but there are few programs designed specifically for those who teach literacy teachers. Common practice has simply been to select a good teacher and give him or her the title of staff developer. For the last two decades we have had the opportunity to teach teachers as well as children. We have undertaken the complex task of preparing people to teach, support, and coach teachers of literacy. Our work with teachers, children, and staff developers in three contexts—Reading Recovery, the Literacy Collaborative, and a two-year research project in Chicago—has helped us identify concepts and skills related to teachers' learning.

This book is based on what we have learned. It is directed specifically to teacher educators—the teachers of teachers—among whose ranks are experienced teachers helping the new teacher in the room next door, university professors standing in front of their undergraduate or graduate classes, groups of teachers working in tandem with their counterparts at other schools, and full- or part-time staff developers.

In the chapters that follow, we refer to the teachers of teachers in various ways (as teacher educators, teacher leaders, literacy coordinators, consultants, staff developers, professional developers) and in various contexts (schools, districts, universities) because we recognize the variety of ways the role can be approached and intend the book to serve a range of needs.

You can use the ideas in this book to provide both short-term and long-term support, but we particularly value long-term systemic efforts. To be most effective, professional development must be broad-based, an ongoing system with interrelated components, including demonstrations, discussion, and in-class coaching. Also, lasting change in literacy education can occur only if professional development is situated within a good *design* for change, one that takes into account political and social factors as well as the barriers that must be overcome. This book contains the theories and examples you need to bring about positive, long-lasting change in K–6 literacy programs.

Section 1 lays the foundation of the book, sharing ideas about how we can overhaul our approach to professional development. Chapter 1 discusses what staff developers need to understand about literacy and adult learning in order to offer teachers of literacy a reflective, inquiry-oriented program of professional development. It also touches on the important ways in which individuals join together to form learning communities. Chapter 2 presents an integrated comprehensive literacy framework for professional development, one that focuses on integrated learning rather than a series of separate activities focused on unrelated topics. Chapters 3 and 4 detail the critical processes in literacy learning and teaching in the context of a broad-based literacy framework.

Section 2 is a practical guide for professional development based on the "learning spiral." Chapter 5 introduces professional development as an integrated, coordinated system. Chapter 6 provides specific directions and guidelines for planning an effective professional development program over time. Chapter 7 describes how to assess the classroom and the school and gather vital information about the teachers. Chapter 8 offers some practical ways to introduce new approaches to teachers and help them try out new ideas.

Section 3 focuses on specific examples of supportive coaching within the instructional contexts that make up the literacy framework. Coaching is based on analysis; one of the difficult tasks of the literacy coach is to analyze lessons quickly and determine precise actions that will help the teacher move forward in his or her learning. Chapter 9 takes a general look at important things that must be in place (organization, efficient use of time, rapport with students) for literacy to be taught successfully. Chapter 10 shows how to analyze writing, reading, and word study lessons using specially designed scales. Chapter 11 focuses on how to bring about a shift in teaching behavior. It includes a number of coaching examples and calls attention to some helpful language. Chapter 12 discusses how to help teachers become more analytic and independent.

Section 4 shows how to extend professional development and places it within a social and political context. Chapter 13 suggests ways to support learning over time through study groups, action research, peer coaching, and other initiatives. Chapter 14 highlights a very important staff development challenge: the best way to bring about lasting change is to design professional development with change in mind. Chapter 15 discusses the concept of this design for change in detail—the benefits of a design, prerequisites for a good design, steps in the design process. Included are classroom and whole-school examples. Chapter 16 returns to the concept of the spiral of learning, reemphasizing the many ways there are to approach professional development. A summary of a year of learning underlines our conviction that teaching is a lifetime of learning.

Carol A. Lyons
Gay Su Pinnell

Developing Teachers' Conceptual Knowledge and Skills

S ection 1 is the foundation of this book, providing specific information about classroom and adult learning. The staff developer must be expert not only in how children learn but also in how adults learn.

Chapter 1 discusses the basic concepts of adult learning, an important one being that all effective learning takes place within a supportive community. Staff developers must create communities of learning within which teachers can try out new ideas in a risk-free environment and experience the support of their colleagues.

Chapter 2 lays out a framework for the effective professional development of literacy educators. This framework is structured around the dynamic process that occurs whenever teachers take on new learning. It offers staff developers a way to think about their work, from gathering important information about teachers' current understanding and the contexts within which they work to establishing a culture of analysis and reflection about teaching and learning.

Chapters 3 and 4 provide important background information about learning and teaching literacy. In Chapter 3 we examine the processes of learning to read and write. It is essential that staff developers of literacy teachers understand these processes and are able to identify evidence that students are moving toward their goal. Chapter 4 discusses the teaching of literacy, identifying a range of interrelated instructional approaches that make up a balanced literacy program and that figure prominently in later chapters.

Understanding and Supporting Adult Learning

It is becoming clear that schools can be re-created, made vital, and sustainably renewed not by fiat or command, and not by regulation, but by taking a learning orientation.
—*Peter Senge* The Fifth Discipline *(5)*

Today the cry for school reform is very definitely being heard in the land. It finds its way into speeches delivered by congressmen, educators, presidents and CEOs of corporations, and community leaders. Parents, teachers, politicians, religious leaders, businesspeople, all have suggestions for improving education in the United States. The ideas may be different, but the goal is the same—to provide educational experiences that will allow every child in America to become a successful learner.

Responsibility, of course, is always placed squarely on the teacher. The phrase "hold teachers accountable" appears frequently in newspapers, popular magazines, and educational journals. And one particular area is deemed critical in creating a competitive and productive citizenry: every child must learn to read and write, a tall order given the diversity of our nation's students and the complexities of the communities they live in and the schools they attend.

Our primary hope lies in the professional development of literacy teachers. There must be a strong commitment to provide initial and ongoing high-quality professional development for all members of the schoolwide literacy team, although it need not be the same for each member—teachers will need more intensive training in specific instructional approaches than the school psychologist or a parent, for example. Nevertheless, the support staff and parents should be helped to understand what the classroom teacher is doing and why. At all levels of professional development, participants should be given the opportunity to examine and discuss classroom data and reflect on the issues and concerns the data reveal. In doing so, they develop a shared understanding that underpins the school-wide literacy program.

Your responsibility as a staff developer is to help teachers improve their practice so that students learn. The educational goals you select, what you teach, the way you organize and present the material, and how you manage and interact with the group stem directly from your ideas about teaching and learning. The staff developer who directs and controls the context and lectures to teachers while they take notes is operating under different beliefs from those of a staff developer who collaborates with the group in selecting the topic and setting goals.

Experts in professional development (Joyce and Showers 1995; Lambert et al. 1995) identify three major skills that effective staff developers exhibit:

◆ They draw on teachers' knowledge and validate teachers' past experience.
◆ They manage the group effectively.
◆ They systematically observe group dynamics and determine individual strengths, limitations, and needs.

Developing these skills is fundamental to organizing and implementing an effective professional development program, and they cannot be acquired unless you know and understand theories related to adult learning.

Adults as Learners

Adult learners share the same essential characteristics exhibited by younger learners. Every individual, at any age, always has the potential to learn. Adults, like children, bring their knowledge, beliefs, perceptions, and assumptions to new experiences and construct new knowledge or refine previous understanding to gain meaning. But in order to gain this meaning, learners of all ages must be motivated to learn and must actively engage in the process.

Learning also requires ownership (*wanting* to learn the information), self-regulation, problem solving, and reflection. Problems are not someone else's to fix or solve. They are an obstacle *you* must overcome to achieve a goal. Learning something difficult is satisfying, much more gratifying than repeating an answer or doing what you are told without questioning. Learning something difficult builds self-confidence and motivates you to seek additional learning challenges. In order to motivate teachers to continue to learn, staff developers must help them solve their own problems.

Some characteristics of adult learners distinguish them from young learners (Friend and Cook 2000):

1. Adults bring with them a vast amount of prior knowledge, wide-ranging experience, and a great number of skills.
2. Along with this wealth of information and experience and these well-developed and practiced skills, adults have acquired ideas, beliefs, values, and passions about learning, developed after years of success and perhaps failure during the years they have spent in schools.
3. Adults are goal oriented. They generally have a set of goals and/or issues they are facing at a particular time, and they want to resolve these problems or issues *now*.
4. Adults are more likely to be flexible learners, because they have had to adapt to many different learning contexts, teaching approaches, and teacher personalities.
5. Adults have high expectations. Teachers know what they want from professional development sessions and expect to get it. They have worked with many different kinds of children and families and have developed a sense of good or poor learning contexts.
6. Adults have many commitments and many demands on their time.
7. Adults are generally motivated to learn. Teachers are accountable for their students' learning and are motivated to try new teaching approaches and techniques that will improve their practice.

These seven fundamental characteristics of adult learners should serve as a foundation for any professional development you provide.

Principles of Constructivist–Based Teaching

The constructivist theory of education (see Steffe and Gale 1995) holds that our past experiences and beliefs influence how we interact with others, learn new ideas, and discard or refine old ones. Our personal perspectives are shaped and changed as we engage in cooperative social activity, conversation, and debate with others around common purposes, concerns, and interests. In the process, we build new knowledge and extend our understanding. Constructivism has been generally accepted as the best approach for working with adults and has emerged as an important educational paradigm for professional development (Garmston and Wellman 1999; Joyce and Showers 1995; Lambert et al. 1995; Lyons, Pinnell, and DeFord 1993).

In order to be effective, staff developers and teachers must acquire deep conceptual understanding about the reading and writing processes, about how students and adults learn, and about how to create opportunities for them to learn effectively. The constructivist theory of learning suggests a set of principles for organizing and implementing a professional development course (see Figure 1–1).

Principle 1: *Encourage active participation*

Learning is an active not a passive process: participants must take part in a shared experience that becomes a catalyst for thinking and conversation. Live or videotaped demonstrations, samples of children's work, children's literature, transcripts of lessons, and/or other artifacts will interest participants and prompt them to communicate with one another. Lectures are deadly and lead learners to become passive. Of course, information must often be presented—learners expect to be informed; but you also engage participants in small-group discussions to find out what they already know about the topic and encourage them to formulate their own questions. Then when you offer a rationale for a new technique or instructional procedure, what you say will be relevant to their questions or concerns.

Constructivist Principles of Teaching

1. Encourage active participation.

2. Organize small-group discussions around common concerns.

3. Introduce new concepts in context.

4. Create a safe environment.

5. Develop teachers' conceptual knowledge through conversation around shared experiences.

6. Provide opportunities for teachers to use what they know to construct new knowledge.

7. Look for shifts in teachers' understanding over time.

8. Provide additional experiences for teachers who have not yet developed needed conceptual understanding.

Figure 1–1. *Principles of Teaching: A Constructivist Perspective*

Principle 2: *Organize small-group discussions around common concerns*

Learning is a social process and more likely to occur when people with a common concern share ideas, give advice, inquire, and solve problems together. One of the best questions you can ask a group of teachers is, *What is your most pressing need right now and how have others attempted to resolve the problem?*

Principle 3: *Introduce new concepts in context*

Introduce a new procedure or way of teaching with a live or videotaped demonstration of the technique being used in a classroom. Then let participants discuss the approach and the impact it had on student learning.

Principle 4: *Create a safe environment*

Adults, like children, want to feel safe and need to be confident that when they attempt something new, they will be supported. Encourage teachers to try out a new procedure in their classroom and share what happened with a small group of colleagues (teaching the same grade level or working with developmentally similar students—poor, average, or excellent readers, for example) who have tried the same procedure. Each member of the group will have had a different experience and must be encouraged to tell her or his story. Have a number of groups synthesize what they learned. Then generate a plan of action for trying the new procedure again, this time with a clearer and deeper understanding of what to expect.

Principle 5: *Develop participants' conceptual knowledge through conversation around shared experiences*

Learners must have many opportunities to make sense of new or expanded information and construct meaning for themselves in order to develop conceptual knowledge that generates further understanding. Conceptual knowledge is developed through conversation about a shared experience. Listening to others' experiences, thereby developing independent and collective rationales for and ideas about the impact of a specific technique on student learning, shifts the whole group's understanding. Providing rationales and evidence grounded in student work and behavior stimulates further questioning.

Principle 6: *Provide opportunities for participants to use what they know to construct new knowledge*

Do not assume every teacher is going to come to the same understanding. Provide time for small groups of teachers to use what they know to interpret the new information they've heard from you and/or other group members. Ask questions that prompt teachers to connect what they know and believe to their practice. Make sure these conversations are specific to student work or observations of student behavior. Talking in the abstract does not facilitate clear communication. Teachers will draw on the examples to express what they know and reshape this knowledge in new and meaningful ways.

Principle 7: *Look for shifts in teachers' understanding over time*

Conceptual understanding is acquired during a series of temporary developmental stages. Look for evidence that teachers have reorganized, refined, or revised their thinking about a procedure, process, or concept as they have worked with students or colleagues. Most teachers continually acquire new knowledge and/or conceptual understanding. Acknowledge these shifts in understanding.

Principle 8: *Provide additional experiences for participants who have not yet developed the needed conceptual understanding*

People must construct their own understanding; you cannot do it for them. Teachers are much more likely to develop conceptual understanding if they:

◆ Observe a clear demonstration by an expert teacher of specific instructional approaches of interest to them.
◆ Discuss the demonstration and reasons for actions and decisions with the expert teacher.
◆ Ask questions about the observation.
◆ Try procedures learned from the expert teacher several times, videotaping the sessions.
◆ Analyze the videotaped sessions privately and determine strengths and weaknesses.
◆ Select one of the videotapes to share and discuss with the expert teacher.

Teachers examine records to learn more about their students' needs.

◆ Decide what they will do differently the next time they teach.

Creating a Community of Learners

As under siege as our educational system is, there are schools in impoverished urban, rural, and suburban neighborhoods in which disadvantaged students, some of them considered learning disabled, are learning to read and write. Why? Because every administrator, classroom teacher, and specialist assumes responsibility for the literacy achievement of every student in the building and is committed to that goal. Together, they have created a community of learners (to include parents) with a common vision for the education of all students. They have created a common understanding about how students become literate and become more proficient readers and writers as they progress through the grades. They also take responsibility for tackling unforeseen problems and finding mutually agreed-on resolutions. A sense of community and spirit engenders a "together we can do it" attitude. Indeed, Allington and Cunningham (1996) argue that without *collaborative* mechanisms for providing high-quality instruction to all students and ongoing professional development for teachers, any schoolwide literacy program will fail.

Successful collaborative efforts are not the result of a top-down administrative directive to adopt a schoolwide comprehensive literacy program or buy a commercial literacy program with prescribed materials designed for the masses. Successful collaboration means every classroom and specialist teacher, every administrator, every member of the support staff, every parent are working together to create a shared vision, mission, and purpose, as well as collaborative ways to accomplish their goals. Although individual talent, energy, resolve, and commitment are important, no one person can initiate and sustain schoolwide literacy reform. The cumulative effort of many individuals sharing ideas, concerns, and skills for improving schoolwide literacy achievement makes the difference.

Creating a successful community of learners is not easy. In the final analysis, who members of the team are and how they interact with one another can make or break a schoolwide team. To be successful, colleagues must feel comfortable discussing and/or demonstrating what they know and what they do not know—a big risk for many adults. Where collegiality among members of the group is strong, communities of learners and practice grow. Where it is weak, the community falters and retreats to its former top-down authoritarian decision making and practices. When this happens everyone—teachers, parents, students—loses.

A critical factor distinguishing more effective literacy initiatives from less effective ones is the commitment of administrators and teachers to implementing them. School-based teams must manage and monitor the program. Using standardized assessments and classroom data collected throughout the year, the team monitors every student's work and decides how to help the students who are not making expected progress.

Characteristics of Collaborative Learning

Some time during your professional career, an administrator or a principal has probably asked you to serve

Colleagues share ideas about how their guided reading lessons are going.

on a committee charged with completing a specific task in a limited time (choosing basal textbooks or developing literacy curriculum guides, for example). Generally, the large group is broken up into subgroups (according to grade level, interest, or content) that work on specific parts of the task. Everyone works very hard, but often not wisely, especially if there is little collaboration among the subgroups. The result can be a fragmented report, with each subcommittee offering different objectives, goals, and advice.

Creating a culture for collaboration that supports teacher learning is vital to the health and life of the school. Anyone who has ever taught will attest to the enormity, difficulty, and complexity of the job whatever the grade level. In order to be successful, teachers need to know how to use their knowledge and experience to inform their practice, they need to receive support and encouragement for their efforts, and they need to participate in ongoing professional development to improve, refine, and expand their skills. Most important, they need to know how to work with others as equals and colleagues.

Collaboration enables group members to use idiosyncratic expertise and skills to focus on a common issue, exchanging ideas and talking through differences of opinion constructively. In a collaborative network of learners diversity is viewed as a necessary resource (Garmston and Wellman 1999; Lambert et al. 1995). Certain characteristics are critical for schoolwide literacy teams to work effectively:

1. *Trust.* An atmosphere of trust is essential to the creation and ongoing development of effective and meaningful collaborative work relationships. Rapport with one another breeds a trust in the collaborative process as the most productive and efficient way to communicate. Trust that individual members won't let the group down builds collegiality and enables individuals to work together constructively.

2. *Diverse leadership.* Effective schoolwide teams believe every member of the team has valuable insights, knowledge, and experience to contribute to the group effort and can be a responsible committed leader. Principals must acknowledge the collective knowledge and experience of group members and con-

vey an attitude that building a community of diverse leaders is the most efficient and effective way to solve diverse problems. In an atmosphere like this, an individual's leadership tendencies are more likely to emerge. The principal becomes a contributing member of the group, not the leader.

3. *Partnerships with parents.* It is well documented that when parents/caregivers are actively involved in and informed about their children's learning, children and teachers are more successful. In effective schools, parents are not just informed about their child's learning but equal partners in the education of their children. School teams develop a culture that encourages parents to identify problems and possible solutions.

4. *Shared responsibility and credit for success.* While it is important to the development of a collaborative community of leaders that everyone shares responsibility for discussing and resolving issues, it is equally important that all members of the group receive credit for success. Visible schoolwide success replenishes the individual personally and professionally.

5. *Time to engage in the collaborative process.* One of the main reasons groups have difficulty forging common understanding and agreement is lack of time. It takes time, especially at the beginning of the collaborative process, to establish trust and rapport with one another. It takes time for teachers to reflect on and discuss their own experiences, listen to experiences of others, find effective ways to work together, and establish common goals. Unless time is dedicated, the collaborative process is doomed.

6. *A language for communication.* In effective collaborative schoolwide groups, administrators, primary and middle grade teachers, resource teachers, support staff, and parents develop a language for talking about their work. Values and beliefs about learning and teaching, collegiality, and interrelationships are all shaped by personal reflection and interaction. Engaging in reflective conversations helps build shared understanding and also helps individuals clarify personal thinking.

7. *Respect for diversity.* Effective collaborative teams respect the diversity of their members—classroom teachers, specialists, parents, administrators, and students—because the group learns more and better when diverse viewpoints are acknowledged and valued. Effective teams look for and attend to different viewpoints, seek opportunities to explore alternative ways of addressing a situation. Passionate differences of opinion are remarkably effective in resolving issues. Respect for diversity builds a culture of inquiry.

8. *A focus on student data.* Effective collaborative teams evaluate their educational programs by continually collecting and analyzing student data. Without these data there is a tendency to maximize or minimize the impact of the literacy program on student learning. Focusing on student outcomes prevents the group from pointing the finger at individual teachers.

9. *Problem-solving skills.* The first step in collaborative problem solving is to identify the problem and use student data to illustrate and frame it. The idea is that every problem has a resolution. Collective knowledge and experience are much more practical and effective than individuals working in isolation.

10. *A vision of what is possible.* Teachers who are part of effective collaborative literacy teams construct a vision of what is possible and make a solid plan for realizing it. In a team approach to solving literacy problems, there is continuing tension between the realities of current practice and the ideals of the desired outcome. This tension becomes particularly acute when students are not making adequate progress. Teachers who accept the status quo will merely reproduce last year's solutions to the problems.

Getting Started

Here are some specific suggestions to help you design a professional development program.

Establish Team Membership Be flexible here. If the team becomes too large, decision making will become less efficient. Attendance at particular meetings will depend on the purpose or problem being addressed. For example, a middle grade teacher probably won't attend a meeting to discuss instructional techniques specific to kindergarten, but any teacher with experience working with deaf students can contribute to meetings centering on those techniques.

Group members' sense of ownership is vital to the success and effectiveness of the schoolwide collaborative team. To initiate the process, invite the entire school community—administrators, faculty members, support staff, and parents—to attend a three-day awareness meeting just before the school year begins.

Establish an Overall Plan of Operation Shared understanding, ownership, and responsibility for student learning are critical to the success of the schoolwide literacy team. Establish these principles at the start, and use them to guide the collaborative process throughout the year. At the initial three-day meeting, share and discuss student reading and writing data at all grade levels. With representatives from each grade level as facilitators, examine student work and developmental milestones in each grade and discuss the curriculum and impact of learning as students progress through the grades.

Encourage Cohesiveness Any collaboration requires that team members have enough trust in and respect for one another to be willing to engage in the process. If participants have successful experiences early on, trust will grow. Conversely, if a colleague shares confidential information, fails to contribute to the work of the group, or dominates a discussion by putting forth what he insists are the right answers, trust is likely to be damaged. Cohesive schoolwide groups stick together.

To build a cohesive team all faculty, administrators, and staff need to develop shared goals, identify and set priorities, clarify who will complete what tasks when, ask for and use colleague feedback, and be very careful not to exhibit either a defensive or a know-it-all attitude.

Monitor Student Outcomes If a school team approach is to be effective, students' ongoing progress must be monitored through the grades. Using existing data collected via standardized and other assessments (e.g., running records, writing samples), monitor student growth over time. Compile and share portfolios of student work at each grade level so team members can see what teachers expect every child to learn about reading and writing and how students acquire this knowledge and skill as they progress. Then address the needs of students who may be falling between the cracks.

Build a Network of Support Outside the School Working within the school to build a culture for learning is important, but it is also necessary to develop support from community and business leaders. Becoming isolated, unaware of the bigger picture, will impede progress. The business community has a high stake in supporting the work of the schools: every businessman wants students to become capable members of the workforce. It is important to keep groups outside your school informed about what you are doing and how it is affecting student achievement. Schools, like teachers, must learn to reach beyond their borders to share their successes, find solutions to their problems, create support for their work, and find resources to help with future endeavors.

Teachers examine and discuss text difficulty and matching books to students' needs.

Benefits of Creating a Community of Learners

Developing a common vision and a commitment to shared goals and responsibilities is essential to developing confidence among a community of learners. The benefits to group members working in such a community and to the students they serve are huge:

1. *Every student in the school becomes a reader and a writer.* When individuals work together for a common cause and take collective responsibility for every student in the school, their work becomes a joint enterprise. In schools where this sense of collective responsibility among group members is strong, students make larger gains in mathematics, reading, science, and history than in schools where the teachers feel responsible only for the students in the classes they teach. (These outcomes appear to be especially true for minority students and students from low socioeconomic backgrounds; see Garmston and Wellman 1999.)

2. *Every teacher becomes more effective, efficient, and expert.* A school team approach to education provides classroom and specialist teachers opportunities to assume leadership roles in curriculum and instruction and to think about individual and collective strategies for working more efficiently and effectively with students. Providing mechanisms and time for members of the school-based team to work together has direct and important consequences for student learning.

3. *Faculty, administrators, and parents learn how to function in professional learning communities that work.* Conversations between colleagues in a learning community help build the professional culture so vital to academic success for all students. They encourage the sharing of roles and responsibilities, collaborative problem solving, and negotiation of purpose and task. Effective professional learning communities enable classroom teachers, support teachers, administrators, and parents to live and work in a less stressful environment.

Suggestions for Expanding Your Skills as a Staff Developer

1. Examine your own beliefs about the learning process:
   - What impact do these beliefs have on your thinking about professional development and your work with teachers?
   - How do you view your role in a professional development session?
   - Does your view of learning influence how you organize, manage, and implement professional development?

2. Observe a group of teachers attending a staff development program provided by someone else. What are the basic assumptions behind the design of the program? (Keep in mind that you cannot assume the internal belief systems of individuals. The staff developer may be influenced by time and resource constraints.)

3. Interview several teachers and ask them how they learn best: by reading and studying alone? by reading and discussing materials with others? by experimenting with teaching practices and discussing the results? etc.

4. Interview several teachers and ask them to describe an inservice session that they believe taught them many new things. How was this inservice organized and implemented? What role did the staff developer play? How was the information presented.

5. Select a videotaped lesson, a demonstration lesson, or student work to use as a shared experience while working with a small group of teachers. Ask them to describe what they notice. Characterize their responses as focused on either student behavior or teacher behavior. Discuss the relationship between and among the student and teacher interactions.

6. Interview several teachers about their views of working collaboratively with others. Discuss:
   - The impact of the experience on their personal and professional growth.
   - Positive outcomes of the collaborative process.
   - What they learned.
   - Why they would or would not become involved in a collaborative team again.

7. Observe a collaborative school-based team meeting. Look for examples of the ten factors related to effective collaborative efforts discussed in this chapter.

8. Select one member of the observed team that you perceived as a leader. Discuss how he or she appears to view this role and its responsibilities within the group.

9. Select one member of the collaborative team who did not seem to be an active participant. Ask him or her about his or her role within and responsibility to the team.

10. Ask each individual selected above (leader and passive participant) how he or she would like to see the schoolwide team organized and managed.

Chapter 2

A Framework for the Professional Development of Literacy Educators

Teacher education still has the honour of being simultaneously the worst problem and the best solution in education.
—MICHAEL FULLAN CHANGE FORCES *(105)*

As a teacher educator, you analyze teachers' current learning and knowledge, assess what else they need to learn, and provide professional training and support that improves their teaching. Ideally, this support is provided in such a way that teachers become more independent in their learning, able to use new procedures, sample student behavior as evidence of learning, and refine their techniques accordingly. New teachers (or teachers new to particular approaches) need assistance at every step of the learning process.

The Learning Spiral

Providing professional development for teachers requires different processes at different times. Teachers' knowledge varies; they have different backgrounds and experience; the schools they teach in are different. The same presentations or classes will not be right for all. Of course, it is nearly impossible to meet every individual need completely, but just like all learners, teachers have the right to learn every time they participate in a professional development session or a staff developer coaches them in their classroom.

Varied learning experiences allow teachers to connect procedures, theories, and observations with their own practical problems in the classroom. Therefore, you need to design experiences of various kinds—some class sessions, some individual interactions—always thinking about what teachers know and need to know.

Ten basic processes related to teacher learning roughly define a sequence, or "spiral," of learning (see Figure 2–1); they are recursive in that we use them again and again to teach different approaches to instruction. These processes can be used both in professional development sessions and in teachers' classrooms, although some are more specific to coaching in classrooms.

How the Learning Spiral Works

Key initial steps in teacher learning are providing clear demonstrations of new procedures while at the same time offering the rationales. Then, teachers try out the new procedures as you help them organize materials and implement the necessary routines. As teachers implement the approach, at first tentatively, they ground the procedures in observations of student behavior.

You also help teachers analyze and reflect on teaching in order to become more sensitive to children's behavior as evidence of learning. Procedures are refined as teachers gain a deeper understanding of the interplay between teaching decisions and student learning. Finally, observation, theory, and procedures are integrated into

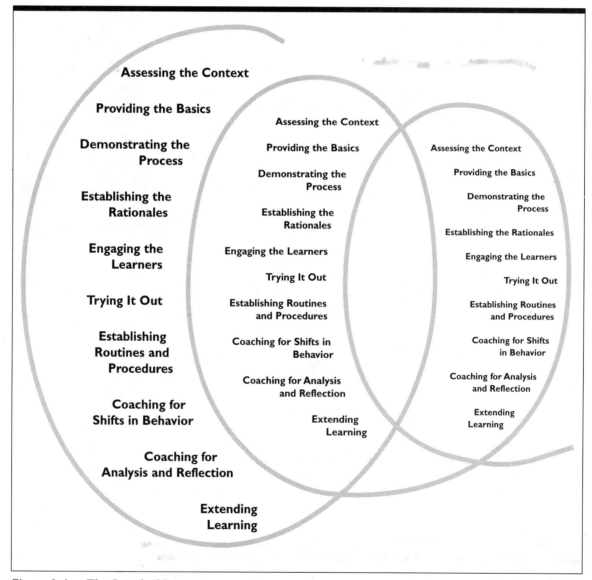

Figure 2–1. *The Spiral of Learning*

excellent teaching that seems effortless, automatic, even "intuitive," but it is learned.

Rationales are an important component of teacher learning, no matter what the content. Teachers want something practical and immediately useful—something we might even call directive or prescriptive. This need must be satisfied, but not without offering and discussing good rationales for why the procedure might be helpful to children. So rationales—the reasons why—are provided early, but only after teachers have engaged in the process with support and assistance can they deeply understand the underlying theory.

Another key concept is grounding procedures in observation. Observing students brings a teaching approach to life. Sharpened, systematic observational skills allow teachers to test their decisions and reflect on them. For example, matching books to readers is a key skill in teaching guided reading. Teachers refine their choices when they prepare the book introductions. Then, using running records as well as what they observe "on the run," teachers are able to test their "matches" several times a day, determining that the text is neither too easy nor too hard and that the students are processing it productively. Observational skills, which can be directly taught and then supported in professional development sessions, open a window of understanding that helps teachers keep on learning.

Finally, the process "comes together" as teachers coordinate their own accumulated and organized understanding into a theoretical framework. At this level, teachers act and interact without conscious attention to routines and procedures, giving full attention to student responses. Conversations flow naturally but are powerful in supporting learning. Teachers can still profit from examples brought to their attention, and they can offer reflections and rationales when asked. But most of the time they make appropriate moment-to-moment decisions without having to think about it.

Using the Spiral of Learning

Analyzing teachers' strengths and knowledge in the context of the spiral of learning lets you find the right approach to help teachers learn. It guides your presentation of a new technique from introducing and demonstrating it (which means finding out what teachers already can do and are thinking) to coaching and extending learning.

This learning spiral is repeated each time you present a new procedure, introduce new materials, or teach a new technique. Over time, as the teachers you work with develop professional expertise, the process becomes much more efficient and is accomplished more quickly. For example, a teacher who has excellent organizational and management skills will apply these skills when any approach is undertaken. On the other hand, new contexts may disrupt the process and require more support. For example, if teachers are teaching a new grade level or using new texts, they will move through the learning spiral more slowly and deliberately.

Using a Framework

In this book, we conceptualize professional development around a framework for planning, problem solving, and coaching based on the processes in the learning spiral. This framework (see Figure 2–2) recognizes the need for specific, explicit examples of and guidance in managing the practical routines of teaching. For every new procedure or approach teachers learn, they proceed from specific how-to-do-it direction to the kind of sophisticated analysis and reflection required to perform the procedure or approach powerfully and efficiently.

Assessing the Context

Assessing context is not something you do once and then forget about. Instead, you examine school classrooms and teachers' understanding again and again, throughout every step of the planning, problem-solving, and coaching framework. Contextual variables influence your decisions as you plan and implement effective training. The goal of assessing the context is to find out what teachers already know and what they are doing that is effective and ineffective. Another goal is to observe teacher-student talk—how is purposeful conversation initiated, sustained, and integrated into daily routines and literacy events? A third goal is to gather information on student achievement. Contextual variables center around three areas: the students, teacher knowledge and skills, and school culture.

A Framework for Professional Development in Literacy Education

Components	Process	Goal
1. Assess the Context	Observe teaching and learning in the school. Identify student factors. Learn about community. Identify teacher factors. Learn to know people in the school.	◆ To find out what teachers already know and what they want to know. ◆ To discover what teachers are doing that is effective and ineffective. ◆ To gather student achievement data. ◆ To gather information about the school context.
2. Provide the Basics	Provide limited number of materials for first trials of processes. Provide concrete examples of organization and routines. Walk through routines.	◆ To equip teachers with the basic materials they will need to try the new approach. ◆ To help them learn how to organize and use materials.
3. Demonstrate the Process	Demonstrate the procedures explicitly. Provide good examples from experts.	◆ To provide clear, explicit examples of the approach or procedure to be learned.
4. Establish the Rationales	Make rationales visible in writing and in talk. Engage participants in stating rationales.	◆ To help teachers understand why the approach or technique is important to learn. ◆ To bring student learning to a place of high attention.
5. Engage the Learners	Show and discuss examples. Link observation of student behavior to procedures.	◆ To engage teachers in active learning and exploration. ◆ To help them visualize the approach in action. ◆ To help them imagine performing the techniques themselves. ◆ To help them begin to analyze student behavior and teacher behavior.
6. Try It Out	Encourage teachers to try the new techniques for themselves. Share the experience and results. Analyze the process for efficiency and good management. Analyze the process for evidence of learning—what was powerful? Why?	◆ To enable teachers to use specific instructional approaches. ◆ To encourage "risk-free" approximations as a way of getting started. ◆ To work toward automatic use of routines by teachers and children.
7. Establish Routines and Procedures	Provide concrete suggestions for changes in teacher behavior and/or organization and use of time. Establish plan of action. Support refining of procedures.	◆ To provide specific guidance for establishing good, efficient routines. ◆ To practice the teaching behavior related to the approach. ◆ To refine and polish the sets of actions that make up the approach.
8. Coach for Shifts in Behavior	Observe the process in the classroom. Analyze and discuss examples from the teacher's own teaching. Connect teacher behavior and student behavior. Discuss changes for greater student learning and/or better management.	◆ To provide opportunities for teachers to become sensitive to the impact of their instruction on student behavior. ◆ To help them analyze their own teaching. ◆ To provide specific suggestions for changes in behavior that will make the approach more effective.
9. Coach for Analysis and Reflection	Coach to support reflection. Coach to widen the repertoire of teaching actions. Coach to promote analysis. Act as a co-investigator.	◆ To help teachers engage in analysis and reflection on their own. ◆ To support them in the continual refining of their teaching.
10. Extend Learning	Lead group conversations about theoretical ideas in connection with observations of children's behavior. Use teachers' classrooms as laboratories. Bring teachers together as co-investigators. Bring teachers together so they help one another learn. Provide give-and-take coaching, according to teachers' specific circumstances and needs.	◆ To help teachers form tentative theories that they then test against the behavior of their own children. ◆ To help them examine examples from their own classroom or from their peers' classrooms and to build theory from their observations. ◆ To help them apply theoretical constructs in their classroom work. ◆ To help them formulate their own goals for extending their understanding. ◆ To encourage self-coaching through assisted reflection. ◆ To support a variety of independent learning experiences for teachers.

Figure 2–2. *A Framework for Professional Development in Literacy Education*

Date Driven

Students Records of student achievement include records of reading behavior and writing samples as well as assessments administered at the beginning of the year. Endemic to the act of coaching is observing children in classrooms. In order to coach teachers in their classrooms, you have to know enough about student behavior in general and about the particular students in the class to give good feedback, select good examples, and achieve credibility as an expert. To that end, you need to be a quick study of student work and the children who produce it, a task that is easier when you are based in the school. Working for several years in one school, you come to know many children individually and build a level of trust with the teachers with whom you work. This consistent contact over time enables you to extend your own learning and become a more proficient and expert staff developer.

Teacher Knowledge and Skill A teacher's knowledge and expertise is key to training him or her effectively. These kinds of variables will strongly influence your decisions about what to "teach for" or "coach for" in the classroom. Any elementary school faculty includes new teachers as well as very experienced teachers. Moreover, even many experienced teachers need to enter the learning spiral at the beginning if an approach is totally new. In fact, ingrained habits and knowledge may actually interfere with new learning.

First, think about some very basic ways to support a teacher in trying new approaches. Providing materials and helping the teacher organize them is a first step: teachers cannot try new approaches without materials and organization. Then, show them how to manage their classroom, use their time efficiently, and introduce simple procedures.

You can gather specific information regarding a teacher's learning process by talking with her, touring her classroom, and observing lessons. Here are some questions to keep in mind:

◆ Is the classroom organized so that the new approach can be tried? Are there materials? Are the materials accessible?
◆ Does the teacher know how to use basic management routines that will facilitate the process?

◆ In general, is the classroom orderly and do students know what is expected of them?
◆ Does the teacher know how to "teach the task" to students so that they can participate?

If the answer to any of these questions is no, you need to start with basic management concepts. A teacher who is struggling with overall management and has very poor communication with students needs a great deal of help. If in general the answers to those questions are yes, you can teach the instructional procedure. If some answers are yes and some no, go ahead with the new approach but pay particular attention to areas related to management and organization. Explicit in-class demonstrations may be in order, or you may have the teacher visit other classrooms in which the approach is being used effectively.

Evaluating the situation is not simple. The answers to these management questions might be yes for some teachers and no for others. In this case, the teacher may need support working with specific students. If the teacher has already tried the new approach and is implementing it with some efficiency, be ready to help him refine procedures and make a stronger link with the student behavior that provides evidence of learning.

It is always a good idea to check your assessments. Assumptions about what teachers know and can and cannot do should be tentative and verified by talking with the individuals in question. Just because a teacher's behavior doesn't conform to our expectations doesn't mean she has no knowledge or understanding. For example, a teacher might be well aware that her students don't understand her instructions but not know what to do about it. Uncovering her frustration may give you the opportunity to help her be more explicit. On the other hand, procedures may look like they are going smoothly, but the teacher may be confusing teaching with performance, applying the technique mechanically. She would need to be helped to see that teaching is helping students develop a processing system.

School Culture Talking with teachers, administrators, parents, and community members about the school as a whole will help you make your professional development the most effective it can be. For one thing, schedules and other logistical matters that affect what you do will become apparent. Then too, you will acquire information across the grades, to include special areas of instruction.

Providing the Basics

If their first attempt at a new instructional procedure is to be a positive experience, teachers must be given:

◆ The materials they need to get started.
◆ Directions for and examples of how to organize and use the materials.
◆ Demonstrations of specific routines for initiating the new approach successfully.
◆ Demonstrations of how to teach the routines to children.
◆ Directions on how to establish the task so that children know what is expected of them.

Let's look at some specific examples of what this might entail.

To introduce interactive writing (see Chapter 4), a teacher educator set up an easel, a name chart, and a simple word wall so teachers could easily see what materials would be needed and how to organize and use them. Then she role-played how to introduce interactive writing to children for the first time and showed a short videotape of an interactive writing session. Finally, she gave the teachers the materials they needed to try interactive writing themselves.

Another teacher educator introduced teachers to writing workshop with a videotape of the process. Then he discussed how to work with children on the first day of writing workshop and provided folders and writing books for teachers to use in their classroom.

Providing the necessary materials removes a major barrier to teachers' willingness to try new approaches. Initial inservice sessions should be devoted to examining and analyzing the materials the teachers are expected to use in the classroom.

It is also important to ground teachers in the basic routines and organizational structures that will help them be successful the first time they try an approach. Of course, it is unlikely they will teach skillfully the first time out when the approach is completely new, and they will no doubt feel awkward and unsure. If they have some explicit routines to follow and materials

are organized and available, however, they will be able to see the potential of the procedure and be more willing to keep working at it.

Demonstrating the Process

Using information gathered from assessing the context, you will select the specific instructional approaches you wish to introduce. (It's always better if teachers have expressed an interest in learning particular procedures or approaches or in learning more about them.) Your goal in demonstrating the process is to provide clear and explicit examples of the approach or procedure to be learned. Procedures are usually demonstrated in one of three ways:

◆ Showing videotapes of exemplary classroom sessions.
◆ Working with children behind a one-way glass while the teachers watch.
◆ Letting teachers observe peers who are implementing the approach effectively.

When teachers observe a live or videotaped demonstration, make sure they know that even though you want them to know how to do the particular procedure, you also want them to notice children's responses and think about what they mean. In other words, you are not simply saying, "Watch this and do just what the teacher does." You expect them to *analyze* what is going on. Having two or three examples (preferably involving children at different levels of learning) minimizes the tendency to imitate precise words or actions and allows teachers to generalize an overall framework for the procedure. Related articles about the procedure can also be helpful; however, it isn't necessary to have a large number of handouts.

Establishing the Rationales

Even though teachers' main interest may be in "how," it's important to make the "why" apparent from the beginning, since the "why" is related to developing reading and writing processing systems. Rationales don't require long lectures on theory. Brief, precise reasons (presented orally or in charts or one-page handouts) are all you need. Here are two examples:

◆ While observing a guided reading session (see Chapter 4), a staff developer pointed out to teachers that the book introduction helped students know what to expect in the text, which in turn supported their predicting and solving words. These brief comments alerted the teachers that the introduction is undertaken for a particular reason, not just because you are "supposed to."

◆ During an observation of interactive writing, a teacher educator drew attention to the process of composing a text, saying that writing with an authentic purpose helps children remember the words and be able to read the text later.

Embedding rationales into the initial teaching of procedures sets the scene for later reflection and provides links to the theories we want teachers to construct. Teachers are assured that there are reasons for what they are doing and internalize language they can use to extend their learning.

Putting teachers on the spot by asking questions that require them to suggest rationales before they have had a chance to understand them can undermine trust and collaboration. Questions do play a role—in guiding teachers to notice children's or teachers' behavior, for example. But part of your job is to provide rationales clearly and concisely.

Engaging the Learners

Learning is active. No live or videotaped demonstration is effective unless the learners act on the material in some way. The teachers you work with need to discuss the examples, talk about the learning involved, or analyze what they see happening.

The goals here are to:

◆ Engage teachers in active learning and exploration.
◆ Help them visualize the approach in action.
◆ Prompt them to imagine performing the techniques themselves.
◆ Encourage them to notice important children's behavior.

With these four goals in mind, there are various ways to engage learners. For example:

◆ Have them point out the strengths in children's writing samples before they watch a videotape of an interactive writing session.
◆ After they watch a guided reading lesson, have them examine some books and decide which text characteristics will support these children in further learning.
◆ Have them examine a large collection of books, noting characteristics that support and challenge learners and placing them within a gradient of difficulty.
◆ Have them examine observational records of the reading behavior of a group of children they have just observed in a guided reading lesson.
◆ While they observe a guided reading lesson, have them identify teacher prompts and match them with student responses.

No one way of engaging learners can be used over and over. Use your ingenuity! You'll know you've succeeded when teachers are talking animatedly about a topic or technique and contributing their own examples.

Trying It Out

Once the materials are available and the basic management routines are in place, teachers can try out the procedures and, in the process, learn more about how to use them efficiently. Your goals here are to help teachers begin using the new technique and then improve their skill with it through practice, evaluation, and reflection. If the technique is completely new, first attempts will be approximations. Reflection and evaluation will produce adjustments. Teachers may need to relook at examples of the tech-

The literacy coach and teachers analyze students' writing samples.

nique in action and discuss their experiences in trying the new technique and the work students have produced.

Establishing Routines and Procedures

At the same time they begin trying out a procedure or approach, teachers begin to establish routines. They get better at the actions included in the procedure each time they use it. The thing to concentrate on here is creating smoothly operating patterns of action and letting students know exactly what is expected of them. Initially, teachers tend to concentrate on management and on their own actions, sometimes following directions step by step (the sequence of a mini-lesson, for example). As they grow more confident and the new behavior is internalized, they do not have to give it so much attention.

You can help by demonstrating, helping to organize materials and plan lessons, providing feedback, and making suggestions. Eventually teachers will make evaluations like the following themselves:

- Were my materials accessible and well organized?
- Did I keep children engaged?
- How did I use my time? Was I able to finish the lesson? Was it too long? Did the children get tired and restless?
- Did I establish a real purpose?
- What worked well and what didn't?
- Did I see evidence that the children were learning?

In helping teachers refine procedures, you need to work both with individuals and with the group as a whole. You will also need to provide direct instruction in the procedures, allowing teachers to ask questions, no matter how detailed or trivial. (In a risk-free atmosphere, no question is insignificant.) At the same time, you need to encourage flexibility, so that the procedures don't seem rigid and prescriptive. The structure of a strong, supportive how-to-do-it framework results in automatic routines that provide security. Only then are teachers and children free to weave a flexible conversation about learning.

Coaching for Shifts in Behavior

When teachers have tried the new procedure and are implementing it with most routines in place, you are able to coach for shifts in behavior. Pedagogy shifts from observing examples and talking about routines to analyzing and discussing lessons as they play out in the classroom. You can suggest changes that will support more powerful teaching and greater student learning.

The following questions will help you gather information about teachers' thinking:

- What did you notice about how the children responded to the lesson?
- What did these children already know about the topic?
- How did you feel you used your time?
- What do the children need to know next?
- Why did you select this activity?
- What learning did you expect to take place?
- Did the children perform as you expected?
- What worked well? What didn't?

Here are some phrases for suggesting change:

- Next time you might try . . .
- Is there another way to reach your goal?
- There are some suggestions in [a book or article] that might be helpful.
- Here's another way to get at the goal you've identified. [Demonstrate or role-play.]
- Let's come up with a specific plan for tomorrow.
- I noticed that you did [a specific action successfully used previously] yesterday. Try that tomorrow with this group.
- You were very successful in helping the children when you [point out a specific moment in the lesson]. Could you do more of that?
- You're really thinking about your goals and priorities for these children. Here's something else to try.

The purpose of a coaching conversation is to use teachers' own thinking—what they want to accomplish—as a springboard to show them how to change their behavior. Help them begin to ask themselves these questions as they refine the techniques. In these first coaching situations, you are always thinking about positives and negatives. The last thing you want is to make teachers afraid or intimidated or have them view your suggestions as nonconstructive criticism. The trust you have built while working on routines and management of the procedures will ease the shift to this kind of evaluative thinking. The more you use teachers' own perspectives and priorities to segue into change, the more effective your coaching will be.

Coaching for Analysis and Reflection

Through coaching, you can help teachers establish the analysis and reflection that leads to independent learning. Over time teachers need to be able to select instructional actions that will best fit particular children. The goal of coaching for analysis and reflection is to:

◆ Help teachers become flexible in their instruction.
◆ Enable them to fine-tune their teaching to meet children's learning needs.

This concept is important: as children grow and change, they have different needs. The routines and procedures for many instructional approaches have a basic structure—steps to be followed. But teachers work very differently with children who are just developing early reading strategies (one-to-one matching, for example) than they would with children who are reading silently from chapter books and need to think about how characters change.

Again, you will need to gather information about teachers' perspectives in order to make appropriate suggestions. Here are some questions you might ask:

◆ What did you hope to accomplish?
◆ What processes did you want the children to learn?
◆ Why did you select that particular teaching point?
◆ What did you teach the children today that they can use tomorrow?
◆ Were any children not learning effectively in the lesson?

Here are some suggestions for moving teachers toward analysis:

◆ You said that some students were not learning as well as you'd like. How could you adjust the lesson to change this?
◆ Are there any other ways to teach this process?
◆ What other parts of the curriculum could

you use to develop knowledge in that area?
◆ How can you connect this lesson with tomorrow's lesson?

Of course you always need to be sensitive to whether a teacher can or cannot answer these questions. The best and most effective interactions have a conversational quality. Over time, you want teachers to develop expertise across the framework and have a rich repertoire of teaching actions to chose from as they make teaching decisions in the classroom. If the process is working well, you become an assistant in the process rather than the motivator of it.

Supporting Extended Learning

Finally, all the knowledge you and your teachers have developed needs to be generalized by everyone in a group setting. This shared process is very important: teachers support one another and learning is accelerated. The goals are to:

◆ Help teachers form tentative theories, generalized from their own work over time.
◆ Make theoretically based interpretations of examples of their own and others' teaching.
◆ Apply these theoretical constructs in the work they do in the classroom.

The idea is for teachers to build networks of understanding that they continually revise as they test hypotheses with children and observe their behavior. Teachers are ready to look at examples from their own classrooms and those of their peers. They can look at lessons, analyze children's behavior, and make hypotheses about what needs to happen next for a group of children.

Learning will be greater if:

◆ An atmosphere of trust has been established.
◆ It is clear that everyone is learning and no one is expected to be perfect.
◆ The group shares a common vision for student achievement.
◆ The group shares high expectations.
◆ The group members make a mutual commitment to asking for and receiving criticism.
◆ Challenge is expected and valued as part of the discussion.
◆ Teachers in the group are listening and talking to one another rather than only to you.

The quality of this kind of interaction is facilitated by small details such as room arrangements: having everyone sit in a circle rather than in rows facing you makes a statement and influences the group in a positive way.

Extending learning is an ongoing process. It is give and take during which teachers take control of their own learning. The goals are to:

◆ Help teachers formulate their own goals for learning.
◆ Encourage reflection.
◆ Support a range of learning contexts such as action research groups, study groups, and peer coaching.

The particular focus depends on the group's goals and needs. At this level, you and the teachers you work with are partners in learning. You are profiting from the experiences and learning of one another. By sharing, challenging, and exploring together, you are learning to make connections across the literacy framework that will make instruction more efficient and maximize learning. Once an approach to instruction is deeply known, you can see it within a bigger picture—the overall curriculum—and make the powerful connections that accelerate learning.

Teachers discuss student progress, documented by records.

Working with the Planning, Problem-Solving, and Coaching Framework

The components of the planning, problem-solving, and coaching framework are resources—different approaches that you can use to match an individual's experience and level of development. When introducing any new procedure, begin by engaging the group and giving an explicit demonstration; then move to other levels. At any point in a teacher's development, any of the types of assistance or coaching may be appropriate. For example, a teacher may be skilled in analyzing writing behavior and need coaching that will expand her understanding of theory. This same teacher might be less experienced in teaching reading (or find it harder for some reason) and need coaching for shifts in behavior that will make her teaching more effective.

The basic question you must always ask is this: *In what areas does* this *teacher need to shift and change?* You may decide to coach a group of teachers in guided reading for several weeks and focus class sessions and readings on that topic. But your in-class assistance will vary from one teacher to another. In one classroom you might work on organization and selection of books; in another, you might observe lessons and help the teacher use prompts effectively. The classroom is where you individualize your teacher education program. That is why coaching is so important.

Teacher educators who work in school settings must be expert at analyzing the process. If they are good analyzers, they will be far more effective than teacher educators in college and university classrooms have been in the past. A rigorous, continuing professional development program for teacher educators is essential if we are to achieve the high literacy achievement that policy makers expect.

Suggestions for Extending Your Skills as a Staff Developer

1. Use the spiral of learning to think about your own learning. Select something that you have learned as an adult. It may be something at which you are now expert or something that you still need to learn more about. (Some ideas are golf, sewing, arts and crafts, or any aspect of teaching.)

2. Look at your learning in relation to the spiral.
   - How expert are you?
   - Where would your learning be best supported on the spiral?
   - What was your learning like at previous points?
   - What helped you move forward in your learning?
   - If someone helped you, what did that person do?
   - Did you receive any other kind of help (from a videotape or a tutorial, for example)?
   - Where do you need to go next?
   - What would most help you to extend your learning?

3. Now think about a professional development program you have attended (a one-day session or series of sessions); it can be on any subject.
   - Where on the planning, problem-solving, and coaching framework would you place your learning about the particular topic?
   - At which component of the framework was the professional development targeted?
   - What actions can you remember by the staff developer, consultant, or trainer? Where would they fit on the framework?
   - What made the session effective for you as a learner? Find those actions on the framework.
   - What could have made the session more effective for you as a learner? Find those actions on the framework.
   - To what extent was there a match between your own level of learning and the session?

4. Discuss what you've learned with a staff development colleague. How will this framework inform your work?

Chapter 3

Learning to Be Literate

The first years of school are crucial, because they lay the foundation in literacy learning of all the verbal learning that follows in an individual's school career. That foundation needs to be sound.
—*MARIE CLAY* BY DIFFERENT PATHS TO COMMON OUTCOMES *(130)*

Becoming a competent reader and writer is an essential foundation, for education and for life. How do children learn literacy? What is the best way to teach them? The knowledge and skills a teacher needs are so complex they are difficult to describe, but here goes:

◆ A broad understanding of the reading and writing processes—what literacy users understand and do.
◆ In-depth familiarity with how literacy processes are acquired—the progression of behavior that serves as evidence of increasingly complex learning.
◆ An understanding of the structure and complexity of written texts.
◆ Knowledge of the particular learners in *this* classroom, arrived at by ongoing observation and assessment.
◆ A repertoire of effective instructional approaches learned and practiced over time.

Given that foundation, teachers are then required to:

◆ Observe and interpret the behavior of individual learners as a basis for making decisions about instruction.
◆ Interpret behavior in light of literacy processes and literacy learning.
◆ Discern patterns as a basis for planning group instruction.

- Conceptualize sound plans and organizational frameworks that support learning.
- Evaluate and select appropriate reading and writing materials that match the strengths of readers and writers.
- Interact with individual students via powerful moment-to-moment decisions.
- Adjust instruction in response to behavior.
- Assess the effectiveness of instruction.

It's no wonder that at the end of a scant one hundred hours of teacher education classes, most beginning teachers are just starting to develop as professionals. Information from research has sent a clear message that learning to teach is a lifelong process requiring support and assistance at every level. An experienced teacher who grasps the complexities of the skills listed above can help a novice, but even experienced teachers need help in taking on new instructional approaches. The role of "teacher of teachers" requires an additional layer of knowledge—a complex understanding of how adults learn and, specifically, how teachers learn to be effective. Some guiding principles apply:

- Only those who have good understanding of teaching and learning can be effective as teacher educators.
- The educator of teachers of literacy must know, specifically, how children learn to read, write, and develop language.
- Good teacher educators are themselves good teachers of children.
- Good educators of literacy teachers are themselves good teachers of reading and writing.
- Teacher educators must develop a specific body of understanding and specific skills in order to be effective.
- Learning to be a teacher educator takes time, study, practice, and support.

We can think of the specific knowledge related to the delivery of good literacy education in three layers:

1. What teachers need to know about literacy learning.
2. What teachers need to know about teaching children to read and write.
3. What educators or staff developers of literacy teachers need to know in addition to the knowledge required in layers 1 and 2.

While most of this book is devoted to the third layer of learning, the foundation provided by the first two layers is essential.

Understanding the Reading Process

Reading means quickly and (by and large) unconsciously processing continuous print with understanding. The goal of all reading is comprehension: the degree to which you understand what you read is the degree to which you will profit from and/or enjoy it. Reading without understanding is not reading.

Accessing Sources of Information

Readers need information, and they get it by orchestrating a number of in-the-head strategies. Reading is not linear; at any moment, readers use many different sources of information as they perform the operations mentioned above (as well as others we have not listed).

Using Meaning Within the Text A text consists of words combined as language. Of course, readers depend on the meaning of words; however, using meaning is a far larger concept than individual words. Even the meaning of a simple word like *run* has a web of understanding around it. We have mental images of what running looks like: going for a run is different from running for a plane. Then we increase the complexity by thinking about running for office, having a runny nose, eating a runny egg, watching the river run under the bridge, or letting children run wild. Vocabulary isn't simple.

The meaning of words is related to the context in which we find them. This context begins with phrases, embedded in sentences, embedded in paragraphs, sections, complete texts. Readers search for meaning far beyond the word level. As we read a text, we are always thinking about what we have previously read; we derive and interpret information because we are building meaning across a text. The more we understand about a character, for example, the better we can predict what may happen next. As adult readers, we build interest and momentum as we read a novel. In an informational text, we use previous information from that text and others to help us understand what we are presently reading.

Using Information Outside the Text Not only do we build meaning as we read through a text, we build meaning across texts. For example, as we read a mystery novel, we access information, based on our previous reading, of how mysteries are organized—how they "work." If we are reading a book by a particular author, we probably remember something about how that author uses language or the kinds of settings and characters that are likely to be included. If we are reading a biography of someone, we might recall information about the person or period from other reading we have done or documentaries we have seen. The more information we bring to a text, the better or richer our comprehension.

Readers also access information from their own life experiences. Someone who has traveled to South Carolina will remember things he saw there when he reads *Midnight in the Garden of Good and Evil* (Berendt 1994) or *Beach Music* (Conroy 1994). A person who rides horses will respond to and understand *The Horse Whisperer* (Evans 1995) differently from someone who does not.

This is not to say that we always need direct experience with something to enjoy reading about it; the joy and value of reading is that it broadens our world vicariously. Through reading we make connections with universal human experiences—the relationships we have with family and friends and the experiences we have in our own communities. Very few of us have had the background experiences necessary to identify with the heroine of *Memoirs of a Geisha* (Golden 1997), but we do have experience with and/or can empathize with her humanity. We also may have learned something about Japan through reading or some other educational experience, and that information is available as a source of meaning.

Everything we have experienced directly, have read about, or have seen on film is a source of meaning as we read texts. Readers access three categories of information, or "funds of knowledge" (Moll 1990), related to meaning:

1. Their personal experiences.
2. The knowledge they have gained by studying various subjects.
3. Other texts they have read.

Using the Rules of Language Readers also use their knowledge of language as a source of infor-

Independent reading.

mation. We all can quickly and automatically attach meaning to words that are organized according to the conventions of our particular language. Here, we are not speaking of the rules of grammar; we are describing the way word parts go together to make words and the way words are combined to make sentences.

For example, arrange the following fourteen words into a sentence:

rose
the
shape
smaller
with
power
distance
the
its
gigantic
the
smaller
thrusting
aircraft

You might have come up with:

- With thrusting power, the aircraft rose, its gigantic shape growing smaller in the distance.
- The gigantic aircraft rose with thrusting power, its shape growing smaller in the distance.
- In the distance, its gigantic shape growing smaller, the aircraft rose with thrusting power.

There are probably several more syntactically acceptable renditions of this combination of words. Here's one that fits grammatically but doesn't make sense:

- With smaller power, the thrusting aircraft rose, its shape growing gigantic in the distance.

Now try arranging these fourteen words into a sentence:

difference
took
made
the
that
by
traveled
I
all
the
less
has
one
and

This time you may have recognized words from familiar lines by Robert Frost: "I took the one less traveled by and that has made all the difference." Many of us, encountering the words *traveled* and *less,* immediately think of Frost's poem.

Our knowledge of language rules, as well as of specific texts, guides our arrangement of words. Not only must it make sense, it must also "sound right" according to what we know about words. If what we read doesn't fit with what we know about language, we take a closer look.

Using Visual Information Readers know how to look at visual information—the form of letters and words—and connect it to language. We are extremely efficient as we scan print. Without consciously attending to every letter, our eyes move rapidly over print, matching visual information with what we know about language and the world.

As adults, we are almost always unaware that we are sampling visual information—even though we are. We become aware of it only when we encounter a discrepancy—if we misread a word and the meaning becomes unclear or if we encounter a word we're not sure of. For example, we might mistake *turbid* for *turgid.* Looking closely at the visual information, we need notice only the difference between *g* and *b* and then recall specific meanings for each of the two words.

Efficient readers pick up information from print in a way that requires the least effort; their primary attention is directed to interpreting the text. Although we *can* figure out a word letter by letter, we use letter clusters, larger chunks of words, and spelling patterns. For example, rather than attempting to connect one letter to one sound, a competent reader of English automatically processes *ough* according to whether it is found in *rough, trough,* or *though.*

Using Cognitive Strategies

In accessing and orchestrating meaning, language conventions, and visual information, readers use a wide range of cognitive strategies. In thinking about these strategies, it helps to remember two important points:

- There are probably hundreds of strategies. The categories we identify are merely a tool for thinking about cognitive actions.
- Cognitive strategies are not linear "steps." They are employed simultaneously, in an orchestrated way, with unimaginable speed.

The strategies categorized in Figure 3–1 help us think about the reading process.

Sustaining Strategies Sustaining strategies make reading possible. Readers solve words using meaning, language structure, and visual information. At the same time, they monitor whether the information in the text looks right, is consistent with the language rules they know, and makes sense. Readers sustain fluency by accessing the deeper meaning of the text and dividing it into meaningful units. When reading aloud, we call this fluency *expression.* Competent readers also recognize words automatically and

Cognitive Strategies for Reading	
Sustaining Strategies	**Expanding Strategies**
◆ Solving words	◆ Making connections
◆ Monitoring	◆ Inferring
◆ Gathering information	◆ Summarizing
◆ Predicting	◆ Synthesizing
◆ Sustaining fluency	◆ Analyzing
◆ Adjusting reading	◆ Criticizing

Figure 3–1. *Reading Strategies*

unconsciously and solve problems against a background of accuracy so that few—if any—words are unknown.

Sustaining strategies include:

1. *Problem-solving words.* We have a flexible range of strategies for solving words. Some words we simply recognize immediately. We orchestrate meaning, language conventions, and visual information. We can "take words apart," using relationships between letters and letter clusters and sounds as well as other word-analysis techniques.

2. *Monitoring.* We use meaning, language conventions, and visual information to monitor our reading as we go along to be sure we understand and have read accurately.

3. *Gathering information.* We pick up essential information from print as we go along, gathering words and constructing basic understandings.

4. *Predicting.* As we gather basic information, we form predictions about what comes next. Anticipation takes place at the phrase/sentence level because we understand the rules of syntax, but it also takes place at the text level because we are thinking about what will happen next. Anticipation does not negate word solving; word solving and anticipation work together to propel reading.

5. *Sustaining fluency.* Forward motion is evidence that we are using language and meaning and recognizing and solving words quickly. Reading the punctuation is important here; competent readers reproduce the phrase units intended by the writer, thus reaching the deeper meaning of the text.

6. *Adjusting.* We read different kinds of texts (for example, poetry, instruction manuals, or novels) in different ways. We may slow down in order to problem-solve, provide emphasis (in oral reading), or pay close attention to complex information; then we speed up again. The way we read varies with the purpose and difficulty of the text.

Expanding Strategies We use an important set of strategies to extend our understanding before, during, and after reading a text. The list below begins with seven, to emphasize that all these strategic systems occur (and are learned) simultaneously.

7. *Making connections.* We continually make connections between what we are reading and our homes and communities, our experiences in the world, the knowledge we have gained from reading and studying in various disciplines, and other texts we have read. These connections support reading, make it interesting and understandable, and allow us to comprehend ideas beyond the text.

8. *Inferring.* We hypothesize beyond the text about what the writer really means. We infer from characters' behavior what they are thinking and feeling. We read about processes and infer reasons and relationships.

9. *Summarizing.* We summarize the important details we gain from a text as we go, consulting and revising this summary as our comprehension increases.

10. *Synthesizing.* We not only gather information and summarize it, we integrate it with what we already know.

11. *Analyzing.* As we become more sophisticated readers, we subject a text to analysis. We recognize structure—where the plot reaches a climax, for example. We examine aspects of the writer's craft—how this writer manifests cultural contrasts, for example, or shows rather than tells how a character feels.

12. *Criticizing.* Critical reading is an essential strategy. As competent readers, we constantly evaluate what we read. We think about whether the writer really drew realistic characters and situations, decide whether

informational texts are accurate, look at the tenor, or tone, of articles and news stories.

In one sense, the sustaining and expanding strategies we've just listed are ordered in terms of sophistication: very young children are just learning to solve words and gather information from text, while older students are learning to analyze and criticize texts. In another sense, however, we realize that even young children can make judgments about a text or can talk about what the main character learned.

Understanding the Writing Process

Writing is different from reading in that we *construct* words designed to evoke complex understanding in those who read them. Writers put language together. Many people are *competent* writers, but few people are truly *good* writers. The development of writing skill takes many years and much practice. The competent writer:

◆ Sees writing as a way of recording and expanding experience.
◆ Writes for many different purposes.
◆ Thinks of ideas and composes these thoughts into written sequences of words.
◆ Writes ideas and messages word by word while maintaining a sense of the overall meaning of the text.

Independent writing.

◆ Spells many words quickly and automatically.
◆ Has a flexible range of strategies for spelling words, including how words sound, look, and mean.
◆ Connects words.
◆ Constantly rereads and revises the composition to reflect the evolving message.
◆ Uses feedback from readers as a basis for revision.
◆ Reflects on writing to evaluate how it conveys the intended meaning.

The writing process may seem like a series of actions. First, you think of what you want to write; next, you conceptualize it linguistically; then, you "encode" it (translate it into words on the page); and finally, you read and revise it. The process is much more visible and probably more understandable than reading, but we should not make the mistake of thinking it is simple *or* step by step. It is recursive: within any piece of writing you constantly cycle between composing, encoding, and revising.

Audience
All the time we write, we are thinking about *our audience:*

◆ What they know.
◆ What will interest them.
◆ What information will be important to help them understand.
◆ What will engage them.

For some kinds of writing, the audience is ourselves. We might write lists of things to do, take notes about what we observed during a research project, summarize an article or book we've read, make entries in a diary. If we are writing for others, however, a prime consideration is how to communicate clearly and completely with both familiar readers and distant unknown readers.

Writing Strategies
Always thinking about the audience, writers use a range of strategies to accomplish the purposes of communication:

Reading and writing have strong connections.

1. *Probe experiences for topics.* Writers delve into their experience, sometimes assisted by notes, sketches, or photographs, to compose written text.
2. *Put thoughts, reflections, and experiences into words.* At bottom, writers put their thoughts into words. They decide on the precise sequence of words that will best represent what they want to say.
3. *Select the appropriate form or genre.* Form follows function, in writing as in engineering. Part of learning to be a writer is being able to select from a wide repertoire of structures the one form best suited to purpose and audience.
4. *Decide perspective or point of view.* Writers of informational text decide whether to talk directly to the audience (using *I* and *you*) or use the third person. Writers of fiction have an even more complex decision: whether to write in first, second, or third person and which character's perspective to emphasize. These decisions depend on what we want to convey and to whom we want to convey it.
5. *Organize text to express meaning.* Writers need to think about the way they organize the information they want to present. For example, a story can be told in chronological order or as a series of flashbacks. An informational text can be organized by topic (a treatise on ants, for example, might have sections on what they eat, their method of reproduction, the parts of their body, and their importance to the ecology), by temporal sequence, or by concept.
6. *Select words that convey the tone or voice they want to use.* Here, writers think about clear communication with the audience. A piece of writing is carefully crafted, and word choice is part of the process. Writers who have an extensive vocabulary have power over words.
7. *Write (spell) the words, phrases, sentences, and paragraphs that express meaning.* Writers employ a range of word-solving strategies as they put their ideas in writing. They have to write words, thinking about letter-sound relationships, grammatical patterns, and meaning. Competent writers automatically know most of the words they write.
8. *Use punctuation and other conventions appropriate to the meaning and tone of the piece.* Writers realize that conventions are important, that they facilitate clear communication with the audience. Punctuation helps readers re-create the phrases a writer uses to communicate meaning. Also important in communicating with readers are paragraphing and other organizational features of text.
9. *Reread to assess the extent to which the piece of writing conveys meaning.* Good writers evaluate their writing to be sure it conveys the meaning they intend. As they write, they assess; after they finish, they read the piece several times, revising as appropriate.
10. *Proofread for conventions.* Writers proofread to be sure that proper spelling, punctuation, and grammar presents their work in the best light.
11. *Reflect on writing to learn about the process.* Writers reflect on their writing, getting better at communication and the use of conventions each time.

These competencies may seem a long list. Obviously, there are some important differences between writing and reading. If we take a larger view, however, writers and readers access and apply some of the same kinds of information. Writing is a language process, as shown in Figure 3–2.

Learning to Read and Write

One of the most difficult things for a young child to understand is what people do when they read. Children look at us, puzzled, as we sit silently turning pages. The process becomes more visible when we read aloud, yet there is no way to convey the complexity of the reading process. Children must learn it for themselves, but we can help them considerably.

Writing is somewhat more accessible because children can see us making marks on paper, but here again the connections with language are subtle, as indicated by Marie Clay's description of her daughter making marks on paper and then asking, "What did I write?" (Clay 1975). Just how these markings are connected with meaning is a mysterious process.

Learning to read and write involves a broad continuum of understanding, developed through experience over time.

Early Learning— Emergent Readers and Writers

Young children notice print in the environment and respond to it if it is meaningful. They begin to connect language with print as it is used in meaningful ways. Important early concepts and behavior emerge. They soon begin to understand the concept of *word*

and recognize that words are made up of letters. They learn that print carries the message in reading and that you move left to right and top to bottom as you read. Phonological and orthographic awareness are important concepts:

1. The phonological system is the sound of language. It's what you *hear*. For young children, phonological awareness means hearing the sounds in words. As young children hear nursery rhymes and poetry, they begin to realize that certain words sound the same at the beginning or at the end. They may connect certain sounds to the sounds of their names. They also begin to realize that words are made up of sequences of sounds. This concept is essential for learning to take words apart.

Writing as a Language Process

1. Writers use knowledge gained from their personal and world experience to:
   - Compose written language that provides information to readers about important events, processes, or other phenomena.
   - Create detail that makes meaning clearer to readers.
   - Add information and detail in the process of writing.
   - Evaluate the accuracy of the communication and revise as needed.
2. Writers use their knowledge of language to:
   - Recall and select words that make meaning clear.
   - Recall and construct language structures that make meaning clear.
   - Apply rules of syntax to construct sentences.
   - Apply knowledge of text organization to place sentences into a meaningful text.
   - Revise a text, evaluating words, sentence structure, and organization.
3. Writers connect ideas and sources of knowledge in order to:
   - Quickly jot down ideas.
   - Think of what to write next.
   - Revise their writing.
4. Writers make connections between reading and writing in order to:
   - Learn more about the writer's craft.
   - Acquire new knowledge or organize existing knowledge.
   - Learn more about language.
   - Read and reflect on their writing.
5. Writers are familiar with the conventions of written and oral language, which they use to:
   - Encode the writing.
   - Write many words quickly with standard spelling.
   - Proofread.

Figure 3–2. *Writing as a Language Process*

2. The orthographic system deals with the form of the letters and the spelling patterns within words. Orthographic awareness is what you *see*. It requires visual perception. For young children, this means learning to look at print. They have to be able to notice the very small differences between letters in order to distinguish one from another. This distinction is essential before the child can connect a letter and a sound.

Young children develop phonological and orthographic awareness and integrate this new knowledge with their growing sense of how print works. At the same time they are learning about the nature and structure of language as they hear written language read aloud.

Young children also become aware of the conventions of written language. They learn that:

◆ Letter-sound relationships provide valuable information in reading and writing.
◆ Reading and writing have to make sense and sound right.
◆ There are spaces between words in written language.

Teaching for strategies.

Building an Effective Reading Process over Time

As readers and writers progress in their learning, they develop networks of understanding that connect language and orthographic processing. A *self-extending system* means that readers and writers have the ability to learn from the very acts of reading and writing in which they engage (Clay 1991). In other words, every time they read, they expand their ability to read; the same is true for writing. Children who are learning to recognize words, for example, are at the same time building a system of strategies for learning to recognize words. As they read, they are learning more sophisticated ways to use language. They use language systems, which incorporate meaning and syntax, to monitor and correct their reading. At first these processes are overt; we have evidence from children's behavior that they are using meaning, language conventions, and visual information in a unified process.

As shown in Figures 3–3 and 3-4, Fountas and Pinnell (2000) have described characteristics of readers and writers along a broad continuum. While it is a challenge for elementary school teachers to understand all levels of this developmental learning process, it is essential to keep this continuum in mind as you work with teachers at different grade levels. The challenge is to tune in to learners in every phase of development, and they will not fall neatly into place.

The evidence of learning you observe in classrooms adds up to a unique profile for each student. Teachers have the complex task of assessing each student's needs and adjusting the curriculum and their moment-to-moment teaching decisions to meet that student where she or he is. As a staff developer, you have the equally complex task of assessing students' needs, observing lessons, and advising teachers on how best to adjust their instruction. Of course, it is impossible to know in depth every student in every classroom, but it is necessary to become an expert at picking up evidence quickly. Remember that teachers are your best informants. Probe their observations of the students they work with.

The idea of grade level isn't much help when we are talking about a continuum of development. We would not expect all students to

Building an Effective Reading Process over Time

Emergent Readers [Levels A–B]	Early Readers [Levels B–H]	Transitional Readers [Levels H–M]	Self-Extending Readers [Levels M–R]	Advanced Readers [Levels R–Y]
• Become aware of print. • Read orally, matching word by word. • Use meaning and language. • Hear sounds in words. • Recognize name and some letters. • Use information from pictures. • Connect words with names. • Notice and use spaces between words. • Read orally. • Match one spoken word to one printed word while reading one or two lines of text. • Use spaces and some visual information to check their reading. • Know names of some alphabet letters. • Know some letter-sound relationships. • Read left to right. • Recognize a few frequently encountered words.	• Know names of most alphabet letters and many letter-sound relationships. • Use letter-sound information along with meaning and language to solve words. • Read without pointing. • Read orally and begin to read silently. • Read fluently with phrasing on easy texts; use the punctuation. • Recognize most easy frequently encountered words. • Check to be sure reading makes sense, sounds right, looks right. • Check one source of information against another to solve problems. • Use information from pictures as added information while reading print.	• Read silently most of the time. • Have a large core of known words that are recognized automatically. • Use multiple sources of information while reading for meaning. • Integrate sources of information such as letter-sound relationships, meaning, and language structure. • Consistently check to be sure all sources of information fit. • Do not rely on illustrations but notice them to gain additional meaning. • Understand, interpret, and use illustrations in informational text. • Know how to read differently in a different genre. • Have flexible ways of solving words, including analysis of letter-sound relationships and visual patterns. • Read with phrasing and fluency at appropriate levels.	• Read silently; read fluently when reading aloud. • Use all sources of information flexibly in a smoothly orchestrated way. • Sustain reading over texts with many pages that require reading over several days or weeks. • Enjoy illustrations and gain additional meaning from them as they interpret texts. • Interpret and use information from a wide variety of visual aids in expository texts. • Analyze words in flexible ways and make excellent attempts at new, multisyllable words. • Have systems for learning more about the reading process as they read so that they build skills simply by encountering many different kinds of texts with a variety of new words. • Are in a continuous process of building background knowledge and realize that they need to bring their knowledge to their reading. • Become absorbed in books. • Begin to identify with characters in books and see themselves in the events of the stories.	• Read silently; read fluently when reading aloud. • Effectively use their understanding of how words work; employ a wide range of word-solving strategies, including analogy to known words, word roots, base words, and affixes. • Acquire new vocabulary through reading. • Use reading as a tool for learning in content areas. • Constantly develop new strategies and new knowledge of texts as they encounter greater variety. • Develop favorite topics and authors that form the basis of life-long reading preferences. • Actively work to connect texts for greater understanding and finer interpretations of texts. • Consistently go beyond the text, read to form their own interpretations, and apply understanding in other areas. • Sustain interest and understanding over long texts and read over extended periods of time. • Notice and comment on aspects of the writer's craft. • Read to explore themselves as well as philosophical and social issues.
Texts: Simple stories with one or two lines.	*Texts: Longer books with frequently encountered words and supportive illustrations.*	*Texts: Texts with many lines of print; books organized into chapters; harder picture books; wider variety of genres.*	*Texts: Wide variety of long and short texts; variety of genres.*	*Texts: Wide variety of genres and a range of purposes.*
Approximate Grades: K–1	*1–2*	*2–3*	*3–4*	*4–6*

Figure 3–3. *Building Reading Processes over Time.*

Reprinted with permission from Irene C. Fountas. From Fountas, I. C., and Pinnell, G. S. 2000. Guiding Readers and Writers, Grades 3–6: Teaching Comprehension, Genre, and Content Literacy. Portsmouth, NH: Heinemann.

Building an Effective Writing Process over Time

Emergent Writers	Early Writers	Transitional Writers	Self-Extending Writers	Advanced Writers
◆ Write name left to right. ◆ Write alphabet letters with increasingly accurate letter formation. ◆ Hear and represent some consonant sounds at beginnings and ends of words. ◆ Use some letter names in the construction of words. ◆ Sometimes use spaces to separate words or attempted words. ◆ Label drawings. ◆ Establish a relationship between print and pictures. ◆ Remember message represented with letters or words. ◆ Write many words phonetically. ◆ Write a few easy words accurately. ◆ Communicate meaning in drawings.	◆ Write known words fluently. ◆ Write left to write across several lines. ◆ Write 20 to 30 words correctly. ◆ Use letter-sound and visual information to spell words. ◆ Approximate spelling of words, usually with consonant framework and easy-to-hear vowel sounds. ◆ Form almost all letters accurately. ◆ Compose two or three sentences about a single idea. ◆ Write about familiar topics and ideas. ◆ Remember messages while spelling words. ◆ Consistently use spacing. ◆ Relate drawings and writing to create a meaningful text. ◆ Reread their writing.	◆ Spell many words conventionally and make nearly accurate attempts at many more. ◆ Work on writing over several days to produce longer, more complex texts. ◆ Produce pieces of writing that have dialogue, beginnings, and endings. ◆ Develop ideas to some degree. ◆ Employ a flexible range of strategies to spell words. ◆ Consciously work on their own spelling and writing skills. ◆ Write in a few different genres. ◆ Demonstrate ability to think about ideas while "encoding" written language. ◆ Can use basic punctuation and capitalization skills.	◆ Spell most words quickly without conscious attention to the process. ◆ Proofread to locate their own errors, recognize accurate parts of words, and use references or apply principles to correct words. ◆ Have ways to expand their writing vocabulary. ◆ Understand ways to organize informational writing such as compare/contrast, description, temporal sequence, cause/effect. ◆ Develop a topic and extend a text over many pages. ◆ Develop pieces of writing that have "voice." ◆ Use what they know from reading texts to develop their writing. ◆ Recognize and use aspects of the writer's craft to improve the quality of their writing. ◆ Write for many different purposes. ◆ Show a growing sense of the audience for their writing. ◆ Critique own writing and offer suggestions to other writers.	◆ Understand the linguistic and social functions of conventional spelling and produce products that are carefully edited. ◆ Write almost all words quickly, accurately, and fluently. ◆ Use dictionaries, thesauruses, computer spell check programs, and other text resources; understand organization plans for these resources. ◆ Control a large body of known words that constantly expands. ◆ Demonstrate a large speaking and listening vocabulary as well as knowledge of vocabulary that is used often in written pieces. ◆ Notice aspects of the writer's craft in texts that they read and apply their knowledge to their own writing. ◆ Critically analyze their own writing and that of others. ◆ Write for a variety of functions—narrative, expressive, informative, and poetic. ◆ Write in various persons and tenses. ◆ Write for different audiences, from known to unknown. ◆ Write about a wide range of topics beyond the present time, known settings, and personal experiences.
Texts: Simple labels and sentences with approximated spelling.	*Texts: One or more sentences around a single idea; some conventionally spelled words.*	*Texts: Longer texts with several ideas; mostly conventional spelling and punctuation; simple sentence structure.*	*Texts: A variety of genres; conventional use of spelling and punctuation; more complex sentence structure; development of ideas in fiction and nonfiction; a variety of ways to organize nonfiction.*	*Texts: A variety of long and short compositions; wide variety of purpose and genre; literary quality in fiction and poetry; variety of ways to organize informational text.*
Approximate Grades: K–1	*1–2*	*2–3*	*3–4*	*4–6*

Figure 3–3. *Building Reading Processes over Time.*

Reprinted with permission from Irene C. Fountas. From Fountas, I. C., and Pinnell, G. S. 2000. Guiding Readers and Writers, Grades 3–6: Teaching Comprehension, Genre, and Content Literacy. Portsmouth, NH: Heinemann.

exhibit grade-level expectations; our goal is consistent progress. Too, no one reader or writer will fit exactly the characteristics at any particular level. Readers may have excellent word-solving skills, for example, yet be only starting to be aware of the organization of fiction versus nonfiction. Other students may read voraciously in one or two genres but be either reluctant or afraid to read more widely. In any one classroom, you will find profiles of students that span every point on the continuum. The charts in Figures 3–3 and 3–4 help us think about that range. We can see that the pattern of progress moves

- From reading and writing very simple texts to a wide variety of genres.
- From a few approximately spelled words to employing a flexible range of word-solving strategies.
- From recognizing the uses of print to reading and writing for a wide range of purposes.
- From oral to silent reading.
- From composition of simple to complex written texts.

Moving students along this continuum of progress requires a rich, broad-based combination of literacy activities over several years of elementary education. The task of staff developers in this process is to provide the support teachers need to meet this challenge.

Suggestions for Extending Your Skills as a Staff Developer

1. Observe one or more students in reading and writing contexts:

   - Select one student (or, consecutively, two or three students of different ages).
   - Observe the student closely during an entire language arts period.
   - Take detailed notes of what the student does *in the process* of reading and writing.

2. Afterward, reflect on your observations:

   - What was the range of reading and writing that the student experienced?
   - How much time did the student spend reading continuous text? writing a text?
   - Was there evidence that the student *voluntarily* did any reading or writing?
   - What reading and writing behavior did you notice?
   - Was there evidence that the student enjoyed reading or writing?
   - What was the evidence of new learning during the period?
   - How did the curriculum and the teacher support the student's learning?
   - Did anything get in the way of learning?

Chapter 4

Teaching Literacy:
What Teachers Need to Know

*What needs to be acknowledged is that teaching techniques are learned
inside a school culture where adults are always seeking to learn more
about their students and their craft.*
—ANN LIEBERMAN AND LYNNE MILLER
TEACHERS—TRANSFORMING THEIR WORLD AND THEIR WORK *(64)*

Providing the learning environment and the teaching that students need to move along the continuum from transitional to advanced levels of literacy is a challenge. The goal is consistent progress, knowing where to meet students as readers and writers, and knowing where to go next. Students need time, materials, and instruction. Progress will not be possible unless we are serious about providing time to read every day. We also need to provide the appropriate books and other reading material that will challenge and support our developing students.

With so many content areas to cover, it may seem difficult to find time to teach reading in the intermediate grades. Even students who read well need instruction, but it can be coordinated with work in content areas. Students need to read widely, and some of that reading (and writing) can and should be on topics that are appropriate for content area study. Reading informational literature can contribute significantly to students' content area knowledge and at the same time offer an opportunity to learn more about the reading process (Freeman and Person 1998). It is obvious that as students learn more about literacy and take on the tasks for themselves, the pattern of instruction must change. Teachers:

◆ Expect students to use the full range of skills they currently control.
◆ Provide just the right amount of support to help students reach beyond present levels.

In all reading and writing contexts, students can do more with teacher support than they can working alone (Vygotsky 1978). The language/literacy curriculum offers a balance of instructional contexts, within which the teacher provides information to students, demonstrates processes, gives direction, provides opportunities to apply concepts, and encourages and supports independent action. No one component of the framework is the key to literacy learning; its effectiveness lies in the range of learning contexts that are included.

There are a range of effective instructional approaches for helping students become readers and writers in both the primary (K–2) and intermediate (3–6) grades. As teachers of literacy we spend a great deal of time thinking about the literacy experiences we want our student to have.

We think about the content and topics we want them to read and write about, and we plan the necessary experiences. But most important, we think about our students—their individuality, their strengths, their habits, attitudes, and needs. Knowing our students is critical to teaching literacy successfully, because *they bring* knowledge and experience to the literacy processes. Recognizing what the students bring to reading and writing powers our instruction. The meaning and the pleasure of literacy reside within the individual. As Paulsen (1989) writes eloquently in *The Winter Room*:

> Books can't have light.
>
> If books could have more, give more, be more, show more, they would still need readers, who bring to them sound and smell and light and all the rest that can't be in books. (p. 3)

Within a comprehensive literacy program a range of *reading, writing,* and *word study* con-

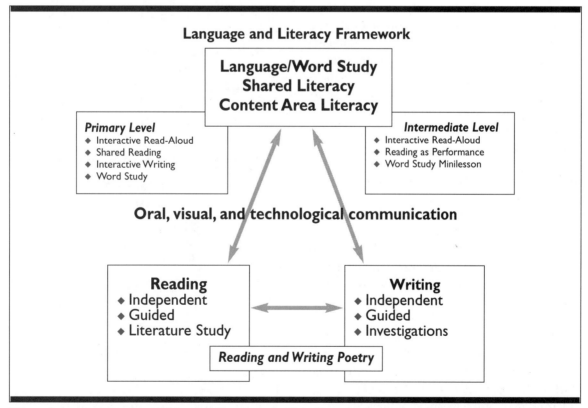

Figure 4–1. *Language and Literacy Framework. This framework is printed here with permission from Irene C. Fountas and the Literacy Collaborative at Lesley University. It is adapted from I. C. Fountas and G. S. Pinnell,* Guided Reading: Good First Teaching for All Children *(Portsmouth, NH: Heinemann, 1996), and I. C. Fountas and G. S. Pinnell,* Guiding Readers and Writers, Grades 3–6: Teaching Comprehension, Genre, and Content Literacy *(Portsmouth, NH: Heinemann, 2000).*

texts supports children's learning in many different ways. The overarching framework, shown in Figure 4–1, implies a range of reading and writing contexts at both primary and intermediate levels. In any professional development system, you will be working toward competence in some combination of these approaches. Remember that creating a curriculum to support learning means more than simply collecting approaches. It is the connections that teachers make across contexts—the "echoes" across the curriculum—that make the difference.

Reading Instruction

The balanced literacy framework involves children in a range of reading contexts that can be adjusted and varied to meet students at different levels of competence and with different interests.

Interactive Read Aloud

Reading to children provides models of complex written language that children can internalize. They learn how stories and informational texts are organized and they expand their vocabularies. As students grow increasingly sophisticated, it is still important to read more complex texts to them. Intermediate teachers read aloud short stories, nonfiction texts, and chapter books that lead to interesting discussions. Reading aloud is a very good way to introduce new genres.

Shared Reading, Choral Reading, and Readers Theater

Reading with children (shared or supported reading) helps them learn about the conventions of print. Children read in unison, usually from an enlarged text. For many children, shared reading is their first experience in what it's like to be a reader; they begin to understand the differences between written and oral language.

For older students, reading may become performance, either as choral reading, which is practiced unison reading, or readers theater, in which parts are assigned. Performance reading requires interpretation of the meaning of the text.

Guided Reading

Guided reading brings children who have similar needs together for small-group instruction (see Fountas and Pinnell 1996 [grades K–2] and Fountas and Pinnell 2000 [grades 3–6]). The teacher chooses a book that is challenging for the group but within their control and guides them in the development of effective reading strategies for both comprehension and word solving.

Guided reading is important throughout the elementary grades, from children's development of early reading behavior to their processing large amounts of text. In the intermediate grades, teachers bring students together in small groups to develop the range of strategies described in Chapter 3. It is also a way to help students learn to read in various genres.

At both primary and intermediate levels, guided reading lessons follow the basic structure show in Figure 4–2. Although this essential structure doesn't vary from kindergarten through sixth grade, what you see from classroom to classroom might look considerably different.

Selecting the Text Based on her knowledge of students' reading abilities (derived from assessment and observation), the teacher selects a text that is "just right" to help students move forward in their development of a reading process. In the primary grades, teachers consider text characteristics such as layout, language structure and pattern, known words, and topic familiarity. Early texts have large, clear fonts with good space between

---

Structure of Guided Reading Lessons

Selecting the Text

Introducing the Text

Reading the Text

Discussing the Text

Teaching for Strategies

Extending Meaning (Optional)

Word Work (Optional)

Figure 4–2. *Structure of a Guided Reading Lesson*

words so that it is easier for students to read word by word and notice visual aspects of language. If children know only a few words, it is important for teachers to consider frequently encountered words and topic familiarity. Good texts for primary students offer some challenge in that the language is different from oral speech, but teachers are judicious in selecting texts that offer recognizable language patterns.

Interactive writing in kindergarten.

In selecting texts for intermediate students, teachers make decisions about texts based on:

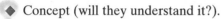

◆ Concept (will they understand it?).
◆ Linguistic difficulty (how complex is the sentence structure and the organization of the text as a whole?).
◆ Theme (is it appropriately sophisticated?).

Teachers gather a varied collection, including longer chapter books in different genres as well as "short reads" (articles, short stories, and excerpts from informational texts).

Vocabulary does play a role in text selection, but it is not an isolated factor. Teachers recognize that words are embedded in a larger text. We've all had students who can read words accurately but don't understand them. In selecting texts for guided reading, teachers think about student comprehension before, during, and after they read; that includes word solving and an overall understanding of the way the text "works" (recognizing and working with organizational features).

Think about the way narrative texts are organized, for example. There are characters and a setting; events usually take place in sequence; there is a high point or climax, followed by a quick ending. Expository or informational texts are different. They use a variety of organizational structures, including:

◆ Description—of places, objects, people, and events.
◆ Temporal sequence—a series of events over time.

◆ Explanation—the cause producing an effect.
◆ Comparison/contrast—of phenomena, characters, events, and texts.
◆ Definition—clarification of concepts and ideas.
◆ Problem/solution—identify and analyze problems, pose solutions, and document results.

While layout, words, concept familiarity, and language complexity are important, genre, or type of text, is another major factor in selecting books for intermediate guided reading. We want students to be able to read texts of increasing difficulty, but we also want them to achieve breadth as readers. They need to learn how to read biography, autobiography, history, fantasy, mystery, historical fiction, realistic fiction, and poetry. Reading in the primary years sets the scene through text variety in reading aloud, guided reading, and independent reading, but in the intermediate years this breadth experience is deepened.

Introducing the Text Taking into account readers' strengths, as well as text characteristics, the teacher introduces the text to students. The purpose of this introduction is to:

◆ Help students understand how the text "works"; that is, organization, theme, and language patterns.

- Familiarize students with some unfamiliar words or concepts.
- Provide vital information that will support comprehension.
- Focus students' attention on the meaning of the text.

The text introduction is the key to "upping the ante" in students' reading. It mediates a first reading of the text, encouraging students to bring their prior knowledge to bear, helping them look at the organization of the text, and discussing and explaining new concepts.

Reading the Text After the introduction, students read the whole text or a unified part of the text softly or silently to themselves. A difference between guided reading and traditional forms of small-group reading instruction is that all students read the entire assigned text during the lesson (in the traditional approach students read aloud one at a time). The teacher observes, "listens in," and may briefly interact with individual students. Since all students are reading a text that has been carefully selected and introduced, they are able to continue processing the print on their own while the teacher focuses on individuals. There is no down time; every student reads—a lot.

Students in kindergarten and first grade read aloud to themselves in whispers or very soft voices; older students read silently. When the teacher interacts with individuals, she simply asks them to raise their voices and continue reading wherever they are in the text. This sampling of oral reading tells the teacher how well students are processing the text and also provides a chance to make a quick teaching point or to prompt the student to use effective strategies previously taught. As older students read longer books, they spend more time reading independently. The teacher may introduce a text, let students read it on their own over a couple of days, then call them together for a discussion.

Discussing the Text After reading the text (or at selected breaks in a longer book) the teacher brings students together to discuss some aspect of the text. It might be the characters and how they changed, or it might be a prediction of what is likely to happen in the plot. The teacher might ask students if there were any parts they didn't understand or might revisit difficult vocabulary. The discussion provides a great deal of information about what students have understood and gives them a chance to voice their responses.

Teaching for Strategies Following the discussion, the teacher makes one or two specific teaching points related to her ongoing observation of students' reading behavior—word solving, making inferences, or any other aspect of reading. The goal of teaching in guided reading is to help students expand their independent reading strategies.

Extending Meaning (Optional) Depending on the text and students' needs, the teacher may decide to extend their work on the text through longer discussions, sketching, journal writing, interactive writing, drama, or other activities that will deepen their understanding and enjoyment. Teachers often use extensions to help students make their understanding explicit; examples are identifying themes, diagramming text structures like compare/contrast, making timelines, and writing and evaluating summaries (see Fountas and Pinnell 2000).

Word Work (Optional) For children who need more experience in how words work, the teacher spends one or two minutes focusing on spelling/phonics principles. Students may use magnetic letters or white dry-erase boards to examine and manipulate words. A brief gamelike activity like this can help students learn to make connections between words; learn that you can make new words by changing the beginnings, endings, and middles of words; or learn about letter clusters as well as prefixes, suffixes, and inflectional endings. Not all students need this work with words, and the goal is to learn something *about* the spelling of words rather than simply to recognize words.

Ongoing Assessment: Running Records Guided reading groups are flexible and change often as the teacher applies ongoing assessment techniques. The running record[1] is a systematic way of coding reading behavior so that the teacher can later analyze the behavior and make hypotheses about the use of strategies. It is most useful in the primary grades. The running record helps the teacher:

- Identify an accurate reading level for a student and select appropriate texts.
- Analyze children's development of reading strategies.

◆ Group children who are similar in their reading development at a particular time.

Teachers can use informal reading inventories, reading records, reading response journals, and interactions with students after reading to assess and group older students. A thorough discussion is provided in Johnston (1997) and Fountas and Pinnell (1996).

Independent Reading

Independent reading gives children a chance to "put on miles" as readers by reading a great deal of material both at home and at school. The dramatic results of a study by Anderson, Wilson, and Fielding (1988), in which they examined the relation between the amount of reading students do and their reading achievement, confirm the importance of doing a large amount of reading. Every day (for periods ranging from eight to twenty-six weeks), 155 fifth graders wrote down how many minutes they spent on out-of-school activities. Of all the activities they listed, time spent reading books was the best predictor of achievement. Students in the 98th percentile rank, for example, read books an average of sixty-five minutes a day (4,358,000 words a year!). On the other hand, students in the 10th percentile read six seconds per day (fewer than 8,000 words per year).

Children begin to learn about independent reading in kindergarten as they look at books the teacher has read to them and gradually begin to read little books for themselves. Many primary teachers use "browsing boxes," which are filled with books students have previously read in guided reading as well as books that will be easy for the particular group.

Older students read independently during reading workshop, a block of time that also includes guided reading and literature discussion (see Atwell 1998; Fountas and Pinnell 2000). Each student selects a book to read, keeps a list of the books he's read (including the genre), and keeps lists of books, topics, and genres that he wants to read. Students

write each week in a reading response journal, to which the teacher writes a response. This ongoing written dialogue promotes reflection on reading and provides the teacher with information about students' response to and understanding of books. Independent reading for older students follows a structure that includes:

◆ A minilesson by the teacher on some aspect of reading.
◆ Silent reading and conferring with the teacher.
◆ Sharing and discussion.

While students are reading silently, teachers can bring small groups together for guided reading.

A Gradient of Text

A key concept in supporting independent and guided reading is the use of a leveled collection of books. This collection consists of a wide variety of fiction and nonfiction texts organized along a *gradient* of difficulty. The texts have been carefully analyzed according to the characteristics that support and challenge readers. Each increment along the gradient identifies books at that level of difficulty, making it easier to match books and readers for guided reading, independent reading, and home reading.

Not every book in the classroom will be part of the leveled collection. Teachers will have a range of fiction and nonfiction books to read aloud to students and to assist them in their

The literacy coach observes an upper elementary guided reading group.

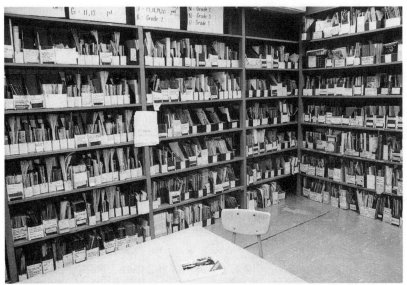

A book room to support guided reading, K–5.

Independent Writing

Through *independent writing*, children learn specific writing strategies and produce pieces of writing on their own in a number of genres: essays, personal narratives, fiction, and poetry. Independent writing during the writing workshop follows a structure that includes:

◆ A minilesson by the teacher on any aspect of writing.
◆ Writing by students while the teacher confers with individuals.
◆ Sharing and discussion.

research; however, the gradient is essential for developing reading strategies.

Many schools have a separate book room for housing the common leveled collection. Multiple copies of a rich array of fiction and non-fiction titles are organized along a gradient from kindergarten through grade 6. (A photograph of a book room is shown in Figure 4–3.)

Writing Instruction

The range of writing contexts is equally rich.

Language Experience, Shared Writing

In supported group writing such as *language experience* and *shared writing,* students produce a common text and in doing so come to know that writing has a purpose and also learn how to compose an extended piece of writing. When teachers work with a group to compose stories and informational pieces on an easel, they can demonstrate important concepts about how print works and illustrate how to spell words.

Interactive Writing

Interactive writing incorporates all the advantages of language experience and shared writing; in addition, it involves children in the mechanical production of some of the writing. While the group composes, individuals are selected to come up and fill in letters or words. The teacher decides where she wants to focus her students' attention.

Guided Writing

In *guided writing,* teachers bring students together in a small group for direct instruction on a specific aspect of writing—conventions, composition, revision, whatever. Guided writing can be used to help students organize their writing, select precise words, and learn how to write in a wide range of genres.

Investigation

In an *investigation* students use reading and writing skills as tools for learning. They learn research skills like note taking and scientific observation, and they organize information in various ways for clear communication. They may present what they've learned in a range of genres: reports, memoirs, narratives, and hypertext presentations. For young children, using writing for investigation begins with interactive writing, in which the teacher guides them to record their observations and summarize what they found out from experiments or explorations.

Reading and Writing Poetry

Reading and writing come together when students participate in *poetry workshop.* Younger children explore poetry by hearing poems read aloud and by engaging in shared reading. Even with older students, poetry should be read aloud again and again. It can be incorporated into readers theater and choral reading. Exploring poems leads students to write poems of their own.

Word Study

A balanced curriculum includes direct attention to phonics and spelling. A word study program uses minilessons followed by application. The minilesson is based on what students need to learn about letters, sounds, and words. The emphasis is on teaching important principles so that students become "word solvers" who know the inner workings of words. For example, sounds are represented by letters or by letter clusters that make spelling patterns. Students can begin to make categories of these spelling patterns. Knowing that you can make connections between words to solve them is another important idea; that is, if you know *tree* and *my*, it is easier to spell the word *try*. Students need to learn both simple and complex letter-sound patterns and be able to apply these principles in their reading and writing.

A minilesson[2] is a brief, powerful piece of instruction provided by the teacher. For example Kristen, a second-grade teacher, had observed that some of her students were using contractions in their writing but weren't spelling them accurately or using apostrophes correctly. They had been encountering contractions in their reading for some time and knew some of the easier ones (*I'm,* for example). Kristen made a chart on the easel and showed them explicitly how contractions worked, using some of the examples they knew. Students then suggested additional examples, and Kristen wrote them on the chart, inviting the children to identify the two root words as well as what letters had been left out. For each, they also noticed where the apostrophe was placed. She proceeded from easy contractions to those that were a little harder, *won't,* for example. Many of her students knew *won't* as a word but had not connected it with contractions. The finished chart was placed on the wall in the classroom as a reminder. Examples of contractions were also placed on the "word wall" (a display of words in the classroom). Finally, Kristen reminded students to select three contractions for their spelling lists that week and to think about contractions during their writing that day.

Adjusting the Curriculum to Meet Local Goals

A comprehensive literacy framework includes a range of reading and writing contexts. Some involve demonstrating and showing students what to do; others involve students in discovering principles and engaging in independent work while the teacher provides supportive guidance. Both are necessary.

Teachers and administrators find they can adjust this curriculum to meet the goals they have for their students. For example, they may see that their students are reading well but not developing as writers, so they allocate more time to writing instruction. They may find that they need to provide activities that broaden students' experience and develop vocabulary. The curriculum for any school or school district is created with the students in mind; the time in school must focus on what they need to develop as readers and writers.

As a staff developer, you may be helping teachers develop skills across this wide range of reading and writing contexts, or you may be working on a particular approach to add to an already established repertoire. In either case, you need to understand adult learning and be familiar with effective ways to introduce and develop new ways of teaching.

Suggestions for Expanding Your Skills as a Staff Developer

1. Analyze the curriculum used by a group of teachers:
   - Meet with a group of teachers from a school, a district, or various districts.
   - Ask them to discuss their goals for their students and provide examples of the current literacy curriculum.
   - List the instructional contexts you identify and ask teachers to describe them in greater depth. How do they typically organize their teaching time? What is the approximate time frame for each reading or writing activity? What do they see as most valuable? What is least valued?

◆ Ask them to talk about what they feel they do very well, as well as what they feel least confident about. What would they like to learn more about? What is missing altogether?

◆ After the meeting, compare your findings with the framework described in this chapter. What approaches do teachers currently use? What should their professional development sequence include?

2. Share the information gathered above with your staff development colleagues, with administrators, and with teachers, providing examples. Showing that you know what teachers are doing will establish your credibility. A habit of collecting information like this lets you design much more effective staff development programs.

Endnotes

[1]The running record was developed by Marie M. Clay. For further information about how to take and analyze running records, see:

1. *An Observation Survey of Early Literacy Achievement* (Clay 1993a), which provides a comprehensive overview of running records, including underlying research and thorough directions for coding, scoring, and analyzing records of reading behavior.

2. *Knowing Literacy: Constructive Literacy Assessment* (Johnston 1997), which provides valuable information about running records, including many examples and directions.

3. *Guided Reading: Good First Teaching for All Children* (Fountas and Pinnell 1996), which provides directions for taking running records and using them in guided reading.

[2]For detailed descriptions of minilessons see Fountas and Pinnell (1998).

SECTION TWO

Implementing High-Quality Professional Development

Section 2 makes specific suggestions for implementing an effective professional development system. Chapter 5 discusses the concept of professional development as "system thinking" and itemizes the components of an effective, coordinated professional development program. The remaining chapters provide detailed descriptions and examples of how staff developers can work with teachers at various levels of development.

Chapter 6 offers specific suggestions for planning a professional development course for teachers.

Chapter 7 addresses the very important task of assessing the context within which teachers work. We offer specific tech-

niques for assessing what teachers understand and can do as well as the ambiance of the school. Effective staff developers assess the context as they begin their work, but they continue to notice and use their knowledge of contextual variables throughout the development process.

Chapter 8 describes effective ways to introduce new procedures to teachers and support them as they try them out. We discuss ways to engage adult learners and demonstrate these techniques in action.

Organizing and Implementing a Professional Development System

Overload and fragmentation are the enemies of success.
—*ROBERT GARMSTON AND BRUCE WELLMAN,*
THE ADAPTIVE SCHOOL *(23)*

A s teacher educators, we expend enormous effort to create pleasurable, rewarding experiences for teachers; yet often we see that in the long run our work has made very little difference. Classrooms are pretty much the same or show only a few superficial changes. Alternatively, classrooms change but student achievement does not.

It's not surprising that professional development seldom results in the changes we intend. Most efforts are scant, piecemeal, and scattered. There is no cohesive *system* to assure learning for either teachers or students. Efforts are not rewarded with lasting improvement; resources, while not completely wasted, do not achieve the intent of the investment.

A system is an arrangement of things so intimately connected that they form a unified whole. A system is greater than the sum of its parts. The components of a system work together in *synergy*, producing an effect greater than each could accomplish alone.

There is no perfect analogy to help us understand the synergy that emerges from a coordinated system, but a symphony orchestra comes close.

When each instrument's voice is combined with that of all the other instruments, the music we hear is very different from that produced by any instrument alone. The instruments are combined in complex, ordered ways:

◆ Each component (strings, woodwinds, brass, percussion) has a role.
◆ Each role is necessary.
◆ Each role must be well performed.
◆ All players have defined responsibilities and actions that they must fulfill.
◆ The sections must work together in harmony (literally as well as figuratively!).

As the piece of music is performed, the combination of notes of varying pitches and timbres creates different sounds and carries different meaning. If you focus on only one component, you miss the overall experience.

The conductor holds the group together and oversees the action, based on a clear understanding of how the piece should sound. A good conductor simultaneously hears, evaluates, coaches, and leads every individual player, the sections, and the group as a whole. She or he controls the tempo, volume, and timing, solving problems as the piece unfolds. Every symphony sounds different as interpreted by the particular orchestra and the particular conductor. Even the acoustics in the room make a difference.

An orchestra doesn't play only a single symphony; there are many choices in the repertoire. Nor does one listen to a symphony just a few bars at a time. A symphony tells a story from beginning to end and needs to be experienced thus. Finally, one would not usually listen to a bit of one symphony and then a bit of another, no matter how beautiful the bits are. You want to hear the entire composition.

As a staff developer, you have responsibilities similar to a conductor. Rather than a loose collection of meetings and experiences, professional development forms an organized, interrelated whole. From the individual teacher's point of view, the learning experiences are extensive, ongoing, and connected. What happens in one session builds on another. In-classroom support and coaching are related to after-school sessions. The data collected about children's achievement are related to the topics that have been studied.

As the staff developer, you have broad knowledge: you know what is going on in classroom across the grades; you understand the reading and writing processes; you know how instruction shifts to meet the needs of developing learners. You simultaneously monitor each teacher's needs and check on student progress. You design a staff development program that meets the various needs of various staff members. Each person on the staff will contribute in unique ways, but all the actions fit together.

You also help teachers build a sense of responsibility for their role as well as a commitment to working with other members of the team. You give them the "big picture" of learning within the school, help them see each cohort of students as moving along a continuum of learning from one grade to the next. One year of good instruction doesn't produce competent readers and writers. Every teacher helps every other teacher improve practice; good practice is articulated from grade to grade so that each student's learning is continuous; and certainly, year after year of *good* teaching is essential for every child to reach his or her potential.

Professional development, therefore, is an interrelated system whose components form a unified whole. "System thinking" is the only way to improve literacy education and create more satisfying roles for teachers. The interconnected components of the system include:

◆ Ways to start an exciting, relevant program of professional development.
◆ Initial training courses.
◆ In-class demonstration and assistance.
◆ Coaching for shifts in teaching.
◆ Shared experiences that extend teachers' learning.
◆ Ways to work toward independence in learning and development.
◆ Ways to monitor and assess the professional training program.

System Thinking as a Base for Professional Development

A systems approach to professional development is based on information. Figure 5–1 outlines a series of interrelated actions, all of which are essential in creating an effective professional development plan that will have lasting effects.

Ten Actions Leading to Effective Professional Development

1. Gather information about the school, initially and throughout the process.
2. Design a professional development system with interdependent components.
3. Create awareness and work for clear goals and common vision.
4. Assess and focus resources—time, people, and materials—where they will make the greatest difference.
5. Provide training on specific, clear instructional procedures.
6. Create a culture that encourages reflection, honest feedback, mutual support, and collaborative problem solving.
7. Provide in-class demonstrations and coaching.
8. Use student achievement to assess impact and inform professional development plans and actions.
9. Monitor the impact of professional development on teaching in the school.
10. Design ongoing, in-depth professional development over longer periods of time.

Figure 5–1. *Ten Actions Leading to Effective Professional Development*

Obtaining Vital Information

It is always wise to begin by learning something about the school. (If you are working with teachers from several schools, apply these ideas across the district.) As a staff developer, you collect and use many different kinds of information from a variety of sources. It is essential to gather information about the school, the students, and the staff before designing the plan.

Spend as much time as possible talking informally with the principal and teachers. These informal conversations show that you value their perspectives and previous experiences. You are not conducting a formal study or coming to conclusions about the school; you are getting a feeling for the school as a place to start. Ask questions about the students and the way the school operates. Gathering information about how teachers see their work, their knowledge, and their strengths and the previous professional development they have had will:

◆ Show them that you recognize the knowledge and skills they bring to the mix.
◆ Help you design experiences that build on existing knowledge and skills.
◆ Help you avoid duplicating something teachers already know.
◆ Enable you to make the best use of your resources.
◆ Begin to create a context of shared ownership for new initiatives.
◆ Suggest ways to build community.
◆ Set the scene for problem solving and independence.

A conversation is just that—some questions, some sharing, some give-and-take. We are not recommending an interview and certainly not an interrogation. You will want to formulate some questions, however, and examples are listed in Figure 5–2. You probably won't use all these questions or comments; select ones in areas that are of most interest, and by all means adapt them to your own style of speaking. (And remember that you will be asking questions throughout the professional development process.)

Your initial interviews will uncover common concerns, individual issues, and shared goals, even though the staff may not currently recognize them. The tone of the interviews will tell you something about how satisfied teachers are with the job they are doing as well as student achievement. You can find out the goals individual teachers have for themselves and the school as well as what they see as "getting in the way." You can identify the existing curriculum and materials as well as the philosophy of instruction at each grade level. You can discover skills and strengths you can drawn on as your plan unfolds.

If you have the time, broaden your initial information gathering by examining student records and interviewing parents and other interested parties. In general, the more information you have, the better plan you can develop.

Designing Interrelated Components

A plan encompassing a wide variety of learning experiences is essential, but a "scattershot" approach will accomplish little. Time is the most valuable commodity in any school. If the school is embarking on a significant professional development effort, chances are that extra time has been allocated for these programs. You may call

Sample Questions to Ask in Initial Interviews	
Purpose for Gathering Information	**Questions/Statements to Get Conversation Going**
1. To get information about a person's perspective on the school as a whole and what he or she sees as good education as well as the roles of teachers and administrators.	◆ I'd like to get to know as much as I can about this school, the students, and the community so that we can make a good plan for professional development. What do you think is important for me to know? [Or, what can you tell me that is important?] ◆ What are the strong points to recognize in this school? ◆ What is important for me to know about the students [the parents, the staff, and the administration]? ◆ Please describe your ideal school. What would it be like? What would students be able to do? How would people work with each other? What would be going on in classrooms? How would the administrators support teachers?
2. To learn about the sense of community that exists among school staff members and gain information about how to work with them.	◆ We know that it will be important for all of us to work together. Can you give me some advice that will help this group [grade level or whole staff] work as a team? ◆ What role would you like to have in working with the other teachers on the team?
3. To gain insight into a person's expectations or "standards" for achievement.	◆ What do you expect your students to be able to read/write by the end of the year? ◆ How many do you think will achieve that level? ◆ Can you think of some students who met your expectations last year? What were they like?
4. To learn how instruction is managed within the school day.	◆ How much flexibility do you have in designing your day? ◆ How is your schedule working now? How would you like to change it? ◆ Often, teachers find it really hard to find enough time to do what they want to do in literacy and language. Do you have any suggestions for increasing the amount of time available for teaching, planning, and reflecting on your teaching?
5. To learn what materials are available and what additional materials the person would like to have.	◆ What kinds of materials do you find most helpful in teaching reading, writing, and language arts? [Ask them to show you some examples if possible.] ◆ What would you like to have if you could buy new materials?
6. To gain insight into what a person sees as successful and unsuccessful in teaching.	◆ Tell me about your teaching in the classroom last year [or so far this year]. What are some high points when you really felt successful? ◆ Were there any low points? What were they? Could these "lows" have been prevented or handled better? ◆ What tends to get in the way of your doing your best teaching?
7. To learn what data are presently available as a basis for instructional decisions and to gain insight into what a person thinks is good assessment.	◆ What do you learn from the evaluation/assessment systems you now use to find out what your students know? ◆ What would you like to know about your students that you aren't getting from your present assessment system? ◆ What kind of assessment have you found to be especially helpful in your teaching?
8. To learn about a person's expectations for professional development and to make a beginning assessment of what the person sees as important to learn.	◆ I'm going to be working with some of your staff in a seminar and also assisting with your teaching in classrooms. What do you hope will come out of this professional development activity? Is there anything you'd like to work on in your teaching? ◆ How do you help your colleagues do better teaching? How do they help you? ◆ If you had a chance to participate in your ideal professional development program, what would it look like? How would it help you? What kinds of experiences would you have? What would it help you do [or do better]?
9. To learn a person's perspective on needed changes in the school.	◆ You described your ideal school. What changes would need to be made to make this school more closely match your ideal? ◆ What tends to get in the way of achieving your vision for the ideal school?
10. To learn a person's perspective about the power of collaboration to achieve larger goals.	◆ Have you had an experience as a member of a successful group—a time when you achieved a significant goal that you could not have reached alone? Tell me about it. ◆ What did your group do to achieve your goal?

Figure 5–2. *Ten Questions to Ask in Initial Interviews*

what you are doing a "course of study" or an "inservice series." The idea, however, is not simply to fill up a series of meetings with one topic or another. Even a series of meetings or sessions on the same topic does not constitute a professional development system.

There are five critical ideas to keep in mind when designing the interrelated components of a professional development plan:

1. Lay out a possible series of meetings and topics in a sequence over time—preferably two or three years. (Precise dates will be ironed out later.) Designate intensive periods of training during the first year, less (but valuable) time during subsequent years.

2. Be sure teachers return to topics recursively so their experiences are shared and their knowledge becomes more analytic over time. Find ways and time to weave learning across the content areas of the course.

3. Follow up class sessions with in-class demonstrations, assistance, and coaching. Find ways and time to connect observations, coaching, and class sessions.

4. Promote and find time to reflect on and refine techniques that are learned.

5. Create feedback loops that will systematically inform the group of the effects of their changing practice.

Presenting an Awareness Session

You are at the school because either its teachers or administrators have already acted on a desire to improve instruction. Teachers expect to learn exciting ways to work with students and/or extend what they already know about specific instructional techniques. Your preliminary information will give you ideas for generating enthusiasm for your professional development plan.

Unanimous commitment is your goal, but don't expect it right away. Some members of the staff may already be excited and willing to participate, but not everyone will be. Most experienced teachers have had many dreary hours of transmission-style inservice that did not meet their needs, was poorly delivered, or presented material they already knew. You will be doing something different—providing explicit, engaging instruction but also working with teachers in their classrooms. The introductory session should give them a very clear idea of what is coming.

Decide Who Should Attend In general, an open invitation to all staff members is best. Certainly the principal should attend to show his or her support. You may also want other high-level administrators to attend to assure staff members of the value they place on the training. Base your decision on what you know about the context. Usually administrators' presence helps. Sometimes a more informal, intimate gathering where teachers feel free to ask questions is a better way to go.

Create a Pleasant, Inviting Atmosphere First impressions are lasting impressions. Start by showing participants how much you value their willingness to spend this brief time with you. When you are looking for a place that will meet your needs, remember the difference between meeting in a warm, cozy living room or in the school gym. You can hold the meeting in your own classroom if you are teaching in the school; otherwise, place children's work on the walls of whatever room you use (perhaps the staff lounge or similar meeting room). Offer refreshments,

Meeting to examine and learn together.

attractively arranged, perhaps with a tablecloth or flowers. Display an assortment of professional books and children's books teachers can browse through to anticipate what they will be seeing and learning.

Use and Show That You Value Teachers' Voices
Present some of the information you learned during your informal conversations, concentrating on common themes. Look at the initial comments in Figure 5–3:

◆ How has this leader recognized the thoughts and contributions of people in the school?
◆ How has she recognized the ideas and goals people hold in common?
◆ How has she shown that she values their commitment to children?
◆ How do comments like these contribute to a feeling of community?

Be sure your comments are honestly derived from the data, not just empty phrases. Of course, not everything you hear during your preliminary conversations will be positive. Unless it is overwhelmingly negative however (in which case you have a more serious problem than initiating a professional development plan), you will find grounds for a positive beginning. Elementary teachers almost always share common goals and have children's interests at heart even if they disagree about particular instructional approaches (or are simply unfamiliar with them). Collaboration will increase as they grow to know each other as individuals working to refine their teaching.

Briefly Describe the Professional Development Project A lengthy treatise on the project will not make a good impression here. You simply want to give people a clear idea of what you will be doing and why. You may want to refer to children's work or show a few minutes from a videotape. (Don't show a lengthy videotape; participants' attention will wander, and they may react negatively to some unimportant detail.) Describe the advantages of the project as well as how much commitment it will require. A one-page handout that lists your expectations and goals may help.

Make Good Use of Your Time and Invite Discussion Be sure to start and end on time. Punctuality shows that you respect the participants' time and sets a precedent for future meet-

---

An Example of Start-up Remarks

Thank you for all the time you spent with me and for your honesty. I was amazed to see the many similarities across grade levels as well as within grade levels. You have [or are moving to] a common vision for what you want your students to achieve.

I noticed collective goals; some were specifically related to grade levels. Also, you are all individuals, and you have your own goals. I can facilitate the problem solving here, but you are the people who will make it happen.

You did a great job, too, of identifying the challenges that you share, and I heard again and again that you are willing to work together. You also are ready either to learn some new approaches or refine approaches you are already using. We have all the components to build a good team. I have some ideas about how we can proceed together to meet your expectations.

I am inspired by your commitment to your students and feel that I want to work with you. The goals are yours. My job is to guide the process and provide some pretty specific instructional procedures that are based on research. I've been learning how to use these procedures. I want to help you develop a flexible plan for putting these techniques into action and support you in the process.

To begin, we will have a series of meetings to examine these procedures; I'll provide examples and directions. Then, we will try them out in classrooms. I'll come in to demonstrate and help and coach you. We'll continue our group sessions to delve deeper into the procedures and solve problems as we go. We'll give ourselves permission to make some mistakes as we try new approaches and learn. It's not important to be perfect; it's more important to keep learning and making the process more effective.

Figure 5–3. *Example Start-up Remarks*

ings. Keep the introductory session to about an hour, and be sure to allow plenty of time for questions. What they have to say is more important than what you have to say.

Apportioning Resources

Work with the school team and administrators to make wise use of resources to support your professional development plan. Don't spend too much money the initial year, and evaluate each expenditure carefully. The resources at your disposal include time, personnel, and money. Budget sensibly, making sure expenditures are consistent with your goals. Be sure you know what materials are necessary (for example, see Pinnell and Fountas 1999 for suggestions on numbers of books needed for guided reading).

Specific resources you may need include:

◆ Professional books for teachers.
◆ Time for teachers to meet together for training sessions on a regular basis (during the school day or after school).
◆ Books to support instruction (to read aloud to students and to use in independent and guided reading, for example).
◆ Other materials to support reading, writing, and language development.
◆ Video cameras and equipment.
◆ Audio tape recorders.
◆ Time for teachers to observe in one another's classrooms.

Mounting a professional development program for a school is almost always affordable within the budget as a whole; it just needs planning and adjusting.

Providing Instructional Training

Ideally, the actions we've talked about so far take place before formal sessions begin. Because the start-up process will gradually involve more and more of the school staff, group ownership of the decisions should be in place when classes do begin. Once you have a calendar for at least the first year, you can begin to provide some very specific training. (We use the word *training* here because we are talking about specific teaching actions. Chapter 6 itemizes the elements that might be included in a professional development course related to literacy education.) From the beginning, however, you need to share *why* the techniques are worthy of use. Revisit these rationales again and again as teachers work with an instructional technique. A concept is understood at deeper levels throughout the experience of learning about it, trying it, reflecting on it, and refining it.

Here are some general characteristics of good training:

◆ Techniques are clearly described, demonstrated, and revisited many times.
◆ Clear rationales are provided for each technique introduced.
◆ Instructional approaches are consistent within an interrelated framework of activity that is research based. They are not an unconnected potpourri of "activities."
◆ Training sessions are balanced as to presentation, discussion, and example.
◆ Participants bring their own examples and student data to sessions for sharing and analysis.
◆ Participants begin by observing and analyzing others' teaching but learn to share, reflect on, and analyze their own teaching through description and videotaped examples.
◆ Participants look closely at individual and group data.
◆ Class sessions are closely connected to coaching in classrooms.
◆ The leader shares his or her teaching experiences and student data, modeling reflection.

It's important for teachers to meet in an attractive room where they feel comfortable. Ideally, a school has a special room set aside for professional development, but that is not always possible. Try to find an area where you can establish permanent displays of children's work and keep professional materials and workshop supplies.

Creating a Learning Culture

You are implementing a challenging and dynamic professional development plan, and you expect change. Remember that change is exciting but risky. You will want to establish a supportive environment within which people feel free to mention their mistakes and ask questions. Learning must be shared honestly. Over time, learning groups become highly skilled at talking with one another, but they are usually not able to do so right away. Your role is critical in establishing norms for group conversation.

Talking During Class Sessions Group conversations during class sessions are key to establishing a trusting environment. Teach the group some simple principles for talking together and model this kind of language yourself:

◆ *Avoid using a judgmental or accusatory tone.* Be objective; it is clearer and less threatening to describe behavior than to make judgments or inferences. For example, it is much better to say, "Three children were looking around. What do you think was going on? Is it possible they couldn't see the book?" rather than, "You weren't getting their attention" or "You can't control your group." Focusing on what happens helps everyone be more analytic.

◆ *Stay focused on important points and issues rather than unimportant details.* One major point may take care of a number of minor points. For example, in guided reading, selecting the appropriate text goes a long way toward ensuring student success, confidence, and engagement. Rather than spending time arguing about how to make students behave, work on important instructional moves that will lead to greater learning *and* better behavior.

◆ *Invite participants to back up their statements with evidence or rationales.* Sometimes being asked to say more or give an example helps teachers shape their thinking more clearly and communicate it to others. Sharing many examples helps them look across cases and form larger concepts rather that fixating on whether a technique is "right" or "wrong."

◆ *Encourage individuals to bring problems to the group for shared problem solving.*

Anyone trying something new will only approximate the technique at first; as a group, you expect problems and partial responses. You may want to devote a part of every session to talking about problems and sharing possible solutions. Invite the group to discuss how they would resolve issues everyone is facing.

Developing the Schoolwide Learning Community While formal group meetings are important in building community, you will also want to establish larger contexts. Keeping professional development material, instructional material, and children's books in your break room or staff lounge encourages teachers to talk casually about their work during breaks and over lunch.

Being a staff developer on location within a school affords many opportunities to promote a learning community. You can talk with teachers on your way into the building, in the corridors, during lunch. You can invite teachers to stop by your office to ask a quick question, make a request, or tell about something interesting that just happened in class. You're free to pop into classrooms to give teachers materials and books or just say hello.

Schools are most effective when teachers talk across grade levels, share new things they've learned, are aware of what their colleagues are working on, ask questions of one another, laugh about mistakes, and visit one other's classrooms. Open doors encourage an open atmosphere.

The literacy coordinator and a teacher look at the framework for learning.

Demonstrating and Coaching in Classrooms

Our university graduate classes are filled with new research and its implications for instruction. Professors show videotapes of classroom instruction and invite teachers to describe their practice. But imagine your university professor coming back with you to the classroom as you try a new instructional approach, perhaps even demonstrating it with your students and then discussing it with you. Working with the approach, you would learn more about it, and you would have your instructor's observations and suggestions to help you. She would be able to observe your students while you taught the lesson, giving you feedback on student engagement and learning.

This is exactly the kind of assistance you can give your adult students in the professional development program we propose. You will introduce, describe, and demonstrate topics in class sessions and then be able to provide direct assistance and coaching in classrooms. Through ongoing reflection, evaluation, and collaboration, teachers will gradually refine how they use the techniques you teach them.

A teacher who is first using a new approach is likely to focus on actions—new behavior requires conscious attention to steps and materials. As the new routines are learned, these actions become more automatic and the teacher can give more attention to observing children's behavior and making powerful teaching decisions. These moment-to-moment interactions make the difference in student learning. The best instructional approaches set the scene for powerful teacher-student interactions.

Coaching teachers in their classroom has many advantages:

◆ Teachers have another "eye" to help them assess student learning.
◆ Teachers feel more confident in trying new approaches because they receive specific demonstrations and on-site assistance.
◆ Techniques are implemented beyond superficially "trying them out."
◆ You gain valuable information that informs your class training sessions.

Assessing Student Achievement and Refining Your Program Accordingly

Part of an effective professional development system is working with the group to teach them assessment techniques that are closely aligned with the new approaches. In many schools data are collected but not interpreted or used as a basis for instruction. Often, teachers see no purpose in data collection other than satisfying the administration. Using a professional development system like ours, you will develop the group's ability to analyze and use data to inform their instruction. Teachers will learn how to collect the information they need to track student progress as a result of their work, creating a sense of shared ownership and a willingness to change.

Although it is sometimes necessary to gather a standardized and consistent set of data for a large number of schools (to evaluate a new program, for example), it is best if teachers have a voice in deciding what data to gather when. Useful sources of data for measuring literacy progress include:

◆ Systematic observations of early reading and writing behavior such as *An Observation Survey of Early Literacy Achievement* (Clay 1993a).
◆ Records of books read by students.
◆ Records of reading progress along a gradient of text difficulty.
◆ Reading observations using running records or informal reading inventories.
◆ Spelling tests.
◆ Writing samples, evaluated with a rubric for conventions and craft.
◆ Story retellings, both oral and written.
◆ Reading response journals, which reveal students' comprehension of the texts they read.
◆ Writer's notebooks, which provide information about what students notice and use as writers.
◆ Poetry notebooks and personal poetry anthologies.

Certain data are particular to the age of the child; other data, such as reading progress, must be kept over time. And don't forget to involve students in the process—selecting pieces for their permanent portfolio, for example.

Standardized measures also enter in. Almost all schools require tests at various points; these days, high-stakes proficiency tests in third or fourth grade are particularly prominent. These tests don't offer very much feedback in terms of instruction; nevertheless, they do allow you to relate new instructional approaches to student performance. Many of the skills required to perform well on these tests are the same as those taught in a literacy program. For example, proficiency tests usually require students to infer beyond what is stated. As you work with teachers in guided reading or reading workshop, help them see how students' making inferences can be part of oral discussion and/or written work following reading. In your professional development sessions, make specific connections to the kinds of behavior that will be required on the proficiency tests. (For a thorough description of how to embed test-taking skills in reading instruction, see Fountas and Pinnell 2000.)

Monitoring Changes in Teaching

An effective professional development system includes systematic monitoring of the impact it is having. The bottom line is whether or not changes are taking place in school classrooms. The many professional development courses provided every year should produce tremendous changes in classrooms, but sadly that is not the case. For a variety of reasons, individuals may participate in and even enjoy inservice sessions but make almost no changes in their daily practice.

You will want to establish a systematic way to detect progress you and your colleagues are making in implementing new instructional approaches. There are several questions your group can address as they monitor change:

◆ How is our group working together? Do we help each other? Do we collaborate?
◆ What kinds of changes are taking place in practice?
◆ What impact are these changes having on students?
◆ What are we learning from our practice?

We are not talking about going into classrooms with a checklist. That kind of heavy-handed supervision leads only to subterfuge or to temporary, superficial change. Explore the questions above in your individual observations and conferences with teachers as well as in your interactions with the group as a whole. Find time to address these questions regularly so that everyone is aware of their importance. Connect these discussions to

the overall vision of the group: each individual member is different, but you are all moving toward the same goal. Teaching actions relative to specific grades may also be different, but they represent a coordinated effort.

To help you, take lots of notes and set up a system for keeping records of:

◆ How teachers use their time and resources.
◆ The engagement, interest, and independence of students in classrooms.
◆ How teachers use the routine procedures of various instructional approaches.
◆ The reflections and perspectives of individual teachers as they talk about their work.
◆ How teachers are able to analyze children's strengths and needs, as shown by their record keeping and their discussion of their students.
◆ Your in-depth analysis of how well teachers have integrated new techniques and procedures into their practice.

It's best to keep a file or notebook for each teacher, so you can go back through your observations easily. (Some examples are provided in Chapters 7 and 9.) You'll find points to bring up in class sessions as you ask participants to talk more about their observations of children or experiences in implementing a particular technique. Sometimes a two- or three-minute piece of videotape will spark discussion among the group.

The close connection between class training sessions and classroom coaching shows participants how important their work is and helps connect theory and practice. It makes the course come alive: teachers are talking about something that is recent, relevant, and directly related to their own experience. They become expert sounding boards for one another by talking not about perfect practice but about what they have learned and their students are learning from them. The spotlight can be turned on how to pace a lesson to keep children engaged or on how to select materials in keeping with students' needs and interests.

This flow of information illustrated in Figure 5–4 demonstrates how the components of a professional development system loop back on each other to inform your work as a staff developer. Knowledge shared in class sessions results in changes in practice, which you support and observe. Your individual conferences with teachers provide the particular help they need and give you feedback as a teacher of teachers. You make systematic observations and analyze them in depth. All this information offers up excellent examples to share in class sessions and helps you plan additional sessions. The process builds ownership, because teachers see that their own teaching is informing the process. The information is current and directed toward their immediate needs. Immediacy is not the only benefit, however; by building experiences on previous experiences, teachers are gradually developing an overall picture of teaching and learning with a cohesive theoretical base.

You, of course, learn as well. Your experiences over time will allow you to recognize patterns of learning, and you will get better at analyzing what teachers do and what they need. You'll begin to get "ahead of the curve," antici-

pating areas in which you need to do more intensive or explicit work. You'll see when a technique you have "taught" in a class session hasn't been "learned" by teachers. You'll identify procedures that are more complex or harder to relate to theory. Don't forget, however, that there will always be surprises: you are working with unique individual teachers as well as unique groups of children. Nevertheless, the more you can anticipate, the better job you will do.

Designing Ongoing Learning Opportunities

It takes several years of professional development to create powerful instruction. The information cycle described above is established during the first year of the professional development project but is continual and ongoing. You will want to make a big initial commitment to your program—in the first year or two, we recommend thirty to forty hours of class time

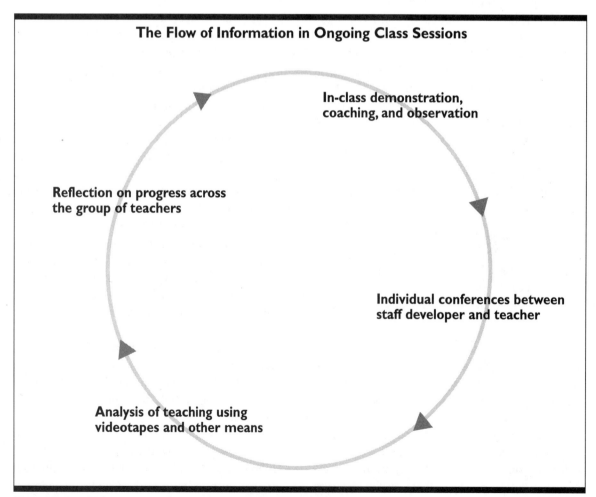

Figure 5–4. *Information Flow in Ongoing Class Sessions*

accompanied by frequent classroom coaching sessions. During subsequent years you will provide less frequent class sessions and offer in-class coaching and assistance as needed.

The effort may seem daunting; however, teachers take an increasingly larger role in the process. They will have learned a great deal about analyzing their own teaching and can begin to help one another in the process. They can examine student progress and decide what they need to do more effectively. Some ongoing professional development activities for teachers who have become well versed in using particular instructional approaches are:

◆ Forming study groups to read new professional books.
◆ Engaging in targeted action research projects to look at aspects of teaching and learning.
◆ Observing and analyzing one another's teaching.
◆ Creating systems for record keeping.

As time goes on, teachers set their own priorities and work in smaller groups. You will be able to accommodate more diverse interests. At this more independent level of professional development, teachers will be better able to profit from attending conferences and/or working with outside consultants. Instead of bringing in someone to provide generic inservice, they will invite an expert to provide the specific new information they need.

The Recursive Nature of System Thinking

Putting a professional development system into place is not a linear process. *All ten components* are critical to the success of the effort, and after you get going, *all ten components* take place simultaneously. It is the combination of components that makes the difference.

Professional development takes enormous amounts of energy and time. We are not talking about something simple, short term, or easy; we *are* talking about something that is very important to success. Manufacturers spend a great deal of time training their workers; computer systems engineers spend a large proportion of their time

updating their skills. Teaching is as demanding and complex a profession as any other and influences our children's lives. It is important to make the effort.

A professional development system within a school allows teachers to target energy and become more efficient and effective. The system expands so that more is accomplished. Teachers become more independent; you no longer have the entire responsibility for class sessions or coaching. Becoming more aware of their impact on students motivates teachers; and the more they learn, the easier it gets. The synergy of the group produces greater results than any one person can accomplish alone.

Suggestions for Expanding Your Skills as a Staff Developer

1. Start by gathering information about a school or group to which you have access. If you can, work with several colleagues who are also interested either in providing professional development or working as a team to provide it.
2. Using the sample questions in Figure 5–2 as a base, create a guide for informal conversations with between five and ten people. Even if you are planning to work with teachers at only one grade level, include teachers of other grades as well. Also include the principal. (You can also question a group of people at the same time, but you will probably get different information.) Some general suggestions regarding these conversations are:
   ◆ If you take notes (and you'll surely want to), be sure to alert the person that you're going to do so.
   ◆ Establish a conversational tone with give-and-take. That may mean giving some examples and ideas of your own rather than acting like an interviewer.
   ◆ Ask for specific examples.
   ◆ Listen closely and ask for clarification if you do not understand.
   ◆ Have the conversation in a quiet place where you will not be disturbed.
   ◆ Keep it short—fifteen to thirty minutes, unless there is a specific reason to talk longer.

3. After each conversation, take a few moments to remember details and expand your notes so that when you go back to them you will have an accurate picture of what was said. It is not necessary to tape-record and transcribe the conversation.

4. Reflect on all of your conversations and draw out some common threads. Bring your data back to another meeting with your professional development colleagues. Discuss:
   - What are the strengths revealed in these conversations?
   - What common goals were detected?
   - What issues emerged that will be important to this school staff?
   - What do they know and what are they interested in learning?
   - What do they see as their needs for professional development?
   - Where would be a good place to start in developing a professional development plan for the group?

5. Now think about potential opening remarks for an awareness session. What would you say? (Use Figure 5–3 to help you.) Go back to one of your interviewees and share your informal observations of what you have found out about the school staff's perspectives. Choose someone that you know will help you check out your perspectives.

6. Ask for feedback. How accurate were you? Did you get some of the important information? Did you miss something?

7. Report your feedback to your professional development colleagues.

Chapter 6

Planning a Professional Development Course for Literacy Educators*

Participation and professional development are seen as one organizing concept: Learning means having access to multiple, sustained opportunities for participation.
—LINDA LAMBERT
THE CONSTRUCTIVIST
LEADER *(55)*

A professional development course allows you to acquaint a group of teachers with new instructional approaches. You cannot teach every person individually, and true learning requires social support. Group learning is also more efficient than individual work.

The course must be a cohesive, interrelated set of experiences rather than a string of isolated presentations. One-shot inservice sessions have little effect and, in general, waste time, money, and energy. A consultant may provide motivation or some very specific input that fits with the staff development plan as a whole; however, the real payoff lies in a well-organized sequence of learning experiences that builds knowledge over time. Some basic characteristics of effective professional development are listed in Figure 6–1.

A well-planned professional development course creates a "learning group" of people who share what they know and develop a common language for talking with one another. For example, once members of the group know precisely what they mean by terms like *strategies* or *story introductions*, they don't need to spend time clarifying or arguing about definitions. They can focus on the examples that help them learn.

Some complex decisions need to be made with regard to any professional development course:

*We are indebted to Irene Fountas for her contributions to this chapter.

- Who and how many should attend?
- How many sessions are needed?
- What topics should come first, second, and so on?
- What is the best balance between presentation, discussion, and small-group work?
- How can you connect the course to classroom practice?
- How do you balance what you know that teachers need to learn and what they see as their most relevant problems?

Let's take a look at the planning process in detail.

Practical Considerations

Before preparing the course outline, which is a conceptual document, there are some practical considerations in launching a successful course.

Participants

Knowing the participants is the key to implementing the course successfully. The preliminary information you've gathered will help a great deal here. In addition, you will want to determine how many people will attend the course. The optimal number is between five and fifteen participants. If you have fewer than five, you will do better to think of it as a "study group" rather than a formal course. Of course, there is no hard-and-fast rule. There may be practical or political reasons for admitting more than fifteen. However, one staff developer working full time can provide in-class assistance and coaching to only fifteen people.

It's also essential that the staff developer spend some time working directly with children. Teaching skills not practiced are quickly eroded. In addition, trying new approaches with children builds credibility.

Ask participants to make a commitment to attend the entire sequence of sessions, because you will be introducing and revisiting information systematically, looping ideas backward and forward, building each session on the ones that precede it until the whole emerges. Think in terms of twenty or thirty sessions total, in sequences of ten, each sequence building on the next. It is better to have a smaller group of participants who are committed to the series than a larger number who come and go. (Think how

---

Characteristics of Effective Professional Development

- Complex ideas are experienced, discussed, and analyzed in a variety of learning contexts.

- It is grounded in the practice of teaching children.

- It involves learning conversations surrounding the act of teaching.

- It is supported by a learning community who share a language they can use to communicate complex ideas.

- There is a balance between demonstrating specific teaching approaches and reflecting on and analyzing the process of teaching.

Figure 6–1. *Characteristics of Effective Professional Development*

easily someone who comes into a session with no background can disrupt the ongoing learning of the group!)

It's also best if all participants work directly with children in the classroom. Teaching and observing children are essential elements of the course. Every member of the group is responsible for sharing experiences and perspectives that are directly related to their work with children. Participants who are not applying what they learn in class sessions will of necessity alter the focus of the discussion. If you do have persons (the principal, for example) who want to participate in the class but do not work with children, arrange for them to meet with small groups of students or work in a classroom regularly.

Participant Expectations

There is much more to it than attending the sessions and working with children. A member of a group is responsible not only for her or his own learning but for contributing to the learning of others. The group learns more because of synergy—all members help one another. To be a contributing member of the group, each participant must:

- Attend all sessions except in case of illness or some other unavoidable reason.

◆ Read and reflect on materials before the session and relate them to work with students.

◆ Contribute to the group's learning via discussion.

◆ Try out new instructional techniques in the classroom.

◆ Invite the staff developer into his or her classroom to observe, demonstrate, and coach.

◆ Participate in individual conferences with the staff developer.

◆ Bring student artifacts and data to group sessions for analysis.

◆ Be willing to be observed by peers and, with the support and advice of the staff developer, share videotaped segments of her or his teaching (short lessons or very brief interactions with students).

◆ Reflect on his or her practice and set goals for continuing improvement.

It may take some time for a school staff to reach the kind of commitment implied in the above list. Preliminary leadership-team meetings and awareness sessions may be necessary over a period of months or even a year before a group is able to make a commitment to this ongoing work. Once they do, however, they are well on their way to improving their teaching dynamically.

Number, Timing, and Length of Sessions

The number of sessions you will need depends on your goals for the program. You may be exploring a limited topic—guided reading or writing workshop, for example. The teachers you work with will also have ideas about what they want to accomplish. Analyze the topic and estimate the number of sessions you'll need to explore it in enough depth that there is a good chance it will be incorporated into the instruction of the school. No topic worth its salt can be explored in one or two sessions. For example, guided reading, as a focused topic, could be explored pretty well in about ten sessions over the period of a year. More ambitious efforts will take longer.

If your goal is to incorporate a broad framework of literacy teaching and learning that includes many integrated approaches, you will want to establish longer sequences of sessions. A professional development course of study like this will probably require each staff member to put in about forty hours during the first year and twenty hours during each subsequent year.

The timing of class sessions is important as well. It might seem sensible to meet for five solid days and "cover" a topic, but that's not the most productive way to learn about teaching. You may schedule an intense period of study in which to get started and teach some specific techniques, but spaced meetings are much more powerful for adult learners. Teachers need time to explore topics and techniques with their students in their classroom. The experience they then bring back to the group makes learning more powerful for everyone. They also need to address the same topics again and again, each time achieving greater understanding.

You want teachers' experiences to inform each and every class session, and they need time to reflect on their learning and come up with new ideas. None of this learning can be accomplished simply by putting in hours. Meeting every week probably doesn't put enough space between sessions and may be a too demanding schedule for your participants or for you. Remember, we are talking about professional development over an extended period of time. Meeting once a month allows too much space between sessions: participants tend to forget

Looking at teachers' records to plan class sessions

assignments or to do them quickly in the last week before class. It is hard to build momentum. Meeting every other week or every third week seems to be a reasonable schedule.

Unfortunately, most staff development sessions take place after school. Getting teachers released from their classrooms to study and work with one another is ideal, but today's educational climate makes this policy very difficult to implement. Substitutes are hard to get and many of them are not highly qualified. Also, teachers shouldn't be away from their classroom too often. Usually, you can strike a good balance between after-school work, a few half-days of released time, and some summer sessions.

How long sessions should be is another consideration. Nothing of importance can be achieved in forty-five minutes. You might as well not waste your energy. On the other hand, long, exhausting after-school sessions take their toll on the participants and on you. You can fill a day or half-day of released time with varied segments and activities. If your sessions are after school or at night, limit them to two hours. (We repeat: it's essential to start and stop on time.)

Facility

The facility in which staff development takes place should visibly attest to the fact that professionals are working there. Light, pleasant colors, and the proper temperature all show your participants that their time is valued. They'll work together better in a comfortable facility. Everything you can do to make your session professional shows that you respect your group.

It's best if you're able to use the same room for your whole-group, small-group, and individual meetings rather than moving from place to place. Stability and organization make things go more smoothly. The room should be inviting and clean, with comfortable chairs and tables. You may want to bring in fresh flowers or cover display tables with bright cloths. (Take note of publishers' displays at the next conference you attend—they do all they can to make them attractive!) Light refreshments are okay—water certainly needs to be available—but don't go overboard on food. It takes time and is not essential.

Place children's work and pertinent quotations from professional reading on the walls.

Display new children's books or professional books. Ideally, your meeting room will be in the school, so you can visit classrooms when you wish. You will need easels, a child-size one for demonstration and a regular one on which to record participants' comments. It is also good to have a number of small round or rectangular tables so that small groups can face one another as they work together. Rectangular tables allow very flexible arrangements, and can be combined into a large square table at which the whole group can see one another. Participants can also sit in a large circle. During your presentations they will face front, but it is very important that every participant be able to see all the others during group discussions. Figure 6–2 lists characteristics that make a facility an excellent one for class sessions. The more of these characteristics your meeting room possesses, the more positive the atmosphere will be.

A Variety of Learning Experiences

A professional development course is more than a series of presentations and discussions. While some direct presentations will of course be necessary, you will have greater success when you explore a topic through a variety of learning experiences.

Live or Videotaped Observation

Observation is just that: the group watches a teacher work with children and discusses what they see. As the staff developer, you guide the observation, pointing out important behavior and asking participants to share their reactions. Hearing many perspectives helps them sort out their thinking. Sometimes it's a good idea to introduce a particular technique with a brief overview and then a good example. Of course, more than one example will be necessary. Instructional approaches are complex, and every group of children is different.

Live Observation Class sessions that take place during the school day can easily include a live observation in a classroom, which is very effective in helping teachers learn. You can also ask class members or other teachers to work with one or more children during an after-school session. Watching a teacher work with children

Characteristics of an Effective Meeting Room

♦ A light and airy atmosphere.
♦ Comfortable chairs and moveable tables.
♦ Light refreshments (especially important if the meeting is held after school).
♦ Open space so that participants can sit in a circle instead of in rows.
♦ Flexible space to accommodate various forms of instruction—whole group, small group, pairs, individuals.
♦ Wall space for displaying children's work and other learning materials.
♦ Storage space for artifacts and materials.
♦ Permanent, protected space for a professional library.
♦ Place to display and store children's books so that they are available for discussion.
♦ Materials to facilitate discussion: easels, a whiteboard, an overhead projector and screen, a video player.

Figure 6–2. *Characteristics of an Effective Meeting Room*

behind a one-way glass lets you observe and talk at the same time, which makes the experience more interesting. If you are observing in a classroom, caution participants not to talk with one another or interfere with the ongoing instruction. There are a variety of ways for them to take notes during an observation in order to be able to talk about the experience afterward, but it's best to keep your guidelines broad and to use open-ended forms rather than checklists.

Videotaped Observation Videotapes are a convenient way to introduce a teaching technique, especially if participants can see a number of short segments showing different examples. (Since we all have a tendency to do what we *see*, the examples need to be varied rather than imply one precise set of actions.) Tapes do not take the place of live observation, however. It's best to use a combination. Try to ensure that the range of examples teachers see clearly demonstrates the approach's basic moves, as well as how teachers make decisions and adjustments to meet students' needs.

You will collect good videotaped examples as you work with teachers over time. To get good examples, choose teachers who are very clear and explicit in their use of a particular instructional approach and coach them before the lesson. You can also tape your own teaching. These videotaped examples don't need to be perfect—in fact, that isn't possible. But they should be clear enough that they do not misrepresent the approach or confuse the participants.

When using videotapes, there are several things you need to keep in mind:

◆ Sometimes participants may bring in tapes of their own teaching. Use these with caution. Teachers who are just beginning to learn about a technique need good examples. You will not want them to imitate one another while they are approximating the approach in their own practice.

◆ It is very hard for teachers to learn to give and receive criticism. A videotaped early approximation of a technique invites one of two actions: too much criticism or no criticism at all even though there are obvious problems.

◆ Videotaped lessons can have a "deadening" effect if they are too long or aren't good examples. Select brief, well-paced lessons *or parts of lessons* that can engage adults and provide material for discussion.

◆ Having only *one* example can actually get in the way of learning, especially with beginning teachers. They may think the example is the only way and copy it inappropriately.

◆ The tape must be of good-enough quality that participants can tell what is going on. Videotape picks up every sound and makes the classroom seem noisier than it actually is. When taping, you will want to be sure there is relative quiet.

◆ Think about what you want participants to look at. Some suggestions for working with videotaped examples are listed in Figure 6–3.

◆ Focus on student behavior and on how the teacher responds to that behavior. Ask questions that help participants become descriptive and analytic rather than judgmental as they watch a tape.

◆ You can use the same video several times for different purposes. Early on, it may sim-

Suggestions for Working with Videotaped Examples in the Literacy Course		
Before	**During**	**After**
◆ Set the context for viewing the lesson, including information on students and the purpose and focus of the lesson. ◆ Examine artifacts that are relevant to the lesson (student writing samples, running records, etc.). ◆ Make hypotheses about what you will see these students doing in the lesson to be observed. ◆ Focus the observation on a particular aspect of teaching—procedures, student response, teacher's skill in various areas.	◆ Ensure that all members of the group can see and hear. ◆ Have participants watch the tape, taking notes in response to the focus questions. ◆ If appropriate, stop the tape at planned intervals for discussion. ◆ Make sure the length of the tape is appropriate (a few minutes to no more than twenty minutes).	◆ Invite open responses to the tape by asking participants simply to describe—not judge—what they see. ◆ Focus discussion by asking participants to talk about student behavior, teacher behavior, and teachers' skills such as use of materials. ◆ Ask participants to talk in pairs or small groups, focusing on specific aspects of the lesson. ◆ Involve participants in deeper and more extended analysis of the lesson as they gain experience. ◆ Conclude the session by asking participants to summarize their descriptions and what they have learned.

Figure 6–3. *Suggestions for Working with Videotapes*

ply introduce an approach, and your participants will focus on the "nuts and bolts" of the task. Later, they can analyze how the teacher is supporting students' construction of meaning.

◆ As in live observation, you guide the talk. After viewing a tape, you can have participants discuss it in pairs and then come together as a larger group, or you can invite an open response immediately.

◆ Focus the discussion on the aspect of the lesson that is relevant for this group at this time. As they grow more sophisticated in their use of the routine procedures related to an approach, you will want to "up the ante" by stimulating more detailed and in-depth analysis of the lesson.

Presentation

Observation is more effective than talking about it when introducing a particular topic, but inevitably you will need to make some direct presentations that provide clear, essential information. To that end, these presentations must be well organized and focused. Preparation and

organization show that you respect the group's time. Figure 6–4 lists some suggestions for making effective presentations.

Effective presentations are brief and elicit interaction. They address practical concerns important to teachers. It is essential to include many concrete examples, taken from your own teaching or from the participants' classrooms. (Your own work with children will be a real resource for current, up-to-date examples.) Also, think about your audience. If you are working with a group of fifth-grade teachers, for example, it is risky to have a large number of examples from younger students. Kindergarten teachers may not be interested in reading the response journals of fourth graders. You will also want to be sure that your material does not include dated information and is consistent with current research.

Interaction and Discussion

Sessions are lively when the participants interact. You will want to invite and encourage discussion. Figure 6–5 presents some suggestions for inviting group discussion.

Making Effective Presentations

- Design presentations with the audience in mind.
- Have materials and ideas organized so that the presentation goes forward smoothly and quickly without wasting time.
- Keep presentations brief, and intersperse interaction and discussion.
- If participants need information that, for efficiency, must be presented rather than discovered, be honest about what you are doing and tell them how long it will take; then invite interaction.
- Be sure any visual aids are clear and readable.
- As you present, stand beside the overhead projector and point to material on the wall or screen; touching the transparency makes the print move around on the screen.
- Show the entire transparency at once rather than trying to reveal a point at a time; if you must indicate places on the overhead either point to the screen or lay a pencil on the transparency.
- Be relaxed and conversational.
- Use humor when possible but avoid being flippant. In other words, it's always all right to laugh at yourself but not at someone else.
- Try to communicate that you are talking *with*, not *at* people in the group.
- As much as possible, use your own examples from real classrooms rather than hypothetical situations, sets of directions, or lists of "shoulds."
- Don't overuse quotes or long lists of theoretical ideas without concrete examples.
- Be sure your transparencies have print that is large enough for participants to read; if you have a page of small print, summarize the points orally instead of projecting the page.
- Be sure your information is up to date.

Figure 6–4. *Making Effective Presentations*

Lively discussion is part of every effective professional development learning experience:

> Through language interactions with others in the group, we try out our ideas to formulate or reformulate understandings of a particular phenomenon. The process is rooted in what Halliday (1975) has described as "learning how to mean."
>
> Throughout the teaching process, whether with children or adults, dialogue is central to the learning situation. (Lyons, Pinnell, and DeFord 1993, p. 47)

Through discussion, teachers build the common language they use to share meaning, a language tied to experience and to children's work.

As the leader, you challenge participants to make statements and back them up with evidence, challenge them to articulate what they observe, explain it, provide specific examples, and justify what they think. The process places high-level cognitive demands on the learner.

Discussion does not mean simply sharing opinions; it reflects the value that participants place on ongoing learning and problem solving. Central characteristics are tentativeness, posing hypotheses, and exploring problems rather than rushing to judgment. Group members talk about what *might* be happening or why the teacher *might* have made a certain decision. They explore the possibilities for student learning. This "hesitancy reflects (1) valuing ongoing inquiry and (2) recognizing the complexity of students' learning and its relationship to the social context" (Lyons, Pinnell, and DeFord 1993, p. 48).

You can stimulate discussion among the whole group, within small groups, and between pairs. It's highly effective to vary these contexts, moving from one to another as appropriate. Participants need to interact with one another directly, not just with or through the leader, sharing insights and asking questions. Someone may confirm a conclusion by referring to something she's read. Someone else may interpret the quo-

Figure 6–5. *Inviting Discussion*

tation differently. Thus new shared understanding is created.

Inquiry

In inquiry, participants investigate a question or solve a problem. Presenting a problem engages your group and helps them expand their thinking. Inquiry is high-level thinking related to scientific investigation. In fact, it's fun. You are inviting your group to function as an action research team.

Here's an example. Laura asked a group of teachers she was working with to examine documentation related to a small group of first graders' reading. They looked not only at the level of texts students could read but also at the kinds of behavior they exhibited. These teachers were experienced interpreters of run-

ning records, so they were able to make hypotheses about the level and type of text that would provide maximum opportunities for these children to learn. Next, they examined a group of texts and selected some that would provide good next steps for the children. Finally, they watched the group of children in a videotaped lesson and compared their own hypotheses to the decisions the teacher made. Their preparatory investigations sharpened observation and discussion.

Examination of Student Work

Examining student work—reading behavior, writing samples, or other products produced in the classroom—is a good way to promote active inquiry.

Artifacts Artifacts are designated student samples, sometimes called *protocols*, that illustrate learning. These artifacts may be related to the videotapes you use, or they may simply be good examples for teachers to study and analyze. You will collect these artifacts over time, either from your own classroom or the other classrooms in your school. Artifacts are most effective if they come from students you know personally, but you can also use those given you by your staff development colleagues.

Many staff developers assemble "class sets," artifacts produced by a group of students in the same classroom, usually over a period of several months. These class sets can be used for a number of purposes:

Discussing how to introduce a book.

- Analyzing children's progress over time.
- Learning to form reading groups.
- Looking at a range of progress.
- Learning to evaluate writing samples.
- Analyzing running records as a base for teaching decisions.

Work with the teachers in your group to develop class sets that will be helpful not only this year but in subsequent years.

Case Studies You also want teachers in your group to collect examples from their own work with students. Class sessions come alive when teachers share running records, writing samples, and assessment results from their classrooms. Data like these should not be incidental, nor should they overwhelm teachers. It is very informative to follow students over time. Have teachers select a few students to follow and design observations and assessments to be administered periodically. These students should represent a range of achievement, unless your training is centered on lower-achieving students.

Reading

Reading alone won't help most teachers improve their practice; however, reading to learn new information is an essential part of a quality inservice course. Literature in the field, used effectively, is a rich resource. A goal of effective professional development is to encourage and motivate teachers to keep on reading throughout their career.

It is best not to overwhelm teachers with too much reading. Many staff developers rely on a large number of handouts and assignments. Making quick references to sources will help participants learn to use them on their own. Select references carefully and then use them in class sessions. For example, when you are observing readers on videotape, you can refer to a fluency rubric (see Fountas and Pinnell 1996). Evaluating reading fluency will, over time, build an internal sense of fluency. Figure 6–6 lists a number of effective ways to use readings.

Select your readings just as you would any good collection—art, jewelry, etc.—remembering that resources are limited. In the case of teacher education, you have only so much time to invest; busy teachers can cope with only a limited number of out-of-class readings; you can discuss only a limited number of readings in class.

Whenever you assign a reading, ask:

- What did teachers in my group learn from reading this?
- How did they respond to it?
- Did they refer to it as they talked about their practice?
- Did it make a difference to the quality of the class?
- Is there evidence of rereading or of reading beyond the assignment?

Eliminate readings that do not have big payoff. At the same time, constantly look for new readings that will serve your purposes. You are better off having participants read, understand, and use one good reference than asking them to skim through four or five.

Out-of-Class Work

Because teachers' time is limited, be cautious about giving extra out-of-class assignments. They

---

Using Readings Effectively

1. Use readings that you know very well yourself. Study them before using them with participants in your class. Don't include readings you will not be using.

2. It is not wise to give participants lengthy reading assignments. Make short assignments that are directly related to the topic of interest.

3. If assignments are made, they should be used in class. Otherwise, participants probably won't read future assignments.

4. Visit sections of the reading during class; for example, have participants look at a paragraph, chart, example, or short section in small groups and bring forward interesting ideas to the whole group.

5. Take every opportunity to move participants into the readings as they are related to the topic. For example, you may find something in the text that helps to explain reading or writing behavior or something that will assist participants in their analyses. Go right to the section and look at the text. This action will help participants learn to use good references on their own.

Figure 6–6. *Using Readings Effectively*

---

will be reading as well as working on student case studies, which requires record keeping, analysis, and reflection.

If you are working with teachers over a long period, however, you may want to have them analyze their teaching in depth. This kind of advanced learning would probably be overwhelming for beginners, but many teachers learn a great deal from analyzing videotapes of their own teaching, either individually or in pairs. At first, you will want to focus on one or two important factors—group management or interactions that support comprehension, for example. This focus keeps them from jumping to an overall judgment of the lesson as "good" or "bad." The important thing is to look closely and objectively; everyone learns from the *process* of analysis.

Framework for Class Sessions

A routine structure for class sessions is sometimes helpful. Whether or not you establish routines will depend on your own style and on the group you are teaching. Routines help teachers learn what to expect; they can prepare themselves mentally for the session and for joining in the discussion. A suggested framework is illustrated in Figure 6–7. This example is not the only way to organize class sessions, and it certainly isn't meant to suggest that every single class would play out in exactly the same way.

Blending Presentation, Inquiry, and Interaction to Help Participants Construct Their Own Knowledge

It is difficult to find a balance between giving participants needed information and helping them construct their own understanding. If you "tell" everything, you will be able to cover a great deal of material, but the understanding participants develop is likely to be superficial at best. On the other hand, trying to develop *all* understanding through interaction, discovery, and construction takes too much time. The trick is to decide what you need to tell and what participants need to extend through inquiry and arrive at a strategic blend of telling and inquiry.

Suggested Framework for Course Sessions

1. Have individuals interact briefly, sharing their successes and concerns in teaching.
2. Link today's topic with the previous class session.
3. Introduce session activities.
4. Engage participants in inquiry, group discussion, and analysis, integrating presentation and active group work.
5. Link concepts presented in the session to readings.
6. Summarize new or key understandings from the session.
7. Connect key understandings to student work examples (videotaped or actual).
8. Set goals for the next week(s) (until the next session); make assignments if appropriate.
9. Finalize coaching schedule and connect goals to coaching.

Figure 6–7. *Suggested Framework for Course Sessions*

Sometimes it is effective to design an activity that will raise teachers' awareness, engage them in inquiry, and help them use what they know. At other times, teachers may need certain information right away rather than being allowed to discover it for themselves; a good, clear presentation will meet their needs. At other times, you can combine presentation, demonstration, and inquiry. You decide which comes first—demonstrating, discussing, or telling.

Several examples of blending presentation, discussion, and inquiry are presented in Figure 6–8. The examples illustrate what might happen first, second, and third within a given class session devoted, respectively, to using running records, implementing literature circles, introducing storybooks, understanding the purposes of interactive writing, and using word sorting. These ideas may be applied to many other topics as well.

All group inquiry involves discussion, but *group discussion is not necessarily inquiry*. It is useful for group members to talk with one another, but talk serves many different functions. Through talk, participants build social relationships and share their experiences. Focused talk, however, is different. Here, participants explore a problem and build shared meanings.

Organizing and Sequencing Topics

We have discussed a great many factors related to planning a professional development course in order to emphasize that *how* you conduct professional development is as important as the specific topic. Finally, however, we've come to which topics to choose, which you might think should be your first concern.

Deciding What to Teach

Of course you want to choose topics that will be of most benefit to the teachers you're working with. The initial data you gathered will help you decide. You'll also want to consider these factors:

◆ *Which topics/teaching approaches are easier to understand and implement successfully?* Sometimes it's a good idea to introduce "easier" topics first to build competence and confidence. There is no substitute for early success.

◆ *Which topics/teaching approaches are essential to understand and implement before others?* For example, it is essential for interme-

Examples of Class Design		
1 →	2 →	3
Teachers bring some observations of reading behavior (or running records). The session begins with a quote from an assigned reading, and then small groups talk about their observations. They look for evidence of the kinds of behavior referred to in the reading material. (I)	Each group talks about new insights and shares them with the larger group. They talk about how that will affect their teaching tomorrow. (D)	Briefly, the leader takes the group to an appropriate section of the readings to solidify and confirm learning. (P)
Teachers participate in literature circles using books provided by the leader. They read the books prior to the session, form small groups, and have a discussion about their books. (I)	In the large group, the leader leads participants in analyzing and then summarizing the kinds of processes in which they engaged in their group. (I)	The leader makes a list of the processes in which participants engage and invites conclusions as to what this might look like as they work with their children engage in literature circles within the classroom. (P and D)
The leader makes a brief presentation on introducing storybooks to children, referring to the readings. (P)	In small groups by grade level, participants discuss the introductions in the guided reading resource, noting what teachers were doing in each of the story introductions. (I)	The leader presents a videotape of an introduction (shared experience) and invites participants to describe and interpret the observation by writing down two key teaching moves that the teacher made during the introduction and talking about them with a partner before sharing with the larger group. (I and D)
Teachers are asked to bring a piece of interactive writing. In grade-level groups they share the purpose for the writing, talk about their teaching decisions, and talk about something children learned in interactive writing that will help them in independent writing. Colleagues analyze the pieces for learning potential. (I)	Each group lists new insights on chart paper and hangs them on the wall. Further discussion in the whole group follows. (D)	The leader extends learning through a brief presentation on how to make interactive writing more powerful. (P)
The leader prepares a number of word sorts that will invite teachers to look at words in different ways and sets up tables that resemble a word study center. Participants engage in several different planned activities, finding out more about words. (I)	In the large group, participants brainstorm a list of principles or understandings related to how words work and organize the principles from easier concepts to more difficult ones. (I)	The leader facilitates a discussion of the application of their understandings to the word study centers they are planning for their classrooms. The leader guides them to further reading on the topic of letters, words, and how they work. (D)

Figure 6–8. *Blending Presentation (P), Discussion (D), and Inquiry (I)*

diate teachers to implement independent reading, in which students learn how to read silently and use response journals, before working with small groups in guided reading. Once independent reading is well established, students will be productively occupied while you pull out small groups for focused instruction in guided reading.

◆ *What topics do participants see as important in meeting their greatest needs?* If you can do so without disrupting the coherence of the course, it's a good idea to address "hot" topics first so that teachers see the experience as meeting their needs. Otherwise, assure participants you will be addressing hot topics soon.

Figure 6–9 is an example of topics for a literacy professional development course for primary teachers; Figure 6–10, an example for intermediate teachers. These examples illustrate how topics build on one another. Assessment information is provided early in the course so that participants know how to gather data from students. The overall set of understandings, the framework, that the course will introduce is set out. And in both cases, organization and management are also early topics, so that the classroom functions efficiently and the necessary materials are introduced and explored. (*Early, later,* and *ongoing* refer to experience with topics rather than time of year. An early word study topic, for example, might come in the middle of the course.)

The courses for both primary and intermediate teachers involve active observation and analysis of children's behavior, examination and discussion of texts, and observation and analysis of instruction. In the course for intermediate-grade teachers, participants engage in the processes and routines they will expect their students to take on. For example, they work in their writer's notebook for several days and produce a series of drafts (called "discovery drafts"), finally editing and publishing their work (see Fountas and Pinnell 2000). Then they reflect on the process and the routines and materials that will support their students in engaging in these routines as they write on different topics and in different genres.

Participants are taught *why* topics are important and are actively involved in exploring

them. Basic processes such as reading aloud are established as priorities. Subsequently, instructional approaches such as guided reading are introduced and explored. Each of these topics is a foundation for the next, and each will be explored again and again in different ways.

Moving from Introduction to Analysis

When you introduce a topic, many participants will be experiencing it for the first time. You may make a presentation, provide a demonstration, or use what participants already know about the topic; but that is only the beginning. In an effective professional development course, participants go on to try out the technique in their classroom and continue to work on the approach to gain confidence and skill. Learning really begins when participants start to reflect on their own teaching.

Connecting Theory and Experience

Connect each topic you introduce to the teachers' own experiences. Even if they are observing others' teaching, they can introduce their own perspectives in the discussion. What you observe in classrooms is the best source of ways to connect theory and practice. As you work toward understanding instructional approaches and their theoretical bases, you can bring in examples and ask teachers in the group to talk about them.

Evaluating the Course

There are several ways to evaluate the success of a professional development course. Ultimately, of course, the best evaluation is whether children are learning, which you will discover as you collect classroom artifacts. It is important, though, to conduct both formative (during the process) and summative (after the process) evaluations of the course.

Individual sessions may be evaluated by observing the participants and asking:

◆ Did every member of the group participate in inquiry and discussion?
◆ Was interaction intensive, problem-centered, and substantive rather than just "chatting"?
◆ Did the group make good use of readings?

Organizing Topics for an Initial PD Course in Literacy for Teachers (Grades K, 1, 2)
[Time = 1 1/2 to 2 1/2 Years]

Early	Later		Ongoing
Curriculum and Organization			
◆ Overview of language/literacy framework	◆ Making connections across the framework	◆ Making instructional decisions with the framework in mind	◆ Using connected instruction across the framework to meet students' needs [based on observation]
◆ Organizing the literate environment	◆ Evaluating the environment for opportunities to read/write	◆ Evaluating the environment for efficiency ◆ Using extra personnel effectively	◆ Adjusting the environment to account for students' new learning
◆ Schedules and routines	◆ Making and implementing a workable schedule	◆ Analyzing time and efficiency	◆ Adjusting the schedule to account for students' new learning
Reading and Exploration of Text			
◆ Concept of text gradient ◆ Exploration of texts ◆ Analysis of levels	◆ Matching books to readers—using observation and leveled texts	◆ Selecting and introducing texts	◆ Analyzing text selection and introductions in relation to readers' behaviors
◆ Demonstrate and try out guided reading	◆ Components of guided reading lessons—making them effective and efficient	◆ Working across lesson components to teach for strategies	◆ Interacting with children to support strategy development while reading
Writing: Convention and Craft			
◆ Demonstrating and trying out shared and interactive writing	◆ Efficiency and effectiveness in shared and interactive writing	◆ Analyzing gradient of text in shared and interactive writing	◆ Analyzing shifts over time in shared/interactive writing ◆ Meeting students' needs
◆ Demonstrating and trying out minilesson ◆ Principles: what makes a good minilesson?	◆ Using minilesson structure for writing ◆ Minilessons on managing routines ◆ Planning minilessons (use observation/data)	◆ Minilessons on the conventions and craft of writing ◆ Using observational data ◆ Refining minilessons	◆ Analysis of reading and writing behaviors as basis for minilessons on craft and writing
◆ Demonstrating and trying out conferring with writers	◆ Conferring with writers—what do you learn?	◆ Holding powerful conferences with writers ◆ Connecting minilessons with conferring/group share	◆ Analysis of changes over time in writing behavior ◆ Adjusting minilessons, conferring, and group share to meet writers' needs
Language, Literature, and Word Study			
◆ Demonstrating interactive read-aloud ◆ Noticing students' behavior through rereading of text ◆ Selecting books to read aloud ◆ Social/cultural diversity in books to read aloud	◆ Connections—reading literature aloud, reading and writing ◆ Connections—reading literature aloud and word study ◆ Connections—reading aloud and oral language development	◆ Building concepts through reading aloud ◆ Building knowledge of text characteristics through reading aloud ◆ Selecting read-aloud texts for variety in genre ◆ Evaluating books to read aloud	◆ Introducing and discussing characteristics of genre through reading aloud ◆ Introducing and discussing literary elements through reading aloud
◆ Poetry reading ◆ Poetry as part of the language/literacy framework ◆ Building appreciation for poetry	◆ Reading and enjoying poetry ◆ What children learn from poetry ◆ Creating a rich text base in the classroom	◆ Learning more about poetry over time ◆ Benefits of knowing poems ◆ Selecting poems ◆ A gradient of text in poetry	◆ Connecting poetry with reading, writing, and literature study ◆ Analysis of children's response to poetry
◆ Word study—phonics and spelling ◆ Demonstrating word study minilesson ◆ Components of language ◆ Connections between word study and other parts of framework	◆ Using minilesson structure for word study ◆ Minilessons on managing word study activities ◆ Learning how words work—language concepts	◆ Making explicit connections for students across the framework ◆ Matching minilessons to students' needs ◆ Developing a repertoire of minilessons	◆ Analyzing student behavior to plan minilessons and word study activities ◆ Observing behavior in word study to inform reading/writing instruction
◆ Observing students' behavior ◆ Specific techniques for analyzing reading and writing behavior	◆ Refining use and analysis of observational techniques	◆ Using observation to inform interactions in reading and writing	◆ Using observation to inform planning, lessons, and interactions in reading, writing, word study

Demonstrate ➤ Establish Rationales ➤ Engage the Routines ➤ Try It Out ➤ Routines/Procedures ➤ Shift Behavior ➤ Analyze

Figure 6–9. *Organizing Topics for the Literacy Course [Primary]*

Organizing Topics for an Initial Course in Literacy for Teachers [Grades 2, 3, 4, 5, 6]
[Time = 1 to 2 Years]

Early	Later	Ongoing	

Curriclum and Organization

Early	Later	Ongoing	
◆ Overview of language/literacy framework ◆ Three blocks: language word study; reading workshop; writing workshop	◆ Making connections across the framework ◆ The language/literacy curriculum and content study ◆ The language literacy framework and genre study	◆ Making instructional decisions with the framework in mind ◆ Connecting reading and writing workshop and language word study across the framework	◆ Using connected instruction across the framework to meet students' needs [based on observation and examination of reading/writing products, formal assessment]
◆ Organizing the literate environment ◆ Organizing materials for independent use	◆ Evaluating the environment for opportunities to read/write	◆ Evaluating the environment for opportunities to read/write	◆ Adjusting the environment to account for students' new learning
◆ Schedules and routines ◆ Creating a workable schedule ◆ Variations in the schedule to create blocks	◆ Teaching students about schedules ◆ Creating a good working culture ◆ Creating a community of learners	◆ Analyzing time and efficiency ◆ Analyzing independence of students	◆ Adjusting the schedule to account for students' new learning ◆ Adjusting the schedule to create new learning opportunities

Language and Word Study

Early	Later	Ongoing	
◆ Demonstrating and trying out interactive read-aloud ◆ Value of reading aloud to older students	◆ Interacting with students while reading aloud ◆ Using picture books and short stories	◆ Using reading aloud as basis for literature discussion ◆ Using reading aloud as basis for craft of writing ◆ Using reading aloud to study genre	◆ Analyzing students' responses in interactive read-aloud ◆ Analyzing students' connections from read-aloud to other areas
◆ Demonstrating and trying out word study minilesson ◆ Important principles about how words work ◆ Word study and spelling as part of the framework	◆ Evaluation—what makes a good minilesson in word study? ◆ Trying out active word study activities ◆ Trying out word study system	◆ Refining independent use of word study application activities ◆ Refining independent use of word study system [spelling]	◆ Analyzing students writing as basis for planning minilessons and application activities ◆ Using assessment of spelling in connection with word study
◆ Response to poetry—exploring your own response ◆ Creating personal anthologies ◆ Connecting poetry with your own writing	◆ Reading poetry to students ◆ Observing ◆ Getting students started in poetry study/poetry anthologies	◆ Exploring poetry as language ◆ Expanding students' personal collections ◆ Writing poetry ◆ Poetry workshop	◆ Studying and discussing poetry ◆ Genre and poetry ◆ Poetry and the writer's craft

Reading and Exploration of Text

Early	Later	Ongoing	
◆ Building rich text base—books and other ◆ Text characteristics ◆ Exploring your own response and knowledge ◆ Concept of a gradient of difficulty	◆ Characteristics of text—demands on readers ◆ A gradient of difficulty based on text characteristics ◆ Analysis of levels ◆ Matching books to readers	◆ Evaluating text collections—diversity in culture, race, language group ◆ Gradient of informational text ◆ Selecting and introducing texts for guided reading	◆ Analyzing text characteristics in relation to selection and introduction ◆ Analyzing text characteristics—supports for readers learning more ◆ Analyzing texts in relation to readers' behavior
◆ Reading workshop—independent reading ◆ Demonstrating and trying out independent reading ◆ Exploring your own reading through independent reading ◆ Book talks	◆ Getting started with independent reading in the classroom ◆ Minilesson structure for independent reading ◆ Conferring and discussing ◆ Giving book talks	◆ Refining procedures for independent reading ◆ Observing and interacting with students in independent reading ◆ Helping students use effective strategies in independent reading	◆ Analyzing reading behavior as a base for minilessons in independent reading ◆ Making connections between guided reading and independent reading
◆ Literature study ◆ Exploring your own response to literature ◆ Connecting literature with your own writing	◆ Establishing routines for literature discussion ◆ Using reading aloud in connection with literature study	◆ Literature study of different genres ◆ Literature study of literary elements	◆ Analyzing students' understanding of the writer's craft in literature ◆ Analyzing students' understanding of informational texts
◆ Demonstrating and trying out guided reading	◆ Components of guided reading lessons—making them effective and efficient	◆ Working across lesson components to teach for strategies	◆ Interacting with children to support strategy development while reading

Figure 6–10. *Organizing Topics for the Literacy Course [Intermediate]. Used with permission of Irene C. Fountas and Lesley University Intermediate Training Course.*

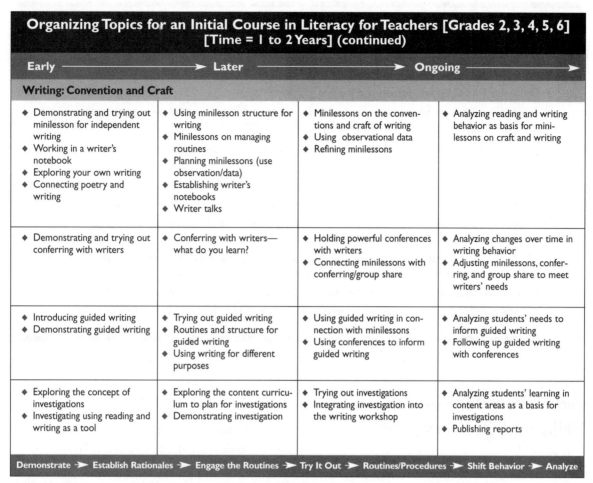

Early →	Later →	Ongoing →	
Writing: Convention and Craft			
◆ Demonstrating and trying out minilesson for independent writing ◆ Working in a writer's notebook ◆ Exploring your own writing ◆ Connecting poetry and writing	◆ Using minilesson structure for writing ◆ Minilessons on managing routines ◆ Planning minilessons (use observation/data) ◆ Establishing writer's notebooks ◆ Writer talks	◆ Minilessons on the conventions and craft of writing ◆ Using observational data ◆ Refining minilessons	◆ Analyzing reading and writing behavior as basis for minilessons on craft and writing
◆ Demonstrating and trying out conferring with writers	◆ Conferring with writers—what do you learn?	◆ Holding powerful conferences with writers ◆ Connecting minilessons with conferring/group share	◆ Analyzing changes over time in writing behavior ◆ Adjusting minilessons, conferring, and group share to meet writers' needs
◆ Introducing guided writing ◆ Demonstrating guided writing	◆ Trying out guided writing ◆ Routines and structure for guided writing ◆ Using writing for different purposes	◆ Using guided writing in connection with minilessons ◆ Using conferences to inform guided writing	◆ Analyzing students' needs to inform guided writing ◆ Following up guided writing with conferences
◆ Exploring the concept of investigations ◆ Investigating using reading and writing as a tool	◆ Exploring the content curriculum to plan for investigations ◆ Demonstrating investigation	◆ Trying out investigations ◆ Integrating investigation into the writing workshop	◆ Analyzing students' learning in content areas as a basis for investigations ◆ Publishing reports
Demonstrate ➤ Establish Rationales ➤ Engage the Routines ➤ Try It Out ➤ Routines/Procedures ➤ Shift Behavior ➤ Analyze			

Organizing Topics for an Initial Course in Literacy for Teachers [Grades 2, 3, 4, 5, 6] [Time = 1 to 2 Years] (continued)

Figure 6–10. *Organizing Topics for the Literacy Course [Intermediate] (continued)*

◆ Did new learning occur? What evidence shows that it did?

◆ What changes do I need to make next time to get greater involvement?

It is a good idea to ask participants for a more formal evaluation, either orally or in writing, several times a year—possibly in December, March, and May (the summative evaluation). A quick way to get good information is to ask participants to list five things about the course that are helping them learn and five things they suggest changing. In this way, you force some constructive suggestions. You can make it clear that it may not be possible to change everything but that you want to hear their perspectives and to think about their ideas. All evaluation is directed toward making the learning experience more effective for participants. One of the best ways to get good information is to ask participants at the end of the year to help you plan the course for

next year's group as well as their own continuing professional development.

Recognizing Participants' Accomplishments

Teachers begin a challenging and time-intensive experience when they make a commitment to your literacy professional development course. The concepts may be new and difficult. It is important that their beginning steps receive positive reinforcement. It's also important to offer encouragement and celebrate their successes. Some suggestions for showing participants that you appreciate their accomplishment are listed in Figure 6–11. These suggestions are not clichés; they should be delivered as honest expressions of your regard for the effort they are expending.

Helping Participants Realize Their Accomplishments

- Remain aware of the difficulty of trying new approaches for the first time.
- Give positive comments on beginning steps.
- Compliment self-awareness on the part of participants.
- Ask for feedback on your tone of voice or demeanor when interacting with participants.
- Be clear about expectations without being authoritarian.
- Provide rationales for trying new approaches rather than evoking authority (such as central administration).
- Be on a first-name basis with everyone.
- Periodically, ask participants to think about what they have accomplished in the last month(s).
- Establish some milestones (such as completing the leveled book collection or holding reading groups for all children) and celebrate them.
- Make sure that rewards (being acknowledged in meetings; having examples or photographs displayed) are bestowed on everyone in the group.
- Plan celebrations at key points and at the end of the course; invite authority figures.
- Create a visible way to recognize participants' accomplishment such as certificates or pins.

Figure 6–11. *Helping Participants Realize Their Accomplishments*

Suggestions for Expanding Your Skills as a Staff Developer

1. Design a course on a selected topic. Choose something that your observations suggest is relevant for the group of teachers with whom you are working. Start with a clearly defined topic, such as a particular instructional approach, rather than something so broad it would take several years to accomplish. An example might be reading workshop, guided reading, or literature study.

2. Use this chapter as a guide to ensure that your course:
   - Includes a variety of learning experiences.
   - Lets participants know what to expect.
   - Introduces topics and moves to a deeper analysis over time.
   - Is connected to teachers' classroom experiences.
   - Is related to the overall professional development plan.

3. Work with professional development colleagues or meet with a group of teachers from your school. Ask for feedback on your course design.
   - Is it complete? Does it show what to expect? Is there enough detail to help you conduct the course effectively?
   - Do you clearly show how you connect hands-on experiences, demonstrations, and presentations?
   - Will the learners be actively involved instead of just listening?
   - Will the topics and activities interest the learners? Are they likely to be relevant to them?

Chapter 7

Assessing the Classroom Context

We shall need to adopt an image of teaching that takes account of the possibility that the teacher herself is a resource in managing the problems of educational practice.
—MAGDALENE LAMPERT
THE COMPLEX WORLD OF
TEACHING *(269)*

Effective teaching starts with what the learners already know. The first thing a good teacher says to a student (either explicitly or indirectly) is, *Tell me [or show me] what you know about this.* Think about learning to use a computer, for example. Sometimes you know so little, you find it impossible to articulate the problem. You have to demonstrate what you are doing. A good technology expert will ask you to describe what you see on your screen and how you got to the place you are. Then she talks you through what to do next. Step by step, she helps you solve your problem. Afterward, she may ask you to articulate the steps you are going to take if the problem arises again. Or she may walk you through the steps again, this time providing less support, so that you can get used to doing them on your own. You may even get some additional information about what to do if you encounter variations of the problem. In any case, your learning is ongoing: you become more independent as you go through the same processes again and again. Now consider the computer expert who sits down at your computer and "fixes" the problem so quickly you can't tell what is happening. Your problem is solved, but if it recurs, you will again need to send for the expert. The expert who guides you through the process, letting you do it with support, is the more effective teacher.

The attitude of the expert is critical:

◆ How do you respond when the "hot shot" computer user is respectful, patient, and confirms your progress?
◆ What are you thinking when the expert says how easy this problem really is, implying you are wasting her valuable time?
◆ What if she barks orders rapidly?

- What if she starts teaching you more operations than you want to know so that she won't have to come back and she won't get any more questions from you?
- How do you respond if the expert fixes the problem impatiently and refers you to a book or to one of those help lines that put you on hold for endless minutes?

Learning is a human process. To you, the computer problem is not simple; you are at the edge of your learning and need support and direction so that you can move on. You are the learner and the goal is yours. It's your time, not the computer expert's, you want to save, and you will learn only as much as you truly believe you need to learn. You probably don't want to sit down and have an hour lesson in operations that you see no need to know *right now*. Your learning is rooted in immediacy. You learn best when you own the problem, you seek a solution, and you participate in the solution. The expert offers just the right amount of help at the right time; your learning is at the cutting edge and it "takes."

As a teacher educator your students are adults, but the principle of knowing the learner applies and is just as important as—and even more complex than—when you are working with children. Your knowledge of the learning context influences how you plan, how you organize the topics that need to be addressed, how you interact with teachers and the children in their classes, and how you assess your impact.

Here are some important questions to ask yourself about the teacher, the teacher's students, and the classroom:

- *The teacher.* What is the teacher currently doing in his classroom? What kinds of materials does he select? How does he talk with children? What does he notice about the children's behavior as evidence of understanding? How does his teaching change relative to students' work? How does he adjust his teaching over time to meet students' changing needs?
- *The children.* What are students doing in this classroom? What evidence is there that they are engaged? What materials are they primarily using? What kind of work are they doing? What evidence is there that they are reading and writing continuous

text? How do they work with other children in the room? What do they say about their work? What do they say to the teacher and one another? How do they respond to the teacher's directions and information? Is there evidence that they know what is expected of them? What is the quality of student work in writing and reading? What is the evidence of learning?
- *The culture of the classroom.* What kind of student work is displayed and therefore valued in the classroom? How do the teacher and students use their time? Is the atmosphere peaceful and productive? Is the classroom inviting? Are materials organized and available? How do children work and talk with one another? What evidence is there of collaborative work? How does the teacher address the children? Is there evidence that the people in the classroom like to be there (do you see smiles and occasionally hear laughing)?

To answer these questions, you need data. Some of this information comes from observation; other information will be available in student assessment reports. Rest assured there are systematic ways of gathering, interpreting, and using information to improve your work with teachers.

When to Assess

Planning and problem solving are recursive: you move backward and forward within the process, selecting the action you need at the time. Assessing the context would seem to be step one, and it is: nothing can happen unless you have some good information before you start. You will, however, assess the context again and again, for different purposes. It's impossible to lay out with any accuracy how you will assess a particular context. Good staff developers are constantly gathering information about teachers' ongoing learning. Nevertheless, there are three times when assessment is critical.

When You Begin a Professional Development Program
Chapter 5 describes the process of beginning a professional development program. Gathering

Observing in a classroom.

Of course, the comprehensive professional development program you are developing may include new approaches of which participants are not yet aware. In addition, they may be unaware that certain areas of their curriculum, management, or teaching need improving. Or they may not be fully aware of how their particular strengths and skills can be applied in new ways. (For example, certain teachers in the school may be very skilled at implementing classroom routines; they can easily apply these skills to new instructional approaches and help other teachers do so as well.) A good staff developer makes those connections.

Part of your assessment, therefore, is to take a nonjudgmental look at the environment in the school and classrooms and also to observe teachers and children working. Your goal is to uncover strengths on which your new program will build. You may identify teachers who:

◆ Are already using or approximating some parts of the new approaches you want to establish in the school.
◆ Are likely to take on new learning quickly because they can link it to what they are already doing.
◆ Can become resources on specific topics.
◆ Will need more support because what they are currently doing is quite different from the new approaches.

Being nonjudgmental is important. You want to see teachers' real strengths rather than compare what they are doing with specific instructional ideals. You want to look beyond any particular curricular approach to discover management, interaction, and conceptual skills teachers are applying. For the most part, whatever the curriculum, a good manager is a good manager. An organized person will be able to plan and organize all kinds of materials. A teacher who has positive, warm, and caring interactions with children will do so whatever the subject or method. Someone who thinks about his teaching and works to make it better will be successful in just about all approaches. Of course, the school and district climate also has a great deal to do with teachers' ability to use their strengths and to improve.

As you assess the context, think of yourself as a learner rather than an evaluator. Classroom

data is central. Working with teams of teachers, administrators, and others, you discover the information that will help you successfully launch a program participants see as meeting their needs and for which they take ownership. This kind of assessment may involve visiting some classrooms and certainly means getting a sense of community and the physical layout of a school. Most of your time here will be spent talking with people about their perspectives and their hopes.

When You Plan the Professional Development Course

In planning the professional development course, you need much more specific information. You will want to talk with individual teachers, grade-level teams, and the staff at large to find out what knowledge and skills they see themselves as already bringing to the new program and what they think they need to learn next. As much as possible, the program should be consistent with what learners think they need.

teachers can give you a very good idea about what their students are like, thus helping you do a better job as a teacher educator. Also, verify your observations with the teachers. You may be missing something or misinterpreting something. Your observations in the classrooms will help you. The more you know about what a teacher does every day and what the students in her class are learning, the easier it will be to have positive conversations.

While You Are Coaching

Finally, assessment data informs the coaching you do. Because you are working with the teacher in very specific ways, you need to know what learning interactions go on in that classroom. This information should be closely tied to literacy instruction: generic interaction patterns are not particularly helpful. To coach a teacher effectively you need to:

◆ Be specific about the particular learning context you observe. Often the teacher will choose what he wants to be coached in (for example, guided reading or minilessons for writers workshop). Sometimes the specific learning contexts are linked to the topics you have introduced and demonstrated in class.

◆ Be sure the teacher has seen demonstrations and had the opportunity to try the approach with support before you begin to coach.

◆ Find out something about the children and their learning before you observe the lesson. (Quickly observe children reading, look at some running records, or ask the teacher to describe what they can do.)

◆ Notice the setting for instruction, including what materials are available and how they are organized.

◆ Notice typical teacher behavior and learning interactions.

Obviously, preparing to coach an individual teacher requires very detailed information. Even then, you will need to be tentative, because teachers and children change every day. If a teacher needs a great deal of support, you'll need to gather even more information, perhaps working in the classroom for several days.

Think about this process in terms of a camera with a zoom lens. You can select a wide angle to capture the broad landscape that gives you a sense of the whole (a forest, for example). This setting will give you a panoramic view, which parallels the kind of information that helps you become generally aware of a school or a group. If you zoom in a little more, you see details—differentiation among trees and perhaps the outlines of a lake. This view parallels the kind of information you need to design your professional development system. Zooming in still more allows you to see much more detail—individual trees, animals, smaller plants, and the edges of the lake. This view parallels your careful observations in classrooms, your detailed conversations with teachers about what they do, and your analysis of children's work. Finally, you zoom in very close to look at individual trees, the shape of their leaves, perhaps even leaf veins and dewdrops. This kind of close and detailed look at classroom learning is essential for effective coaching.

Figure 7–1 illustrates this concept:

1. In the initial planning phase you need information from a broad spectrum of the school community and a general sense of what the school is like and what kind of teaching and learning go on there.
2. Planning and preparing for the professional development course is based on information about the school as a whole but also requires specific detail from observation in classrooms.
3. Coaching requires information about the teacher's ways of working in addition to the information inherent in 1 and 2.
4. Coaching also requires information about individual learners—both teachers and children.

Assessing School Culture

A culture consists of the ideas, customs, skills, and arts of a group of people. These ideas are passed along from one generation to another over time. A culture is not "fixed": it is changed by new ideas and skills, as well as by external forces, as long as the changes are adopted by the people within it. Assessing the culture of the school and classroom provides important basic data for you in working with teachers.

Schools are places in which individuals live

and work together for a substantial part of the school day. Research on schooling indicates that every school has a culture of its own (Sarason 1982). For every school, we want to know:

1. What's it like here?
2. How do people feel about being here?
3. What do people spend most of their time doing here?
4. How do people work with one another here?

Schools are embedded within the culture of the district; they are susceptible to state and national norms for education. Yet we know that schools within the same school district are quite different from one another. Some schools are warm and inviting; others are full of tension. These differences are not necessarily related to the characteristics of the student body or the community; the culture of the school is a manifestation of the relationships and values of the people within it. Cultures develop over time.

You are working with teachers in classrooms that are embedded within *this* school culture, so it is important to gather information about the atmosphere or tone of the entire school. It is hard for teachers to try new techniques within a negative atmosphere. As you talk with school personnel during the awareness phase (see Chapter 5), you will get an idea of the factions and norms that exist. Figure 7–2 suggests some questions to guide your ongoing observation.

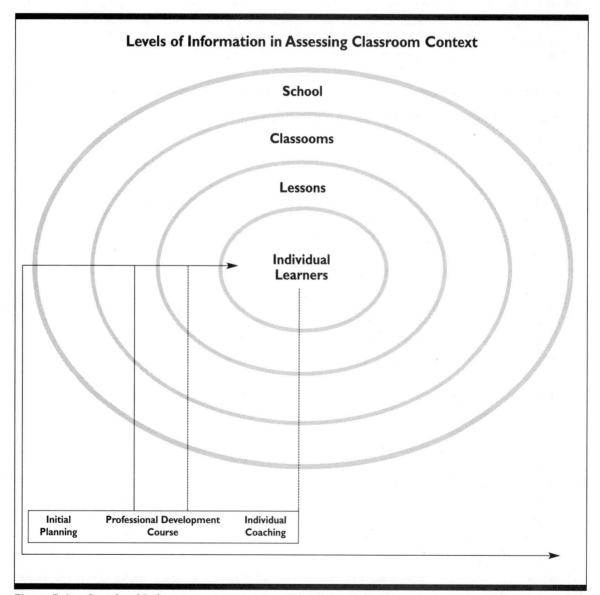

Figure 7–1. *Levels of Information in Assessing Classroom Context*

A physical facility that is clean and attractive is an indication that the teachers and students who work there are respected. Look for the ways students, their families, and the community are visibly reflected in the school building—that will give you an idea about what is truly valued there. Questions 14, 15, and 16 in Figure 7–2 are critical: can and do school staff members see students and the community as having strengths? Positive comments about students in general are a sign of a good school culture.

Also notice how people talk to one another and what they talk about. Teachers who talk about their work in a positive way, perhaps discussing students' learning in some depth, are satisfied teachers. Of course, everyone has bad days and complaints, but you don't want to hear an overwhelming number of negative comments. Happy teachers share ideas with one another. Part of the task of professional development is to work with administrators and staff to create a welcoming and dynamic learning culture.

Assessing Classroom Culture

Classroom cultures are influenced by the school culture; all of us respond to the larger environment. The school influence, however, is not necessarily pervasive. Teachers create the cultures within their own classrooms. We have all walked through an "uninviting" school only to enter a warm and highly productive classroom. (It's also possible, though less likely, to have a harsh and punishing atmosphere in an individual classroom even when the overall school culture is excellent.)

Students moving from class to class often change their behavior remarkably as they enter the different cultures. A teacher's interactions with students set the tone for all interactions. The

---

What to Look for in the School Culture

1. As you enter the building, what do you see?

2. Is there a welcoming atmosphere?

3. Is the building as a whole clean and attractive?

4. Is the school office a welcoming place where people are acknowledged and helped?

5. Are the classrooms, cafeteria, office, and library clean and attractive?

6. Do staff members speak respectfully to students and do students talk in respectful tones to one another?

7. What is happening in the yard or playground? Are students playing? Are teachers interacting with students?

8. Are the students and their community a visible part of the school? Is student work displayed and valued in the corridors, office, library, and other gathering places?

9. How available are books? Can students find books to read in places besides the library?

10. Is the principal accessible? Does the principal interact in a friendly way with students, staff members, and visitors?

11. Do people in the school talk with one another? What do they talk about? Do they talk about their work?

12. Are professional development books and materials available?

13. Do teachers have a place where they can meet and work together? Is it attractive and welcoming?

14. When asked about the school, what do people say? Are their comments positive?

15. When asked about the students in the school, what do people say? Are their comments positive?

16. When asked about the parents and the community, what do people say? Are their comments positive?

Figure 7–2. *What to Look for in the School Culture*

What to Look for in the Classroom Environment

General Atmosphere
1. As you enter the classroom, how do you feel? Is there a welcoming atmosphere?
2. Is the classroom clean, orderly, and attractive?

Space and Room Arrangement
3. Is there a place for every student to sit?
4. Are there comfortable places for students to work independently and in small groups?
5. Are there comfortable places for students to write and read?
6. Is there a defined meeting place where the whole class can work together? Can every student see and hear?
7. Is the place where the teacher works with small groups of students centrally located?

Materials and Supplies
8. Are there adequate and varied supplies for writing?
9. Are materials well organized, each kept in a labeled place?
10. Are the materials students need to use daily easily available for them to retrieve and return? Are directions for using materials posted?
11. Does the room contain *only* materials that are needed and used? Is there no unnecessary clutter?
12. Are there special places for students to store and retrieve their work (crates or baskets, for example)?

Books
13. Is the room well supplied with books?
14. What kinds of books are available?
15. Is there a range of levels so that every student can find something to read independently?
16. Are the books that students read accessible to them?
17. Are books displayed and accessible to students in many parts of the classroom?

Evidence of Routines
18. Is there evidence that routines have been established to use and return books and other materials?
19. Are directions for routines posted when necessary?
20. Are the directions understandable to any student or visitor?

Displays—What Is Valued?
21. What is displayed on the walls of the classroom?
22. To what degree are the materials on the walls produced by students or collaboratively by the teacher and students?
23. Are the display materials current and related to the topics students are studying?
24. Are the display materials useful in instruction; that is, can students learn from them (as opposed to their being merely "decoration")?

Figure 7–3. *What to Look for in the Classroom Environment*

way the classroom looks, its physical organization, and the way materials are used are the building blocks of culture.

Environment

You can get a great deal of information simply by looking at an empty classroom. Figure 7–3 lists some important questions to ask yourself. Look carefully at what is displayed—it shows what is valued. The material should reflect students' participation, provide opportunities for student learning, and be current. The more the materials reflect the students (instead of being commercially produced), the more inviting the classroom.

Readers and writers need comfortable spaces in which to work, and they need to have texts and other materials readily available. Have you ever tried to write something at home and been interrupted by weekend guests, your son's birthday party, or some other pressing task? It's easier to get back to your writing if your materials are organized and you have a quiet place to work. It's next to impossible if you have to move them from place to place.

The students in classrooms are novice writers, so they need to learn the habits of organization and continuity. Examine the classroom to find out where students work; there should be comfortable space for individual work as well as for small- and large-group meetings. Examine the group meeting area. Can all the students sit comfortably and still see and hear? If they can't, their attention will wander.

It's best to set up central places for storing students' ongoing work (reading response journals, writing folders, spelling folders, etc.) rather than let them keep it in their desks. Having trays and baskets for student work in different parts of the classroom lets the teacher examine that work quickly. All work storage places should be labeled, both the basket or tub that holds the materials *and* the shelf where it goes. Many teachers post simple directions for using and returning materials next to the storage space.

Finally, the text base of the classroom is vital. The classroom collection should include enough books to accommodate the range of reading levels, interests, and needs of the classroom. Good classrooms have books to read aloud, informational texts for research, references such as dictionaries and thesauruses, interesting books for independent reading, books students recommend to one another, books for literature study, books of poetry, and leveled books for guided and independent reading. Like other materials, books should be very well organized (in labeled tubs or baskets, for example) and attractively displayed. A book that is displayed face out rather than spine out is more likely to be read.

Routines

As you observe the teacher and students working in the classroom, you will get an idea of the degree to which routines have been internalized. Routines are important because they establish a set of predictable actions that, once learned, don't have to be thought about. Routines reduce anxiety: students who know what is coming next can monitor and control their behavior. Good routines give the teacher more time for learning conversations and real teaching.

One kind of routine is a predictable action that involves the whole class, such as taking attendance or turning in homework. Other routines require self-awareness—modulating the voice in different settings, for example. There can be routines for almost everything:

◆ Using and returning different kinds of materials.
◆ Modulating the voice.
◆ Coming into the room and getting started.
◆ Gathering in the meeting area.
◆ Sitting and working individually.
◆ Reading and returning books.
◆ Working in independent centers.
◆ Leaving the classroom for various reasons.
◆ Dealing with visitors.
◆ Participating in a whole-class meeting.
◆ Participating in small groups.
◆ Signaling when you want a turn to speak.

Teachers shouldn't go overboard here: a harsh, rigid atmosphere is uninviting and unproductive. But just think how routines help you get through the day—getting dressed in the morning, cooking, driving, and so on. You don't have to think about them; they're automatic. Routines are not punishment; they are simply "standard operating procedure."

Too often, teachers assume that students already know routines or can learn them with just a few suggestions. Routines must be taught like lessons. If you are working with a beginning teacher, you may have to help her establish classroom routines *before* you can have her try new approaches and coach her in presenting literacy lessons.

Time

One of the most challenging issues for teachers is managing their time: there's never enough of it. When you ask teachers what interferes with time, you may end up with a list like this:

◆ Taking attendance and completing other paperwork.
◆ Announcements over the intercom.
◆ Constantly getting students into and out of the classroom.

- Assemblies.
- Getting kids to settle down.
- Disruptive students who don't remember what they're supposed to do.
- Getting started in the morning.
- Broken concentration because of approaching holidays.

These complaints are very real. When the school day is broken up into many short periods, interruptions are more frequent and it is harder to teach and learn. Solving the time problem may involve working with the whole school to eliminate unnecessary assemblies, reduce time spent on seasons and holidays, and build in larger blocks of time. You can help individual teachers make their classroom routines more efficient. But the first step is to find out how the teacher uses time.

Engagement

The word *engage* has two definitions, both of which apply to classroom practice. One meaning is to attract and hold attention; so *engagement* means that students are interested in and attending to the task in which they are involved. A second meaning is to be busy or occupied; it makes sense that when students are attending, interested, and busy, they will be learning productively. Of course, someone can be busy but not truly engaged; both kinds of engagement are necessary for learning, whether students are involved in individual, small-group, or whole-group activity.

Students are engaged in whole-group or small-group lessons if they are:

- Looking attentively at the teacher and/or at other students.
- Responding to questions.
- Volunteering responses.
- Providing responses that build on the teacher's or other students' comments.
- Showing that they understand ideas and concepts.
- Not distracted by outside noise or others' behavior.

Students are engaged in their independent work when they are:

- Sticking to the task.
- Not distracted by other events or behavior.
- Highly focused rather than moving around the room.
- Making progress on the task.
- Asking for help only when necessary.
- Talking to others only when necessary.

It is easier for some students to be engaged than others. Some students are highly distractible and require a great deal of structure and support from the teacher. Engagement also depends on the level of interest the task holds for the student.

Inexperienced teachers will need help engaging students during lessons. When teachers are trying something new, both the students and the teacher sometimes feel insecure. The new actions will probably seem awkward at first. Engagement can easily become an issue, so your support is essential. As a first step, observe the teacher working in familiar lessons, noticing the routines she uses and the extent to which students are engaged.

Figure 7–4 is an example of an open-ended observation form on which to gather information about the use of time, level of engagement, and routines in classrooms. (A blank reproducible form is included in Appendix C) You can use this form to note all the events that take place in a particular period or interval. Don't ignore transitions

Observing a guided reading group.

Use of Time, Engagement, Routines

Observer: GP

Date: March 10

Classroom/Teacher : Peg B.

Grade: 1

School: Saddleback

Number students: 24

Instructions. Note exact time an instructional activity starts. Change to new instructional activity any time the teacher changes focus, moves to a new area with different materials, moves the students, or signals in some way that the instructional activity is changing. For example, when a teacher at the easel changes from reading aloud to interactive writing, this requires a new line. For a "transition" (for example, when students are moving from one area to another, sharpening pencils, getting materials, etc.), use a line, write *transition* as the instructional activity, and note the time started.

The STARTING TIME for each new instructional activity noted is also the ENDING TIME for the previous instructional activity. This form accounts for every minute of class time, with no gaps between the instructional activities noted on the lines. A guided reading or interactive writing lesson should be noted in this guide, with the time started. Then, switch to the form for that activity. This form should reflect the appropriate box and time for guided reading and interactive writing. The INSTRUCTIONAL ACTIVITY describes whatever the teacher and students are doing—individually or as a group. ESTABLISHED ROUTINES are those activities that you note as being routines of instruction or procedures for student behavior.

Rubric for engagement:
1 = Only a few students are on task and attending to the instruction. There are many distractions, including noise and movement. Instruction is severely undermined.
2 = About half of the students are on task and attending to the instruction, but there are many distractions, including noise and movement. Instruction is undermined.
3 = Most of the students are on task and attending to the instruction. There are occasional distractions, and some students are moving about. Instruction, in general, is being provided most of the time.
4 = Almost all students are on task and attending to the instruction. Instruction is being provided almost all of the time. There are only a few distractions.

Time Started	Engagement	Instructional Activity	Note Established Routines
9:00	1 2 3 4 / NA	Students come into the room. Teacher walking around. Does 1 running record.	Hang up coats. Go to book boxes. Turn over card to register attendance.
9:05	1 2 3 ④	Flag and song with intercom. Two announcements. Calendar—count the days. Daily oral language—edited 1 sentence by noticing capitals and periods.	At tables. Move to meeting area— orderly; have place to sit.
9:07	1 2 ③ 4	Shared reading of 1 big book. Shared reading of completed interactive writing. Read-aloud—Curious George Goes to the Hospital. Conversation about yesterday's trip to a hospital.	
9:30	1 2 ③ 4	Minilesson on writing—directions on how to get started and think of something to say. Teacher gives examples. Generated list—what you like best. Generated list of words they might use—teacher wrote on board. Some discussion.	Raise hands.
9:40	1 2 3 4 / NA	Teacher passes out paper; children sharpen pencils one table at a time.	Orderly, but quite a gap from minilesson to getting started.

Figure 7–4. *Use of Time, Engagement, Routines*

Time Started	Engagement	Instructional Activity	Note Established Routines
9:50	1 2 3 ④	Children get started writing. Teacher walks around; confers with 4 students.	Some children still working on getting supplies.
10:05	1 2 3 ④	Guided Reading Group 1.	Group of 5 goes to table; others write. All have started.
10:20	1 2 3 ④	Guided Reading Group 2. Teacher reminds children to keep writing during transition.	One student taps members to come.
10:30	1 2 3 4 NA	Bathroom Break and Snack	Lots of movement; other classes involved; snack takes a long time.
10:50	1 2 ③ 4	Guided Reading Group 3. After introduction, teacher listens to all children for about 1 minute. Then, children read to themselves while she walks around.	Some students finished writing; draw pictures.
11: 15	1 2 ③ 4	Group Share 10 students share writing. Teacher comments on how they've used capital and period. No discussion.	Back to meeting area.
11:25	1 2 3 4 NA	Lunch	
	1 2 3 4		
	1 2 3 4		

Figure 7–4. *Use of Time, Engagement, Routines (continued)*

and "bathroom breaks." Significant amounts of time can be lost here, with an accompanying breakdown in student engagement.

The information you gain about what goes on in the classroom will provide a valuable base for working with the teacher. It will give you a clear picture of how efficiently the teacher uses time. For example, if you notice that a great deal of time is lost at the beginning of the day, you can help her streamline activities. If time is lost moving from one activity or subject to another, you can problem-solve ways to make things happen more smoothly and organize materials more efficiently. You will have an idea of the routines that the teacher uses productively as well as those that may get in the way of good instruction. Your observation will reveal where the teacher might be able to adjust the schedule to gain more time for instruction.

The form in Figure 7–4 also lets you evaluate student engagement in the activities you observe. If an activity does not lend itself to this analysis (lining up, for example), simply ignore that column for that activity. Ways of using the simple engagement rubric included on the form will emerge from your conversations with teachers in which you build a working definition of what engagement really means. Using this rubric will help you pinpoint when the teacher loses the children's attention. For example, you might notice that engagement is high at the beginning of the morning meeting but dwindles after about twenty minutes. Either too much time is being spent on the activity or it isn't interesting—or both. Rank engagement here as a 1 or 2, but make notes that will help you and the teacher analyze and remedy the situation.

Why include all this basic classroom-management material in a book directed toward improving the teaching of reading and writing in elementary schools? Because, although a welcoming, peaceful, orderly classroom does not guarantee *effective* teaching, a chaotic classroom guarantees *ineffective* teaching. Neither the teacher nor the students want to be there. Nothing is accomplished. Routine, predictability, and good relationships are necessary, although not sufficient, if reading and writing are to be well taught. Many effective staff developers do a great deal of work with teachers making sure that good management is in place. That doesn't mean you have to wait to introduce teachers to any new approaches; sometimes the new approaches are quite helpful in bringing order to instruction. But it does mean attending to routines, organization, and time as you go.

Quality of Interaction

As you observe teacher-student interactions, notice the tone of voice the teacher uses. Does he include and engage all students or only a few? Are students sitting so that they can see one another as well as the teacher? Also note the kinds of interactions that are taking place. Your concerns are general here: you don't need to examine the specific language associated with a lesson; however, it's important to have good interaction in a classroom before introducing a new teaching technique. Some questions to help you assess the situation are listed in Figure 7–5.

Assessing Student Learning

The major concern in any classroom is what and how much students are learning. They are always learning something, but your job is to help the teacher assess whether they are learning in accordance with stated goals. You'll want to address questions such as:

◆ What is the current level of learning across the language arts?
◆ What is the quality of work?
◆ What progress are students making over time?
◆ How is learning being assessed?
◆ What do students think about what they do every day?
◆ What do they think they are learning?
◆ How do they assess their own progress?

Test scores will not be much help to you as a staff developer. They will give you a general idea of achievement in the school and perhaps in a particular classroom, but they won't tell you much about how to begin offering professional development. You need more detailed information. Use your own assessment skills (the same ones you want to develop in teachers) to find out something about student learning.

Looking at Records

All teachers keep records of student progress. Your goal is to be sure teachers have systematic

---

Questions to Ask About Teacher-Student Interactions

1. What do teachers and students talk about? Do they discuss work, personal experiences, and opinions? Do they have shared memories to which they refer?

2. Is most of the talk centered on what students are learning rather than on controlling their behavior?

3. What kind of language are they using? Does the teacher ask all the questions, with students responding? Or is there give-and-take?

4. Over a period of a few days, does every student have the opportunity to talk in large and small groups? Are there established ways to get a turn in these discussions?

5. Is there a conversational tone to the interactions in the classroom? Do people look at one another when they talk? Do they listen and respond?

6. Are voices modulated appropriately for conferences and small- and large-group interactions?

7. Is there a balance of student and teacher talk?

8. Do people address each other respectfully?

Figure 7–5. *Questions to Ask About Student/Teacher Interactions*

ways of keeping examples of student work and recording evaluations. You also want their records to provide useful information rather than mechanical documentation. If you are concentrating on interactive writing, independent writing, or guided writing, it makes sense to look at students' writing folders and get a sense of what they are learning over time. For reading, you can look at informal reading inventories, running records of reading behavior, or progress graphs. This process is most successful if you can sit down with the teacher and ask her to talk you through the evidence you're looking at. The collaboration will be very helpful later when you observe lessons and coach the teacher.

Observing in Classrooms

You can get useful information about students' learning by observing and interacting with them as they work in the classroom. You can see what they are producing; you can listen to them read and take some running records yourself. You can ask students to tell you about their work, have some conversations about books, or work with a small group on your own. You simultaneously get a feel for the overall operation of the classroom and get to know particular students.

Observing Lessons

You can also look for evidence of learning as you observe whole-group and small-group lessons.

Figure 7–6 is a simple open-ended form for taking notes (it includes a space for listing potential topics to talk with the teacher about later). Or you can simply take a writing pad, draw a line down the middle, and organize your notes that way.

Getting to Know Students over Time

School-based staff developers have the opportunity to follow children's and teachers' learning over longer periods of time and get to know many of them very well. In any professional development system, this kind of continuity is integral. For example, Gayle had been a literacy coordinator in the same school for four years and knew more about that year's third graders than their teachers did. She had been in kindergarten, first-grade, and second-grade classrooms frequently over the years. She had worked with teachers to examine and analyze the behavior of individual children. Imagine how helpful she was to the third-grade team, especially the new teacher in her first year. She was able to illustrate her points by referring to one or another child's behavior and help the teachers identify progress.

Your situation may not allow this level of continuity. University teacher educators, for example, are at quite a disadvantage because they must talk about learning in very general terms. District-based teacher educators are a little closer to teaching as it is practiced in specific classrooms, but school-based teacher educators

Observation of Lessons

Teacher/Grade: Raquel-Gr. 3   **Focus of Instruction:** Word Study Minilesson

Observer: CB   **Date:** 3/00   **Time:** 9:00–9:45

Teacher	Student(s)	Notes/Questions
Focus—Contractions	Whole class—23 students.	
Two clear points written on the easel. Good meeting area.	Students engaged and attentive. All have place to sit. All can see.	Good organization and set up.
"A contraction is two words put together. You take out some letters and put in an apostrophe."		Clear explanation.
Explains the main point of the lesson. Provides several examples. *can not–can't, did not–didn't, will not–won't* Invites more examples. Says *lots* is plural and moves on. Teacher writes clearly; moves quickly through examples. Tells them the two words within contraction. Talks about taking out letters and using apostrophe. Writes *can't've*—no discussion.	Students come up with: *should not–shouldn't, have not–haven't, does not–doesn't.* Sam gives lots. Sarah gives wants. Carl gives *can't've.*	Five students [Sarah, Sam, Ben, Ilia, Carl] offer all examples. Writes examples but doesn't demonstrate taking out letters. Could have students do more talking about what's taken out; also come up with words in contraction.
"Now today choose three contractions for your spelling list. We'll put *can't* on the word wall."	Students move to independent work.	

Potential topics for discussion:

To be more powerful:
1. Get more interaction.
2. Get them to talk about what's left out when you put in the apostrophe.
3. Get them to figure out the words in the contraction instead of telling them.

Figure 7–6. *Observation of Lessons*

are able to ground their work thoroughly on what's happening in classrooms. The closer to practice you can make your work with teachers, the more effective it will be. If your base of operations is not a single school, you can still learn about children and use this knowledge in the teacher education setting:

◆ Look at some records of children's behavior (for example running records) and some samples of writing before you visit a classroom to observe or coach.
◆ Ask teachers to talk about individual children prior to a visit.
◆ Encourage teachers to compile an ongoing video library of their work. Prior to coaching, observe a videotaped class lesson so that you get a feel for student learning and behavior.
◆ Right before observing and coaching a teacher, spend some time (about half an hour) looking at the writing displayed on the walls, talking with the students, and observing them at work.

Assessing What Teachers Know and Can Do

Always remember that the teacher is a learner and that your job is to help that person learn. But the learning is reciprocal: in the process, you will learn much more about your own teaching and extend your own skills. Working with the teacher, you must try to understand what he knows:

◆ What does he understand about the reading and writing processes?
◆ What does he notice as evidence of learning in students?
◆ What does he know about analyzing and selecting texts?
◆ How does he decide what students can do independently?
◆ Is he able to determine what students should learn next?

There are no "tests" that give you this information. You need to talk with the teacher and observe him in the classroom.

Talking with the Teacher

In a sense, you are always finding out more about what teachers think as you interact with them in class sessions and in their classroom. Staff developers value quick, casual conversations with teachers, picking up a lot of valuable information on the run. A brief conference prior to visiting a classroom either for observation or for coaching is also helpful. A framework for a conference like this is suggested in Figure 7–7. (A blank reproducible version is provided in Appendix C.)

Observing Specific Lessons

You cannot work on everything at once with any teacher; that would be overwhelming. Each observation serves many purposes; it affects your work with the teacher over time as well as your future class sessions. You need to be able to access the information quickly, not have to plow through hundreds of pages of detailed notes.

When you are teaching specific instructional approaches, you will no doubt focus your observation on specific components of the new approaches. A form like the one in Figure 7–8 will help you keep track of the things you notice (in this example, William observed Karen teach a guided reading lesson). If you require more space, simply turn the form over and write on the back. Voluminous notes aren't necessary or even advisable. Trust your own observational powers and jot down only the most significant behavioral patterns you see.

Observing During Staff Development Sessions

Your staff development sessions, if they are interactive, will also help you know the teachers with whom you work. As they share insights into their students' work, you gain important information about what they notice and value. Then you can focus on these areas.

Relative to guided reading, for example, teachers can share running records and discuss whether books were right for students; they can look at text characteristics and talk about introductions that provide just the right amount of support—not too little, not too much. Talking about these things helps them develop "case knowledge." Over time, they encounter hundreds of examples, from which they generalize a theory of teaching.

Reflection Prior to Classroom Visit

A Guide for Thinking About Coaching

Observer: <u>W.T.</u>   **Date:** <u>Word Study Minilesson</u>

Teacher: <u>Karen</u>   **Grade:** <u>2</u>

Think about:

- ◆ What kinds of questions does the teacher ask you?
- ◆ What are some of the confusions the teacher expresses?
- ◆ Are there differences between the way the teacher talks and what you observe in the classroom?

- ◆ What kinds of behavior provide evidence of the teacher's strengths and skills in classroom work?
- ◆ What does the teacher say about children? To what degree does he/she describe children's behavior as evidence of learning?

The goal is to create a context in which "good dissonance" can take place. Criticism is offered in a constructive and positive way through nonthreatening conversations.

Make notes in response to the questions below:

1. What are your perceptions of the teacher's strengths?	Highly organized classroom. Students know what's expected. Materials organized and accessible. Procedures for guided reading in place; she knows all steps. Lessons efficient unless the book is too hard.
2. What do you think the teacher needs to learn **next** (conceptually) to reach another level of understanding?	May want to work on book introductions, helping her understand how to get children more involved. Selections generally good and will work with stronger introduction. She's searching for reasons why her lessons bog down.
3. What are the **teacher's** perceptions of his/her strengths and needs?	Likes her book collection and organization. Says she feels good about guided reading but lessons bog down and kids get antsy. Asks whether she should choose easier books.
Notes from preconference:	

Figure 7–7. *Reflection*

Observation of Guided Reading

Observer: W.T.   Teacher: Karen   Date 12/5

Grade: 1   Number of Children in Group: 5

Preparation	Independent Activities
Text selected: *Shopping* **Level:** B **Notes:** Easy text; familiar topic; some hard words.	**Number:** 3 **Engagement[1]:** 1 2 3 4 **Types represented:** Reading in library center; writing in journals and drawing pictures; worksheet on word families.

Introduction of Text	**Engagement:** 1 2 ③ 4	**Start:** 10:10 **End:** 10:26
Teacher's Language	*Children's Language*	*Other Observations*
"We're going to look at the pictures and you're going to tell me about the story. Brendon, tell me the whole story." Goes from child to child, asking each to tell about pictures. Points out the picture and says the word *escalator*.	Children are labeling things in pictures and talking about them. Michael (C2) begins to read the story w/o attending to teacher. Children notice and point to picture of escalator.	They may not understand this as a story. Teacher is attempting to get them involved, but this won't help them understand how the story works. Lack of focus.
Reading the Text	**Engagement:** 1 ② 3 4	**Start:** 10:26 **End:** 10:33
Teacher's Language	*Children's Language*	*Other Observations*
Instructs children to whisper read. Interacts with 3 children. Points out *ing* on *going* and *shopping* for two. All interactions focused on helping children with difficult words.	All 5 children have difficulty with the text. Difficult words include *sitting, going, stores*. No evidence of fluency or phrasing. Process breaking down for all children.	Children are doing some wild guessing at words; no evidence of comprehension. Toward the end, teacher used shared reading to finish. Reflect on the introduction.
After Reading the Text	**Engagement:** 1 ② 3 4	**Start:** 10:33 **End:** 10:45
Teacher's Language	*Children's Language*	*Other Observations*
No discussion of story. Worked on hard words that were in the book; used white board—*going, sit, shop*.	Repeated words.	Routines of guided reading in place; work on selection and introduction of text.
Word Work: None		NOTE—Talk about optional word work in class.
Extension/Assignment: None		NOTE—Introduce idea of extension.

[1]RUBRIC FOR ENGAGEMENT: 1 = Only a few children are on task and attending to intruction. There are many distractions, including noise and movement. Instruction is severely undermined. 2 = About half of the children are on task and attending to the instruction, but there are many distractions, including noise and movement. Instruction is indermined. 3 = Most of the children are on task and attending to the instruction. There are occasional distractions and some children are moving about. Instruction, in general, is being provided most of the time. 4 = Almost all children are on task and attending to the instruction. Instruction is being provided most of the time. There are only a few distractions.

Figure 7–8.   *Guided Reading Observation*

Teachers constantly compare examples, analyzing one in terms of another. As they watch their peers teach lessons, they gain new information they can apply to their own teaching.

Suggestions for Extending Your Skills as a Staff Developer

1. Look at the form in Figure 7–4. At first glance, it may seem there is not much information here, but conduct a time analysis:
   - At what times does the instruction appear to be going well (at least in terms of pace and efficiency)?
   - At what times does it appear to lag?
   - Where is the teacher using time well? Where is she losing time?
   - What organizational features of the schedule might interfere with good instruction?
   - What advice would you give the teacher?
2. Conduct a similar analysis for Figures 7–6 and 7–7.
3. Identify a school and/or group of teachers you are working with (or will work with in the future). Using the ideas in this chapter, assess the culture and context of several classrooms.
   - Ask several teachers to describe life in their classroom. Identify each teacher's perspective on the classroom context she has established. What does the teacher value? What aspects of classroom culture are missing?
   - Assess the learning context in one classroom. Using the questions on pages 79 and 85, analyze teacher and student behavior during literacy learning.
   - Visit a classroom and map the physical layout of the classrooms. Notice whether the materials and books are well organized and accessible to students. Use suggestions presented in this chapter to guide your observations.
   - Interview several teachers, some primary and some intermediate. Ask each teacher to discuss her strengths and the areas in which she would like more support.
4. Observe a professional development colleague's class session.
   - How do teachers talk about their students or respond to case studies?
   - What level of specificity do you notice when they describe reading behavior?
   - How do they interpret running records or other records of reading behavior?
   - Identify patterns of behavior and think about what they mean.
   - What would be a good next step for this group of teachers? Do they know what is expected? Do they have enough background knowledge? Do they need more demonstration?
5. Drop in the teachers work room or lunch room in a nearby school.
   - What do the teachers talk about?
   - How do they talk to one another?
   - Is there a positive or negative tone to the conversations?
   - Do they share frustrations, challenges, and celebrations?
   - What do they say about the principal?
   - What evidence is there that students and their families and community are valued?
   - What evidence is there that they are advocates for students?
   - What do they say about the support staff and other teachers?

Chapter 8

Introducing, Demonstrating, and Trying New Procedures

*Critical factors for a
solid framework of professional
development are the melding
of theory and practice; robust
initial training followed by
continuing support, collegiality,
and guidance; and accountability
for children's progress.*
—JANET GAFFNEY AND
BILLIE ASKEW
STIRRING THE WATERS: THE
INFLUENCE OF MARIE CLAY *(76)*

Teachers are always being asked to try new instructional procedures in their classrooms. Sometimes they are eager to do so, but often change is either required or strongly encouraged by the administration. Many of the approaches beginning teachers are expected to use require new learning. Typically, teachers are introduced to new techniques in an inservice workshop; in a well-designed session, they may observe live or videotaped examples and have a chance to discuss the new techniques.

What happens after that is usually left to chance. Teachers go back to their classrooms and, working alone, try out the new procedure. Most of the time, they have little support. Often, they use makeshift materials. The one or two examples they have seen are not enough to help them adjust the procedure to *their* students. Still, many teachers persist, going through the steps of the process again and again, refining them, learning by trial and error. They read more about the technique, compare their new experiences with previous experiences, and look for evidence of learning. They've developed their own systems for taking on new learning. For them, successful experiences lead to more successful expriences.

Many other teachers find the process of new learning frustrating, even frightening. Changing what you do in your classroom and departing from a prescriptive curriculum can make you feel vulnerable. Sheer labor is involved in rearranging materials and collecting new ones. Trial and error can produce anxiety. Ultimately, the new approach may be dropped, modified so radically that it does not accomplish the intended goals, or implemented in a mechanical and superficial way that undermines its effectiveness. Careful consideration of basic materials, organizational plans, and processes is essential.

A good staff development program provides support systems built around the four components of learning:

1. Provide basic materials and clear demonstrations of processes.

2. Engage the learners in active exploration of the approach.

3. Establish the rationales by clarifying reasons for each element of the approach.

4. Support participants as they try out the approach themselves.

These components make up a "spiral of learning" (see Figure 8–1) in which learners expand their knowledge by coming back to a particular point or topic many times, considering it differently each time. A spiral expands continuously, but it is not linear in the sense of having discrete steps. In other words, as a staff developer, you don't simply introduce and "cover" a technique like guided reading in one or two ses-

Figure 2–1. *The Spiral of Learning*

sions and considered it "learned." Learning to teach means developing and refining the repertoire of approaches you have at your disposal; most important, it means integrating information about the reading process, how children learn, and the procedures of instruction. The spiral represents a kind of moving around in critical areas of learning in a way that connects information and experience.

Providing basic directions and materials is probably the first step in introducing any new instructional procedure, but in very short order you will be working on all four of these components simultaneously: constantly providing more demonstrations and helping teachers get the materials they need, supporting them with practical suggestions, bringing in connections to the underlying theory or research. This "theory" is not necessarily—or even ideally—presented in the ponderous language of textbooks; for the most part, it takes the simple form of articulating what children are learning from the activity.

Providing Basic Materials

For each new approach you want to establish through your staff development program, think about what teachers really need to get started. You want to make it easy, not discourage or overwhelm them. We're not recommending you do everything *for* them; that would be smothering. But the necessary materials and equipment must be provided if a teacher is to try a new technique. (Figure 8–2, for example, lists the materials needed to implement guided reading.)

Some materials are simple; some imply being able to use additional techniques; others require a great deal of support to implement. Here are three examples:

◆ A leveled book collection will take some time to organize and acquire.[1] You will want the teachers to look at texts over time, their goal being to understand the characteristics they must consider (layout, length, difficulty of concepts, difficulty of vocabulary, and complexity of language) in assigning texts a place in the gradient. You may need to start with a limited number of books already arranged by level—examining the characteristics of these texts will help teachers

---

Basic Materials Needed for Guided Reading

◆ Table or area for a group to work comfortably.

◆ A leveled book collection, appropriate to grade, with multiple copies of titles at each level.

◆ A clipboard for teacher's records and guides.

◆ Individual book boxes/tubs *and/or* group book boxes/tubs for independent reading.

◆ An easel for writing on chart paper.

◆ A small whiteboard and/or a Magnadoodle[1] for illustrating how words work.

◆ Student writing folders.

◆ Lowercase magnetic letters for working with words—three or four sets organized on a cookie sheet or in divided plastic containers so they are easy to find.

[1]Small dry-erase whiteboards and markers can be obtained from most office supply stores. A Magnadoodle is a board with iron filings under a plastic surface. You "write" on it with a magnetized pencil and erase by drawing a bar across the board. Teachers like small whiteboards and Magnadoodles because they are convenient to use and provide a very clear, framed surface for examples.

Figure 8–2. *Basic Materials Needed for Guided Reading*

---

become more independent with the gradient, make better text selections, and introduce stories with greater skill.

◆ A whiteboard is a very simple piece of equipment, easily acquired; however, selecting words to bring to students' attention in order to show them the principles of how words work involves complex decisions.

◆ To set up browsing boxes, teachers need only assess students' reading levels and gather a number of appropriate books; but using browsing boxes in connection with guided reading means knowing students well, teaching routines, and gradually building up books that are just right for each group.

Supplies are not always within your control, but you can certainly survey teachers to see what is available. Often, when teachers want to learn a new technique, they take matters into their own hands and convince administrators to order necessary materials. (This kind of positive action is a sure sign the training you provide will produce positive results!) If you are working closely with the administration, make purchasing materials part of the overall plan and budget.

A final note of caution: being given new materials for our classroom is exciting, but none of us wants to cope with too much too soon. For guided reading, a good but *limited* set at the beginning will make the task of selecting and introducing books less overwhelming. You may want to purchase materials throughout the year rather than all at once. In addition, when teachers help acquire the books themselves, they learn more and own the process.

Demonstrating Basic Processes

Teachers expect a trainer to provide clear, specific information about a new technique. While they will discover a great deal as they work with the technique, they need basic information to get going. More complex instructional techniques, like guided reading, require prerequisite skills, so the overall plan for introducing them is also complex. Teachers have to know where to start.

By "the basics," we mean the "nuts and bolts" of any given teaching procedure. In a sense, you are asking teachers to trust you, to try something new by following a series of steps leading they're not sure where. You will, however, always discuss *why* each step is necessary in terms of children's learning.

Teaching Prerequisite Skills

Analyze the instructional technique and identify what a person has to know *going in* to implement it successfully. For guided reading, for example, teachers need:

◆ Good observational skills.
◆ Ability to use running records, informal reading inventories, or other excellent and detailed methods for gathering information on readers.
◆ Adequate information to be able to group readers.
◆ At least a beginning understanding of text characteristics and the gradient of text.

◆ Knowledge of some of the texts that they will be using with students.

When teaching prerequisite skills, be sure participants understand *why* they are learning the technique and how it will help them teach better. The worst approach is to tell participants that training is "required by the district." They need to understand the larger goals of the project and what it means to them and their students. (Of course, the real value of the technique will ultimately be internalized only as they use it.)

Teach each prerequisite skill by providing clear demonstrations and then letting participants undertake the action with your encouragement and support.

1. To teach running records, for example, you could give a brief, direct explanation of the coding techniques and have participants practice them by simulating children's reading errors. Then ask two participants to work with a child who is reading—one taking the running record, the other observing. Immediate hands-on experience like this gives them a lot to talk about right away.

Discussing a demonstration lesson.

2. Another example: the best way for teachers to learn about text characteristics is to give them a limited set of books and ask them to rank them in order of difficulty. Through this process, they plumb their existing knowledge of children's books, which is usually considerable.

Selecting Clear Examples

People who are just beginning to learn new skills need simple, clear examples. Some general demonstration principles include:

◆ Provide more than one example, so that, from the beginning, observers know that there will be variations.

◆ Try not to include "noise." While there is no perfect lesson, try to get as good an example as you can without unusual "props," interruptions, and adjustments that take a great deal of explaining.

◆ Keep the examples simple. A teacher might have a very good reason for including an extra step or giving a student special treatment; at first, however, it is best to stick with examples that will work with most students. Introducing a special technique in the initial stage may convince participants to make it part of the routine for all students.

◆ Be sure that the demonstration reflects excellent teaching and doesn't leave room for misunderstanding. Beginners will be inclined to reproduce exactly what they see.

Ways of Demonstrating Processes

There are six ways to demonstrate instructional processes: all have their strengths and weaknesses (see Figure 8–3).

Live Demonstrations Watching "live" teaching is highly valued because it's real. As they observe, trainees notice details of student and teacher behavior and can appreciate the moment-to-moment decisions teachers make. Classroom demonstrations, observations through a one-way glass, and demonstrations over fiber-optic networks provide opportunities to observe live teaching.

Guided Observations Being able to guide an observation is very beneficial: you can answer participants' questions immediately and call their attention to important moments, and they can describe significant behavior as it happens. Guided observation can't take place in a classroom, because talk must be suspended. Demonstrations accomplished via a one-way glass, a fiber-optic connection, or videotape all allow you to guide the observation.

Simulation A simulation is very easy to implement; in addition, it lets you slow down the process so that the routines are easier to understand. Sometimes participants just need to walk through the steps of an instructional approach in order to see the framework better.

Authentic Engagement: Teachers as Readers and Writers Authentic involvement in language and literacy processes is one of the best ways to help teachers see themselves as learners and see instruction from the student's point of view. For example, teachers can read works of children's literature or adult literature and share their personal responses and the connections they made while reading. They can record in a notebook their thoughts and responses to things they read or their memories of past events. They can write and "publish" within their group. They can move through the routines and procedures of the reading workshop or writing workshop and afterward reflect on their own learning and how the process was supportive. Adults, like children, enjoy engaging in literacy for authentic purposes. When implementing authentic engagement, you want to be sure that the process is appropriate. The level and subject matter must be such that your adult learners can engage with the material. You are not asking adults to pretend to be children but to find their own way into learning and sharing what they've learned. If you work with a group over time, they form a learning community, a process that they can also apply to their work with students. In general, the higher the grade level your participants teach, the easier it is for them to engage with the experiences authentically and then apply them to their work with students.

Using Videotapes Images on film have great power; people tend to do exactly what they see, especially if they watch something several times. It is difficult to produce videotapes containing clear examples, however. You will need to spend a great deal of time taping lessons to get a few that show the process with great clarity and little "noise."

Ways of Demonstrating Teaching Approaches

	Advantages	Disadvantages
1. Live Demonstrations *Description:* Bring groups of participants into classrooms to observe teaching.	◆ Participants see real teaching "on the run," so it has credibility. ◆ Participants can usually talk with the teacher before and after the lesson to get more information on the students and teaching decisions. ◆ Participants can usually see and hear very well. ◆ Sometimes participants can interact with children before or after instruction. ◆ Materials (for example, books) and children's work are readily available for examination. ◆ Observers can select individual children to focus on so that they build detailed knowledge.	◆ Instruction is fast paced, so observers must follow very closely; taking notes diverts their attention. ◆ Participants cannot talk with one another during the observation. ◆ The leader cannot guide the process by pointing out specific aspects of instruction. ◆ It is often difficult to arrange visits and work around teachers' schedules. ◆ The number of observers must be limited to keep classroom disruption to a minimum. ◆ Travel to schools is sometimes difficult to arrange. ◆ The observation has to take place during school hours. ◆ Normal interruptions, like fire drills, can be expected to occur.
2. Demonstration Using a One-Way Glass *Description:* Observe children in a classroom setting or small groups in a special facility through a one-way glass.	◆ Participants see real teaching "on the run," so it has credibility. ◆ Participants can talk with the teacher before and after the lesson to get more information on students and teaching decisions. ◆ The leader can point out important aspects of instruction and evidence of learning. ◆ Participants can ask questions and talk with one another during the lesson. ◆ Participants can usually see and hear very well. ◆ Materials (for example, books) and children's work are readily available for examination. ◆ Observers can select individual children to focus on so that they build detailed knowledge	◆ The one-way glass and sound system may be difficult to acquire and make functional. ◆ Instruction is fast paced, so observers may miss some critical moments. ◆ The number of participants are limited to those that can comfortably assemble behind the glass. ◆ The number of children are limited to those that can work in the space provided. ◆ Usually the space is not the children's own classroom, so there is some artificiality. ◆ There are logistic difficulties involved in transporting groups of children to a facility.
3. Demonstration on Videotape *Description:* Collect videotapes of specific teaching techniques in classrooms.	◆ A lesson captured on videotape can be shown several times for different purposes—noticing children's behavior, teacher's technique, management, etc. ◆ You can choose to watch a small segment of a lesson for a particular purpose or an entire lesson. ◆ Videotapes are generally easy to use if you have a player. ◆ Other than equipment, no special arrangements are needed. ◆ Observers can ask questions during viewing. ◆ The leader can guide observation, either by talking while the tape is playing or by pausing at appropriate spots. ◆ Teachers who need to see the examples again can take them home and watch them.	◆ The information provided on videotape is limited to what the camera captures; observers are limited to the lens. ◆ Sometimes action captured on teacher-made videotapes has poor quality and sound. ◆ Videotapes that show less effective techniques will be seen over and over. Since the tendency may be to copy the teaching in detail, ineffective or inappropriately applied techniques may be perpetuated. ◆ In showing videotapes, you sometimes experience technical difficulties. ◆ On videotape, the classroom seems noisier than it does when you are there, leading to false impressions. ◆ It is hard to see students' work; you may miss significant student responses.
4. Simulation *Description:* Engage participants in "walking through" the steps of an instructional approach themselves.	◆ You can simulate a technique anytime, anywhere, with no equipment and very few materials. ◆ Simulation slows down the process so that participants can understand, question, and discuss each step, making it clear. ◆ You can address questions and concerns relative to the approach because you are moving through it. ◆ Participants are actively engaged in the process.	◆ Simulation is artificial by definition. Participants are not really seeing the technique in action. ◆ Some participants may feel somewhat foolish and not be engaged at the level they should be. ◆ Participants are "practicing" in the absence of children, so one aspect of instruction—that it fits the child—is missing. There may be a tendency to view teaching as performance.

Figure 8–3. *Ways of Demonstrating*

Ways of Demonstrating Teaching Approaches (continued)

	Advantages	Disadvantages
5. Authentic Involvement in the Process *Description:* Engage participants in reading, writing, and language processes that mirror procedures to use with students but allow for real participation at an adult level.	◆ Participants experience learning for themselves. ◆ Participants learn the routines for the procedures very well because they have worked through them. ◆ The authentic reasons for engaging in the activity become apparent through participation. ◆ Participants can see the procedure from the point of view of the students. ◆ The process is highly engaging. ◆ Participants not only learn the new procedures but also form a learning community. ◆ The process lends itself to reflection and analysis.	◆ Some procedures designed for young children do not lend themselves to authentic adult participation; instead it becomes role-playing. ◆ Some procedures can be modified for adults, but they are changed so much that teachers cannot see what it would be like for young students. ◆ Engaging in authentic language and literacy processes takes a great deal of time, which may not be available. ◆ Participants must be willing to engage in authentic processes and reflect on them rather than simply being shown what to do.
6. Connection by Fiber-Optic Network to Live Classroom [Distance Learning] *Description:* Participants in one setting view ongoing live teaching at a remote location, connected by fiber-optic network. They can interact with people at the site.	◆ Participants are watching live teaching as it occurs in classrooms. ◆ Usually, participants can see and hear reasonably well, especially if two cameras are used. ◆ The leader can guide the process. ◆ Participants can talk and ask questions. ◆ It has the convenience of bringing remote areas together. ◆ The network is convenient to use, especially since no transportation of students or participants is required. ◆ You can bring great variety and diverse cultures into the realm of participants' experience. ◆ Expertise from one area can be available to other geographic areas. ◆ Students and teachers are in their own classrooms; after they become used to the camera, they tend to ignore it.	◆ The equipment and line fees make distance learning quite expensive. ◆ Teachers, school administrators, and parents must agree to allow cameras in the classroom. ◆ It takes time to establish relationships and set up the fiber-optic connection. ◆ If there is a delay between talking and hearing, the whole process is tedious. ◆ Participants are seeing the lessons through a camera, so some things will be missed. ◆ It is hard to see children's work—what they are writing, for example. ◆ The staff developer must acquire technical expertise or have a technician handy. ◆ Interrruptions and technical difficulties often interfere with discussions, momentum, and sustained attention.

Figure 8–3. *Ways of Demonstrating (continued)*

Videotapes should be good enough technically that viewers can see and hear everything that is going on, which isn't easy. In a videotape of a group lesson, for example, you may see and hear the teacher but be unable to tell what students are doing and how they are responding. It is very hard to see students' written work on a videotape or notice individual reading behavior in detail. Good videotapes require professional sound engineering and two or more cameras to truly capture classroom lessons—an expensive process beyond the capability of most schools, districts, and universities. You can purchase good professionally produced videotapes, but they probably won't zero in specifically on what you are trying to teach. In addition, the children and teachers on the screen will undoubtedly be somewhat idealized.

Combining Ways of Demonstrating

Since you have several options for providing demonstrations, you will want to vary what you do. For a combined approach, for example, you could:

◆ Introduce the process with a brief talk.
◆ Show a video that clearly illustrates the procedure.
◆ Walk participants through a simulation (which will be informed by the video) or engage them as readers and writers.
◆ Show another example that illustrates how the procedure varies according to the needs of students.
◆ Discuss the procedure, bringing out questions.
◆ Go into a classroom and observe a live demonstration.

Learning to teach is not a matter of seeing one or two demonstrations and then using the procedure. That's just a way to get started. Seeing many demonstrations, provided in a number of ways, will allow teachers to generalize the procedure, which is your goal. Once they understand a framework of actions and how they can vary their teaching decisions based on student response, they will be able to learn from their own teaching.

Balancing Demonstration and Description

Is it ever appropriate to tell a teacher what to do? Absolutely. Teachers need and demand some very specific information to get started with a new technique. Telling, however, is not as powerful as demonstrating. And teaching is more than telling. You will want to keep your descriptions and explanations brief and interesting. Avoid long lists of "rules" or "don'ts." Move into some kind of demonstration as soon as you can and involve participants in discussing what they see and hear. If you explore a procedure in depth through demonstration, authentic engagement, and discussion, you will find that the learners are more active.

Establishing Rationales

Designing professional development is not a question of either theory *or* practical suggestions. Dichotomous thinking like this leads to two problems:

◆ When you explain theory in detail, with copious references to research, before you introduce practical aspects of an approach, learners find the going much too difficult. Of necessity, they are always much more concerned with what they have to do tomorrow than with purely theoretical learning. When the separation between theory and practice is too great, the theory doesn't take. A session like this can even be counterproductive in that teachers reject the new learning. "Exclusionary" language doesn't get you anywhere.

◆ When all you do is describe and demonstrate an approach, giving every practical suggestion you can think of, you risk having participants think of it as today's trick or tip.

They may quickly discard the idea because they do not understand its importance in terms of children's learning. Also, they may apply it mechanically to no good result.

Teachers shouldn't be asked to take on any new instructional technique without a clear explanation of what it means for children's learning. Unless you provide the "whys," teachers have the right to reject an approach.

It is essential, then, to embed theoretical understanding within the learning of new instructional approaches. It might be easier to think of rationales or reasons instead of theory. It's simply a matter of knowing why you are doing what you are doing. For every instructional approach you teach, think through the reasons yourself. Put your statements into simple, everyday language. If you are having difficulty coming up with these clear statements or with rationales for the approach, you may want to do more teaching of children and studying it yourself before embarking on the daunting task of training others.

It will help to talk over these statements of rationale with a friend; try them out to see whether they are clear to someone outside the field of education. Also, you may find some very clear statements in the books you read, but be careful about quoting too much material. Your trainees won't want to listen to long quotes read aloud. If you use a quote, be sure it's one they can discuss and relate to specific demonstrations of teaching or to their own experience. Your role is to make explicit connections between the theoretical statements and the teaching and learning shared among the group.

Avoid educational jargon or convoluted theoretical statements. Look at the difference between these two reasons for providing an introduction to a new, more challenging text in guided reading:

Statement I: Think of your introduction as a conversation that gives readers the information they need to read a new text. This conversation helps them remember and use what they already know as they read a book that is a little bit more difficult than they can read easily. They are better able to solve problems as they read, and they learn more during the process.

Statement 2: From a sociocultural perspective, the book introduction provides a scaffold that helps readers work within the zone of proximal development, accessing prior knowledge, predicting, hypothesizing, and confirming hypotheses as they process continuous text in new and challenging material. It is essential for students to work within the zone so that they take on new cognitive strategies.

These two statements provide essentially the same information. Statement 2 is accurate and informative; these sentences might well appear in a dissertation on reading theory. But think about the prior knowledge it assumes! Unpacking the statement will be difficult for teachers who do not know the work of Vygotsky or Bruner or who understand that work only superficially. Conversation about books is, indeed, a social and cultural event; solving problems while reading does work to expand strategies. But don't make your adult learners work so hard on the language when they are also taking on many new actions while at the same time organizing materials and managing time. Your role is to acquaint them with basic logistics by way of clear, accurate explanations with a theoretical base. Over time, these theoretical explanations will be elaborated.

In the beginning, steer clear of detailed discussions of theoretical foundation. Participants will no doubt offer some excellent observations that you can tie into theory during demonstrations, discussion, and other active learning. If you have begun with very clear rationales, you can and will come back to them again and again.

Engaging the Learners

People learn by acting on information. In the process they use their prior experiences to construct new knowledge. As noted in Chapter 1, social interaction, participation, reflection, and application support learning for both children and adults. Conceptualizing teachers' professional development as *active* rather than *passive* requires that we carefully design training sessions to provide a balance between telling and doing.

Giving specific directions in clear language and demonstrating processes both imply passivity on the part of the learners, and that's what you don't want. Use your ingenuity to structure class sessions so that teachers are always active instead of simply observing. Reading Recovery, for example, uses "talking while observing": teachers watch lessons through a one-way glass, talking out loud about what they see and hypothesizing about what it means (see Appendix A). This active process is intensive but leads to deep learning. Figure 8–4 lists some ways to promote active learning on the part of your group of adult learners.

Participants need to be actively engaged every time you provide a demonstration, in as many ways as possible. For example, you might:

1. Have teachers look at students' written products from a particular classroom.
2. Have them analyze the work and make hypotheses about what these students know about writing.
3. Encourage them to think about what kinds of minilessons would be appropriate for these students.
4. Ask them to provide rationales for their hypotheses.

Talking about a reading lesson.

5. Show a videotape of the teacher of these students presenting a minilesson focusing on some aspect of writing.
6. Have them discuss the minilesson in light of their earlier analysis of student work.
7. Ask them to talk about whether their hypotheses were validated or not.
8. Provide some samples of work these students did during the week after the minilesson.
9. Ask them to analyze these samples for evidence of shifts in student learning.

In any one session, don't focus on too many things. And remember that watching long videotapes tends to put participants to sleep. Active exploration is critical. Show brief, focused teaching interactions or parts of lessons rather than long sequences. Five to ten minutes of a powerful example is sufficient. Figure 8–5 offers some suggestions for selecting videotaped examples.

You need to think very hard about any videotape you show: it must relate to what you are teaching the group (ask a friend's opinion if you're not sure). Ask yourself:

◆ How will the example on this tape help teachers understand the procedure?
◆ What will they see and understand from watching this tape?
◆ Do I need to provide background information or student artifacts to make the learning come alive? What kind?
◆ What part or parts of the tape should I show?
◆ How should I balance viewing and discussion?
◆ What impression will this piece of video give viewers of the life in this classroom?
◆ Can participants connect the example on tape with the theoretical foundation of the instruction?

Engaging Adult Learners

During a live demonstration, focus learners' attention on something specific:

- ◆ Teacher's language.
- ◆ Students' language.
- ◆ Management techniques.
- ◆ Use of text.
- ◆ Intersectional patterns.
- ◆ Use of time.

When using videotapes, engage learners in the kinds of observation mentioned above and also involve them in closer analytical work:

- ◆ Looking at a part of a lesson several times, noticing procedural details and comparing them with other lessons.
- ◆ Looking closely at individual readers or writers and analyzing their processing.
- ◆ Look at interactional patterns across groups.
- ◆ Make a close analysis of language, perhaps using a written transcript.
- ◆ Make a close analysis of how the teacher engages students.
- ◆ Reflecting on an aspect of the lesson.

Bring students' written products to the session and have teachers analyze them for:

- ◆ Changes over time.
- ◆ Spelling development.
- ◆ Quality of writing.
- ◆ Range of topics or genres.
- ◆ Letter formation.
- ◆ Text layout.
- ◆ Sense of audience and voice.
- ◆ What children know.
- ◆ What students need to know next.

Bring records of students' reading into the session and have teachers analyze them for:

- ◆ Specific behavior indicating evidence of strategies.
- ◆ Changes in behavior over time.
- ◆ Range of texts that student have read (reading lists).
- ◆ The quality of reading response journal entries.
- ◆ What students know.
- ◆ The extent to which texts students are reading allow them to use what they know.
- ◆ What students need to know next.

Figure 8–4. *Engaging Adult Learners*

Suggestions for Selecting Good Examples from Videotapes

1. Show only good, clear examples of teaching.
2. Select tapes that reflect good planning and organization on the part of the teacher, so that the basics are in place.
3. Select segments that are directly related to what you are teaching your class.
4. Make sure that the materials the teacher is using are good (appropriate, high-quality books that provide opportunities for students to learn, for example).
5. Look for segments that clearly show students' responses, including variety among responses.
6. Look for segments that clearly show teacher-student interactions around points that are related to what you are teaching your class.
7. Use segments that are high enough in technical quality that participants can hear and see teachers and children.
8. Avoid segments that provide bad examples or show inappropriate behavior on the part of students or teachers. Use poor examples only with highly advanced groups who are well able to analyze and learn from them.
9. Be sure your examples reflect our diverse society by including people of color and English learners.
10. Find segments that show teacher and student faces as much as possible.

Figure 8–5. *Suggestions for Selecting Videotapes*

If you were present in the classroom when the tape was recorded (or you taped it yourself), you'll "hear" and "see" it differently because you'll remember the actual lesson. You'll also find it more interesting and be less aware of its length. Try to see it from the novice or unconnected observer's point of view.

Nevertheless, making your own videotapes is a very good thing to do. It may require many "takes" to get one that you feel comfortable showing; however, you will learn a great deal in the process. The lesson doesn't have to be perfect, in fact probably shouldn't be, but it must be a good, clear example.

Also think of videos as having multiple purposes. It takes a great deal of time to prepare a good video accompanied with artifacts. Once achieved, however, this "package" can be reused until it becomes outdated. (Remember, your own knowledge and skill will increase year after year.)

Trying It Out

Once materials are available and participants have seen some clear demonstrations, they will be ready to try the approach or technique themselves. Don't let too much time elapse between your introducing a new procedure and the teach-

ers' trying it out—anxiety can build. And don't get into the habit of providing demonstration after demonstration. Teachers need to get their feet wet as soon as possible. A first attempt is simply an approximation to get the feel. The goals are to:

◆ Get started using the procedure or a component of the procedure.
◆ Make approximated attempts without fear of failure.
◆ Engage in the teaching moves and decisions related to the procedures.
◆ Reflect on and adjust teaching moves and decisions.
◆ Gradually establish routine actions, so that it is easier to observe and respond to individual students.
◆ Build confidence and expertise.

There are a variety of ways to help teachers try out the procedure in their own classroom. Some will need more support than others. Figure 8–6 delineates decreasing levels of support. (Many teachers won't need the highest level of support represented by the top box on this chart.)

The teacher will be learning the procedure by approximation. Sharing the task with him or her is a good way to simplify the process. For example, you could provide the book introduction for a guided reading lesson and help the children read, letting the teacher lead the discussion of the text. Or the teacher can discuss an interesting experience with the children or read a favorite book aloud to them, while you help them compose and write a short piece of interactive writing.

As teachers become more independent, you can provide suggestions that will help them manage the process better. Don't try to fix everything at once. One or two suggestions per visit are about all you will be able to make—so select your suggestions carefully. The goal is to help the teacher reflect on his own teaching so that you can begin to coach for greater understanding. The first, second, or third time a teacher tries a new technique, he probably doesn't want to be asked questions like:

- How did the lesson go?
- What did children learn?
- What did you notice about students' response?
- What do you need to do differently?

Those are excellent questions to use *later*, because they prompt analysis. But asking them when the person doesn't know the answer will be highly threatening and can be seen as manipulative. Instead ask questions that help you understand the teacher's thinking:

- What kinds of books are these students interested in?
- What were you thinking about when you selected the book?
- I noticed the students were really interested in looking at the pictures. Is that what you expected?

Then model some ways of talking about children's behavior and evidence of learning.

In the beginning, the teacher probably has questions about organization and procedures and wants to be reassured that she is "doing it right." That can be tricky, because you don't want to judge her teaching nor do you want to give the impression there is only one right way. Any procedure will have many variations depending on the teaching decisions required for a given group of students at a particular time.

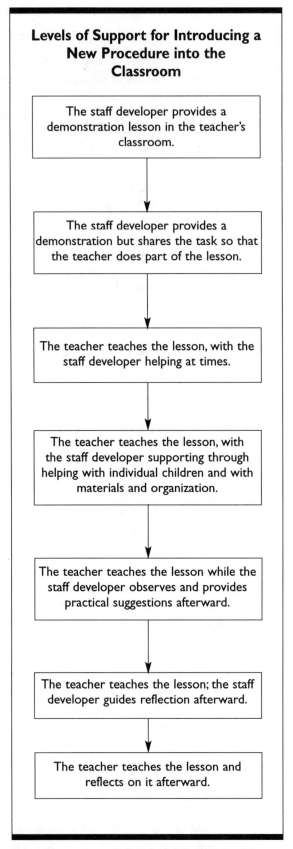

Levels of Support for Introducing a New Procedure into the Classroom

The staff developer provides a demonstration lesson in the teacher's classroom.

↓

The staff developer provides a demonstration but shares the task so that the teacher does part of the lesson.

↓

The teacher teaches the lesson, with the staff developer helping at times.

↓

The teacher teaches the lesson, with the staff developer supporting through helping with individual children and with materials and organization.

↓

The teacher teaches the lesson while the staff developer observes and provides practical suggestions afterward.

↓

The teacher teaches the lesson; the staff developer guides reflection afterward.

↓

The teacher teaches the lesson and reflects on it afterward.

Figure 8–6. *Level of Support for Trying New Procedures*

Give feedback to the teacher in the form of clear, nonjudgmental descriptions of what you saw happening in the lesson. Be direct in making one or two suggestions that will make an immediate difference. There is nothing wrong in saying:

◆ "I have a suggestion for the next lesson with these students."

◆ "Here are a couple of books that might be good for these students to read next. Which do you like best?"

You may also demonstrate a way to use materials more effectively or efficiently or recommend particular language.

Invite questions and comments from the teacher. The discussion after a lesson should be a real conversation. If teachers feel free to bring up issues and concerns without being evaluated, they will share their frustrations. Out of this conversation will come some goals for making the teaching more effective. As they become more comfortable with particular techniques, teachers will take on more self-analysis, using you as a resource.

From Action to Awareness

Trying out a technique in a risk-free setting allows teachers to draw on the expertise they already have. For example, they have ways of interacting with people and managing events. Even a new teacher has probably led a group in some way or other. Teaching draws on all of those skills.

Marie Clay (1998) refers to a process she calls "from acts to awareness." She points out that children do not always have to articulate processes in order to engage in them. We believe this concept applies to teaching as well. As teachers do whatever is needed to try out the new approach, they become more aware of:

◆ The way materials are selected and used, mentally evaluating those that are more and less effective.

◆ Students' behavior and their responses to instruction, mentally noting evidence of learning.

◆ How time is used, noting what takes too much time or when the lesson drags.

◆ Their on-the-spot decisions, noting those that lead to good student response and those that don't.

◆ The language they are using and whether it is clear to students.

By using a procedure, teachers begin to see relationships among processes as well as how they fit into the bigger picture. As a staff developer, you can raise awareness by focusing attention on factors like those listed above. Gradually, as routines are established, more time and attention can be spent reflecting on important aspects of teaching and learning.

A Spiraling Learning Process

For any new technique, a staff developer thinks through essential processes to support teachers' learning. Providing basic materials, demonstrating processes, establishing rationales, engaging learners, and trying out the new approach are interrelated and essential processes. Each must be carefully considered with regard to what you want to teach. The processes are not discrete steps—and if they are used as such, they will not be powerful.

Also, it is good to remember that while one approach may be established to the point that teachers are trying it out and refining their teaching, another may still require basic demonstrations. The spiral of learning does not reflect teachers' development over time; instead, it refers to processes that you employ given the familiarity and ease teachers have with specific kinds of instruction. Still, as you work with teachers over time, it may be easier for them to learn new approaches because they will develop internal systems for taking on new ideas and trying them out. Teachers who need only a brief demonstration or can take on a new approach simply by reading about it have developed these learning systems. No matter how much expertise you have, however, it is always helpful to share the learning process with others.

As a staff developer, you will be constantly moving within this spiral of experiences; in the process, you will learn more about how adults learn. You will develop expertise relative to instructional approaches: which ones require a great deal of demonstration? Which ones require only a little support before teachers can try them out? Using this spiral as a tool, you can use your observations and experiences to become a better and more knowledgeable teacher educator.

Suggestions for Extending Your Skills as a Staff Developer

1. Select an instructional approach to record on videotape. For example, you could record an interactive read-aloud with discussion, a minilesson on word study, or a guided reading lesson. You can teach the lesson yourself or you can tape a colleague's teaching.

2. Collect samples of children's work (observations of reading behavior, reading interviews, writing or spelling samples, whatever is appropriate) before and if possible after the lesson.

3. Tape the entire lesson, being sure that the camera is positioned to capture the best view possible of the teacher and children.

4. Afterward, watch the entire tape. Select a five-minute segment that illustrates some aspect of teaching within the approach.

5. Meet with a group of colleagues and show your five-minute tape. Discuss:
   - Why you selected the segment you did.
   - What the segment illustrates about the instructional procedure.
   - What the segment illustrates about teaching and learning.
   - What theoretical ideas the taped segment would help people learn.

6. Reflect on the process. Write three or four clear statements that explain the learning theory that underlies the instructional technique you are working on—particularly that illustrated by the five-minute segment you chose. Ask someone outside education to read the statements and give you feedback on their clarity.

Endnote
[1] Resources for acquiring and establishing a leveled collection are delineated in *Matching Books to Readers* (Pinnell and Fountas 1999).

Enabling Professional Development Through Coaching

Section 3 focuses on coaching, the professional development context that can make the most difference in teachers' ability to implement new ideas effectively.

Chapters 9 and 10 address the important skill of analysis. Staff developers must be able to "size up" situations and pinpoint essential characteristics of instruction. Staff developers in literacy education must also be able to conduct in-depth analyses of literacy teaching. These two chapters discuss specific tools that will help staff developers sharpen their powers of analysis and select important points on which to coach teachers. Each chapter includes examples of lessons and shows how staff developers might go about analyzing them.

Chapters 11 and 12 focus specifically on coaching. Chapter 11 includes examples of lessons and related coaching conversations that will help teachers have more impact on student learning. Chapter 12 discusses how to coach teachers to develop a cycle of analysis and reflection that will support their independence as they learn from their own teaching.

The rating scales introduced in this section have been created specifically to help you improve your analytic capabilities as a foundation for coaching. They are not intended to be used to evaluate students or teachers but instead to weigh student learning against the instruction that you see going on in classrooms and pinpoint productive areas for discussion.

Chapter 9

Analyzing Teaching in Preparation for Coaching

The structure for intimate colleagueship that we see as the peer-coaching study team is the building block of an organization that provides both caring support and the reflection necessary as people think out instructional decisions and work to enhance their professional repertoire.

—BRUCE JOYCE AND BEVERLY SHOWERS
STUDENT ACHIEVEMENT THROUGH STAFF DEVELOPMENT *(165)*

Once teachers have been prepared to try out new instructional approaches and are doing so in an organized way, staff developers can coach them toward higher levels of competence and confidence. Effective staff development involves professionals in an ongoing spiral of learning that includes demonstration, inquiry, reflection, and experimentation. According to Darling-Hammond and McLaughlin (1996) "effective professional development is . . . sustained, ongoing, and intensive, supported by modeling, coaching and collective problem solving around specific problems of practice" (p. 203).

There is growing support for the notion that coaching teachers in their practice is the most powerful means to increase their knowledge and improve their practice (Costa and Garmston 1994; Garmston and Wellman 1999). Being a coach is also a staff developer's most difficult role. There is no widespread understanding about how to help staff developers become effective coaches and no guidelines for helping a staff developer select powerful "coachable moments."

Studying literacy coordinators during coaching sessions (see Lyons 1999, 2000 and Pinnell and Lyons 1999), we found that more and less effective coaches are differentiated by their:

◆ Knowledge of the reading and writing processes.
◆ Capacity to use this knowledge to call attention to critical parts of the lesson.
◆ Ability to select points that will lead to new learning.

- ◆ Ability to engage teachers in reflection as a way to improve their skill.
- ◆ Ability to create a trusting relationship within which critical feedback is valued.

Coaching will be effective if staff developers learn how to analyze teacher-student interactions during a reading or writing lesson, determine what changes a teacher must make immediately to improve student learning, and then bring about a shift in that teacher's knowledge and practice.

If teaching is complex, coaching teachers is even more so. Coaching requires analytic and inferential skills: the key is good observation and analysis. You have to know how to look before you can decide where to direct a teacher's attention and what suggestions to make. As one literacy coordinator said, "My biggest coaching problem was deciding which segments of the lesson illustrated critical areas that needed improvement. Once I learned how to use the interactive writing and guided reading scales, my coaching focus became crystal clear."

An Example of Analytic Coaching

Let's join Lisa, a staff developer, as she observes Marian teach a guided reading lesson to a group of five first graders. Marian has good organizational skills and has been working for several weeks on guided reading, but the approach is still new to her.

Before the Observation

Before the observation Marian mentions that even though she provides detailed introductions to books, the children in her groups always seem to be struggling to read the words. Can Lisa help? Lisa decides to look at four specific factors:

- ◆ Are the books Marian selects appropriate for the children in the group?
- ◆ Are Marian's book introductions effective?
- ◆ Is Marian providing appropriate support during reading?
- ◆ Do children really understand what they are reading?

During the Observation

Lisa observes the lesson from beginning to end: the book introduction, the children's reading of the text, and Marian's teaching after the reading.

Looking at the Text Marian has selected *Animal Homes* (Hartley and Armstrong 1997), a text filled with interesting drawings of animals, a different group on each page. Each group has a different habitat—*burrows, caves, nests, hives,* and so on. The pattern of the text is quite easy, with each page beginning, "Some animals live in . . . [caves, hives, logs, etc.]." On the last page is the question, "Where do you live?" This is the only place the pattern changes.

Right away Lisa, an experienced teacher, knows that this book is probably quite a bit harder than Marian may have thought at first glance. The language pattern is easy and repetitive, and most of the words are easy; however, the concepts are quite difficult. The concept of a "cave," for example, is probably unfamiliar to many kindergartners, and they almost certainly will not recognize the word in print. The illustration on the cave page shows both a bear and a bat, with only the suggestion of a cave in the background. Lisa predicts that text features may present significant difficulty on every page. She asks herself:

1. Does this text have concepts that are meaningful to the children?
2. Can they read and understand most of the words?
3. Are the illustrations supportive?
4. Is the language structure recognizable?

She can answer "yes" only to the fourth question.

Introducting the Text Marian's introduction to the book is extensive, lasting more than fifteen minutes. She goes over every page, using some of the language. She says the names of most of the animals and discusses them carefully (although she herself does not know the names of two animals shown in one of the illustrations). Children contribute examples from their own experiences: being stung by bees, seeing bears at the zoo, hearing stories about turtles. It is hard to help children grasp the idea of various kinds of animal "homes," most of which are not truly depicted in the illustrations, so Marian provides long explanations. She also has them point to each habitat name and notice the first letter.

As she observes the introduction, Lisa takes notes:

- ◆ Marian's materials are very well organized; she's getting right into the introduction.

- She is engaging children in conversation, using some of the language of the book and asking children to predict what they might be reading about.
- She is generating a lively discussion; children are engaged; she has good rapport with them.
- There are too many concepts here, and some of them are very hard to understand.
- Looking at the illustrations may not help the children understand how the book works. The animal names are not even used in the text.
- You certainly need a lot of background information to understand this book. Marian is trying to build background knowledge, but the gap is too great.
- When Marian asks questions to get the children involved, they offer experiences unconnected to the information they need to understand this text. They have not encountered these words nor have they seen most of the animal habitats.
- The children may be able to use the first letter as a start in figuring out words, but the meanings of the words are too unfamiliar.
- It may be difficult for some students to get the meaning of this text.
- Marian is teaching intensively and shows enthusiasm for the book; she shares some of her own responses to the animals in the book.
- She has spent a lot of time on this introduction, but students will probably still have difficulty reading this text.
- She has drawn their attention to the first letter of each home, but the word *animal* is also hard and she hasn't helped them look at the first part of that word.
- The level of engagement is good. Marian has involved every child in this discussion and recognized and affirmed his or her responses.

Reading the Text The children begin to read the text, with Marian observing and sometimes interacting with individuals. Marian's frustration is evident as the children struggle to read the text. Some have trouble with the language pattern as well as the words; others have no trouble with the repeated words in each sentence but

bog down on the final "content" word. Still others are trying to use the names of the animals they see in the pictures. The children's frustration becomes apparent as well. Even those who begin strong, completing the lead sentence correctly, are making wild guesses by the middle of the book. Finally, seemingly discouraged, Marian has the children read the text in chorus just to finish it.

Here's what Lisa is thinking:

- This text really is too hard, not because of the sentences or most of the words but because of the concepts. Maybe Marian needs more support in looking at texts for this group of children.
- These children are using some good strategies for reading—noticing first letters, recognizing frequently encountered words, reading left to right with their eyes, searching for meaning in the illustrations. All five of the children, however, are having difficulty. They could better use what they know on an easier text.
- Marian seems to realize the book is too hard, because she is putting an end to the struggle by reading the book with the children. She's observing and listening to the children. I hope she's getting the idea that these words and concepts are too difficult.
- The introduction was not effective because there was too much talk. That's probably because the book is so difficult. Maybe Marian needs to work on shorter, more focused and powerful introductions. I think I need to help her choose a more appropriate book so that she can refine her introductions.

This ongoing analysis gives Lisa a great deal of information. She is searching for the answer to questions like these:

1. What is one change that will help Marian be more effective in teaching guided reading?
2. How can I connect this change to Marian's own concerns about her teaching?
3. What's a good way to start the conversation?
4. What are some positive things about her teaching that I can and should reaffirm?

Discussing the Reading After the group finished reading the book, Marian says, "Some of you had trouble with the word *animal*, and I didn't think you would. This book is all about animals. Every page begins, 'Some animals.' Let's look at that word. Turn to page one." The children find page one, which shows birds in the illustration. The text says: "Some animals live in nests."

Marian asks the children to say the word *animals* and to find it on the page, which all of them are able to do. On a small dry-erase board, she writes the word clearly and asks the children to look at it. She asks, " Do you see anything about the word that you know?"

Two students say, "A." One says, "An."

Covering up all but *an*, Marian says, "Yes, the first part of the word is *a-n*, like the word *an*. That will help you start the word *animals*. Do you see the *s* at the end? Say the word and be sure you can hear the *s*." All the students do so. Marian says, "So when you come to a long word like that, look for something about it that you know and also think of what it means."

Then Marian asks the students in the group to reread page one, which everyone can now do. The session concludes with a brief discussion of how the bird's home is a "nest," as shown in the illustration.

As she observes and takes notes, Lisa revises and elaborates on her thinking:

◆ Marian seems to understand that many pages of the book are too hard for students, because she's not going back and trying to teach every page again. She understands how the book works.

◆ She seems to have an idea of what will help the students. She went back to the easiest page in the book, the one where the topic is most familiar and the illustration is clear.

◆ She gave students a way to solve the word *animal* and prompted them to use that technique again. That was a powerful piece of teaching.

◆ She has helped them use both meaning and decoding, at least on the page where they can do it. That shows she knows her children and is observing them closely.

After the Observation

Lisa takes a few minutes to reflect after her observation of the lesson. She has to think quickly because she wants to coach Marian right away. (Whenever possible, Lisa meets with a teacher

briefly within half an hour after the lesson.) Here's how she sums up her thinking:

◆ Marian has materials in place, manages a guided reading lesson very well, and is able to engage her students.

◆ She is observant and able to adjust her teaching quickly in response to student behavior.

◆ She is positive with students and affirms their efforts.

◆ Given the difficulty children had with the text, Marian's teaching points were well selected. She showed children something that would help them solve words and did so in a meaningful way. I think she is beginning to match children's behavior with the idea that readers use meaning and visual information together.

◆ The thing that will help her most right now is to improve her ability to analyze and select texts with children in mind. That will lead naturally into refining her work in book introductions.

◆ This text was so mismatched that I think she needs some direct help in looking at books. Then her growing teaching skills can be used better.

◆ I think I'll start by going back to her complaint that children seem to struggle in the reading group. She may bring up the notion that the text was too hard.

◆ I'll bring up as an example a page where all the children had a lot of trouble. We can talk about what made that hard for kids. Then maybe I'll point out how much easier the page with the nests is and how right she was to use that page for her teaching points after the reading.

What Lisa Is Doing

This long example is one way a staff developer might use an observation to prepare for coaching. (Remember, no situation you encounter will be just like this example. Also, this one takes place quite early in Marian's work with guided reading.) The coaching hasn't yet begun, but Lisa has applied quite a bit of analytic skill to the process. Several points about Lisa's thinking are clear:

Reflecting on and analyzing observations.

◆ She has very specific instructional procedures in mind.

◆ She is looking specifically at evidence of children's literacy learning and connecting that evidence with Marian's decisions.

◆ She notices positive aspects of Marian's work, particularly basic patterns related to organizational and management.

◆ She is hypothesizing about what Marian knows and can do already.

◆ She is searching for a focus that will make a real difference for Marian.

◆ She is searching for a way to connect her own analysis with what is directly relevant to Marian.

◆ She understands the reading process and can analyze and interpret children's behavior. She also knows how to look at the interactions within lessons.

◆ Finally, she deeply understands from her own experience and study the instructional approach that she is trying to help Marian learn.

Lisa mentally prioritizes the points she wants to make in her conversation with Marian. There are literally dozens of points she could make: she could show Marian better ways to introduce *Animal Homes*, interact with children while they are reading, engage them in a discussion of the story, or help them internalize the concepts in the story. Although those techniques may be impor-

tant in the future, Lisa wants to suggest short-term differences that will have a long-term impact. She wants to use the data from her analysis to inform her coaching, her goal being to help Marian learn something beyond the lesson under scrutiny. She wants to help Marian expand her knowledge and skills in a way that, from that point on, will help her teach better every day.

Lisa's analysis will continue during the first moments of her coaching conference with Marian. She'll search out Marian's analysis of the lesson. What were her concerns? What was she thinking about as she made some of her decisions? Lisa will not put Marian on the defensive by asking dozens of questions, but she may start by saying something like this: "I noticed. . . . How did that fit with your earlier concerns about your students? What are you now thinking about . . . ?" Thus, Lisa will get a bit more information that will allow her to determine whether her own perceptions and Marian's match. Often, teachers exhibit remarkable awareness; Marian may very well start the conference by saying, "Wow, that book just wasn't right. I didn't realize how hard it would be for my kids."

The heart of coaching is this analytic process. No script will substitute for it or circumvent it. Coaching cannot be preplanned as a set of questions or steps, although we will suggest some helpful language. No formula will work for every coaching conference: each one must be specific to time and place but go beyond it. An analysis like this one is a map that guides the coaching conference; without it, your coaching may be ineffective.

How did Lisa develop this ability to analyze teaching? First, she is grounded in her own teaching of children. She has used guided reading successfully for a number of years, so she has a sense of what good teaching looks like in that context. She also knows children from her years of teaching at several grade levels. She has read about and studied the reading process as well as how children learn.

But these experiences are only the foundation for taking this "outside" analytic view. Lisa has observed many teachers working with children; from her training as a staff developer, she has learned ways of working with adults. Finally, she has analyzed guided reading lessons intensively. She can determine where Marian was effective even though, in general, the lesson did not go well. The sum total of her experience and training is paying off in her ability to pinpoint what this beginning teacher needs.

A Rationale for Developing Analytical Skills

Staff developers often go into classrooms to coach only to discover they need to change gears and help the teacher with basic organizational skills. That's the right thing to do in such a case. It is not effective to coach on the fine points of teaching when a teacher is worried about the basics. If the teacher is not organized and is struggling with unfamiliar procedures, she will not be doing her best work with students. It will be hard to pay attention to the subtleties of teaching, including:

◆ Skillfully selecting and using appropriate materials.
◆ Quickly adjusting instruction in response to student behavior.
◆ Using precise, clear language so that students attend to the information that will help them.
◆ Quickly deciding on the most powerful teaching moves at a particular time.
◆ Posing questions that promote problem solving on the part of students.
◆ Interacting in ways that recognize students' attempts and extend their reach.
◆ Introducing routines that save time and make learning interesting and efficient.

Looking at this list of skilled actions brings to mind the old adage that teachers are born, not made. And it is true that some persons seem intuitively to exhibit some of the behavior inherent in the list above. Nevertheless, such behavior can be learned. A good foundation for skilled

teaching may have been laid in other life experiences (participating in sports, being a camp counselor, being in charge of a fundraiser), so some teachers may learn faster than others. But our work in professional development indicates that experience, self-awareness, support, and time are also factors. Coaching is a way to help teachers become more analytic about their work and accelerate the development of skilled behavior that, once learned, begins to permeate all of the contexts within which teachers work with children.

Analytic Tasks for the Literacy Coach

Analyzing teaching is accomplished through a sequence of actions that the literacy coach uses in the process of working with teachers.

1. *Observe and notice significant behavior.* Working effectively with a teacher depends on the coach's ability to notice important behavior and interactions related to learning. This process implies an underlying understanding of content and the ability to use that knowledge in an explicit and analytic way. Observing a teacher introduce a book in a guided reading lesson, for example, a literacy coach notes:
   ◆ The teacher's language.
   ◆ The children's language in response to the teacher.
   ◆ Children's initiated language.
   ◆ The teacher's adjustments and changes in response to children's behavior.
   ◆ The use of text and the way the teacher helps children construct meaning.
   ◆ The use of time.
   ◆ Focus of attention.
   ◆ Level of engagement.
2. *Infer teachers' understanding.* As a literacy coach, you form hypotheses about the teacher's current understanding relative to content. The ability to form these tentative opinions is built by observing many teachers over time. Behavior is indicative of underlying assumptions. For example, during the book introduction, a teacher might focus mainly on introducing individual words as vocabulary items. The coach might infer that the teacher currently understands her role in the introduction as teaching chil-

dren individual words or that the teacher's idea of the reading process is reading individual words rather than processing text.

3. *Select examples to support teachers' learning.* The literacy coach's goal is to point out explicit examples that might expand the teacher's understanding, and, as a result, his teaching skills. Observing and coaching is not a matter of simply telling a teacher what is "wrong" or "right," which would produce prescriptions rather than build the underlying theory that fuels good decision making. The prescriptive approach interrupts the learning process and promotes dependency. Examples from the classroom are selected to promote thinking and reflection on the part of the teacher. For example, the literacy coach might select a particular conversation or interaction about a concept in the story or an illustration. Through this one example, a teacher could learn more about helping children process text for meaning rather than simply how to use a technique for introducing words.

4. *Learn more about the teacher's perspective.* After observation, the literacy coordinator may have hypotheses and examples to consider; however, it is important to talk with the teacher to learn more about her underlying thinking. Coaching is two sided: both persons learn more about their role and build theoretical understanding as they go. Observing a teacher's behavior gives the coach some information, but the teacher's reflections are also valuable. The coach may, for example, ask the teacher to talk about the lesson that was observed, what she thought about while preparing for it, and her reflections on what happened.

Analyzing General Aspects of Teaching

A number of characteristics are generally considered to be related to effective instruction (Lyons, Pinnell, and DeFord 1993). These "generic" characteristics can be applied to any teaching, any age, any setting, any time. They are the basis for many personnel evaluation models in education. For example, research indicates that teachers who relate well to pupils, have good pace and timing, and are well organized are more effective. Clarity is also a characteristic of effective teaching. These characteristics are important and take the teaching a long way.

An Aspects-of-Teaching Scale

Our two-year research project (see Appendix A) revealed that these general principles of teaching are also important in literacy lessons. We created the scale in Figure 9–1 to help us recognize and include ten important general factors in our coaching analyses. (A full-size version of this scale is provided in Appendix C.) Some of these aspects of teaching can be directly taught to teachers; others are more nebulous, develop from their successful work with children, and are learned over time. Then, too, many of the factors are interrelated. Organization, for example, is undoubtedly related to use of time and to pace. Engagement is probably related to rapport and intensity. Below we define each of these factors and briefly discuss its importance.

1. *Materials.* In Chapter 7 we discuss the important role you can play in helping teachers acquire basic materials and organize them so they are accessible. No lesson can be efficient if teachers do not have what they need or if they are constantly looking for it. The flow of the lesson will be disrupted; children will not pay attention.

2. *Organization.* In previous chapters, we have emphasized how important it is for teachers to know the basic procedures required for any kind of lesson. In a well-organized curriculum, the teacher uses the appropriate materials at the appropriate place in the lesson. Routines have been established; everyone knows what is expected. The lesson flows smoothly from one component to another.

3. *Time.* How to allocate their time is one of the most difficult decisions for teachers to make. There's only so much time for any lesson. For many reasons, teachers can end up spending too much time on one component of a lesson, not leaving enough time for other important components. Skillful teachers have an internal rhythm or sense of time so that they work efficiently in all parts of a lesson.

General Aspects of Teaching

Lesson: _____

Teacher: _____ Grade Level: _____ Date of Lesson: _____

Observer: _____ Scale[1] _____

	Rating	Notes
Materials The teacher has materials well organized and available for use in an efficient way during the lesson.	0 1 2 3	
Organization The teacher is prepared, and the lesson flows efficiently from one activity to another.	0 1 2 3	
Time The teacher uses sufficient time appropriate for each component of the lesson.	0 1 2 3	
Pace The teacher makes maximum use of time by keeping the lesson moving; there is limited "down time."	0 1 2 3	
Intensity The teacher is actively teaching on some important aspect of learning throughout the lesson and teaches in a persistent and intensive way.	0 1 2 3	
Feedback/Praise The teacher provides specific feedback of a positive nature; negative feedback is constructive and specific.	0 1 2 3	
Interaction The teacher actively encourages the children to interact, respond, participate, ask questions, and volunteer comments.	0 1 2 3	
Engagement The teacher involves the children in the designated task(s), holding their interest and attention throughout the lesson.	0 1 2 3	
Enthusiasm Through verbal and nonverbal actions, the teacher conveys interest in and enthusiasm for the activity.	0 1 2 3	
Rapport Through verbal and nonverbal actions, the teacher conveys a warm, affectionate, and positive attitude toward children.	0 1 2 3	

[1]Scale: 0 = Not at all true—needs demonstration, teaching, and support to achieve basic level; 1 = True sometimes—needs improvement; 2 = True most of the time—needs some refining; 3 = Consistently true throughout the lesson—an excellent model for this aspect of teaching.

Figure 9–1. *Aspects of Teaching*

4. *Pace.* Pace is related to the use of time, but there are some important differences. Good teaching is fast paced so students pay attention and stay active; lessons don't bog down. Maintaining a good pace doesn't mean racing through a lesson without listening to children or checking on their understanding; it does mean keeping a steady forward movement without getting bogged down.

5. *Intensity* has to do with active teaching. This doesn't mean the teacher is doing all the talking; in fact, he might be facilitating an animated discussion among students. But the teacher maintains a strong focus on the goal of instruction, taking advantage of opportunities to teach. Good teaching is not haphazard, going first one way and then another. A skillful teacher focuses on what children need to learn next; throughout the lesson, he directs their attention to clear examples.

6. *Feedback/praise.* Skilled literacy teachers affirm students not only when they are correct but when they are active as learners. The best praise demonstrates to children that what they are doing is effective; it is specific to behavior and affirms exactly what you want children to do as readers or writers. For example, *you checked the first letter to see if you were right* or *you are almost right; check the ending of the word and try again* are much more effective affirmations than *good job.* Specific praise reinforces the process; approximations show that the child is actively searching for information and are highly regarded. Sometimes teachers need to point out what children are doing wrong—being disruptive, for example. Skillful teachers find positive ways to suggest that a child modify her behavior—*look this way* or *help us find the place quickly* instead of *stop talking* or a long lecture on paying attention.

7. *Interaction.* In a good lesson, children are active; their voices are heard. They have opportunities to speak and respond to others. Children learn by using language themselves rather than being passive recipients of the teacher's lectures. Skillful teachers actively encourage children to interact and

participate; they make sure that every child has a chance and that no one dominates. Teachers who encourage interaction have good ongoing feedback on what children understand.

8. *Engagement* is an important factor in achievement. No matter how well organized the lesson is, students learn only when they are engaged. That is true of all learners in all situations. Skillful teachers constantly sense the degree to which students are engaged, and they adjust time, content, and activity to keep students involved. Engaging learners is not the same as "entertaining" them; in fact, entertaining is not the teacher's role. The goal of teaching is to focus students' attention on something interesting, useful, challenging, and within their grasp.

9. *Enthusiasm.* If you look at a teacher and a group of children involved in a lesson, you ought to see people enjoying what they do. Good teachers are enthusiastic about the content they are teaching; they also find students' ideas and responses interesting. Without enjoyment and enthusiasm, teaching simply isn't satisfying. For example, in guided reading, teachers tend to communicate enthusiasm and anticipation for a text when they have selected one they like and they know students will enjoy. Enthusiasm is not the same as being "bubbly" or "dramatic." It does not require a facade. Enthusiasm is an intangible part of communication among human beings who like what they do.

10. *Rapport.* The relationships between teachers and students are critical to learning. The classroom is a community in which people talk with one another and share meaning. Within a community of learners, both teachers and students listen to and work to understand one another. They value one another's contributions and show one another respect, which is the keystone of rapport. The teacher sets the tone for this kind of communication and interaction within the classroom. The word *warmth* comes to mind here, but that term carries with it culturally bound stereotypes. A teacher may be quiet and soft spoken and

have rapport with children. A teacher with a more dominating style or a louder voice can also have remarkable rapport with her students. The key is whether communication is clear, respect is communicated, and the teacher and students like one another and enjoy being together.

Using the Aspects-of-Teaching Scale

Low scores on a scale like this one indicate ineffective teaching; however, high scores do not necessarily mean the teaching is effective. In other words, a teacher can have good pace, clarity, timing, and organization and at the same time explore concepts that are inappropriate for the particular children in the class *or* use ineffective or inefficient approaches to explain or demonstrate a concept. He may be doing something very well that is simply not worth doing.

These generic characteristics are important but insufficient either to explain the effects of teaching or to improve instruction in general. Teachers who understand the theoretical underpinnings—the why of what they do—are deeply effective in the best sense. These are the teachers who continually evaluate the materials they are given or directed to use. They adjust their instruction for individual children, regardless of the prescriptive curriculum. They make it work because they know and meet students' needs.

Applying the Aspects-of-Teaching Scale to a Specific Lesson

Going back to our earlier example, we see that Lisa is thinking about these general aspects of teaching as she analyzes Marian's guided reading lesson. Although Lisa has encountered this scale while training to be a staff developer, she doesn't apply it formally during her observations. She has internalized the attributes of effective teaching and knows when these fundamental aspects of teaching are not in place. She knows what to look for. She notices when the pace is off or too much time is being spent on something. She tries to uncover aspects of teacher/student relationships by paying attention to classroom interactions. Taking comments from her brief notes and placing them on the aspects-of-teaching scale, we would come up with something akin to Figure 9–2.

Figure 9–2 shows that Marian has an excellent command of the general aspects of teaching.

Reflecting on lessons.

Lisa thought her materials and organization, as well as her rapport with students, was excellent throughout the lesson. Also, Marian was teaching actively; she kept students engaged and encouraged them to participate. She provided praise, although much of it was not specific to particular processing behavior. Except for the frustration she experienced while students were reading, she demonstrated enthusiasm. Nevertheless, these skills were not sufficient to promote maximum learning on the part of Marian's students.

Marian's timing and pace were off, which prompted Lisa to try to determine the cause. She couldn't simply tell Marian to teach faster or cut down on lag time. The underlying reason was the text Marian had selected, which influenced how long the book introduction became and threw the timing of the lesson off. The difficulty of the text also made the lesson bog down during reading, again contributing to the timing and pace problem. (We don't want to imply that text selection is always the issue; the text could have been appropriate but the introduction weak.)

General Aspects of Teaching

Lesson: _Guided Reading_

Teacher: _Marian_ Grade Level: _1_ Date of Lesson: _____

Observer: _____ L.B. _____ Scale[1] _____

	Rating	Notes[2]
Materials The teacher has materials well organized and available for use in an efficient way during the lesson.	0 1 2 ③	Has all materials well organized at the table.
Organization The teacher is prepared, and the lesson flows efficiently from one activity to another.	0 1 2 ③	Has the book read and introduction prepared; well organized.
Time The teacher uses sufficient time appropriate for each component of the lesson.	0 ① 2 3	Introduction too long: 15 minutes. Lesson too long: 30 minutes.
Pace The teacher makes maximum use of time by keeping the lesson moving; there is limited "down time."	0 ① 2 3	Lesson bogged down during introduction; reading laborious. Picked up again at end.
Intensity The teacher is actively teaching on some important aspect of learning throughout the lesson and teaches in a persistent and intensive way.	0 1 2 ③	Teaching very actively all of the time but missing evidence children don't understand book.
Feedback/Praise The teacher provides specific feedback of a positive nature; negative feedback is constructive and specific.	0 1 ② 3	Praises children frequently; little specific praise.
Interaction The teacher actively encourages the children to interact, respond, participate, ask questions, and volunteer comments.	0 1 2 ③	Encourages all children to interact; good participation.
Engagement The teacher involves the children in the designated task(s), holding their interest and attention throughout the lesson.	0 1 2 ③	Whole lesson held children's attention; good engagement.
Enthusiasm Through verbal and nonverbal actions, the teacher conveys interest in and enthusiasm for the activity.	0 1 ② 3	Conveys enthusiasm/ interest; teacher and children frustrated during reading.
Rapport Through verbal and nonverbal actions, the teacher conveys a warm, affectionate, and positive attitude toward children.	0 1 2 ③	Excellent!

[1]Scale: 0 = Not at all true—needs demonstration, teaching, and support to achieve basic level; 1 = True sometimes—needs improvement; 2 = True most of the time—needs some refining; 3 = Consistently true throughout the lesson—an excellent model for this aspect of teaching.
[2]Comments excerpted from notes.

Figure 9–2. *Aspects of Teaching (filled in)*

Opening Our Eyes to Teaching Strengths

As literacy experts, we are accustomed to looking at very specific instructional procedures and assessing how they are used in the classroom. When we work with teachers who are just beginning to implement a new approach, it's important to notice their general teaching skills, which may be masked if we concentrate on specific behavior. As one staff developer said, "Using this scale made me think about what a good teacher Jane is basically. Looking so closely at the content [instructional procedures] had clouded my perspective."

Suggestions for Extending Your Skills as a Staff Developer

This series of activities will be much more productive if you work with a small group of staff development colleagues, viewing the same lessons and comparing your perceptions.

1. Select a teacher, classroom, and lesson for observation.
2. If possible arrange to videotape the lesson so that you can go back to it afterward and check your initial perceptions.
3. Have a preconference with the teacher to determine her/his goals, organizational plan, and concerns.
4. Observe the lesson, trying to get an overall feel for the action.
   - Don't take extensive or verbatim notes. Make brief notes on what strikes you as important. You may want to jot down some words at the top of the page that will remind you of what to look for—materials, organization, interaction, timing, pace, etc. Only note those aspects that you are unaccustomed to noticing.
   - Focus on general aspects of teaching rather than content or specific instructional procedures. Try to "look past" the curriculum to see what is really happening between teacher and students.
5. After the lesson, have a conversation with the teacher, using openers like:
   - "Can you let me in on your thinking when...."
   - "What did you think was happening when...."
   Don't play the expert here. Your real purpose is to see the lesson from the teacher's perspective.
6. Then, reflect on the whole process using the aspects-of-teaching scale. Look through your notes and consider each of the ten aspects. Use the numerical rating but also note comments. Ask:
   - Did I note evidence of all aspects of teaching?
   - What are the weak areas? What are the strengths?
   - For weak areas, what explanations can I find?
   - How do my perceptions match (or not match) the teacher's?
   - What interrelationships did I find *among* aspects of teaching?
   - What interrelationships did I find between aspects of teaching and the success of instructional procedures?
7. Compare your perceptions with others who observed the same lesson—your group of professional development colleagues. Discuss where you differed, offering evidence.
8. Use the aspects-of-teaching scale after observing five more lessons, either in classrooms or on videotape. Ask:
   - Is it getting easier to use the scale?
   - Do I find that I remember aspects of teaching while I observe?
   - Am I finding that my colleagues and I are becoming more reliable (achieving consensus)?
   - Are we constructing a mutual vision of good foundational teaching skills?
9. Continue your conversations with colleagues over time in order to develop common definitions for concepts like *pace*.

Chapter 10

Analyzing Literacy Teaching

Assessing literacy demands that we teachers have an intimate knowledge of literacy and its development so that we can make sense of the literate things students do and the circumstances under which they do them.
—PETER JOHNSTON KNOWING LITERACY: CONSTRUCTIVE LITERACY ASSESSMENT *(1)*

If we want to help teachers understand why they do what they do, we must anchor their thinking in the same cognitive processes they want to instill in their students. While generic aspects of teaching, such as pacing, are important, teachers want to dig deeper into their work and connect it to literacy in functional ways. "Deep teaching" requires intensive analysis, and this process is an ongoing learning agenda throughout a teacher's career.

Good literacy teaching rests on originality, management skills, and effective human interaction, but it also requires the finely tuned application of techniques. Any instructional approach can be less or more powerful depending on the moment-to-moment decisions a teacher makes. Skilled teachers constantly assess student learning and adjust their language, focus, and materials so that students are challenged just enough to learn successfully. How these actions are coordinated differs within and across instructional approaches, according to the goal.

Literacy coaches must first investigate approaches or procedures in detail by using them and observing other teachers use them, thereby becoming familiar with a wide range of possible moves and decisions. They are then able to observe classroom lessons, analyze them, and offer the specific support teachers need.

We have developed scales for analyzing guided reading lessons, interactive writing lessons, and literacy minilessons. (We also provide some guidelines for creating your own scales.) These scales are intended to be used by staff developers, not by classroom teachers; however, you may find that simple adaptations will help teachers who are experienced in particular techniques analyze their own lessons. These scales will help you:

◆ Focus your observations so they lead to informed coaching decisions.
◆ Analyze lessons to determine teaching and learning behavior.
◆ Connect teaching and learning behavior to underlying cognitive processes related to literacy.
◆ Select areas to emphasize that will pay off in terms of student achievement.
◆ Encourage teachers to reflect on their teaching in a way that will help them understand more about teaching and learning and, as a result, make better instructional decisions.

Analyzing a Guided Reading Lesson

In guided reading, the teacher provides the support children need to read a text that is slightly more challenging than they could read without assistance. In the process, the students learn more about how to read. Our scale for analyzing guided reading lessons (see Figure 10–2) is organized according to the four ways readers process text and the components of the guided reading lesson; directions for using the scale are provided in Figure 10–1. (A longer version requiring more detailed assessment is included in Appendix C.) Using this scale, the observer looks across the lesson (before, during, and after text reading) as well as at the text selected in order to make an overall assessment for each of the four functions.

Reading Functions

There are four functions related to effective reading (defined as processing continuous text with understanding). These functions are interrelated and overlapping, but they are broken out in the scale to simplify their analysis. The guided

reading lesson is designed to develop all four functions across the five lesson components:

1. *Text selection.* From a gradient of texts, the teacher selects one that is within the control of group members yet provides opportunities for them to learn more. The teacher uses ongoing assessment of reading behavior to make this determination.
2. *Text introduction.* In a brief conversation, the teacher engages children's interest and provides information that will help them read the text. The idea is to provide enough support that children can be successful in reading a challenging text. The introduction foregrounds comprehension but leaves work for the readers to do.
3. *Text reading.* Each child reads the whole text (or a unified portion of a longer text) softly or silently on his own. The teacher observes and interacts with individuals to support effective reading strategies.
4. *Teaching after reading.* After children in the group have read the text, the teacher selects examples that illustrate effective reading strategies. Examples may involve word solving, comprehension, fluency, or any other aspect of the reading process.
5. *Extending the text and/or word work (optional).* The teacher may engage students in extending the meaning of the text through writing, sketching, extended discussion, drama, or other media. The teacher may also briefly involve the group in decontextualized word work (using magnetic letters or writing). This option is usually selected when working with readers who need more support in solving words.

Function 1: Readers Construct and Extend the Meaning of Texts The purpose of reading is understanding; without that, "reading" is meaningless word calling (Adams 1990; Clay 1991). In every act of reading, meaning must be key. Readers decode words, using letter-sound relationships, in the service of meaning. Across the guided reading lesson, teachers help children construct meaning by bringing their personal, world, and literary knowledge to the understanding of the text. They also help children go beyond the text to make inferences and connect meanings.

Guided Reading: A Scale for Analysis

Directions

The following scale is designed for use in analyzing guided reading lessons. The scale is organized into four functions of the reading process in relation to the components of guided reading lessons.

Functions (the columns):

1. **Readers construct and extend the meaning of texts.** The teacher helps students construct meaning by making connections between the text and their personal, world, and literary knowledge. Teachers also help student develop a range of strategies to go beyond the text—for example, inferring and using other analytic strategies.

2. **Readers monitor and correct their own reading.** Readers use sources of information, including meaning, language structure, letter-sound information, and visual patterns in words, to check on themselves as readers, search for more information, and self-correct when needed.

3. **Readers maintain fluency and phrasing while reading continuous text.** Readers connect the text with language and know how good reading "sounds." They read at a good rate, slowing down and speeding up as appropriate. They read in phrase units and notice and use punctuation to help them in their expressive reading.

4. **Readers problem-solve words "on the run" while reading continuous text.** Problem solving of words takes place "on the run," and the reader does not lose meaning. Word solving takes place against a backdrop of accurate reading.

Lesson Components/Text (the rows):

1. **Text:** The text is the new book or other piece of written language that the students read.
2. **Introduction:** The teacher and students talk about the book before students read it.
3. **Reading the Text:** Each child in the group reads the book/story softly or silently to him/herself.
4. **After Reading:** The teacher and students revisit the text for discussion and specific teaching points.
5. **Extending the Text/Word Work** [optional components]: Experiences such as drawing, writing, drama, help students extend meaning. Work on words involves manipulating letters or writing.

Rating Scale

- Score the lesson for each of the four functions. In doing so, you are really asking questions like this: "Across the lesson, how well did I [or my colleague] help students construct and extend the meaning of the text?"
- To answer that question, look across the lesson—before, during, and after reading. If the lesson included extension or word work, also examine those options. Finally, look at the text selected for reading, making a judgment about the extent to which it supported meaning.
- There's no way to "add up" a score. There might have been more attention to meaning in one component of the lesson than another. Highlight or circle lesson components that were particularly effective for the function. This holistic rating will be a guide to what is happening in lessons. Use the scale below:

  0 = There is no evidence of teaching for this function. There is no evidence that students are learning about this function.

  1 = There is only a little evidence of active teaching for this function. There may be some evidence that students are learning, either prompted by the teacher or spontaneously.

  2 = There is moderate evidence of active teaching for this function. Student behavior provides moderate evidence that they are learning, either prompted by the teacher or spontaneously.

  3 = Across all parts of the lesson, there is high evidence of active teaching for this function. Student behavior consistently provides a high level of evidence that they are learning and/or have learned in this area.

Figure 10–1. *Directions for Using the Scale for Analysis of Guided Reading, Short Version*

Scale for Analysis of Guided Reading Lessons

Is the teacher...	Helping children construct and extend the meaning of texts? 0 1 2 3	Helping children monitor and correct their own reading? 0 1 2 3	Helping readers maintain and support fluency and phrasing? 0 1 2 3	Helping readers solve words while reading continuous text? 0 1 2 3
Text Selection *The guided reading text...*	◆ Contains meaningful and interesting topics and ideas. ◆ Has words most students know the meaning of. ◆ Has words most students recognize.	◆ Has language structure students can say (with some support). ◆ Contains many known words with some problem solving. ◆ Allows children to problem-solve against a backdrop of accurate reading.	◆ Has features that support phrasing, fluency. ◆ Is engaging and interesting. ◆ Provides for problem solving against a backdrop of accurate reading. ◆ Has mostly known words and/or words that can be solved with support and current strategies.	◆ Has mostly known words. ◆ Offers opportunities for teaching about how words work. ◆ Has new vocabulary words that can be solved using current strategies. ◆ Has unknown words that are mostly in speaking/listening vocabulary of children.
Before the Reading *The teacher...*	◆ Helps students activate prior knowledge. ◆ Explains unfamiliar ideas, concepts, and word meanings. ◆ Shows students how to use illustrations as support. ◆ Raises questions. ◆ Engages students' interest.	◆ Assures overall meaning and language structure of text is available to all students. ◆ Rehearses some language. ◆ Explicitly demonstrates problem-solving behavior.	◆ Establishes meaning of whole text. ◆ Makes students aware of and rehearses language structures. ◆ Draws attention to punctuation. ◆ Demonstrates some phrasing.	◆ Talks about meaning of some words and has children say them. ◆ Demonstrates problem-solving behavior. ◆ Selectively attends to words that have generative value. ◆ Draws attention to how to use words, letters, word parts in problem solving.
During the Reading *The teacher prompts students to...*	◆ Use sources of information such as meaning of words, sentences, whole text. ◆ Recall details while reading. ◆ Interpret text in various ways while reading. ◆ Connect words by their meaning.	◆ Use known words to monitor and read accurately. ◆ Use visual information to monitor, cross-check, search, and self-correct. ◆ Orchestrate the use of many kinds of information. ◆ Be flexible, demonstrating if needed.	◆ Read fluently using proper phrasing, demonstrating if needed. ◆ Notice and use punctuation. ◆ Interpret the text (characters, plot) expressively.	◆ Use word-solving strategies: letter/letter cluster; relationship to sounds; beginnings and endings of words; word parts. ◆ Recognize and use unknown words. ◆ Use analogy. ◆ Check word solving with meaning and structure.
After the Reading *The teacher...*	◆ Readdresses questions. ◆ Summarizes to remember text. ◆ Helps students connect to other texts. ◆ Helps students connect to their experience. ◆ Helps students expand word meanings—new words and broader meaning of known words. ◆ Helps students extend meaning through inference and interpretation—via oral language, writing, drawing, drama.	◆ Selects examples from observation that illustrate monitoring, self-correction, searching, flexible use of multiple cues. ◆ Explicitly demonstrates processes that are generative (as listed above).	◆ Reconstructs sections of text to help students notice features such as dialogue, layout, punctuation. ◆ Helps students realize value of fluency and phrasing. ◆ Revisits text with students to practice phrasing. ◆ Talks about how to interpret text, and demonstrates oral reading.	◆ Demonstrates word solving in clear, explicit way (using whiteboard or other visual display). ◆ Revisits word structure through writing, building with magnetic letters. ◆ Helps students notice words that are tricky or interesting. ◆ Helps students further develop vocabulary. ◆ Selects generative examples of word solving (based on reading *this text*).
Extension/ Word Work *The activity...*	◆ Extends meaning through writing, sketching, discussion, drama, or other means. ◆ Concentrates on word meaning connected to word structure.	◆ Uses a language structure students can say (with some support). ◆ Contains many known words with some problem solving. ◆ Allows children to problem-solve against a backdrop of accurate reading.	◆ Has features that support phrasing, fluency. ◆ Is engaging and interesting. ◆ Provides for problem solving against a backdrop of accurate reading. ◆ Has mostly known words and/or words that can be solved with support and current strategies.	◆ Has mostly known words. ◆ Offers opportunities for teaching about how words work. ◆ Introduces and analyzes new vocabulary words. ◆ Uses unknown words that are in speaking/listening vocabulary of students.

Figure 10–2. *Scale for Analysis of Guided Reading, Short Version*

To help readers extend meaning, teachers select texts that have meaningful and interesting topics and ideas. Vocabulary, too, is a consideration. Students should recognize and know the meaning of most words so that problem solving can take place against a backdrop of accurate understanding.

Through their introduction, teachers engage students' interest in the text. Teachers introduce texts in a way that helps students make connections between the text and their own personal experiences as well as their knowledge of the world and of other texts. Activating prior knowledge is a key to understanding. Teachers may also draw attention to illustrations and raise questions.

While students read the text, the teacher looks for behavior (for example, reading in phrases, reacting to a part of the story) that indicates comprehension. She also interacts briefly with students, often prompting them to think about what would make sense or engaging in a quick conversation about some aspect of meaning.

After the reading, the teacher leads students in discussing some aspect of the story; the discussion shores up their comprehension and allows them to express their ideas. During the discussion, the teacher and students revisit the text for some explicit teaching. The goal is to help students expand their comprehending strategies.

Finally, the teacher has the option of involving students in discussion, drawing, drama, writing, or some other activity that fosters deeper understanding of a text. Another option is word work on vocabulary.

The construction of meaning is a primary concern in guided reading lessons. While many teacher actions are directed toward helping students develop related skills, meaning must never be abandoned. Meaning is not fostered only in the introduction of the words or concepts prior to reading, nor is it dealt with only when discussing the story or answering questions about it afterward. Teachers need to be constantly on the alert for signs that students understand (or don't understand) the text and for evidence that they are making inferences beyond the texts.

In the guided reading lesson in Chapter 9, Marian provided an extensive introduction to the text, working very hard to help students understand concepts and sophisticated vocabu-

lary. The level of the concepts involved worked against success, however: the book was too hard. Nevertheless, there is evidence of active teaching here. Marian was using the illustrations, although they did not provide enough information to help her students.

Observing students read, Lisa noticed that they were struggling on every page; the process broke down and they did not understand the story. Marian worked at the word level, trying to help students decode many unfamiliar words. Most students understood the idea of a nest, but not the less familiar habitats.

After reading, Marian didn't discuss the book with the students but taught word solving. In her analysis of the lesson, Lisa noticed how diligently Marian was working to establish students' understanding of the text, selecting the one meaningful page (birds and nests) to make her teaching points. In spite of this work, the difficulty of the text defeated her efforts. Overall, Lisa rated this lesson as a 2 in helping children construct meaning.

Function 2: Readers Monitor and Correct Their Own Reading Good readers monitor their reading continuously. Someone who is reading accurately is actively monitoring—checking to make sure the words make sense and sound right in terms of the syntactic rules of the language. Mature readers are unconscious of monitoring until they encounter discontinuity. Then they stop, search, repeat, or take other action to resolve it, using meaning, language structure, letter-sound information, and visual patterns in words to help them.

Teachers help students monitor and correct their reading by selecting texts that present opportunities for problem solving without being so difficult that the overall meaning is lost. Texts should be largely available to students and offer only a few challenges. In the introduction, teachers call attention to the language structures in the text, particularly those that are literary or otherwise difficult for students; they may even rehearse some language. Also, they can explicitly demonstrate problem solving using more than one source of information.

During reading teachers prompt students to use a flexible range of strategies that combine sources of information—meaning, language structure, and visual or letter-sound information.

They prompt readers to monitor their reading and correct miscues. After reading teachers select examples that illustrate problem-solving behavior, perhaps asking students to revisit part of the text.

In her introduction, Marian drew students' attention to the first letter of each animal home and tried to make connections to the pictures. During reading, she prompted mostly for word solving but also occasionally asked students to also use the illustration or think about the meaning. After reading, she had them look at the word *animal* and also explained that every page started with the phrase "some animals." Lisa recognized that Marion was directing students' attention to processing strategies. Overall, she rated Marion's helping children monitor and correct their reading as a 2.

Function 3: Readers Maintain Fluency and Phrasing While Reading Continuous Text

Readers connect the text with language and know how good reading "sounds." They read at a good rate, slowing down and speeding up as appropriate. They read in a series of phrases and notice and use punctuation to help them. Fluency is strongly related to reading comprehension (Pinnell et al. 1995).

In guided reading lessons, teachers select interesting texts with mostly familiar language patterns. Unfamiliar or difficult language patterns may require teacher demonstration or even some rehearsal during the introduction. Readers will not be fluent if they do not understand a text or if they have to problem-solve too many words. In the introduction, the teacher elucidates the text, perhaps pointing out punctuation, which helps with phrasing. During reading, teachers can prompt for fluency: *read these words all together* or *read it like you are talking*. If students know what fluent reading "sounds like" (from their own experience and through demonstrations), they can also learn to listen to themselves. After reading, the teacher may revisit the text to help students "read the punctuation" or read in phrases. Extensions such as choral reading or readers theater also support fluency.

In her guided reading lesson, Marian had little success teaching for fluency. There were, in fact, no opportunities, because the text was so difficult. Even when she attempted to involve the students in choral reading to finish the text,

Analyzing a guided reading lesson.

she was forced to go very slowly, and some students simply skipped over the words. Lisa noticed that not one student read fluently at any time during the lesson. She rated teaching in this function as 0, or "no evidence." This didn't mean that Marian did not know how to teach for fluency or didn't value fluency. It simply wasn't present in this lesson.

Function 4: Readers Problem-Solve Words "On the Run" While Reading Continuous Text

Readers slow down to problem-solve words, using a variety of strategies in a flexible way. Then they speed up again. This problem solving takes place against a backdrop of accurate reading and does not destroy the momentum of the reading or the comprehension of the reader.

Guided readers know most of the words in the texts selected for them, so they are solving problems against a backdrop of accuracy. In the introduction, teachers can bring words to students' attention, perhaps pointing them out in the text, and ask students to say them aloud. This process is not *preteaching* words; it simply gives students more information to bring to word solving. This attention to words is highly selective, usually only one or two words, and would not include words students can solve on their own.

During reading, teachers prompt for a range of word-solving strategies, including using letters or letters clusters and sounds, word parts, and connections to other words. After reading, teachers revisit the text, often using a whiteboard or easel, to demonstrate ways of solving words. The goal of the teaching is to help students expand their understanding of how words work so that they become more effective at word solving while reading continuous text.

Lisa noticed that Marian was working hard to help students develop word-solving skills. Marian drew students' attention to concept words during the introduction, pointing out the first letter of each type of home and linking it to the illustration; she prompted for word solving in a variety of ways during the reading. Also, she made a skillful teaching point with the word *animal*. She made her point explicit using the whiteboard, pointed out something the children knew about the word, had them locate it on the one meaningful page, and reminded them that they could use this strategy whenever they came to words they didn't know. Even though students were unable to solve most of the words in this difficult text successfully, they were trying to use strategies. Overall, Lisa rated the lesson a 3 in teaching for word solving.

Looking Across the Lesson

The guided reading analysis scale helps you break down the lesson into parts and pinpoint certain areas. If you want, you can use only part of the scale—rating only text introductions, or only teaching for fluency, for several lessons.

As Lisa looked at the whole of Marian's lesson, she noticed some strong teaching for word solving as well as evidence that Marian valued meaning and was attempting to support meaning in every component of the lesson. Lisa had a hunch that Marian was a stronger teacher than her analysis of this particular lesson indicated. She wanted to test that hypothesis by helping Marian select a text at a more appropriate level for the group, observe another lesson, and look for evidence that Marian understands how to help children construct meaning while reading continuous text. The guided reading scale helps

Lisa sharpen her own thinking about lessons. In the next section we describe a similar scale for interactive writing.

Analyzing an Interactive Writing Lesson

"Interactive writing is an instructional context in which a teacher shares a pen—literally and figuratively—with a group of children as they collaboratively compose and construct a written message" (McCarrier, Pinnell, and Fountas 2000; also see Chapter 4 of this book). It is designed to help young children learn about the writing process. Figure 10–4 is the scale we devised for analyzing interactive writing lessons; directions for using it are included in Figure 10–3. (A more detailed version of this scale is included in Appendix B.)

Functions of Writing

The scale itemizes five writing functions as applied to five components of the writing process.

Function 1: Establishing a Purpose for Writing (Planning) Planning takes place throughout the experiences that precede and surround writing. It begins with establishing a purpose and audience for writing, and then involves using knowledge gained from past experience to shape the content, form, and function of the piece. Interactive writing to report the results of a science experiment, for example, stimulates children to remember and use information gained from:

- Their observations of phenomena.
- Note taking.
- Discussion.
- Synthesis of knowledge gained over time.
- Exposure to appropriate reporting formats.

Planning for interactive writing may involve a combination of direct experiences, literature discussions, and inquiry. Typically, a series of related experiences are involved. Planning recurs throughout the lesson as teachers and students continually refer to the reason for writing, to the audience, to information that should be included, and to the appropriate format for the piece.

Function 2: Deciding the Precise Text (Composition) Building on both hands-on and literacy experiences, the teacher talks with the

Interactive Writing: A Scale for Analysis

Directions

The following scale is designed for use in analyzing interactive writing lessons. The scale is organized into five functions of the writing process in relation to the components of interactive writing lessons.

Functions (the columns)

1. **Composition**: *Planning*
   A planning function, which operates throughout the process of writing, includes establishing a purpose and using past experience to shape the content, form, and function of the piece.
2. **Composition**: *Deciding the Precise Text*
   During the composing process, the teacher engages children in conversation designed to compose a precise text that they will then write. The text is negotiated; discussion focuses on the precise words to be used in the text to convey meaning.
3. **Construction**: *How Print Works*
   Text construction includes arranging words in space on the page and using conventions such as space, capitalization, and punctuation to make the text readable.
4. **Construction**: *Word Solving*
   Constructing a text refers to the actions the teacher and students take to inscribe the words of a text, letter by letter. It may involve teaching students to "say words slowly and hear the sounds," notice visual feature of letters, notice letter clusters and patterns, link letters and sounds, connect words, think about relationships between meaning and spelling of words, and use references and resources.
5. **Reading Connections**: *Rereading*
   Interactive writing provides a context for connecting reading and writing. Children reread the text *while* constructing it, *after* writing it, and on an ongoing basis. Reading/writing connections are made at the word level and at the text level.

Lesson Components (the rows)

1. **Text**: The piece of writing that the teacher and children collaboratively compose and produce.
2. **Preparing to Write**: The experiences and discussion that take place prior to composition.
3. **Composing the Text**: The process through which the teacher and children decide the specific message to write.
4. **Writing [Encoding] the Text**: The actions and discussion surrounding the writing [encoding] of the text.
5. **Extending the Text**: The experiences and discussion that take place after the message is written, which will include reading and revisiting the text for different purposes.

Rating Scale

- In scoring the lesson you are asking questions like this: "Across the lesson, how did I [or my colleague] help students learn about how words work?"
- To answer that question, look across the lesson—from planning and composing to rereading and revisiting.
- As you watch an interactive writing lesson, it is not always possible to know how a piece will be used later. Usually, interactive writing pieces grow out of classroom experiences, take several days to create, are reread many times, and are used for different purposes. A truer picture will be gained by observing over time.
- There's no way to "add up" a score. There might have been more attention to meaning in one component of the lesson than another. Highlight or circle lesson components that were particularly effective for the function. This holistic rating will be a guide to what is happening in lessons. Use the scale below:
  0 = There is no evidence of teaching for this function. There is no evidence that students are learning about this function.
  1 = There is only a little evidence of active teaching for this function. There may be some evidence that students are learning, either prompted by the teacher or spontaneously.
  2 = There is moderate evidence of active teaching for this function. Student behavior provides moderate evidence that they are learning, either prompted by the teacher or spontaneously.
  3 = Across all parts of the lesson, there is high evidence of active teaching for this function. Student behavior consistently provides a high level of evidence that they are learning and/or have learned in this area.

Figure 10–3. *Directions for Using Scale for Analysis of Interactive Writing, Short Version*

Scale for Analysis of Interactive Writing

Is the teacher helping the students...	Establish a purpose for writing, and plan the text? 0 1 2 3	Decide on the precise text appropriate to meaning, audience, and purpose? 0 1 2 3	Write the text, giving attention to how print works? 0 1 2 3	Write the words of the text, giving attention to strategies for spelling? 0 1 2 3	Make connections between reading and writing? 0 1 2 3
Text *The interactive writing text...*	◆ Grows out of meaningful experiences. ◆ Involves ideas and topics students understand. ◆ Fulfills a real purpose.	◆ Is one that children can say. ◆ Is related to content, purpose, and audience. ◆ Has potential for learning about the composing process.	◆ Presents opportunities to connect purpose, audience, and layout. ◆ Presents opportunities to learn about punctuation and layout.	◆ Contains words that children can write with support. ◆ Contains useful frequently encountered words as well as words with patterns that illustrate principles.	◆ Is readable with the high support of shared reading. ◆ Has syntactic patterns and words that are in children's oral vocabularies. ◆ Offers opportunities for reading and for making connections between texts.
Preparing to Write *The teacher helps students...*	◆ Understand the purpose for writing. ◆ Think about form in relation to purpose and genre. ◆ Develop knowledge of text organization. ◆ Analyze aspects of literacy texts.	◆ Generate possible language from which they can draw during composition. ◆ Organize ideas into a plan that will guide the composition.	◆ Notice print layout and other aspects of text and print conventions in those they hear read aloud. ◆ Talk about the kinds of texts [genres] that could be used for different purposes and the layout/structure for each.	◆ Notice the structure of words in shared reading. ◆ Use life and literacy experiences to broaden vocabulary. ◆ Use words in specific ways related to content, theme, or genre.	◆ Build experience and vocabulary. ◆ Bring understanding of content, ideas, texts, or events to the composition of the text. ◆ Talk about experiences in a way that will help them bring meaning to the rereading of the text.
Composing the Text *The teacher helps students...*	◆ Remember the content and larger purpose of writing. ◆ Keep audience and purpose in mind. ◆ Think about aspects of text such as coherence, cohesion, clarity, and voice.	◆ Generate and negotiate alternative words, phrases, sentences. ◆ Make connections between this text and others. ◆ Connect text and illustrations. ◆ Think about how to start and end and about events.	◆ Compose a text that requires attention to print conventions (dialogue, punctuation, layout). ◆ Make plans regarding layout/conventions appropriate to genre.	◆ Compose a text that requires problem solving at the word level. ◆ Select words for meaning that conveys the message.	◆ Compose a text that will be readable. ◆ Connect to other books they have heard read aloud or to other pieces of interactive writing that they have produced and reread many times.
Writing (encoding) the Text *The teacher helps students...*	◆ Constantly evaluate the text in terms of purpose and audience. ◆ Revise while writing for consistency with audience and purpose.	◆ Remember the composed text while writing word by word and letter by letter. ◆ Evaluate layout as appropriate to purpose, audience, and the precise message. ◆ Make decisions about punctuation.	◆ Make decisions about text layout, punctuation, and conventions of print. ◆ Shift from thinking about the message to considering conventions such as layout and punctuation and then shift back to message.	◆ Say words slowly and connect sounds to letters and letter clusters. ◆ Attend to visual features of words, including word parts and spelling patterns. ◆ Make connections between known words and new words.	◆ Reread while writing to recapture the meaning and language structure of message. ◆ Use early reading behavior such as word-by-word matching or rereading to search.
Extending the Text *The teacher helps students...*	◆ Reflect on audience and purpose while rereading. ◆ Think about the overall content, purpose, and audience when extending the text through drama, drawing, discussion, and other ways.	◆ Revisit the text to notice and evaluate choice of words, layout, and organization. ◆ Revise the text as needed to reflect the intent of the composition.	◆ Reread the text to notice the way conventions were used. ◆ Apply principles of construction to their own writing.	◆ Revisit the text to locate familiar words, make connections between words, notice letter-sound relationships and visual [spelling] patterns.	◆ Be conscious of and demonstrate fluent, phrased reading. ◆ Analyze the text to think about meaning, audience, and purpose.

Figure 10–4. *Scale for Analysis of Interactive Writing, Short Version*

children about the text they will write. The negotiation is specific to the type of text, the precise words, the layout of text, and the suitability of words, phrases, and sentences relative to the purpose for writing. During composition, children refer to the overall knowledge described in the planning function; however, the focus is on the particular words to use in *this* text.

Function 3: Attending to How Print Works (Construction)

Constructing a text refers to the actions that the teacher and children take to inscribe a composed message or story. Text construction includes writing the actual words, letter by letter; arranging words in space on the page; and using conventions such as space, capitalization, and punctuation to make the text readable. Constructing the text involves continuous conversation using vocabulary specific to writing. For this analysis, think about the format selected (is it appropriate to the purpose?), the arrangement of print on the page, the connection between print and illustrations, and print conventions. Children are learning to use the techniques of putting words into print while at the same time keeping meaning and purpose in mind.

Function 4: Solving Words (Construction)

For this analysis, think about ways in which children learn the structure of words. Within interactive writing, children have the opportunity to construct words they do not yet know. Word solving takes place within the process of writing continuous text. It involves drawing students' attention to spelling principles so that they can learn how words "work." It may involve teaching students to say words slowly and hear the sounds, notice visual features of letters, notice letter clusters and patterns, link letters and sounds, connect words, think about relationships between the meaning and spelling of words, and use references and resources.

Function 5: Connecting Reading and Writing

Interactive writing provides a context for connecting reading and writing. The text that the children compose and write, with teacher assistance, is intended to be read. Interactive writing is used to build up a large collection of readable texts that children can refer to and use as resources throughout the school year. While composing the text, children think about reading it. Children reread the text many times *while*

constructing it and again and again *after* writing it. Reading/writing connections are made at the word level and at the text level. In general, the text that children can read after helping construct it and then reading it together is more difficult than text children would be expected to read on their own in books.

Components of Interactive Writing

Writing processes are recursive: teachers and children are always moving back and forth between composing, writing, rereading, and, again, composing. For example, after a portion of text has been composed and constructed, the teacher and students go back to the kind of general discussion associated with planning a new piece of text.

Identifying a Text The text in interactive writing arises from real experiences and is negotiated by the teacher and children. You can use interactive writing for any purpose—making a list, taking observational notes of a science experiment, retelling a story, writing a letter, and so on. The idea is for the writing to emerge from children's experiences.

In interactive writing, you are not simply "practicing writing." You are writing for a real purpose. While deciding the precise words of the text, the teacher and students are always thinking back to the purpose and the audience. While encoding the text and rereading it, they remember their original word choices but continue to think about audience and purpose. Teachers assist children by helping them say the text several times.

A gradient of text is evident in interactive writing. Very young children who are just beginning to learn about print can be guided to create simple texts that they can write and remember; as they grow more sophisticated, they can compose and write much longer texts. The text is always negotiated; typically, teachers guide composition so that a text will be appropriate for the group and teach something new, but the children are very much part of all decisions.

Preparing to Write Preparation encompasses any activity that naturally leads to writing. Teacher and children may discuss something they have learned or some experience they have had; they may invite someone to visit the classroom; they may make a list of things to include in a book they are writing; they may respond to a story they've heard read aloud. The conversations that surround any of these activities are essential: as children recall and share experiences, they bring to light language they can use as they start to compose the text.

Composing the Text After their discussion, the teacher and children are ready to make decisions about the text. Of course, they will move back and forth between discussing and composing several times in the course of writing even a simple text. The teacher lightly guides the composition of each sentence so that it conforms to the standards of good writing and can be remembered later. As they choose the words for the text, children are invited to think about the precise meaning they want to convey as well as about their audience. The goal—even for beginning work—is clarity, cohesion, and voice. For example, the teacher might ask them to consider several options and decide which one sounds best. It is important, though, that children "own" the language.

Writing the Text *Writing,* here, refers to encoding the text—that is, writing it word by word and letter by letter. Because interactive writing is a group lesson, a lot of discussion and sharing goes on here. The teacher and students talk about how words sound, how they look, and what they mean. The teacher prompts students to think about letters and sounds, parts of words, and how words are connected. In early lessons, students are prompted to say words slowly and even to connect them with their names. Later, students participate in more sophisticated word analysis, such as using *car* to write the word *part.*

The teacher will write many of the words himself to move the writing along. Only when he wants to draw students' attention to something specific does he call students up to the easel to "share the pen." Individual students then quickly write in a letter, a part of a word, or a word. Everyone in the group participates.

During the encoding process, students reread the text frequently in order to keep the whole message in mind. Sometimes they alter their original message to make it clearer. While writing the text, students still consider it as readers and alter its composition in terms of audience, purpose, and meaning.

Extending the Text Students use interactive writing pieces in a variety of ways. They reread them frequently in shared and independent reading. They use them as resources for independent writing. The class may refer to a piece of interactive writing when they find something similar in a book the teacher is reading aloud to them. It isn't always possible to know how the piece of interactive writing in the lesson you are observing will later be used; however, you can pick up clues. For example, skilled teachers explicitly remind children of what they learned that day that they can use in their own writing and reading. They encourage their students to reread the piece or use it in some way.

An Example of an Interactive Writing Lesson

Figure 10–5 is an example of a short interactive writing lesson. Pat, the staff developer, is working with John, who has been trying out interactive writing in his kindergarten for most of the year. The lesson takes place in March, and children know quite a bit about writing. The first column describes the components of the lesson; Pat's notes are shown in the second column.

Applying the Scale Afterward, Pat applied the interactive writing scale to this lesson, considering the five functions across all components. (The five functions parallel the step-by-step components of the lesson, because interactive writing mirrors the writing process. Remember, though, that all five functions have a role in *every* component of interactive writing. In other words, you are thinking about audience and purpose throughout the process, not just at the beginning; you are thinking about word solving from the beginning as you select precise words that convey your meaning.) Here are Pat's ratings for the five functions:

1. *Establishing a purpose for writing (planning).* Pat observed that the text emerged from real experiences and that children were highly engaged both in planning and composing. Several times during writing John reminded them of the purpose of the text, and afterward he again helped them see the "big picture." She rated this function a 3.

2. *Deciding the precise text (composition).* In Pat's view, John was very skillful in getting

An Interactive Writing Lesson	
Description of the Lesson	**Staff Developer—Notes and Analysis**
1. Text The final written text for this lesson was: *We went to the zoo.*	Pat noticed that this text grew out of real experiences and that it contained words that would be well within the children's control at this time of the year. In fact they knew *we, to,* and *the.* All four of the first words were on the word wall. She expected the writing of this text to go quickly and for the group to produce several lines of text.
2. Preparing to Write *[Extended over 2 days; 5 minutes for this lesson]* The day before this lesson, John had taken his kindergarten class to the zoo. Afterward, they talked about the trip and children drew pictures of their favorite animals. As they shared their pictures, they decided that it would be a great idea to write a big book about their trip. They planned that in the book each page would tell about a different animal. Some children liked tigers best and others like sharks or elephants. The interactive writing lesson that day was making a list of the animals to include in the book. All the children's selections were listed. The next day, John took the children back to the list, reminded them of their goal, and had them read the list	Children were highly engaged in composing this piece of writing; it represented something important. Pat indicated in her notes that: ♦ John has created meaningful purpose for writing. ♦ The list helps children organized their thoughts so they can plan. ♦ They are having opportunities to develop oral language. Her ongoing analysis indicated that John was creating rich language opportunities and skillfully involving children in planning their writing.
3. Composing the Text *[10 minutes]* Children had lots of ideas for what should be in the text. They suggested sentences such as "We liked the tiger" and "We went to the zoo." JOHN: What would be a good idea for the first page of the book? How should we start? ALICIA: With a tiger. JAMES: Lions and tigers! Several more children suggested animals, and some children suggested "We went to the zoo." ALICIA: We went to the zoo and saw lots of animals. JAMES: The zoo is full of animals and this book is about animals. JOHN: When people start to read our book, what do they need to know first? ALICIA: That this is a zoo. CINDA: This is a book about the zoo. MARK: We went to the zoo. JOHN: Do you think that would be a good idea? To let them know that this book is about the zoo? CHILDREN: Yes! JOHN: That way, they'll know what to expect when they read about our animals. Which do you like better? "We went to the zoo" or "This book is about the zoo." After some discussion, the group actually came up with "We went to the zoo" as the first page, which John asked them to repeat a couple of times so they could remember it.	Pat noticed that John was helping children think about the organization of the text as they chose the precise message that they wanted to write. She noted that John: ♦ Generated several alternatives. ♦ Gave many children a chance to contribute. ♦ Showed them how to start a text. ♦ Monitored the length of the text so that they have the right amount to write at a time. ♦ Offered two simple alternatives even though several children suggested more complex texts. ♦ Had children repeat the message several times. Overall, Pat's observation indicated that John was skillfully involving children in composing the message, selecting words with the audience and the organization of the text in mind. They seemed to know that they were expected to think carefully about what to say, offer their suggestions, and make choices. The sentences children offered were almost all appropriate for writing, indicating that they understood something about written language. In fact, Pat noted that two alternatives children offered were more complex and might have provided more to learn. She was curious to know why John seemed to guide them to such a simple sentence.

Figure 10–5. *An Example of an Interactive Writing Lesson*

4. Writing *[10 minutes]* JOHN: Where will we start writing? Who knows? Cinda came up and pointed to the left margin. JOHN: That's right. Let's say the word *we* slowly. Children said *we* several times; many spelled it aloud. JOHN: Does *we* need a capital letter? CHILDREN: Yes. JOHN: Why? SEVERAL CHILDREN: Because it's the first word of the sentence. John had James come up to write *we*, which he connected with Wanda on the name chart. JOHN: Let's read what we wrote. Children read *we* and repeated the next part of the sentence. JOHN: What's the next word? CHILDREN: *went.* JOHN: Sarah come up and put your hand here to hold the space. After that, John worked in much the same way on every word in the sentence. Children said words slowly, thought about the letters, and then one child was chosen to come up and write a letter or more. Some children were asked to "hold" the space. At the end, John asked what to put at the end of the sentence, and all children said, "A period!" and one child placed a period there.	Pat had been observing the children in this classroom for a few minutes before the lesson started. She noticed the word wall in the classroom, which contained many frequently encountered words; she looked at many of the writing folders as well as work on the walls. She was pleased to see that most children were well underway in writing. She was surprised to see that John did not seem to be taking children's knowledge into account. He was asking children to be "spacers" when most children were pretty consistent at leaving spaces in their own writing. She noticed that many children were spelling most of the words aloud. She noted: ♦ This segment of the lesson is taking a long time—not necessary. ♦ He's having them say every word slowly—*we, went, to,* and *the* are frequently encountered words and are on the wall. Most of them know them or can find them on the wall, and they also know *zoo.* ♦ He seems to be following a routine rather than thinking about what children need to know. ♦ He should be writing these easy words himself so that they can produce more. Pat observed that encoding was taking a long time and that children were just going over what they already knew.
5. Extending the Text *[2 minutes]* After the first sentence was written, John had the children reread it twice, each time with a member of the group pointing to the words. He reminded children that they would be producing more pages of the book tomorrow.	Pat noticed that John brought children's attention back to the "big picture" of making a book. He encouraged them to reread and to think about tomorrow's work.

Figure 10–5. *An Example of an Interactive Writing Lesson (continued)*

children to produce good alternatives. In fact, two children offered more complex alternatives than he guided them to select. He gave them choices. He reminded them of the precise message during writing as well as afterward. Pat thought John was doing a good job involving children in composition, but given their experience and capability, they might have written something more complex. She rated this function a 2.

3. *Attending to how print works (construction).* John drew the children's attention to the way words were arranged on the page

as well as to spaces. He also asked them to end the sentence with punctuation and to start with a capital letter. Pat noticed this work, but questioned whether children still needed so much attention to this very basic information. John could have worked on more complex ideas if they had written a second sentence. Pat rated this function a 2.

4. *Solving words (construction).* Pat noted that this lesson was far too long for the length of the text generated by the group. John seemed to go through the same routine for every word—saying the word slowly, having

a child place a hand to hold a space, and asking one or two children to come up and write. In Pat's view, this routine wasn't necessary for these children at this time. Most of them knew all of the words. John could have written the sentence himself, had the children read it, and gone on to write one or more additional sentences, making a richer and more challenging text. John was actively teaching, but it seemed to Pat that the children were not learning; in fact, this teaching might be getting in the way. She rated this function a 1 and noted that a place to begin working with John might be in making decisions about word solving.

5. *Connecting reading and writing.* Pat noticed that John was building, over time, a text that would provide good reading material for children in the class. He had them reread the text several times and also helped them make connections between what they were writing and a book that they could read. Pat observed that by writing some of the text himself and producing more lines of print (something that was within children's capabilities), John could have made more connections with reading. She rated this function a 2.

Looking Across the Lesson Pat's analysis helped her determine what John might do to increase his effectiveness in interactive writing. A teacher needs to shift his teaching constantly in order to offer new learning to children. John's skill in planning and composition were evident, but the lesson had unrealized potential for much more learning. Either routines were getting in the way or John didn't realize how to shift his instruction in response to students' writing behavior. He missed opportunities to help them compose a more complex text, and he spent too much time focusing on things the children already knew.

Pat decided to support John in changing his instruction so children will have more opportunities to learn. Her goal was not simply to tell John to do interactive writing another way. In a brief conference, she drew his attention to the children's independent writing so that he could see their capabilities and also invited him to examine his routines. John had thought he was

supposed to work on every word and was relieved when he recognized his role as a decision maker. Shifting teaching in response to what children know and need to know is a "big idea" that will help John in his teaching from now on.

Analyzing a Literacy Minilesson

A minilesson is a brief, powerful, direct piece of teaching that clearly demonstrates a principle or process to students. Minilessons are usually followed by an application activity that involves students in some kind of inquiry and then in sharing and discussion so that students can talk with one another about what they have discovered. Literacy minilessons are used to:

◆ Demonstrate reading processes at the beginning of reading workshop in preparation for independent reading.
◆ Demonstrate writing processes at the beginning of writing workshop in preparation for independent writing.
◆ Demonstrate word-solving strategies.
◆ Demonstrate spelling principles.

Minilessons may also focus on the management of processes like independent reading (for example, how to use browsing boxes), on content knowledge, or on strategies.

An Example of a Word Study Minilesson
Figure 10–6 is an example of a word study minilesson. In this lesson, Melissa is working with her students to help them learn more about words with *ly* endings. As she has observed their reading, Melissa has noticed that her students have difficulty reading words ending in *ly*. For example, several children who were reading *Pinky and Rex and the Spelling Bee* (Howe 1999) had difficulty with the word *hardly*. Later in the book, one student had trouble with the word *really*. At another time, several students reading *Man Out at First* (Christopher 1993) had trouble with *suddenly*. They can decode the words, but they don't seem to connect the sentence structure with their own language use. Often they simply leave off the *ly* ending. Melissa has also noticed spelling errors like *happly/happyly [happily], lonly [lonely],* and *finly/finely/finelly [finally]*. She has

A Word Study Minilesson

Statement of Principle

MELISSA: When you add *ly* to a noun or adjective it makes the word tell how something is done or describes something.

The principle, clearly stated, is written at the top of a chart on the easel (see Figure 10–7). Melissa also has two examples, *hard* and *hardly* in the first column and *happy* and *happily* in the second column.

Points Related to Principle

MELISSA: This week we're going to be studying words with *ly* endings. I've put some on the chart here. This is the word *hard*, and that describes something doesn't it?

JUANA: Like the floor is hard.

DAVID: Or a test is hard.

MELISSA: Yes, but when you add *ly*, the word is different.

DAVID: Like you can *hardly* wait or you can *hardly* do it because it's so hard.

MELISSA: It tells *how* something is done. This word is *happily*. It comes from *happy*. What do you notice?

GABE: It has an *i* instead of the *y*.

MELISSA: Yes, when you add *ly* to some words, the spelling changes. Can you think of more examples of words that would be like *hard* and *hardly*?

GABE: Beautifully?

MELISSA: That's a good one! [Writes *beautiful* and *beautifully* on the chart.] Someone can look beautiful, but to do something in a beautiful way would be to do it *beautifully*.

JUANA: Like to dance beautifully.

Melissa and the students go on to generate *soft, softly; dead, deadly; happy, happily, hungry, hungrily, quick, quickly, angry, angrily, merry, merrily,* and *fantastic, fantastically.*

As students offer examples, Melissa writes them on the chart, placing them in the correct columns.

Discussion

There is quite a discussion about the examples *friend, friendly* and *lone, lonely,* because those words describe what someone is like or how he feels. The students also connect *alone* and *lone* during the discussion. Students are interested in the long word *fantastically,* and Melissa offers *realistically* as another example. When a student offers *only,* Melissa says that it does come from *one* but that the spelling and pronunciation change. After generating the examples, students look at the chart and discuss the differences between words. They select *hardly, happily,* and *fantastically* to go on the word wall.

Summary

MELISSA: Today we have looked at several kinds of words that end in *ly*. We learned that when you add *ly* to a noun or adjective the meaning is changed. The *ly* word can describe how you do something or how something looks or feels. When you add *ly* to words that end in *y* the *y* is changed to *i*. Some long words end in *ally*, like *fantastically*.

Application

MELISSA: Today in the word study center, I'd like you to make words that end in *ly* with word tiles. Start with the base word and then add *ly*. Change the spelling if you need to. Make three of the examples for *hard/hardly* and three for *happy/happily*. See if you can discover more words that fit that pattern. Write three examples of each in your word study notebook.

Each student spends about 10 minutes of independent time working with letter tiles and writing examples in the word study notebook.

Discussion

At the end of the language arts period, Melissa asks several students to briefly share what they have discovered. A few more examples are added to the chart, including *bad, badly, silent, silently, quick, quickly,* and *merry, merrily*. The students summarize what they have learned by adding three points to the bottom of the chart.

Figure 10–6. *A Word Study Minilesson*

decided to focus the week's minilesson on using *ly* endings. (Her plan for the lesson grew from her observations of students' reading and writing behavior, but studying adverbs was also part of her district's prescribed curriculum for the grade level.)

Before the lesson, Melissa writes a clear statement of a principle. A principle is a concept or rule that can be generalized to other situations and circumstances. When students learn principles instead of isolated words, they form categories of connected words. As they encounter new examples, they can apply the principles. This kind of learning is not the same as memorizing a rule. No memorization is required here, nor will it be tested. Melissa's goal is to make the principle come alive through examples.

This minilesson focuses on some very specific learning about how words work. The chart that Melissa and her student make during the lesson (Figure 10–7 shows both the chart as she started it and the chart after the final discussion) is posted in the room and revisited during the week. Also, Melissa calls students' attention to the principle during other reading and writing activities. In the process, they generate more examples and find more anomalies to puzzle over. Melissa does not attempt to teach *every* principle and rule that has to do with *all* words ending in *ly*. Her students' familiarity with such words is heightened, and they will probably create more categories and make more complex associations on their own. Melissa also requires her students to place two examples from each *ly* category on their weekly spelling lists, which they study for a five-day period using a variety of effective learning strategies (see Pinnell and Fountas 1999).

Applying the Scale

Our scale for analyzing minilessons is shown in Figure 10–8. (It's generic, showing the components of minilessons and some overall purposes, and can be used for any kind of minilesson. You can make it more specific as your focus requires.) If you look at Melissa's lesson, you can easily see that she made clear statements and demonstrated principles, used what students knew, engaged them in inquiry, and connected the minilesson to the curriculum.

Of course, she did not accomplish every single action shown on the scale. That would have made the lesson much too long. Scales are not meant to be checklists, in which the more actions you take, the higher the score. The idea is for the staff developer to have an inventory of possible teaching moves from which the teacher selects. This selectivity is the heart of decision making. When you use the scales, you are making an assessment of how effectively a particular combination of actions accomplished an overall function.

Using, Adapting, and Creating Scales

You can use analytic scales like these to:

◆ Analyze and reflect on your own teaching so that you can provide clear demonstrations of specific processes.
◆ Analyze taped lessons that you want to use as examples for your class of teachers. The scales will help you uncover areas that could be problematic as well as effective teaching to point out.
◆ Sharpen your observational skills so that you see the positive aspects of teachers' lessons as they learn more; the scales are expressed in positive terms.
◆ Pinpoint what to focus on instead of overwhelming teachers with many areas for improvement.
◆ Stimulate group discussion about a specific function or component of a lesson.

You can also use these scales in your work with teachers, perhaps asking them to rate their own teaching in one or more components or functions. (This approach is best used with very experienced teachers who are accustomed to analyzing their teaching.) Or you can remove the rating numbers and use the scales as a framework for conversation. We have found, however, that both staff developers and teachers become more invested and engaged if they have to commit themselves to a number they share with others. It sharpens their observational and analytic skills, and they learn from others' perspectives as they explain their reasoning.

You may also want to create your own scales, and you will learn from the process. Figure 10–9 offers some guidelines. The purpose of creating a scale is to increase your observational skills by examining the individual aspects of an instructional approach and how they relate to

Adding *ly* to Words			
When you add *ly* to a noun or adjective it makes the word tell how something is done or describes something.			
hard hardly	happy happily		

Adding *ly* to Words				
When you add *ly* to a noun or adjective it makes the word tell how something is done or describes something.				
hard hardly		happy happily	Add -ally	?
Tell how hard hardly beautiful beautifully soft softly dead deadly final finally safe safely	Describe friend friendly lone lonely	hungry hungrily angry angrily	fantastic fantastically realistic realistically	only
• For words that end in a consonent or silent *e*, you just add *ly*. • For words that end in *y*, you change the *y* to *i* and add *ly*. • For some long words, you add *ally*.				

Figure 10–7. *Chart*

Scale for Analysis of Minilessons

	Use Clear, Explicit Language and Demonstration 0 1 2 3	Connect to Students' Current Knowledge 0 1 2 3	Engage Students in Inquiry 0 1 2 3	Connect to Curriculum 0 1 2 3
Statement of Principle	◆ Select a *single* principle or procedure for the lesson. ◆ State principle in one or two sentences. ◆ Write principle on chart.	◆ Select principle that students *need to know next* and not already know something about. ◆ Ask students what they already know. ◆ Ask students for examples.	◆ Provide opportunities for students to make hypotheses related to principle. ◆ Test hypotheses in a clear, interesting way.	◆ Make connections to observations of reading, writing, and spelling. ◆ Make connections to students' spelling.
Specific Points Related to the Principle	◆ Provide examples that clearly demonstrate process or principle. ◆ Make a few clear points that break down the process to make it understandable.	◆ Select examples that students will recognize. ◆ Ask students for examples. ◆ Write examples on chart or easel.	◆ Promote new hypotheses as points are made. ◆ Ask students to test one another's hypotheses.	◆ Connect points to texts students read, their writing, or content curriculum. ◆ Draw examples from texts students read, their writing, or content curriculum.
Discussion	◆ Engage students in active discussion. ◆ Encourage students to use precise language that will help them internalize principle or procedure.	◆ Invite students to restate principle. ◆ Invite students to share discoveries. ◆ Invite students to ask questions. ◆ Ask students to respond to each other.	◆ Promote new learning through shared examples and ideas. ◆ Be open to questions.	◆ Invite students to make connections to texts they read, their writing, or content curriculum.
Summary	◆ Provide a clear summary statement at the end of the lesson.	◆ Promote active listening to summary statement. ◆ Ask students to assess their own understanding and ask questions if needed.	◆ Be sure students understand summary as a basis for discovering more.	◆ Be sure the summary statement is one students can connect to examples they find in reading and writing.
Application	◆ Demonstrate application activity. ◆ Provide clear directions for application activity. ◆ Provide directions in writing at center or for each student.	◆ Be sure students know they are to use what they know in application activity.	◆ Ask students to connect the summary statement to what they will be doing: "As you are . . . think about. . . ."	◆ Expect students to draw examples from reading, writing, and content curriculum during application activity.
Sharing and Discussion	◆ Restate principle in summary form.	◆ Invite active sharing of discoveries.	◆ Teach students how to learn from one another's examples. ◆ Promote new learning through discussion.	◆ Invite students to describe connections to reading, writing, and content curriculum during discussion.

Figure 10–8. *A Scale for Analyzing Minilessons*

one another. The scale will also help you analyze events and collect evidence to support your analysis. As staff developers, scales will help you be much more specific in your work with teachers. You and they will have a clearer picture of the components of instruction and of what defines good teaching. (See Figure 10–10 for testimonials from staff developers who have used these scales.) The elements/functions on these scales are also related to student gains.

Whether you use our scales or make your own, it is essential for you to increase your analytic powers as a staff developer. Close observation, so important for effective teaching, is even more important for effective coaching. There is no script or preplanned program for coaching a teacher in her classroom with a particular group of students using a particular instructional approach. Your own knowledge of the approach and of learning is critical to your being able to help effectively.

Guidelines for Creating Scales to Analyze Teaching

- Select a particular kind of instructional approach that you know a lot about.
- Observe many examples of the lessons and capture some on videotape. Be sure that your taped examples illustrate different groups of students at different age levels at different times of the year being taught by different teachers.
- With a group of colleagues, look at the lessons. You will need to view each lesson several times.
- Identify the important components of the lesson, from beginning to end. If there are important prerequisites or follow-up components, you can include them.
- Generate clear, brief statements describing what the teacher is doing effectively in every component of the lesson. Also notice evidence of children's learning, but your main focus is what the teacher is helping students do. Focus only on positive actions.
- Discuss what is happening in the lesson, clarifying your descriptive statements. Watching many lessons will be helpful because you will be gathering a large number of effective actions.
- Generate lists of the overall purposes of the instructional approach (for example, to help students learn specific strategies or principles).
- Work until you have several categories for the overall purposes of the instruction. This process will be related to the nature of learning. You can call them functions or process categories.
- Now, see if you can categorize your lists of lesson descriptions under the purposes.
- Arrange a grid that shows statements of processes along several columns. Place your list of lesson components in rows down the left column.
- Place your statements of characteristics along the rows for each component and under the functions. Now you have a beginning grid that is divided by lesson components and the important functions.
- Watch several lessons again. See whether there are any statements you want to add to the grid. Check to see whether there are any functions or process categories you have missed.
- Field-test your scale by using it over time with different teachers at different grade levels. You may not want to place numbers on the scale yet. Get feedback from teachers on the descriptions.
- After collecting data for several weeks, revisit your scale and revise it. This time, place a numeric rating scale for each function (0, 1, 2, 3). Think of wording that fits the instructional technique you are analyzing and will help distinguish the ratings.
- Ask a group of teachers to view videotaped lessons using the scale. Work for reliability in rating and use the ensuing discussion for ongoing revision of the scale.

Figure 10–9. *Guidelines for Creating Scales to Analyze Teaching*

What Staff Developers Say About Analytic Scales

◆ The guided reading scale helped me become a better coach. I never thought about all those parts. When we used the scale, we talked about every part of the reading process. Having something like this helps me focus my support of a teacher. It keeps me from working on everything at once.

◆ The scales helped me develop conceptual understanding about the reading and writing processes. I never knew it was so complex.

◆ The scales were developed by a group of researchers and literacy collaborators who work with kids and have much experience in working with adults. That lends great credibility to the scales.

◆ Until I used the interactive writing scale, I never thought about "planning" throughout the lesson.

◆ The scales work. If you're thinking about five aspects of interactive writing, then you are thinking about helping children become writers.

◆ The scales made me see and understand the reading and writing processes because they were put into words; it became explicit.

Figure 10–10. *What Staff Developers Say About Scales*

Suggestions for Extending Your Skills as a Staff Developer

1. Select one or more of the scales in this chapter and try it out for yourself. (Remember, you'll learn more if you discuss what you're doing with colleagues.)
2. Collect several videotapes of your teaching.
3. Complete the rating scale for yourself so that you are comfortable with the process.
4. Then collect several more videotapes of your own teaching or that of others.
5. Meet with a small group of colleagues and observe a lesson, preferably one taught by someone none of you know (perhaps a teacher from another city or state).
6. First record your ratings individually and silently. Then share the ratings, making a grid that shows everyone's answers. Notice

where you agree. Now talk over the discrepancies. This is your opportunity for a discussion. Ask participants to provide evidence for their ratings. It is not necessary to come to a consensus. The point is the discussion. Ask:

◆ What is the teacher doing that is especially effective relative to each function?
◆ To what extent is the teacher working toward the functions across the components of the lesson?
◆ Where does the teacher need more support?
◆ What is one thing that would help the teacher to become more effective immediately?

7. Select an instructional approach and create your own scale following the guidelines in this chapter.

Chapter 11

Coaching for Shifts in Teaching

The act of sharing ideas, of having to put one's own views clearly to others, of finding defensible compromises and conclusions, is in itself educative.
—THEODORE SIZER
HORACE'S SCHOOL:
REDESIGNING THE AMERICAN
HIGH SCHOOL *(89)*

Professional development gives teachers the power to make effective decisions. It is most strongly supported when:

◆ A teacher reflects on his craft with the support of another teacher who has more experience and training, specifically in assisting or "coaching" colleagues (Joyce and Showers 1980, 1982).

◆ Observation and reflection take place during and after classroom experience (Schon 1983).

Learning is the active process of bringing together what the learner already knows with new information. Instead of simply accumulating knowledge, "taking it in," learners constantly reorganize information and build new structures of knowledge unique to them. Social interaction is important, though, because shared activity and shared meaning help learners make sense of new information. This constructivist view has influenced the design of instruction for children over the past several decades.

A key principle in constructivist theory is the critical role reflection plays in learning. Schon's work (1983) demonstrates that reflection is central to clarifying one's understanding and making sense. Schon suggests that adults' growth and development depend on their ability to:

- Reflect on their learning.
- Adjust their behavior based on that reflection.
- Develop a theoretical framework and set of understandings based on their own experience.

Conversation is the reciprocal medium through which adults construct meaning. But what specifically about a coaching session leads to improved practice? What evidence tells us that teachers are expanding their ability to think about their teaching?

Coaching sessions have several purposes. Coaches provide the feedback teachers need to refine specific procedures, but more important, coaching expands teachers' conceptual knowledge in a way that helps them learn from their own teaching over time. Teachers of teachers must be able to reflect on and analyze the processes related to pedagogical knowledge and decision making. For example:

- They intellectualize their own knowledge of book introductions by forming an explicit understanding of what a powerful introduction achieves.
- They identify evidence that indicates that an introduction has accomplished this goal.
- Then they learn to observe other teachers as they introduce books to children, and analyze and evaluate the conversations and responses they see.

In order to be effective, staff developers must understand the principles and processes involved in facilitating teachers' learning in the coaching and feedback session that immediately follows observation and analysis.

Thinking from the Learner's Perspective

Everyone is a learner; it's part of being human. Think of an instance when you *know* you have learned something. (Every learning experience isn't necessarily a happy one, but in this case, think positive!) It might be the afternoon your tennis backstroke improved, the morning you lofted the golf ball on the green in a single stroke, or the evening you played your violin in a con-

cert. It might be the day you discovered you could converse easily within a language other than your native tongue or fluently read and understand a textbook on an unfamiliar and difficult topic. In each of these examples, learning obviously took place over a long period and more learning will always be needed; but at a certain point, you realized you had moved forward.

Conditions for Learning

If you listed the conditions that led to this example of learning (or one of the examples offered above), you would probably come up with something like this:

- You wanted to learn the skill.
- You thought you had a good chance of becoming skilled—it wasn't beyond your reach.
- The task offered challenges and problems to solve.
- You worked hard.
- You didn't try to learn everything or be perfect all at once; you recognized steps in learning.
- Often, you had a model to look at that helped you understand what you were working toward.
- You had to work to correct behavior that was getting in the way.
- You constantly evaluated and adjusted your behavior.
- You probably experienced some anxiety and tension.
- You were willing to seek and accept help.
- Someone may have helped you (in person, on a videotape, or via books).
- You knew when you were not doing well and when you improved.
- You persevered through setbacks.
- Obstacles seemed to offer opportunities to learn more because you were uncovering problems.
- You learned more about problem solving in the process of learning the skill.
- You learned more about yourself as a learner.

Doing something *hard* gives you a feeling of satisfaction and success. If the task is too easy, you don't learn much. If the task is so difficult as to be impossible, you soon give up. But addressing challenging tasks that are within reach (with effort) is one of the most satisfying experiences human beings can have. If you have a series of successful learning experiences, you will undertake the learning process again and again. You build confidence in yourself. You "learn how to learn."

The Context for Learning

Now, think about the context for your learning. What was it like? Chances are, you would describe it like this:

- There were lots of opportunities to practice *without constant feedback* so that you could get the hang of it.
- The environment was risk free. It was acceptable to fail several times or just to approximate the skill without encountering negative behavior from others.
- The environment was safe. You could try out behavior without hurting yourself or others.
- You could ask for help when you wanted it; someone was available.
- When you reached points where you didn't know what to do next, you could ask someone to observe you and identify the problem.
- You received compliments specific to your improvement; positive comments were justified and earned, not empty clichés.
- You had a feeling that you were sharing the experience with other learners, that you were not the only one overcoming obstacles and improving your skill.

Statements like these make it clear that a learning context is not punitive or judgmental, doesn't raise impossible standards. Imperfection is expected as part of learning. Nor, on the other hand, is there an "anything goes" attitude. Challenge and high expectations provide the "good dissonance" that allow you to struggle with what you want to do.

The Role of the "More Expert Other"

In all learning situations we are more successful if we have another person, with greater expertise, working alongside us. That "more expert other" is a model, a teacher, and a coach who:

- Gives us an idea of what success looks like—just beyond our present expertise.

- Suggests next steps to take in our learning.
- Helps break down complex processes so that we can see and practice parts if necessary.
- Helps us keep the big picture in mind so that we can orchestrate components of a process.
- Offers support and encouragement.
- Identifies critical junctures and provides help at those times.
- Helps us evaluate the outcome and realize improvement.
- Restarts the process at a higher level.

You can connect almost any example of learning with your role as a staff developer and coach. You are the more expert other who creates the context and conditions for the learner; your own behavior and decisions are critical to the teacher's learning process.

The Context for Coaching

The context for teacher education must have the same characteristics as any other learning context. The staff developer creates an environment within which teachers are willing to try new approaches. This environment must be one that accepts that learners are always on the way, not "there" yet, and are working to refine teaching and develop their conceptual and analytic skills.

Chapter 1 discusses ways that staff developers and administrators can work together to create a community of learning characterized by trust and shared endeavor. Within a learning community, teachers feel part of a team. By working on their own teaching, teachers contribute not only to the lives of their students but to the school's vision and mission. Improved teaching helps everyone in the school become more successful.

There is also the expectation that people will help one another get better at what they do. It is a staff developer's responsibility to observe and help the teachers he works with; in the process, he also learns more about teaching both children and adults. A staff developer is not there to evaluate, except in the sense that all of us make analytic assessments all the time. He is there to help, sometimes providing practical and useful suggestions, sometimes demonstrating, and sometimes just listening as a teacher works through her own

Literacy coach demonstrates how to introduce a new book.

analyses. No matter how "expert" a teacher becomes over the years, she will still expect a colleague or staff developer to help her move further in her understanding. A hallmark of the learning community is ongoing development.

Everything a staff developer does contributes to this learning context:

◆ Saying a friendly hello to colleagues every day.
◆ Having informal conversations over lunch and in the corridors.
◆ Working alongside teachers to acquire and organize materials.
◆ Making incidental observations and comments on students' work—noticing how well they are doing.
◆ Interacting with students regularly.
◆ Providing informal help in selecting books in the book room.
◆ Bringing a book related to someone's interests to that person's attention.
◆ Arranging and leading staff development sessions and study groups.

◆ Providing data to teachers that help them understand children's learning.
◆ Being a leader and a supporter rather than an "authority."

Skillful coaching is essential, but success does not depend on coaching style alone. At one time or another, we've all said, "It's not what you said. It's the way you said it." The way you interpret what someone says depends in many ways on the ongoing relationship you have. The trust staff developers bring with them into the classroom is the foundation on which their coaching is based. With trust, you have a much better chance of clear communication; if you misspeak, you can clarify what you meant. People give one another second chances. Never interacting with a teacher and then suddenly appearing at her door won't work, no matter how skilled you are.

There will be dissonance in the coaching situation. When people are learning something new, dissonance is not only inevitable but desirable. Dissonance sharpens your thinking and brings comparisons to mind that clarify understanding. We call this "good dissonance," because it serves a useful purpose in learning. Within a trusting context, dissonance works for you. Criticism can be offered in a constructive and positive way through nonthreatening conversations.

Coaching Conversations

Coaching emerges from the trusting context that surrounds the act of teaching. The staff developer is not a passive observer but is always thinking and doing. An effective coaching conversation has five essential features:

1. It is tied to a specific event that has just occurred.
2. It takes place in the context of the teacher's attempt to learn a specific technique or concept.
3. It makes use of specific teacher and student actions as well as words.
4. It includes reciprocal reflection and constructive dialogue between teacher and coach.
5. It results in new learning and a plan of action to improve teaching.

Think about what a real conversation looks like. There is give-and-take. Both participants:

- ◆ Make statements and ask questions; one doesn't interrogate the other.
- ◆ Offer advice and help.
- ◆ Clarify for each other.
- ◆ Share experiences.
- ◆ Share hunches—that is, wonder about things.

Coaching is a conversation directed toward inquiry: the staff developer and teacher are making hypotheses and searching for information. Their greatest sources of data are their observations of children as they look for evidence of learning. Lindfors (1999) has described two kinds of inquiry:

- ◆ Information seeking, which means clarifying, explaining, and confirming.
- ◆ Wondering, which means reflecting, exploring, and considering many possibilities.

Both kinds of inquiry are evident in the coaching conversation. At the beginning there may be much more seeking of information, but the coach is always urging the conversation toward wondering because it is through these hunches that teachers become active learners in the classroom.

Gathering Information Prior to Coaching

In previous chapters we have emphasized the ongoing analytic work that staff developers do prior to coaching:

1. *Gather information to gain perspective.* Use prior information to form your own perceptions of what the teacher knows and can do. Don't rely on one observation or simply on what teachers say in professional development sessions. Collect data from many sources at different times: observations of the teacher in various contexts, journal entries, questions he asks, examples of students' work, videotapes of his teaching, and informal conversations. You are looking for his strengths.

2. *Make hypotheses about the teacher's perceptions.* Use the same information to make hypotheses about the teacher's perceptions of his strengths and needs. There must be a match between a teacher's assessment of what he does well and needs to know and what you are working toward in your coaching. For example, if a teacher thinks he is doing quite well in implementing interactive

writing, giving him critical feedback will not be the place to start. You may need to start by looking at children's work and helping the teacher deepen his awareness.

3. *Form an idea of what the teacher needs to learn* next. From looking at information and talking with the teacher, decide the one thing that will extend his understanding and make a difference in his teaching *now*.

4. *Develop a tentative plan.* Develop a tentative plan with specific goals in mind. Realize that you may need to change your plan as you get more information and test your hypotheses. The lesson you observe will confirm or disprove some of your expectations. If your hypotheses are confirmed, you will be looking for something in the lesson and/or the teacher's own self-awareness that will help you make the points and draw attention to the examples that will spark conversation and result in positive change. Ground the plan in specific behavior that you want to develop in students.

5. *Hold a preconference to find out what the teacher* wants *to learn next.* Hold a brief, reflective preconference. This focused conversation will help you realize what the teacher is thinking about at the time of the lesson. What does he want to happen in this lesson? Over time, teachers will learn that their own agendas for learning are the most powerful. As a leader, you may have an agenda—something that you know the teacher needs to learn; but you must link this agenda to what the teacher thinks is important. Keep the focus on the students and on evidence of learning. Probe for what the teacher really wants to happen in his classroom.

Thinking About Coaching During the Observation

The preconference provides valuable information that will help you understand a teacher's thinking. During your observation, you match all previous information with what you see. You gather examples that will spark productive discussion related to the teacher's agenda as well as your own.

Using "Instant Replays"

While you are watching a lesson, you are looking for a "way in" to focus the teacher's attention. As

Helpful Language to Use in Coaching Conversations

1. It's wonderful to step into this classroom and see [point out specifics].
2. I noticed that. . . .
3. The children were [engaged, working, etc.] except for. . . . Why do you think that was happening?
4. What were you hoping would happen when?
5. When I was watching, I was excited about. . . .
6. What has happened lately that you felt really excited and pleased about?
7. They were enjoying. . . .
8. They were really learning actively when. . . . Does that fit with your sense of what was going on?
9. What let you know that they were understanding?
10. Can you help me understand what was happening when . . . ?
11. Maybe this will help. Try [a specific action or technique] and let me know how it works.
12. Try this [book, idea] and give me some feedback on how it went.
13. What are your priorities for these children?
14. What do you want these children to be able to do in [time period]?
15. Did they perform as you expected today?
16. Talk about [child, event, book].
17. I was impressed with the children's [independence, enjoyment, oral discussion, reading, writing, etc.]. What helped them learn that?
18. You look like you are really enjoying these children.
19. I was listening to the respectful way children talk to one another. What did you do to help achieve this?
20. You seemed concerned about [event, child, time, etc.]. Can you talk about it?
21. I thought [child] was [attitude, behavior, etc.] Is that right? Can you tell me more?
22. How can I help you in your teaching? [I have a suggestion. Tell me what you think.]
23. They were [behavior]. Is that typical?
24. You [teacher action]. Can you talk about your decision?
25. Was this a typical [morning, reading group, lesson, etc.]?

Figure 11–1. *Helpful Language to Use in Coaching Conversations*

you see good examples of student behavior, you can note them and later describe them specifically. In a way, you will be "replaying" a part of the lesson that has significance. (When you videotape a lesson, you can literally replay brief moments from it.) Coaching time is short, and it is not productive to go over the lesson in such detail that both you and the teacher are worn out. Select the snippets that illustrate the points you want to make.

Remember, too, that these "instant replays" are designed to prompt conversations about student behavior, not to imply criticism of the teaching. Assessing what could change in the teaching comes up naturally during the conversation.

Taking the Right Tone

Figure 11–1 itemizes language we have heard effective literacy coordinators use in conversations with teachers. Remember, it's not enough simply to repeat these phrases mechanically. You want to sound tentative and conversational, not patronizing. Nor do you want to give positive feedback or compliments that you don't mean, so it's not necessary *always* to start with positive comments (especially when they're followed by *but*). Teachers will be waiting for the other shoe to drop. Effective staff developers make specific, direct, and concrete suggestions; they make those suggestions as a respectful and reassuring colleague. They don't waste teachers' time or their own.

Forming an Action Plan

Many staff developers and teachers find it helpful to come up with a brief, *written* action plan at the end of the coaching session. Sometimes the staff developer writes the plan, asking the teacher to contribute, but more often the teacher writes it herself. The plan is really a memo that reminds both parties what they talked about and

Literacy coach and teacher analyzing student's writing

what the teacher is going to try next. As you can see from Marian's action plan in Figure 11–7, this is not an official document with well-stated objectives. It's a record of one teacher's thinking at one point in time. Here's why it's valuable:

◆ Teachers find the plan easy to write and a brief but powerful reminder. It helps them reflect on their goals over the next week or so and review them before the next coaching session. The plan is brief and directly tied to ongoing teaching. The action plan changes over time, so teachers are very much aware they are learning new things. It also reveals when no progress is being made and prompts more intensive work.

◆ Staff developers find the action plan easy and nonthreatening. Although the plan ideally comes from the teacher, they provide enough support that the teacher's plan is appropriate. It helps them focus their coaching on only two or three specific points instead of "beating around the bush." The plan is also a good summary of the coaching session.

You will find your own ways to set up and use action plans. The following suggestions may help:

◆ Have the teacher clearly state one or two areas to work on in the next week or so.
◆ Use an informal way to write down these goals; avoid time-consuming, official-looking forms.
◆ Use an automatic "carbon copy" pad, which you can purchase at any office supply store; you'll both have a copy instantly.
◆ Save these informal plans over time and reflect on them with the teacher at various points.
◆ Use the plans of everyone in your group of teachers to determine topics for professional development sessions.

Reflecting After Coaching

After the coaching session, it is always good to think about what has been accomplished. You may want to make some quick notes, either on your copy of the action plan or at the bottom of the reflection form. In any case, you'll want to think about three critical questions:

1. What did the teacher learn that will make a difference in her teaching?
2. Did you as a staff developer accomplish your goal?
3. Did the teacher accomplish her goal?

Principles for Effective Coaching

There are three essential principles behind effective coaching:

1. Create a trusting context that provides good dissonance so that both you and the teacher learn something new.
2. Attempt to understand what the teacher knows at this point in time and back that up with evidence.
3. Remember that your job is to connect your own agenda with the teacher's agenda so that both of you can meet your goals.

An Example of Coaching–Guided Reading

Chapter 9 includes a description of Marian's guided reading lesson and Lisa's analysis. Remember that Lisa has been working with Marian for some time. Prior to her observation and coaching, she made the notes in Figure 11–2

Reflection Prior to Classroom Visit
A Guide for Thinking About Coaching

Observer: _____L.L._____ Date: ___10/2___

Teacher: _____Marian_____ Grade: ____1____

Think about:
- What kinds of questions does the teacher ask you?
- What are some of the confusions the teacher expresses?
- Are there differences between the way the teacher talks and what you observe in the classroom?
- What kinds of behavior provide evidence of teachers' strengths and skills in classroom work?
- What does the teacher say about children? To what degree does he/she describe children's behavior as evidence of learning?

The goal is to create a context in which "good dissonance" can take place. Criticism is offered in a constructive and positive way through nonthreatening conversations.

Make notes in response to the questions below:

1. What are your perceptions of the teacher's strengths?	Good organization and interactions with children. Using all procedures for guided reading. Prepared for lessons. Excellent engagement. Looking for reasons why her lessons bog down. Recognizes lessons are too long. Shows strengths in helping children think about meaning of text.
2. What do you think the teacher needs to learn **next** (conceptually) to reach another level of understanding?	Lesson bogging down during reading of text; also introduction too long. Whole lesson too long. Introduction ineffective probably because texts are not right; work on text selection first.
3. What are the teacher's **own** perceptions of his/her strengths and needs?	Asked for help with introductions as well as how to get children through the books faster. Lessons are too long. Asked me to look at her book collection and the ones she is using.

Notes from preconference:
Animal Homes has simple language but hard concepts; don't know if children will know them.
Pictures are not really supportive.
Watch to see children's responses during introduction.

Figure 11–2. *Reflection Prior to Observation—Marian*

Preconference: Guided Reading of *Animal Homes*

[about five minutes]

LISA: In class you mentioned that students are bogging down during the reading of the text. Is that something you'd like for us to look at together today?

MARIAN: Yes. Maybe I should be teaching harder to get them through the books. I really spend a lot of time on the introduction—maybe too much! But they still have trouble.

LISA: What about the books? You mentioned looking at the books you've chosen for each group.

MARIAN: I've wondered if the books are too hard. Today I'm going to introduce *Animal Homes* to the first group. It has a lot of words they know and it's repetitive. There's only one line of print on each page. Only one word changes at the end of the line. The last word is shown in the picture, so I'm really going to stress looking at pictures. And the last page, I'll have them say that.

LISA: [Reads through the book quickly.] I think it's good that you are thinking about how hard some of these concepts are. Using illustrations and checking to see if they understand will be a good idea. I'll watch to see whether children are using the pictures to help them and whether they understand the story.

Figure 11–3. *Preconference*

(see Chapter 9 for an explanation of this form), drawn from previous classroom observations, informal conversations with Marian, and observations of Marian in professional development sessions. Lisa often jots down ideas on sticky notes during class and transfers them to folders or forms later. She doesn't need an extensive agenda for a classroom coaching session, but it's very important to have some idea of what the teacher is looking for.

Lisa begins by having a brief preconference with Marian, during which she takes a few notes (see Figure 11–3). Lisa's previous thinking helps her begin the conference. Marian reveals her concerns about book selection and introductions, so together Marian and Lisa are able to establish some common goals.

During the lesson (see Figure 11–4), Lisa observes and takes brief notes, using the guided reading scale (see Chapter 10) as a framework. She notes Marian's excellent organizational and management skills as well as her rapport with students; she also notices some skilled teaching behavior, but she realizes that Marian needs more help in text analysis and selection. For

example, as Marian hinted, the book introduction is too long. Lisa posits two explanations:

◆ Marian typically "overintroduces" material.
◆ The text difficulty is frustrating, and Marian works longer than she usually does because children are giving her feedback that they don't understand the pages.

As Lisa observes children trying to interpret the pictures, she realizes that the illustrations are not at all clear for beginning readers, who tend to focus on the animals in the foreground instead of their "homes" (which sometimes are not even shown). This book is interesting but might be more appropriate for more advanced readers. Lisa's notes are provided in Figure 11–5.

After the observation, Lisa and Marian discuss the lesson (see Figure 11–6), building on their previous conversation. Marian demonstrates a great deal of self-awareness and takes an active role. Finally, Marian writes a few notes as an action plan (see Figure 11–7); they each kept a copy. On this simple form, Marian formalizes two good suggestions to work on between now and their next coaching session.

	Marian's Guided Reading Lesson on *Animal Homes*
Text	Marian had selected *Animal Homes* for a group of four first graders: Brian, Holly, Marie, and Rachel. On every page, the text says: "Some animals live in . . ." and the name of the "home" ends the sentence. The pictures show the animals but do not always show the homes. Names for homes in the text are: *nests, shells, burrows, caves, hives, logs*. On the last page, the text asks readers to look at four houses and find one closest to their own home.
Introduction (10 minutes)	MARIAN: Today you are going to read a book that is all about animals. It's about their homes. Every animal in this book has a home. What's the animal on the first page? ALL CHILDREN: Bird. MARIAN: Yes, that's a bird. And birds live in . . . ? SOME CHILDREN: Trees. SOME CHILDREN: Nests. MARIAN: So this book is all about the way animals live. "Some animals live in nests." What's the first letter of *nests*? ALL CHILDREN: N MARIAN: Find the word *nests*. [They do so.]. That's right. "Birds live in nests." Now look at the next page. What are these animals? RACHEL: Turtle. BRIAN: Lobster. MARIE: Turtle. HOLLY: A worm? MARIAN: That's a crab and a turtle and a snail. Where does a turtle live? HOLLY: In his house? MARIE: On the ground. MARIAN: A turtle lives in a shell. All these animals live in *shells*. That's an *s-h* word. Find it. [Children do so.] MARIAN: Look at page 3. What are those animals? BRIAN: A mouse and a duck. RACHEL: A duck. MARIAN: No it's not a duck. It looks a little like one doesn't it? BRIAN: A gerbil, no, a beaver! MARIAN: This is a platypus. It's an animal kind of like a beaver that swims in the water a lot. The other animal is a kind of mouse. Where do you think they would live? BRIAN: In the water. MARIAN: In a burrow. They live in a burrow. That's a hole in the ground. Find *burrow*. [Children do so.] What does it start with? CHILDREN: B. MARIAN: That's right. Marian continues this routine through the entire book. When they come to the last page, she repeats the question and has them say it together. Then she has each child point to the picture most like his/her home. Then she instructs them to read the book.

Figure 11–4. *Marian's Lesson*—Animal Homes

Reading of the Text (*10 minutes*)	As they read the text, most students are able to produce the idea of *nests,* but two of them substitute *birds* for the word *animals.* After the first page, most readers struggle through the book. All make it through the whole book at a slow rate. Some are able to read the question at the end, but most have difficulty with the shift in pattern. The process is lengthy and somewhat tedious.
Discussion (*5 minutes*)	MARIAN: What did you learn by reading this book? HOLLY: Animals live in different places. BRIAN: A bee has a hive. MARIAN: That's right. Let's look at the first page again. RACHEL: There's the baby birds in the nest. MARIAN: Yes, you see different kinds of nests on that page don't you. Some animals live in nests. Then children talk about what they know about where animals live. Some children offer that bears live at the zoo, and they talk about wild bears living in caves or the woods.
Teaching Points (*3 minutes*)	MARIAN: Let's clap the word *animals.* [They do it together.] Find the word *animals* on the page. [They do so.] What does it start with? HOLLY: A. RACHEL: A-n. BRIAN: That's like *an.* MARIAN: That was great noticing. Marian writes the word *animals* on the whiteboard and shows them the *an.* Then she has students find the word and read the first page again together. She then asks them to find *some* on the first page, first predicting the first letter. Quickly, she has them find *some* again on three more pages. They read one more page together.

Figure 11–4. *Marian's Lesson—Animal Homes (continued)*

Lisa can refer to the plan before she visits Marian's classroom again.

An Example of Coaching— Interactive Writing

Pat's observation and analysis of John's interactive writing lesson is described in Chapter 10 (Figure 10–5). Remember that John skillfully engaged children in planning their writing and composing the text. The writing grew from a real experience and they were eager to produce a book about the zoo. They generated alternatives, and John guided them to select from among them. Although John was working well with the children, he did not really teach them much that was new.

Pat noticed the rich oral discussion that surrounded this piece of writing, and she wanted to encourage John to continue this kind of teaching; she also noticed that John and the students worked on every single word in a very routine way, making the writing unnecessarily tedious and ineffective. As Pat reflected on the observation, she decided that what John needed to know next

Lesson Observation

Teacher/Grade: __Marian Gr. 1__ Focus of instruction: __Guided Reading__

Observer: __L.L.__ Date: __10/3__ Time: __9:00–9:25__

Teacher	Student(s)	Notes/Questions
Routines in place. Has all supplies ready. Introduction: Provides main idea—animals homes. Focuses on the name of the animal. Children predict birds. Asks where birds live. Has them check first letter. Tells them names of animals. Goes through every page with routine of looking at the picture, naming the animal, and finding the word that tells where the animal lives. Ends up telling them the names of most homes. Reading: Has to do too much interacting and telling. Discussion: Asks children to talk about book. Teaching Points: Goes back to easiest page (1). Has them clap *animal*. Puts on whiteboard. Has them find in story and read. Has them find *some* on 3 pages.	Four children: Brian, Marie, Rachel, Holly. This group is struggling more than others. Children know routines. Introduction: Can locate nests and use 1st letter. Don't know names of animals—guess. Call out names. Some are off. Not repeating any of the language. Can't tell from pictures where animals live. Reading: All children struggling. Children trying to use animals' names. Slow pace. Difficulty—shift in pattern. Discussion: Children offering what they know. Still don't seem to understand whole story. They notice 1st part of *animal*. Read in story—no difficulty. Found *some* with no trouble.	Text seems too difficult. Technical words. Picture of animal every page but not of where they live. Animal names won't really help them—may get in the way. Book requires knowing something about the animals. P. 3 very difficult. Pictures don't really help. Introduction off track and too long. Text so difficult that they might not understand it even with a skillful introduction. Going back to p. 1 helps. Good look at 1st part of word. *Some* is frequently encountered.

Potential topics for discussion:
- Talk about text selection—what makes this book hard?
- Talk about how book introduction can help but emphasize book selection?
- Teaching point on *some*—frequently encountered word.

Figure 11–5. *Observation of Guided Reading—Marian—Animal Homes*

Coaching After Marion's Lesson on *Animal Homes*

[ten minutes]

LISA: You asked me to observe children closely while they were reading. I noticed that they seem to have a lot of difficulty after page 2. You're right to be concerned about the reading bogging down.

MARIAN: I really worked on the book introduction.

LISA: I agree. You went over every page and you were prompting them to notice the pictures and think about the meaning. You also had them notice the first letter. You were offering them a lot of support. The guesses they were giving seemed to be mostly animal names. They didn't know some of them.

MARIAN: I think they just didn't know the names for all those animal homes; they were just too complicated.

LISA: Do you think the pictures were helpful enough?

MARIAN: No! After I got going, I saw that some of them were hardly there, and the kids didn't know them anyway. If they didn't know the animal, they wouldn't know the home. This book would be better if it just said "This is a bear" or "This is a bird" and left out the really hard names. But then that might be too easy for this group.

LISA: You've identified a critical problem. The text was too hard. And I like how you noticed that the pictures didn't really help. That might have made it almost impossible for children to read even with your introduction.

MARIAN: I really lost a lot of time and the lesson was way too long. The introduction was too long.

LISA: I agree. You focused on animal names, but those words weren't in the text.

MARIAN: I might have even confused them with going over animal names when they didn't know them and weren't going to read them.

LISA: We don't know, but I think that might be a good insight on your part. For beginning readers it's best to be very careful about the language.

MARIAN: I could have just said *some animals*.

LISA: Yes you could. They might have been more accurate, but would they have known the meaning?

MARIAN: No, they just didn't have the background knowledge.

LISA: Let's look at the books you have and select a book that might be better for this group tomorrow.

Marian and Lisa select a book that both agree will have better potential for the group. Together, they look at the characteristics of the text. The book has more print than *Animal Homes* but easier concepts and more frequently encountered words. After looking at these characteristics, they discuss the introduction and Lisa demonstrates how it might go. Marian makes some notes on a sticky note, which she places on the front of the book.

Figure 11–6. *Coaching Conversation*

was how to decide quickly at which points children should be asked to "share the pen." He also needed to know the reasons for these decisions:

◆ Reserve attention for words that will help children learn something new.

◆ Keep the lesson moving along at a faster pace so that more text can be produced.

◆ Produce a richer text for children to read.

Pat's preconference with John (see Figure 11–8) revealed that he was experiencing some frustration with interactive writing. It was taking too long and interfering with other activities he also valued. John knew that his students had learned a great deal from interactive writing, but he still felt uneasy about how much time it took. Accustomed to high engagement, he also worried that some students were easily distracted.

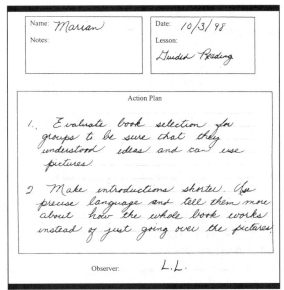

Name: *Marian*   Date: 10/3/98
Notes: Lesson:
                  Guided Reading

Action Plan

1. Evaluate book selection for groups to be sure that they understood ideas and can use pictures.

2. Make introductions shorter. Use precise language and tell them more about how the whole book works instead of just going over the pictures.

Observer: *L.L.*

Figure 11–7. *Action Plan*

John's legitimate concern and suggested that they talk about what might happen during the writing of the text. Since this was John's first year using interactive writing, he had assumed that children should write as much as possible in the session. He was excited about doing more of the encoding himself and quickly grasped the idea that more text could be written.

After the conversation, Pat noted that in the next session with John, she would look again at the encoding of the text, with the goal of helping him refine and expand his already considerable skills in helping children learn to compose texts. The focus at that time might be on composing texts that pose more writing (as well as reading) challenges.

Going Back to the Rationales

In both examples in this chapter, the literacy coaches provide concrete, specific suggestions, but that's not all they do. Using everyday language rather than textbook jargon, these coaches focus on students' reading and writing behavior.

Pat's observation revealed what might be a possible misunderstanding on John's part. If he could adjust the way he dealt with encoding, he might solve the issues of time and attention. In the coaching conversation (see Figure 11–9), Pat addressed the issue directly. She recognized

---

John and Pat's Preconference

At the beginning of the conference John briefly describes the previous work that he and the children have done—their trip to the zoo and the list they have made in preparation for making a big book about animals.

PAT: You've really got a great start on this project. This list will help them keep the big picture in mind as they are writing. You've supported them in organizing their ideas.

JOHN: They're really excited, and I think they've done some wonderful pictures that we can use for illustrations in the book.

PAT: I was also looking at some of their writing that you have displayed. They are doing some wonderful writing!

JOHN: They have come a long way. I don't think I've ever had a class that's writing so much at this time of the year. They just love it too.

PAT: How is your work with interactive writing going? I know that's something new this year.

JOHN: I've done a lot of work on letters, sounds, and words. The interactive writing really helps with this, and they love making their own charts. I do have a concern, though. I've always read a lot to the kids. This year, interactive writing is taking so much time that I don't think I'm doing as much in children's literature. Also, sometimes the kids get really antsy by the end of a session.

PAT: About how long do your sessions usually last?

JOHN: Usually from snack to lunch—about forty minutes.

PAT: That does seem long. I'll watch to see how they can be more concise. You really should be thinking about something between five and twenty minutes. And I really agree that reading to children is so important. We have to find time in your schedule for that.

Figure 11–8. *Preconference with John*

Coaching After John's Lesson

PAT: It was amazing to see how many ideas the children had about the zoo.

JOHN: You should have heard them yesterday. I had a hard time getting them to boil it down to a list. They really loved the zoo.

PAT: I can see that, and you were really keeping them involved. You said that you had some concerns about the length of lessons and I have a suggestion that might help.

JOHN: Good, what?

PAT: When you were writing the sentence, everything seemed to go slower. It took a lot of time. Is that what you felt?

JOHN: Yes! That's when they sometimes get antsy, although that didn't happen so much today.

PAT: When you're writing the text, you can think, What do children already know? You can think about it word by word—that's the way you write it. If most children already know the word, you can just write it yourself and move on.

JOHN: You mean I don't have to have them come up to write every word?

PAT: That's right. You really want to focus on just the words that will help them learn something new.

JOHN: Most of my kids knew all those words—maybe *went* would be a challenge for some. They're all on the word wall except *zoo*, but kids were so excited that they had learned that one too. But what about Annie and Meg, who don't know the words?

PAT: You can spend some extra time with a couple of children or a small group to work closely with interactive writing. The main thing is that you don't want the writing to take so much time.

JOHN: That was really my concern. That only took about twenty minutes, but it kind of dragged.

PAT: That's not too long, but if you write the words most kids know, you could produce more text in the time. Can you think what might be the advantage of that?

JOHN: We could get more done in a day and it would be more interesting to kids.

PAT: Yes, because you'd be getting into words that would help them learn more. I was really impressed with your work with them in composition. What if they'd decided to write the alternative that James posed: "The zoo is full of animals"?

JOHN: *Full* and *animals* would give them something to think about. They know *an*, so that would have been a good way to start *animals*.

PAT: What would you have written yourself?

JOHN: *The, zoo, is*, and *of*.

PAT: So you might think about helping them generate a longer text. You would probably have had time to write one more sentence. They would learn more by reading it later, too. Your kids have learned so much this year.

JOHN: I'm sure they could all read that.

After a little more discussion they end the session by writing the action plan. John's plan is simple. He writes that he would (1) select teaching points for sharing the pen, and (2) try to produce a slightly longer text within a shorter time.

Figure 11–9. *Coaching Conversation with John*

Each session is grounded in evidence and linked to the reason for making changes. Even when simply changing an action or two, teachers deserve to know the underlying reasons for the shift.

Skilled staff developers get teachers to understand the specific concepts that will help them refine specific approaches to teaching. They select specific examples that help teachers understand and move forward. As knowledge and experience build, teachers begin to understand the rationales at increasingly complex levels. While it is important to state the rationales from the beginning, deep understanding will not be possible until teachers have worked in the classroom over time. They build up examples from which they learn; they see evidence of student learning. They build what some researchers call "case knowledge," which they use to form tentative theories. In professional development sessions, you can help them connect their concrete experiences to what they are reading so that they begin to understand theoretical information in a very practical way.

Suggestions for Extending Your Skills as a Staff Developer

1. Extend your own learning by looking back at the figures in this chapter:
   - Lisa's *reflections* prior to the visit (Figure 11–2).
   - Transcript of Lisa and Marian's *pre-conference* (Figure 11–3).
   - Lisa's *observation* of Marion's guided reading lesson (Figure 11–5).
   - Lisa and Marian's *coaching* conversation after the lesson (Figure 11–6).
   - Marian's *action* plan (Figure 11–7).

   These figures represent the structure of coaching when you are working for shifts in behavior: REFLECTION, PRECONFERENCE, OBSERVATION, COACHING, ACTION.

2. Reflect on or discuss with a colleague:
   - What are the values of thinking and action in each component?
   - What is the coach's task/responsibility within each component?
   - How is each component helpful to the teacher?
   - How will each component help the coach learn more?

3. Now work through the series of components for yourself with a colleague who is willing to help you. Afterward, reflect on the process:
   - What steps felt really natural to me?
   - When did I learn the most about the teacher?
   - When was I especially effective?
   - What do I need to work on in my coaching?

Chapter 12

Establishing the
Analytic/Reflective Cycle

Staff development should not be perceived as something we do unto the weaker teacher or reserve for inexperienced staff members . . . There needs to be a genuine feeling that no one has arrived. Everyone needs to be swept up by the deeply engrained value placed on adult learning.
—SHELLEY HARWAYNE GOING PUBLIC: PRIORITIES AND PRACTICES AT
THE MANHATTAN NEW SCHOOL *(251)*

The long-term goal of professional development is not to perfect any one approach to instruction but to promote ongoing learning. Teachers who know how to learn from teaching will go on expanding their skills. Learning gives a lift to life: it makes everything you do more satisfying. Being a learner does not mean you lack confidence; true learners are well aware of their expertise and funds of knowledge, but they are always expanding and revising them.

Teaching involves constant investigation of the organizational structures, plans, materials, and interactions that get the best response from students. Expert teachers hold tentative theories that they test with each new group of students and in every instructional context. Learning for them is not a matter of trying and discarding new methods but instead involves observing and interpreting students' responses as they work with these students in different ways. They look for and document evidence of learning. They learn from their teaching, and that keeps their work fresh and interesting.

In the past, professional development consisted primarily of training programs to instill particular skills—and that was the end of it. Structured courses that introduce something new into your teaching have their place; but for the skilled teacher, that is where learning *begins.* Coaching provides the support teachers need to engage in classroom inquiry.

Looking at an interactive writing lesson.

An Example of Coaching in Guided Reading

Caroline, a staff developer, has had the pleasure of working with Melissa over the several years Melissa has been teaching in this school. When Melissa joined the teaching staff, she had only two years of experience and had not used guided reading or word study. She'd followed the adopted reading curriculum, using mostly whole-class instruction. Now, several years later, Melissa feels quite comfortable in her work with guided reading; she has taught at two different grade levels in the school.

In the guided reading lesson described here, Melissa is introducing *Mieko and the Fifth Treasure* (level M) to a group of her more advanced readers. Melissa wants to help her students become more sophisticated in their interpretations of texts—specifically, to make inferences about the feelings and motives of characters. She also has an upcoming proficiency test in mind, on which her students will be expected to demonstrate understanding that goes beyond literal comprehension. She is seeking some authentic ways to extend their strategies. She feels she can learn from this group of readers and then apply her ideas to her work with her other students. In a preconference (see Figure 12–1) she asks Caroline to be her sounding board.

Melissa has specific goals in mind, and Caroline's presence as an outside expert will allow the two of them as a team to gather more information on the students' reading. The two teachers have a comfortable relationship that allows Melissa to assign Caroline a specific role in the inquiry. Caroline offers her advice freely, and Melissa is able to consider it as such, not as an order. They know their conversation after the observation will be free wheeling; they may even argue.

As described in Figure 12–2, Melissa provides a tight, relatively brief introduction to this 77-page

As teachers learn more about any instructional procedure, the routines become unconscious. Teachers move through the steps, but their attention is on communicating with students. They make smooth, orchestrated moment-by-moment decisions in order to maximize students' learning. It might seem that at this point, coaching is no longer essential. Not so. When you work with teachers over time, they grow in their ability to analyze their teaching, and the collegial support of coaching is even more needed and appreciated. Expert teachers open wide their classroom doors. In the process, conversations change. *You too will learn from* the practice and reflection of the expert teachers with whom you work.

As a staff developer you work alongside teachers in different classrooms, and together you reflect, analyze, and interpret students' work (e.g., writing workshop, interactive writing) and build personal and collective theories of literacy learning. Schon (1983) refers to this collaborative inquiry as reflection-in-action and suggests that the critical component is the examination and testing of different rationales—grounded in student work—to explain the impact of teaching on student learning. As a result of this analytic/reflective process, teachers construct a more complex and complete understanding of literacy learning and learn how to adjust instruction to meet an individual student's needs.

Preconference—Melissa's Guided Reading Lesson

MELISSA: You have me on your schedule today, don't you?

CAROLINE: Yes, I'm looking forward to it. You want to talk about guided reading, right?

MELISSA: Yes, this is a good time because the group with Juana, Gabe, Francie, Michael, and Sean are starting a new book, *Mieko and the Fifth Treasure* [Coerr 1993].

CAROLINE: That's a great one!

MELISSA: I'm going to introduce it for guided reading so we can discuss it later. Depending on how it goes, I'll probably let them finish it on their own.

CAROLINE: What are you working on with them?

MELISSA: This book will present some challenges. It's historical fiction for one thing, and they haven't read much of that. I also notice from their reading lists that the boys are choosing mostly sports stories and even the girls haven't chosen historical fiction as a genre. I did read *Secret Soldier* [McGovern 1999] and they liked that.

CAROLINE: So none of them have read *Sadako and the Thousand Paper Cranes* [Coerr 1993] by the same author?

MELISSA: No, I thought *Meiko* would be a better story to start on because it's not as sad, but I hope some of them will choose to read *Sadako* later.

CAROLINE: Will you be talking a lot about the genre?

MELISSA: That's part of it. Also, they'll be reading about a completely different culture, and they need to try to see how Japanese people might have felt about the atomic bomb being dropped on Hiroshima and Nagasaki. They also need to see calligraphy as art, and I don't think they've ever thought about it that way. There are some interesting Japanese names for things like shoes, but I don't expect that to be a big problem. What I'm really trying to develop is their ability to take other perspectives so that they can explain something from different points of view. I want them to really get into knowing how a character feels and why she does what she does. That's making inferences as they would describe it on the proficiency test.

CAROLINE: How can I help?

[Melissa explains that she will introduce the story, have the group read the first chapter, and then bring them back for a discussion. She asks Caroline's advice on how to help students understand why Meiko didn't want to paint. Caroline suggests using the Author's Note at the end to explain something about calligraphy; Melissa thinks this is a good idea but doesn't want to get sidetracked into a long discussion.]

MELISSA: I know I could go into a whole study of Japan or of calligraphy from this book, but that's not what I think they need to learn from reading it.

[Caroline and Melissa find a couple of passages that will help students connect their own knowledge of Nagasaki with how Mieko would have seen it.]

MELISSA: I thought you might have a conference with a couple of the kids after they've read a few pages. I'll do the rest. Listen to some oral reading for fluency and find out what they're thinking. Then I'd really like you to watch the follow-up discussion.

CAROLINE: That sounds great to me.

Figure 12–1. *Preconference for a Guided Reading Lesson—Meiko and the Fifth Treasure*

text. It takes about ten minutes. She provides enough background and encourages students to think about what they know about the setting; but she keeps the conversation focused on what she is trying to help students learn. She gathers information by interacting with individual students during the lesson and during the discussion that follows. Caroline is a supportive co-investigator.

After the lesson, Caroline and Melissa have the coaching conversation shown in Figure 12–3. Melissa asks Caroline for specific information; Caroline makes some suggestions. The session doesn't end in a written action plan, but Melissa definitely has a plan in her head. Caroline is a conversational partner as Melissa sorts out what she wants to do next with regard to helping

Description of a Guided Reading Lesson Using *Meiko and the Fifth Treasure*

Introduction to the Text

MELISSA: I'm excited about the book we're going to be reading today. It's called *Meiko and the Fifth Treasure,* by Eleanor Coerr. There's Meiko on the cover. Look at what she's doing.

SEAN: She's painting. It looks Japanese.

FRANCIE: She might be writing with a brush. That looks like Chinese writing or maybe Japanese.

MELISSA: You're both right really. Mieko is a girl just a little older than you are now and she lived in Japan a long time ago. She's doing calligraphy, which is a kind of painting that is art but also means something. It's a word picture. Turn to the very last page of the book—right after page 77—where it says *author's note*. [*Melissa reads the first paragraph of the author's note, which explains "characters" as art.*] Look at the character you see there for *mountain*. Do you think it looks a little like a mountain? And look at *tree*. [*Students nod.*] Down at the bottom you see *friendship*.

JUANA: It looks like it could be two girls holding hands or something.

FRANCIE: I could see it might look like two people.

MELISSA: Now look at the back of the book. Read it to yourself. [*Students have a few moments to read.*] This book will be all about the four treasures you read about here. The first four are easy to understand aren't they? They are all the things you need to make those word pictures.

SEAN: The fifth one is treasure of the heart?

JUANA: It's beauty in the heart?

MELISSA: What do you think that could mean?

SEAN: Well, it's like being really nice or happy so that your heart feels good.

FRANCIE: It could be that with your heart you love people like your family, and that would be kind of like beautiful.

MELISSA: You'll read in this book that Meiko's teacher told her about the fifth treasure—beauty in the heart. He said that when you paint, the beauty would flow from your heart to your hand, to the brush, and out onto the paper. So having beauty in your heart would be necessary to be a great artist in calligraphy—or a great calligrapher.

GABE: So it's kind of like you are happy that almost guides your hand?

JUANA: Could it be like when you're really happy if you're going to the beach or something, you might do your work faster and better?

MELISSA: Maybe so. I know that when I feel happy I do better at just about anything. Meiko wants more than anything to be a great artist, but the next paragraph tells you why she is so sad and doesn't have beauty in her heart.

SEAN: It's kind of like *Snowflake Bently,* because he saw beauty everywhere, like in the snowflakes.

[*After recognizing Sean's connection to another text, Melissa and the students discuss Nagasaki. They have heard of Hiroshima and know about the atomic bomb; they learn about the other city and pronounce it. They discuss what kinds of feelings Meiko might have in her heart with her village ruined, her hand badly hurt, and living away from home.*]

MELISSA: There will be some Japanese names for everyday things, like *futon*.

GABE: We've got a futon in our house.

MELISSA: Yes, and Meiko puts on her *kimono* and her *geta*, her shoes. So when you come to words like that, just figure them out by thinking what would make sense. Let's find the word *calligraphy* on page 10. [*Students find it and notice that the word has* graph *in it.*] That's good noticing! We have been doing *graphs* in math. When you see *graph* as part of a word, it always means something to do with writing. In math you write a diagram or chart, but in this book Meiko writes or paints her word pictures. As you read this book, think about how Meiko feels. She doesn't even want to go to school. Use a sticky note to mark a place in the book that the writer really shows you the anger in her heart. Read to the bottom of page 19 and then stop. If you have time, you can make a quick sketch in your reader's notebook to show what you've learned about this book.

Figure 12–2. *Description of a Guided Reading Lesson*—Meiko and the Fifth Treasure

Description of a Guided Reading Lesson Using *Meiko and the Fifth Treasure* (continued)

Reading

Melissa and Caroline let students get started and then go to each, sampling oral reading and interacting briefly. Gabe wonders about Meiko's parents and whether they are dead, but then he searches back and finds that her father is a doctor. Gabe thinks Meiko should be glad to be alive instead of complaining about just a cut hand. Francie is more sympathetic to Meiko but doesn't like Grandpa's belief that the souls of people killed by the bomb have to swim across the River of Death. "I don't think that would be right," she says. In general, students are bringing a great deal of information to the text, and are making some revisions to their knowledge of Japanese culture.

Discussion

The discussion starts by students' sharing the parts of the text that they have marked. Juana has marked the very last sentence on page 19, which sparks quite a bit of discussion: "But a strange school? With children she did not know? And with a hideous, twisted hand?" Juana says she picked this sentence because to her it means that Meiko is really afraid, not just whining. "Everything was different for her, and she really likes beautiful things because she was an artist. She might be afraid that she can't paint again and people won't like her because she can't paint and she has an ugly hand."

Melissa says, "That might be right. The writer is really letting you into Meiko's thoughts, isn't she?"

Another student chooses Meiko's nightmare, because she sometimes has nightmares when she's afraid. They agree that Meiko is also afraid that something will happen to her family.

Then the group generates a list of words that can be used to describe Meiko's feelings.

They also briefly visit any words they found tricky. Francie has noticed the word *gradually*, thinking it can be added to the *ly* word chart in the column for *ally* words, like *fantastically*. After taking off the ending, though, students realize that it belongs in the *ly* column just like the short word *hardly*.

Melissa asks them to read to the end of Chapter 2, finish the quick sketch, and be prepared to discuss more about the book the next day.

Melissa also points out the dedication of the book, which, accompanied by the appropriate calligraphy, says

In the midst of the world's corruption,
A heart of pure white jade.

When they meet again, some students have worked approximations of calligraphy into their sketches.

Figure 12–2. *Description of a Guided Reading Lesson—Meiko and the Fifth Treasure (continued)*

readers learn to make inferences. At the same time, the conversation is valuable for Caroline; she's observed a good demonstration of a teacher working with students to develop comprehension strategies, and she's learned how Melissa looks for evidence of learning.

Does Melissa really need Caroline in her classroom? Shouldn't Caroline spend her time with teachers who are less experienced? In general, that's true. You will not need to spend as much time supporting and coaching teachers like Melissa; however, it is Caroline's coaching support over time that has helped Melissa become so skilled. Experienced teachers benefit greatly from working together as co-investigators.

Melissa highly values collegial conversations: they help her to be a more effective teacher. This process of inquiry keeps Melissa learning more every year; she stays with teaching because it is satisfying and produces positive results. Every person at every level needs the opportunity to keep on learning if we are to meet the challenges in today's educational climate.

Learning from Observation

The first step in moving a teacher toward analyzing and reflecting on his practice is to observe several lessons and listen carefully to how he

---

Caroline and Melissa's Coaching Conversation

CAROLINE: The group was really involved in the discussion!

MELISSA: Yes, I was really pleased with how they could talk about the book. I'm amazed at how much they have learned this year. They were really making connections, and they did know something about Hiroshima.

CAROLINE: I was so impressed when Sean brought up *Snowflake Bentley* and his taking pictures of snowflakes. That was quite a reach.

MELISSA: He does that all the time. What did you find out in your conferences?

CAROLINE: Gabe thought Meiko was kind of a whiner, but I think he understood her more after the discussion. They were all reading very well and I think understanding the story so far.

MELISSA: They started relating Meiko's feelings to their own, so that's good. They can see that even though the story was long ago and in a different culture, the feelings can be the same. I was please with the last discussion, but I think I'll keep them coming back for a while instead of having them finish it on their own.

CAROLINE: They were making connections. Francie even noticed an *ly* word.

MELISSA: Yes, that could have taken us a little off track, so I didn't make a big deal of it, but I do encourage them to make connections with word study.

CAROLINE: What about asking them to do some writing about this book? There's so much in it.

MELISSA: They could just write what they are thinking about.

CAROLINE: Later on in the story, Meiko gets letters from people, but doesn't write back for a long time. They could write what they think Meiko should say in a letter—like whether or not she should tell her parents how she feels—and that would get some good discussion going.

MELISSA: I'll think about that. I'm also going to keep the word chart going. Meiko goes from being angry and afraid to being very lonely and hating everyone. There are some interesting expressions in the book that we can also add—like hatred growing in your heart "like a bad weed."

CAROLINE: Were you pleased with the lesson?

MELISSA: Yes, I think that the brief introduction, without going into a lot of detail about Japan and so on really got them right into the story. I'm working to help them make inferences about characters' motives and feelings, so that's what I was going for, and they really did it.

CAROLINE: So what do you expect to happen over the next few discussions?

MELISSA: I'll keep going with thinking about Meiko's feelings, but I want them to really notice when she changes how she feels and why.

CAROLINE: I really enjoyed seeing your students again today.

Figure 12–3. *Coaching Conversation Following a Guided Reading Lesson*—Meiko and the Fifth Treasure

assesses student progress and describes the processes he wants the students to develop next. Armed with the answers to these two questions, you will be able to determine where the teacher is on an analytic/reflective continuum of learning (see Figure 12–4) and tailor the coaching session to meet his needs.

Coaching is effective when the teacher is already teaching the particular technique pretty well. Up to that time, the staff developer is assisting, guiding, and working alongside the teacher to establish the procedures of the approach. Then

the situation changes. Coaching supports the teacher in analyzing her own teaching, an action that has accelerative value. Once a teacher develops a system for learning from and through her teaching, all new approaches will be easier to implement and adjust to meet students' needs.

The conversation in Figure 12–3 provides evidence that Melissa is able to reflect on and analyze her teaching. But she wasn't always at this point in her learning. When she first implemented guided reading, she was new to teaching. She was very concerned about the routines and

Self-Analysis Continuum

1. Teacher has developed the knowledge and expertise to teach students how to engage effectively in most aspects of the reading and writing processes (see the guided reading, interactive writing, and word study scales in Chapter 10.)

2. Teacher can analyze, reflect on, and assess an individual student's processing across a lesson and provide several plausible rationales for when and why it may be breaking down.

3. Teacher can generate alternative procedures to meet individual needs across the lesson framework that are more appropriate for individual students.

4. Teacher can use the alternative procedures flexibly and fine-tune instruction to meet individual's needs "on the run."

5. Teacher has developed expertise is all aspects of the reading and writing processes across the lesson framework and has a rich repertoire of decision-making and teaching actions that are used in a flexible and efficient way.

Figure 12–4. *Self-Analysis Continuum*

materials, and that was her main focus for a while. She looked closely at elements such as book selection and learned more about them.

Finally, she became so familiar with the procedures that she was able to focus mostly on student behavior. At that point, Melissa began to generate alternative hypotheses about students' responses. By adjusting her instruction, she could test those theories, meet students' needs, and at the same time add to her learning. She might notice something about a student's behavior in guided reading that she would address in an individual reading conference with him. She could use literature discussion to expand comprehension strategies when she noticed students in guided reading had a hard time making inferences from text.

Now, gathering information constantly, she works across the literacy framework instead of treating each lesson as a separate event. Some of her actions may seem second nature, but this kind of dynamic decision making is *learned.* At this point, coaching is the most helpful form of professional development for her, and she is able to learn a great deal from just one session.

Coaching for Self-Analysis

Teachers who are implementing procedures and have all routines in place can profit from coaching that requires them to make their own analyses. In this way, they begin to develop the skills needed to enter the reflective/analytic cycle; but it takes time and work to get to this point.

In the example shown in Figure 12–5, Ellen is working with a group of students who are reading *Amalia and the Grasshopper* (Tello 1994). Ellen anticipates the text will be easy for students, so she provides a concise introduction that nevertheless gives the gist of the story, calls attention to language patterns, and clarifies specific words. Students read fluently, but do not pick up on a very important point in the story—that the grasshopper's legs were the model that helped the little girl learn to jump.

Ron, the staff developer, knows he is observing a strong lesson. Ellen doesn't need his help on the procedures or on book selection. He does notice that students are not accessing prior knowledge adequately while reading; after the reading Ellen has to explain how the grasshopper helped Amelia. The lesson would have been more powerful if students had been able to bring that prior knowledge to the story. In her introduction, Ellen might have checked on what her students knew, reminded them of things they might have forgotten, or done a bit of explaining, thus helping these readers begin at a more strategic point.

The lesson needs only a little refining, and Ron believes Ellen has the knowledge to analyze for herself how to do it. He wants to move his coaching toward encouraging analysis and reflection rather than providing feedback and suggestions. That doesn't mean he will refuse to give suggestions if that's the most efficient thing to do; but he knows that Ellen can be analytic. His observations of her as she reflects on teaching in professional development sessions reveals that she knows a great deal about reading. He also knows he needs to work from Ellen's perspective—what she sees as the essential focus for discussion.

Guided Reading Lesson, *Amalia and the Grasshopper*

Ellen's Guided Reading Lesson

Ellen introduces *Amalia and the Grasshopper* to a group of second graders early in the year. In this story, a little girl's grandfather helps her notice how grasshoppers use their legs to jump high. Amalia, discouraged because she wants to play basketball like her brother, learns to use her legs for leverage and toss the ball high enough to make the basket. The text has complex sentences, some as long as three lines of text with two embedded clauses. Readers are expected to deal with the full range of punctuation.

Ellen's introduction is strong but concise; she leaves work for students to do. She helps them notice some of the language patterns and also focuses on some words that may be tricky. She talks about how difficult it is to be too little to do something. She explains the main idea of the story by saying, "Amalia's grandfather is going to help her solve her problem. Read and find out what will happen."

Students are highly engaged in the story; all read it with high accuracy. Ellen notices strong word-solving skills, and her brief interactions with students are directed toward reinforcing this effective behavior. She also draws students' attention to the punctuation, demonstrating how to read a passage with a dash. After the lesson, she brings students back to a couple of tricky pages and has them practice reading in phrase units. They talk about how to "read the punctuation."

During the discussion, Ellen asks students why they think *Amalia and the Grasshopper* is the title of the book. Several students say it's because there is a grasshopper in the story, but the discussion reveals that they do not understand how the grasshopper really helps the little girl. One child says, "It really should be *Amalia and Her Grandfather,* because he showed her how." Ellen sees this as an insightful comment, but is concerned that only one student understood the role of the grasshopper while reading. The rest of them really don't understand why Amalia thanks the grasshopper instead of her grandfather. She explains how looking at how the grasshopper uses its legs helps Amalia jump very high.

Ron's Observation

Ron notes that Ellen has selected an appropriate text and is using the procedures smoothly and skillfully. Her lesson is organized and fast paced. She brings students into the conversation. Her teaching points are related to her ongoing observations of students' reading behavior.

He notices that students are reading with accuracy and some fluency. Ellen's interactions with them are effective in helping them solve words.

His observation of the discussion indicates that while children can read all the words and generally understand the events in the story, most of them have missed the important information on which the plot turned. He hypothesizes that they need more support in bringing prior knowledge to their reading of the text.

Ron is also thinking that Ellen will probably notice and bring up the children's confusions. He has been working with her for some time. This lesson seems a good example for her to extend her own way of analyzing lessons. So, he decides not to come forward with a specific suggestion for improving the introduction.

Instead, he formulates goals like these:

- I'd like for Ellen to analyze the readers' behavior and notice that some were not effectively using prior knowledge.
- I'd also like Ellen to analyze the lesson, connect it to the reading process, and think of some alternatives that might have been more powerful for these students.
- Finally, I hope that Ellen can use this kind of self-analysis more effectively to vary her instruction.

Figure 12–5. *Guided Reading Lesson,* Amalia and the Grasshopper

In the coaching conversation (see Figure 12–6), Ron begins by focusing Ellen's attention on the students' reading. He wants to know what she noticed. She first focuses on students' ability to read the text accurately; she has been working hard on word solving and is pleased to see them applying these strategies. He then asks her to focus on the discussion, when it had become clear that the students had not understood the importance of the grasshopper. Ellen gets the point right away. She shares Ron's concern that students are not using prior knowledge. His goal, then, is to help her figure out why.

Ron prompts Ellen to connect her readers' behavior to the reading process. He asks her to focus on the specific cognitive demands of the text: "What would readers have to understand to read this book?" Ellen is already expert in selecting texts at appropriate levels of difficulty, so this deeper analysis will really pay off for her.

Ellen wants readers to learn how to access prior knowledge "on the run" instead of skipping over important information. The title should have provided a clue that the grasshopper is important. She doesn't want her readers to finish the book with a significant gap in understanding; she wants them to recognize when prior knowledge is needed and use it to predict what will happen as well as to understand the deeper messages of the text.

Next Ron prompts Ellen to be more analytic about her teaching by asking her to think about what she might have done differently. His objective here is not to help her learn how to do introductions. It is to help her use her own analysis as a basis for varying her teaching. Ellen generates some alternatives; notice her train of thought from a simple solution (telling and showing students the information they need) to more complex thinking. She knows that different approaches are appropriate for different students. She is developing a way of thinking about teaching that she can use in other situations with other students. As Ron continues to coach Ellen, she will analyze many different instructional contexts.

Coaching Conversation Geared to Support Self-Analysis

Amalia and the Grasshopper

RON: I really enjoyed the lesson. Tell me how you thought it went.

ELLEN: They did very well and that was a hard book. They were getting those longer sentences, and I think every one of them was reading just about all the words. The page that starts "Yet as hard as Amalia tried" is really tricky for them. But Devon connected *yet* and *bet* and he went back and repeated it until it made sense.

RON: I saw that too. You were really helping them connect to word study. What about the discussion?

ELLEN: I couldn't believe that they didn't get it about the grasshopper. I thought that would be easy. They really didn't understand why the grasshopper was important.

RON: Would it be necessary? You did explain it afterward.

ELLEN: Well, I guess maybe it wouldn't. They did talk about how her grandfather helped her. But it seems to me that they were missing the whole point of the story. If they don't get it while they read, they won't enjoy it as much. I don't want them just to miss important things like that and depend on somebody to explain it afterward.

RON: I agree. Comprehension happens because you are thinking while you are reading. What would readers have to do to understand this book?

ELLEN: They'd have to understand the dynamics of how a grasshopper's legs work—maybe not all the scientific information but the fact that the grasshopper can jump really high even though it's little. They didn't know enough about grasshoppers so they couldn't bring it in to their reading.

RON: Maybe there's something you could have done in the introduction that would make the difference.

ELLEN: I should have covered it in the introduction?

RON: There were probably several different ways to do it. Why don't you look through the book and think about what you might have done differently in the introduction?

Figure 12–6. *Coaching Conversation,* Amalia and the Grasshopper

ELLEN [*as she looks through book*]: I showed them this page where the grandfather is showing her how to shoot. But I could have had them look at this page that shows a close-up of the grasshopper. The grandfather is telling her to "look and see what it does." Here's the whole point right here. It's the idea that she could learn by looking at what the grasshopper does even though it's very little. Or maybe I could just explain that by talking about it and looking at the grasshopper on the back cover. I was afraid to do too much on the pages of the book because I thought the story would be easy for them—and it was, if you just think about reading the words.

RON: You've got a good analysis, I think. Any of your options could be a good move. How would they help the readers?

ELLEN: Because then, when they got to that place in the book, they would remember the little discussion and what they knew about grasshoppers. They'd use that knowledge to figure out right there what Amalia was going to do instead of waiting to find out. They could predict with it.

RON: Why would that be important?

ELLEN: They'd really be acting like good readers then. That's what they should do when I'm not there helping them and explaining it. It would give them experience in making connections to what they know and using it to predict.

RON: That one change in your introduction would help them expand their strategies, and it's also something that they can keep doing. Would you have done anything after they read it?

ELLEN: If they understood it, I could have just pointed out how remembering about grasshoppers helped them know what was happening.

RON: If they already knew about grasshoppers, you wouldn't want to go over it in depth in the introduction, would you? Every group of students will be different, so your idea of checking could be important.

ELLEN: With another group I might just say something like, "Amalia wanted to learn to jump so she could play basketball. What do you think that might have to do with a grasshopper?" Then, they could talk about it and I'd see what they know. Some might just need a little reminder to use what they know; Devon did understand it. But if they needed more information, I'd know that and could provide more. I wouldn't want to do it for them if they could do it themselves.

RON: I agree. It will be different for every group, but the important thing is that you are looking at the book and thinking about what the readers need to be reminded to do.

Figure 12–6. *Coaching Conversation,* Amalia and the Grasshopper *(continued)*

Varying Coaching to Meet Teachers' Needs

Ron's coaching takes only nine or ten minutes. He can coach Ellen so efficiently and effectively because he has analyzed her guided reading lesson and has observed her closely over time. Just a year ago, when she was first trying guided reading, he wouldn't have been able to accomplish so much simply by asking a few questions. In fact, Ellen might have resented a series of questions that did not offer some concrete assistance. Back then, Ron would have suggested ways to help make her teaching more efficient. He might have described a reader's behavior and asked Ellen to think about what it might mean. He would probably have generated alternatives with her and talked about them. (He would have been coaching for shifts in behavior, as described in Chapter 11.)

But at this point, Ellen is well able to enter the cycle of self-analysis (see Figure 12–4). It's appropriate for Ron to ask questions, but he doesn't turn the conversation into an interrogation. His questions are sensitive and focused. He really needs to hear Ellen talk about the students' behavior, and he also wants to know what she sees as alternatives.

Shaping the Coaching Conversation

The two examples above, as well as all the others in this book, make it obvious that there is no script for the coaching conversation. (Ron's conversation, for example, is shaped by what he knows about Ellen and what she has told him.) Staff developers have a wide repertoire of ways to coach and language to use.

Using Questions to Prompt Analysis

Questioning is a way to prompt analysis, but not if the questions are the same every time or if they are off target. Some purposes for asking questions are to:

1. Help teachers observe and analyze student behavior.
2. Help teachers become aware of their own decisions and the impact they have on students.
3. Help teachers deepen their understanding of reading and writing processes.
4. Help teachers reflect on their own learning.

Figure 12–7 lists some helpful questions relative to coaching for analysis. You will, of course, adjust the questions to fit into the flow of a particular conversation. The point is that each question has a definite purpose; it leads in a certain direction. That direction must be the place the teacher should go and wants to go. Avoid questions that encourage you and the teacher to meander or that are manipulative. None of us like a conversation in which we think the other person is beating around the bush or leading us to the "right" answer.

Being Selective

No one can work on everything at once. Beginning literacy coaches tend to make too many points during a session. It's important to implement only a few critical things; otherwise

---

Questions to Prompt Analysis of Teaching

1. Help teachers observe and analyze students' behavior.
   - Talk about what you noticed during [reading, writing, discussion, etc.].
   - What important [reading/writing] behavior did you notice in your students?
   - What did you noticed about students' behavior during [any component of the lesson]?
   - How were the students different from each other in the way they responded?
   - Where in the text did they have trouble? What do you think caused the problem?

2. Help teachers become aware of the impact their decisions have on students.
   - Why did you select this text?
   - How will this text help the readers?
   - What were you hoping would happen during your introduction?
   - What went well in the lesson?
   - Did you change your plan at any time in the lesson? Why?
   - Did you change your plan because of students' responses? How?
   - Looking back, what changes would you make in your lesson?
   - What are some alternatives to choose from [at any point in the lesson]?
   - What work or problem solving did you expect the readers to do in this text?

3. Help teachers deepen their understanding of reading and writing processes.
   - What did the students learn from this lesson?
   - What did the students learn today that they can use in [reading, writing] tomorrow?
   - How can you help students develop this [knowledge, strategy, process] in other learning contexts [reading aloud, guided reading, independent reading, literature study, investigation, guided writing, independent writing, word study].
   - How would [action, behavior] help readers or writers?
   - Why is [action, behavior] important for readers or writers?

4. Help teachers reflect on their own learning.
   - What have you learned about your teaching today?
   - What will you be working on next in your teaching?
   - How did your analysis of the lesson help you?

Figure 12–7. *Questions to Prompt Self-Analysis of Teaching*

Literacy coach and teacher discussing text difficulty.

teachers feel overwhelmed and don't know what to work on. In selecting coaching points, consider these criteria:

◆ Identify the most important thing for the teacher to learn next.
◆ Find the best example to help the teacher understand your coaching point.
◆ Go for one big idea that will make other things fall into place.

Balancing Telling, Teaching, and Supporting

On any day or during any week, your coaching will vary with teachers' level of experience and by the instructional approach being used. A teacher like Ellen might need coaching for analysis in guided reading but need demonstration or coaching for shifts in behavior in interactive writing. Your coaching will have different purposes at different times.

You will always be moving back and forth between telling, teaching, and supporting:

◆ Telling involves explicitly demonstrating procedures or communicating information. Beginners will need a great deal of telling. Even experienced and highly expert teachers may occasionally need a simple piece of information or a demonstration. Sometimes that's the most sensible and efficient way to work. Not everything must be "discovered." An analytic teacher can take a small piece of information and fit it into the bigger picture.

◆ Teaching means showing how to think about something in a new, generative way. In other words, you might explain something in a way that reveals its broader application.
◆ Supporting means helping and encouraging teachers to formulate new, developing insights. Teachers make their own journeys to knowledge; conversing with a more expert other helps them shape what they know and expand it.

Telling, teaching, and supporting may occur at any time and may appear together in any coaching session. You might provide some information, explain something, and encourage the teacher to put her emerging thoughts into words. Chapter 8, in discussing the "spiral of learning," emphasizes that learners engage in the same kinds of processes over and over but that the concepts are always changing. Nevertheless, the learner never returns to precisely the same place; he has new knowledge on which to build.

As a coach, even if you are telling and teaching, you recognize what the teacher is bringing to the situation. You constantly build on the working relationship you have already established with the teacher; on the teacher's own issues, concerns, and questions; on the teacher's understanding of the reading and writing processes; and on her knowledge of the particular students in her class.

Suggestions from Literacy Coaches

A group of experienced literacy coaches involved in a year of advanced training spent many hours analyzing lessons and leading coaching sessions. They practiced the skills described in this book and analyzed their own work. At the end of the training year, they assembled a rich list of suggestions for staff developers relative to coaching teachers in classrooms (see Figure 12–8). Many of these ideas are embedded in this chapter and Chapter 11. They represent practical advice with a strong theoretical base.

Suggestions from Literacy Coaches

Build on the teacher's understanding and perceptions.
- Build on the teacher's background knowledge of the reading process and of the students in the class.
- Build on the teacher's issues, concerns, and questions.
- Follow the teacher's lead but go farther so that you expand understanding.
- Use the preconference to get information that will help you better understand what you observe.
- Use the preconference to gain insights into the teacher's thinking.
- You may want to help the teacher problem-solve something she is going to do in the lesson or work through her decision making; wait to be asked for advice.
- Don't use the preconference as a "rehearsal" in which you tell the teacher exactly what to do; you may not know the context and will undermine the power of the teacher's decisions.
- Look for evidence of understanding throughout the process.
- Don't assume that just because you have coached for a concept, it is understood in a way that can be applied.
- Use class sessions to gain insights into how a teacher is thinking about his work.

Create a common language.
- Use clear language that the teacher will understand.
- Practice saying complex ideas clearly and succinctly.
- Ask the teacher to restate points so that meaning is in her own language.
- Tie your language and examples to students' reading and writing behavior.
- Constantly summarize and restate so that you rehearse the ideas for the teacher.
- Build coaching on what is happening in the class so that the teacher can easily talk about the important concepts.

Build the coaching relationship.
- Construct a good working relationship with the teacher in many contexts, not just in coaching.
- Achieve conversational give-and-take.
- Make coaching sessions brief and focused.
- Don't make too many teaching points in any one session.
- Ask the teacher if he has any questions or concerns that you can help with.

Keep the focus on important concepts that can be translated into action.
- Keep the focus on the reading and writing process, especially concepts you have explored in class.
- Go for one big idea or concept that will help everything else fall into place for the teacher.
- Weave pieces together so that the teacher can use the information in a new way.
- Help the teacher make a plan of action that will result in forward movement and more learning.
- Provide alternatives for further action and ask the teacher to select from them.
- Before coaching refer to and reread text materials that help you formulate the theoretical ideas clearly.
- Share knowledge in a way that helps the learner make it her own—knowledge then becomes a tool that the teacher can use in problem solving.

Learn from and about coaching.
- Reflect later and look for new ideas as you analyze your observation and coaching.
- Keep practicing coaching and have colleagues observe and give you feedback.
- Watch videotapes of lessons and your coaching with colleagues; ask for feedback.
- The more your understanding grows, the better coach you will be.

Figure 12–8. *Suggestions from Literacy Coaches*

Suggestions for Extending Your Own Skills as a Staff Developer

1. Read over the coaching conversation between Ron and Ellen. If you are working with a colleague, you might even read it aloud as you would a script.

2. Focus on the teacher first. Look at Figure 12–4, and find evidence in the transcript that Ellen can perform the tasks in points 1 through 4 of the self-analysis cycle.

3. Now concentrate on Ron's coaching. What is he doing with his questions? Is he asking Ellen to:
   ◆ Notice and analyze her students' behavior?
   ◆ Become more awa[re] decisions?
   ◆ Probe deeper into [...] ing processes?
   ◆ Learn from her tea[cher]

4. Observe a staff develop[er] who is well into the ana[...] learning. Look at the tea[cher...] Figure 12–4. Look at the coach in relation to Figure 12–7.
   ◆ Is it the coach working with the teacher at the appropriate level of self-analysis? Why or why not?
   ◆ How is the coach helping the teacher?
   ◆ Identify the important coaching moves.

SECTION FOUR

Supporting Lasting Change

Section 4 explores a number of challenging issues in today's educational environment. Teacher education and professional development take place within a larger educational context. Schools, school districts, and other educational systems are resistant to change. Professional development, if it's good, inevitably means change, so staff developers must be aware of the barriers that exist and ways to over come them. Effective professional development is not accidental. Careful planning, awareness of context, and a system design are all essential.

Chapter 13 focuses on ways to help teachers extend their learning through action research and continued study. It includes specific suggestions for working with teachers who are well versed in implementing approaches to teaching literacy.

Chapter 14 itemizes the challenges of professional development and describes how embedding professional development within larger support systems will contribute to its effectiveness.

Chapter 15 explores the concept of design as it applies to the larger educational systems of which professional development is an essential component. It includes examples of how to design systems at the classroom and school level as you work for educational change.

Chapter 16 describes the wide variety of ways staff developers serve schools and contribute to the education of teachers. It depicts the spiral of a "year of learning" that reveals the many practical ways teacher educators can work in a school setting.

Chapter 13

Supporting and Extending Learning

In a learning organization, leaders may start by pursuing their own vision,
but as they learn to listen carefully to others' visions they begin to see that their
own personal vision is part of something larger.
—PETER SENGE SCHOOLS THAT LEARN *(352)*

Learning is continuous and self-renewing. All learners incorporate new information into what they already know, so knowledge builds. In a learning community, everyone is expected to keep on learning but also to contribute to others' learning. Beginners are respected and helped, but advanced learning is made possible.

Extended learning is essential for effective literacy education, because no script or set of procedures can guarantee powerful instruction. Teachers must reach a point where they are able to solve their own problems, make their own analyses, and help others. All the staff development in the world will not improve education if teachers do not become independent. Today's educational reforms "require multiple leaders proficient in process skills; they require the patience and engagement of parents and community; they ask teachers to participate in relationships with students and with one another that were not part of the 'bargain' when they entered teaching. To undertake these reforms calls for a reinvention of schooling" (Lambert et al. 1995, p. 197).

Dynamic extended learning in a school or among a group of teacher learners is the ultimate goal of the spiral of learning described throughout this book.

Characteristics of Extended Learning

Effective systems for extending learning have the characteristics listed in Figure 13–1. Let's examine each of them separately.

Figure 13–1. *Characteristics of Systems for Extending Learning*

The Responsibility for Learning Is Shared

The responsibility for learning is not shouldered solely by the leader. The staff developer may work in a highly supportive way with new teachers but becomes a member of more advanced learning groups. The staff developer and experienced teachers work with new teachers so that they too gradually become responsible members of the learning group. Mentoring takes place, but partners are not assigned. The closeness of the work brings experienced and new learners together. Learners and mentors find one another naturally.

One could describe this environment as a *community of leaders*. Teachers take leadership in areas of learning related to their expertise and/or interests. The principal functions as a learner as well—leading the school in many areas, supporting teachers' learning in others, and always adding to her or his own learning.

There Is a Commitment to Ongoing Learning

Ongoing learning does not take place casually or by accident; it is the result of mutual commitment. Members of the group realize that continually improving and expanding their knowledge and skills is part of their job. Getting this commitment from new members of the staff is very

important. They need to be aware that if they abdicate responsibility to more senior members, they are letting their colleagues down. Commitment involves deciding who will do what rather than letting it hang loose. It means cooperatively working with schedules and duties so that everyone has a chance to learn.

Learning Is Grounded in the Work of Students and Teachers

Extended learning is grounded in the work of students and teachers. Learning conversations focus on students' work, whether it means observing them directly, looking at their products, or watching them on videotapes. People in the group are willing to examine classroom work and decide where education is going well and where it is breaking down. They look for evidence of learning in all contexts of instruction and welcome problems as a way of learning about processes.

Rationales are built on observation; teachers can state them explicitly, with examples. Grounding their learning gives teachers hundreds of case examples, built up over time, to which they can connect theories and new learning. Theories and principles are not "empty" but are instead connected to real events and people. Grounded theory makes complex ideas accessible. Living examples are encountered daily in the classroom.

Learning Takes Place in an Atmosphere of Inquiry

Learners ask questions and search for information: they engage in inquiry. Any learning has some of the characteristics of inquiry; that is how ideas come alive. Our minds are never more active than when we are making discoveries—recognizing problems, formulating hypotheses, seeking data, analyzing and synthesizing information, posing tentative conclusions, and deciding on tentative actions. Inquiry is not an academic exercise; it's how we live our lives.

The learning community is built through professional development that includes inquiry. In extended learning teachers engage in inquiry related to real problems and to ideas that spark their curiosity. Learning is deepened when you work with others. In extended learning colleagues investigate ideas together.

Learning Is Accomplished Through Conversation

Learning involves conversation structured around the development of new knowledge and skills. Conversation takes many forms; all are present within any social group.

- ◆ Casual conversation about an area of interest—home, sports, current events.
- ◆ Focused conversation describing, analyzing, and interpreting events.
- ◆ Dialogue, in which participants, suspending judgment, seek to understand the viewpoints of others and to explain their own ideas clearly.
- ◆ Discussion, in which the talk is directed toward making decisions and the process is clearly delineated.

Any group of people who work together will engage in social conversation, but a characteristic of extended learning is the preponderance of focused conversation, dialogue, and discussion.

We are talking here about more than sharing opinions. When a group engages in true communication with the goal of learning, participants take the responsibility for supporting their statements with evidence from observations of behavior or from their reading. They model the process for others. Members of the group ask the questions that demand evidence to support ideas and opinions.

The communication is substantive in that it sparks thinking. Participants leave the conversation thinking in a different way because people have helped one another expand and synthesize information. They seek to understand one another's viewpoint. They work to uncover underlying beliefs and assumptions about instructional approaches. According to Garmston and Wellman (1999), "much of the work . . . is done internally by each participant as he or she reflects and suspends" judgment (p. 55). The talk itself helps individuals expand and change their thinking.

Focused conversation, dialogue, and discussion are

settings within which no individual dominates. Each member of the group feels responsible for helping everyone participate; those who constantly violate the rights of others to talk are called on their behavior.

Data Are Used for Practical Purposes

In learning communities, people make informed decisions based on systematically collected and examined data. Teachers are always collecting assessment data in classrooms, of course, but we're talking here about something more formal: collecting and examining data in relation to their teaching and the school literacy curriculum in order to identify areas of concern before problems are exacerbated. Running records, for example, reveal an individual student's strengths and weaknesses in reading. If a pattern of weaknesses extends across a large number of students, however, *teaching* must be examined, including all aspects of the literacy curriculum, and the investigation guides further professional development and/or results in new instructional approaches.

Extending learning also involves using data for multiple purposes. The same information that teachers use to plan their daily instruction can be used by the faculty to evaluate the curriculum. For example, a group of kindergarten teachers examining the initial assessments of all incoming children may notice they have little knowledge of print. They don't need to go deeply into the reasons but are alerted to do something about it: gather resources to support reading at home,

Teachers look at achievement results.

extend time for reading aloud to children, use interactive writing intensively. In so doing, they change the world of the school for this group of children.

Teachers also consult others as they interpret this information: teachers from the previous grade or the following grade or specialists of various kinds. They may also read up on a particular topic, take courses, or become involved in action research.

Communication Takes Place Within and Beyond the Community

A learning community is an open community. When first learning any new approach or combination of approaches, teachers naturally focus on their own work in classrooms. Extending their learning, they then reach out beyond the classroom. Understanding precisely what their young readers and writers need, they are able to articulate these needs to others. They work across grade levels and with parents and community leaders to gain recognition or resources for the school or capitalize on community resources.

Contexts for Extended Learning

There are essentially five effective contexts for extending learning. Each incorporates some or all of the characteristics identified above. No one form or context will be right for every group—and each group directs its own learning. The key to success is collaboration: the overarching expectation is that everyone will be involved in something.

Study Groups

A study group (see Figure 13–2) can focus on anything teachers want to learn. Typically, members of the group agree to work together for a period of time exploring a particular concept or idea. A specific goal is necessary: the purpose of a study group is not simply to get together and talk about teaching, even though that might be valuable. A study group implies that new learning will take place. It may involve collecting data or connecting specific observations (live or videotaped) relative to the topic being studied.

The Role of the Leader It is usually a good idea for the group to designate one member as the leader. The leader:

Study Groups

In a study group, peers engage in focused study of a single concept or idea. Groups have clear goals, regular schedules for meetings, and specific expectations for members.

Study groups may be based on:
- Reading and discussing books or articles.
- Analyzing teaching.
- Examining student behavior and student work.
- A combination of reading, analyzing teaching, and examining student work.

Figure 13–2. *Study Groups*

- *Guides the group in setting learning goals.* A study group will be ineffective without specific goals. Members have to agree to read the material and to meet at specific times. If they decide to look at student work or a videotape of teaching, someone has to provide it. The leader finishes each session by clarifying what is needed for next time.
- *Makes practical applications.* The leader guides members of the group to take what they learn and apply it in their classroom. It's not enough just to have "nice talk."

Getting Started As a staff developer, you can help study groups get started. Some simple steps are outlined in Figure 13–3. The main thing you need to communicate is: to make a study group work there must be clear goals and expectations. If some members of the group don't participate fully, others will become frustrated. Serious members of a group want value in return for the time they spend. Study groups are voluntary, but there must be commitment (to attendance, outside reading, and application, for example).

Studying Teaching Study groups can analyze teaching via videotapes of their own work or tapes you provide. This activity presupposes they have already developed some analytic skills and are familiar with using scales like those described in Chapter 10. It is always best to have quite a few examples; you wouldn't want the conversation to center only on one person or one lesson. The greatest knowledge comes from applying analytic skills across many examples.

Getting Started with Study Groups

1. Invite teachers to form study groups as part of their ongoing professional development.

2. Bring interested teachers together and ask them to generate ideas.

3. Don't leap to decisions about topics right away because some participants may take on topics that don't really interest them.

4. Ask participants to get some information on the topics of most interest; discuss how topics are relevant for their work.

5. Form participants into groups that are not too small for discussion and not too large to function—between three and seven is a good number.

6. Ask groups to reach consensus on their topic and be prepared to state why it is important for the rest of the group.

7. Ask groups to identify what they expect the outcome of their study to be.

8. Ask them to designate a leader.

9. Ask them to create their schedule of meetings for the year, placing meetings close enough together so that they have good momentum (for example, every two or three weeks).

10. Assist groups in finding books, articles, and other sources of information on their topics.

11. Ask the leaders to come to a meeting or report progress periodically.

12. Hold a culminating meeting so that groups can share what they have learned.

Figure 13–3. *Getting Started with Study Groups*

Examining Children's Work A study group can analyze students' reading or writing behavior. For example, teachers who meet together to look at running records taken over time learn a great deal about the demands of texts on readers and build ideas about patterns of progress over time. This activity is highly productive when cross-grade-level teams work together. Gradually, they build an idea of how the reading process develops over the primary years. The same process could be used by intermediate teachers examining data from students' reading response journals, observing them in literature discussion, or sampling oral reading.

School writing samples can form the basis for shared expectations. What does first-grade writing "look like"? Participants can develop their own rubric for evaluating writing samples. These discussions can lead to a shared vision of what the standards should be. Don't just get one or two samples; gather enough so that teachers can truly form a picture of the expected behavior and competence within each grade level.

Action Research

In action research (see Figure 13–4), teachers systematically gather and analyze data. They pose a question, identify the information they need to address the question, and collect and analyze it.

In education, action research is conducted for the purpose of improving instruction in a specific environment. Collaborative action research involves teams of teachers working together on a project that will impact the entire school.

Action Research in Response to Problems Research can be directed toward a specific problem. For example, fourth-grade teachers who noticed that scores on a proficiency test were low

Action Research

Educational *action research* is careful, systematic investigation of some practical aspect of teaching and learning. It is conducted for the purpose of improving education in a specific environment. Collaborative action research involves teams of teachers working together on a project that will have impact on the school.

There are two kinds of action research:
1. Research to address a specific problem that arises.
2. Research directed toward assessing the impact of the program.

Figure 13–4. *Action Research*

decided to find out what kinds of items were especially challenging. They discovered that test items requiring readers to take different perspectives were difficult for students. Therefore, they designed a study to discover under what circumstances students *could* take different perspectives and when they found it difficult to do. They systematically collected data by observing students as they studied texts requiring them to take different perspectives and by systematically analyzing reading response journals. They examined a large-enough sample of representative work to be confident about their results.

Action Research to Assess Program Impact

Research can be directed toward assessing the impact of the general curriculum. For example, through research, the above teachers discovered that their students found historical fiction particularly challenging. They communicated their findings to the school faculty and suggested that adjustments be made to the curriculum.

First-, second-, and third-grade teachers joined the collaborative action research team. The team looked at the literacy framework and identified areas where taking different perspectives occurs naturally: reading aloud, accompanied by discussion; literature discussion groups; guided reading; and independent reading and writing. During an exciting discussion, they realized that emphasizing perspective could make reading and writing more interesting to students. As teachers they could build students' skills over the years instead of "teaching" perspective only at one point in the curriculum.

Each grade-level group selected texts to read aloud and to use in connection with writing minilessons. They met monthly to share the progress of their instruction, and gathered data again at the end of the year. Late in the spring, they again examined the proficiency test results and found a definite improvement. They continued to focus instruction on perspective and checked students' work over the next three years; achievement steadily improved.

The Steps in Action Research Figure 13–5 lists the steps within each kind of action research. Action research in education can be very exciting. At every step, teachers are bringing their problem-solving skills to bear. For greatest impact, action research should be collaborative and continuous. The topic can be anything the group decides to focus on. While engaged in this

---

Steps in Action Research

Action Research to Address a Problem

1. You are faced with a problem.
2. You identify existing data that will provide information related to the problem.
3. You identify additional information that is needed.
4. You ensure that the data you plan to collect will answer the question.
5. You devise a way to get the data you need.
6. You collect data in a systematic way.
7. You look at all the data and organize them to address your problem.
8. You come up with tentative hypotheses as to what the data mean.
9. You collect more data if needed.
10. You make decisions about steps to solve the problem.

Action Research to Assess Impact of Instruction

1. You identify an approach that you have questions about or that you want to try as something new.
2. You identify what you want to happen as a result of the instruction.
3. You determine the kind of data that will serve as evidence of learning—for you and for others.
4. You design a way to get the data.
5. You collect data in a systematic way over a sufficient period of time to detect impact.
6. You analyze the data at intervals so that you can look for patterns.
7. You attach actual case examples to the patterns and trends you detect.
8. You set times when you may adjust instruction.
9. You examine and interpret data.
10. You make decisions based on the results and put plans into action.

Figure 13–5. *Steps in Action Research*

research, teachers get good information with which to solve their problems. They also learn to:

♦ Be analytical and strategic in how they approach problems and issues.
♦ Articulate their thinking and base it on real data.
♦ Present their information clearly to people outside their study group.
♦ Work collaboratively with colleagues.
♦ Design and divide work efforts so that everything contributes to the whole and nothing is wasted.
♦ Play diversified roles in the collaborative process.
♦ Focus their energy where it will pay off.
♦ Work within a research paradigm.
♦ Develop analytic skills and efficient ways of working that can be built into their daily teaching.

Peer Coaching

When the learning community is established and teachers are comfortable participating in the analytic cycle, they are able to help one another. The support spreads out: staff developers do not have to provide all the learning. Through experiences with the staff developer, teachers have learned ways of interacting around classroom practice. Peer coaching (see Figure 13–6) is a rich context in which two or more participants can learn a great deal. Peer coaching can focus on any topic or aspect of teaching and could look like any example in this book (see the interaction of Melissa and Caroline in Chapter 12, for example).

In peer coaching, teachers observe and analyze one another's teaching and recommend

---

Peer Coaching

In peer coaching, two teachers or a small group of teachers observe and provide assistance to one another. They may explore any aspect of teaching and learning.

There are two kinds of peer coaching:
1. A more experienced teacher assists a beginning teacher.
2. Colleagues work together to assist one another.

Figure 13–6. *Peer Coaching*

---

adjustments. Joyce and Showers (1995), who are credited with advancing the concept of coaching, caution that *coaching is not evaluation*. Whether focused on implementing new approaches or improving existing approaches, coaching is a learning situation in which people help one another achieve common goals.

A peer is someone of equal standing or ability. That definition is appropriate here: teachers are working together as colleagues who value one another and offer support. One is not the "authority" or the "evaluator" but may have more experience.

Experienced Teachers Helping Novices In one type of coaching, experienced teachers help novices. Novices need a great deal more attention and help than the staff development office or even an on-site staff developer can give. Experienced teachers can provide some of this help, giving the staff developer more time to analyze higher levels of teaching. The learning community is making the most of its resources.

As teachers become expert in an area or technique, they are able to analyze the process in depth and reflect on the steps of their own learning. Well along in the cycle of learning themselves, they can provide clear demonstrations and nonjudgmental support for novices.

Peer coaching like this involves much more than observing and offering suggestions. Expert teachers can offer a wide range of help to novice teachers—in planning, designing instructional activities, organizing a rich learning environment, evaluating one's own instruction, preparing student records, analyzing students' reading and writing behavior, selecting texts for the classroom collection, and so on. The novice teacher can observe or work alongside the more experienced teacher and be observed by the more experienced teacher.

Colleagues Working Together

Teachers who are well along in developing particular instructional techniques can provide valuable assistance to one another. Peer coaching introduces companionship into the act of teaching, which is especially helpful when one is trying new approaches.

Colleagues can plan lessons together, decide on what to look for, and offer one another an "outside eye." They become mirrors for one another, enabling one another to see their work with greater clarity. Peer coaches are not "assigned," although participants in a study group might together agree that they are going to try it out in order to learn about it.

Typically, peers invite one another to be coaches. It can be as simple as one teacher asking another to come in and observe a book introduction and then the two teachers discussing the lesson over lunch. They inquire into the learning and teaching that went on. Together, they reflect on their instructional decisions. They work to enhance each other's professional skills.

Getting Started with Peer Coaching Even though teachers will have been coached by you as a staff developer and be familiar with the process, they will still need help the first few times they provide peer coaching. It is important for them to understand that peer coaching is not evaluation, nor is it for the sole purpose of giving feedback and suggestions. The major value lies in talking about and solving problems related to teaching and learning.

The following steps will help a group of teachers learn how to engage in productive peer coaching:

1. Identify a group of teachers who are successful in analyzing and reflecting on their practice.
2. Invite them to learn about peer coaching and call an initial meeting.

3. Begin with a brief description of peer coaching; clarify how it's different from the coaching they have been receiving from you.
4. Ask them to discuss the benefits of coaching and generate a list of how peer coaching can help them as individuals as well as improve the work of the team.
5. Ask them to select topics or areas they want to investigate and to select partners.
6. Provide a simple structure to help them get started (see Figure 13–7). The structure will help them focus on student behavior and analysis rather than rush to offer judgments and/or feedback.
7. Explain the structure and how it will help them. They'll be following the process step by step in order to learn about it. Any sense of "threat" in the situation will be neutralized because the focus will be on student learning and dialogue.
8. Ask them to return to the group to share their experiences.
9. Ask them to share their statements of learning and/or action plans.
10. Get the group to talk about future ways they can use peer coaching.

Above all, you want these first experiences to be positive. These steps are primarily intended for experienced colleagues coaching their equally experienced peers; you would not ask a novice

---

Structure for Beginning Peer Conferences

1. One teacher invites another to work with her in a peer coaching session.
2. The inviting teacher identifies an area for focus.
3. They decide the context for the observation—small group, whole group, individual.
4. They decide the time and length of the observation, thinking what would be most informative.
5. Together, they decide what will be important to examine—student work, interactions, student behavior.
6. The peer coach observes the lesson, focusing on the areas discussed.
7. After the lesson, the teachers look at the information together, focusing on student behavior and evidence of learning.
8. The teachers work to interpret student behavior and discuss instruction in the light of it.
9. They conclude the session by stating what they have learned and writing one or two simple statements about it (this may be an action plan).
10. They make decisions for another coaching session.

Figure 13–7. *Structure for Beginning Peer Coaching*

teacher to "coach" a very experienced teacher nor want very inexperienced people giving each other advice. But peer coaching is highly rewarding to experienced teachers and will have the additional benefit of building their skill in working with novice teachers.

Special Initiatives

Occasionally, a school staff may decide or be askcd to cmbark on a special initiative that by its very nature becomes the focus for ongoing professional development (see Figure 13–8). Special initiatives are "bigger" than the specific instructional techniques discussed in this book, but they have implications for staff development.

Special initiatives may be the result of policy changes (for example, the inclusion of special needs children in regular classrooms), funding changes, or the sudden enrollment of many students from a population new to the school (for example, students for whom English is a second language). Initiatives are not always related to outside demands, however. They may be the result of an invitation to become a professional development setting for university students or to participate in professional development with other schools in the area. Initiatives may also be the result of a school staff's decision to implement a new program or engage in some intensive, whole-school effort to achieve a common goal.

Special initiatives usually require going outside the school for help—from the literature or from experts. They may require inviting other teachers into the school or visiting these other teachers in their own classroom. Special initiatives always require professional development to achieve their goals. If you have established a learning community, then teachers will be in charge of their own learning. They will be able to analyze the actions needed to meet the new challenge and get the help they need. They will extend their own learning by hiring consultants purposefully and selectively to help them acquire the skills they need.

Continuing Professional Development[1]

As part of your professional development system, bring teachers together for ongoing meetings designed to enhance their learning. Planning these meetings is a challenge.

Your professional development plan must provide for more than initial training or even ongoing training. Then too, if you are developing a broad-based, comprehensive approach to literacy, the initial course may be spread over as much as two years. Your approach to ongoing professional development must be based on what teachers know and need to learn. Here are some suggestions for designing professional development for teachers who have participated in an initial course.

Structure Be sure you communicate the expectation that training and professional development are ongoing and expected in the professional learning community (see Chapter 1). Here are some suggestions for clear communication:

◆ At the end of the year, provide a written plan for next year's professional development.

◆ Outline the content based on the data you've gathered during the year (see below). Set topics even though you will of course be flexible as the year unfolds.

◆ Set meeting times and places and provide a yearlong calendar for teachers so they can adjust their schedules before the school year even starts.

Special Initiatives

A special initiative is a whole-school project that requires collaboration across grade levels and between administration and teachers. The initiative focuses on a single problem or issue that affects everyone.

Special initiatives come from:

◆ Collaborative partnerships with other educational agencies (universities, for example).
◆ The adoption of new materials or programs from outside the school.
◆ Forces within the school attempting to achieve new goals.
◆ Political forces that demand change.
◆ Policy changes at local, state, or district.

All special initiatives require ongoing professional development if they are to be successful.

Figure 13–8. *Special Initiatives*

◆ Set some goals for the year that you can come back to time and again during the year, assessing as you go and at the end for the year (*as you plan for the next year*).

Content Initial training in any approach will focus on procedures (see Chapter 6). As we have noted, it is necessary to have some preliminary long-term information even when you begin. But continuing professional development requires a very strong base of information to help you plan your ongoing content:

◆ Information on the perspectives of teacher participants.
◆ Your own analysis of teachers' progress.
◆ Assessment data.
◆ Information on contextual factors, such as district or state mandates, that reveal the need for new learning.

Teachers' Perspectives Ask teachers to tell you what would be important for them to learn more about next year. This information will help you craft sessions that will be important to these teachers at this time. Invite them to talk with one another about what they think they know and do well and what they need to know and do.

◆ Let them begin with self-assessment. You may discover gaps you—and they—weren't aware of. You may also discover that topics need to be differentiated by grade level, interest, or years of experience.
◆ Ask grade levels to identify their strengths and needs as a grade level.
◆ Ask the principal for her or his input.
◆ Consider whether there might be discrepancies between what teachers feel they are doing well and what actually is going on.

Staff Developer's Analysis Another important source of information is your own knowledge of these teachers, based on the data you have gathered all year. Get out your coaching records and read them through from the beginning to end.

◆ What did the coaching sessions look like?
◆ What agendas were raised?
◆ What specific observations did you note during your visits?
◆ Where did you focus your attention?
◆ Did teaching shift as a result of coaching? How?

Evaluating progress in writing.

◆ Were the goals that you set with teachers met?
◆ How did those goals play out?
◆ What does the evidence show they know and do well?
◆ What does the evidence show they need to know next?

Initial training of necessity hits only the surface. Now you need to go back and get the depth you need. Looking at your notes and reflections will help you know where these teachers are as a basis for ongoing training and provide a broader perspective.

Assessment Data If you are working in a single school, achievement can be the subject of one or two sessions and can help you shape your future sessions. You can use any kind of school assessment to inform planning—achievement tests, teacher-made tests, and systematically collected assessment data. Think about:

◆ Where are our students in their achievement?
◆ What do we need to work on in our

instructional program? (Fluency? The lowest achievers?)

- How are the results interrelated? (Are children overrelying on "hearing sounds in words" and using visual strategies? How should word study instruction shift in relation to interactive writing?)

District/State Curriculum Mandates Often district goals or state mandates become the subject of professional development sessions. For example, if your state has a writing assessment, you could examine:

- How writing instruction across the framework can achieve higher results.
- How school-level writing assessments can provide information about how children will do on the state tests or assessments.
- How school writing standards will be tailored to meet the rising achievement standards.
- How these writing standards and requirements "fit" with what you are already doing and what you plan to do.

Literacy coach and teacher choosing a book.

Differentiated Study

Learning requires being actively involved, not simply listening to a lecture. This active involvement is even more important in the ongoing professional development of teachers. Planning professional development is not simply a matter of gathering "good ideas." Planning rests on what you want teachers to learn or where they need to go in their development.

You may want to use different working arrangements with different members of your group, particularly if you are working with a large group of teachers who have already received a year or two of initial training. Maybe the kindergarten teachers need to focus on using interactive writing more effectively. Perhaps the second-grade teachers want to focus on implementing guided reading. You could separate these groups for the first half of the year, having them meet at different times in separate study groups. After three or four sessions, bring them back together for a session focusing on an aspect of learning that connects both areas. You will want to be careful to maintain a cohesive school

community, so it's unwise to make everything separate all the time.

Have teachers share expectations for what they expect students to be able to do in reading when they enter a grade level. The open discussion will provide valuable information and will also prompt intensive discussion. Networking across grade levels helps teachers:

- Plan better.
- Become more strategic in what they teach.
- Organize their efforts across grade levels in ways that will result in more cohesive, articulated instruction and better results.

The primary staff, for example, might want to take an in-depth look at writing. You might decide to have teachers from all grade levels examine the changes that occur during each grade level or the different ways there are to help children write. This way the entire group will achieve a "big picture" of writing development.

Another approach is to bring cross-grade-level teams together around a single concept. For example, the intermediate teachers in one school agreed to spend a year studying "voice" in writing. They used their class meetings to read about and study how a writer's voice is achieved and expressed: they read and analyzed children's literature; they wrote themselves in order to explore how they developed their own voice as a writer; they read fiction and nonfiction. They then designed student experiences appropriate to each grade level, agreeing among themselves on the degree of consistency necessary, and shared these curriculums across grade levels.

Combining Contextual Structures for Extended Learning

Ongoing professional development is more effective when there is variety and a number of contexts are connected. An ongoing "course," for example, may include only a few whole-group meetings. The rest of the time is spent in study groups, action research groups, and peer coaching.

This variety, in connection with learning partnerships among teachers, creates a new school culture. People work in different ways but are always constructing meaning toward a common purpose, whether working in their own classroom, across grade levels, or as a whole school. By participating in varied learning experiences, they learn more about how change occurs. They learn leadership. They are less vulnerable to the winds of change and are able to consider and commit to the hard, long-term efforts that result in real change.

Suggestions for Extending Your Skills as a Staff Developer

1. Select one of these three alternatives:
   ◆ Observe a study group for two or three sessions. The group may focus on any aspect of teaching and learning and may involve examining the literature, analyzing teaching, observing student behavior, or all three.
   ◆ Observe an action research group that is involved either in addressing a problem or assessing the impact of the program. Observe the group for two or

three sessions in any phase of their process.
   ◆ Observe a school staff involved in a special initiative. Observe two or three meetings in any phase of their process.
2. As you observe the group you chose, think about:
   ◆ How are members of the group using their existing knowledge?
   ◆ What is this experience probably contributing to the knowledge of individual group members?
   ◆ What role is the leader playing in the group?
   ◆ Are all members getting an opportunity to participate?
   ◆ What organizational structures support the work of the group? Look for schedules, goals, assignment of roles and responsibilities.
   ◆ How do members of the group show that they value one another's contributions?
   ◆ Is this a successful group? How can you tell?
   ◆ Is anything going wrong? How can you tell?
   ◆ Are members of the group working to solve real problems? Problems important to them? Problems that will make a difference for students? Why or why not?
3. After your observation, reflect on the work of the group:
   ◆ What was working well? What can you learn from this group about your own work in supporting extended learning for teachers?
   ◆ What would you change about the way the group is working?
   ◆ What would help these teachers work better together?
   ◆ What would help them achieve their goals?
4. If possible, discuss your experience with a staff development colleague.

Endnote
[1]We are indebted to our colleagues Diane Powell and Susan Hundley, of Lesley University, for much of the material in this section.

Chapter 14

The Challenge of Professional Development

In education or any field, lasting fundamental change grows out of, and is sustained by, a compelling vision.
—KEN WILSON AND BEN DAVISS
REDESIGNING EDUCATION (26)

Educational reform is at the forefront of the national agenda—and rightly so, because higher levels of skill will be expected of today's students than of any generation in our history. Discussions of schooling center on literacy: we can only guess at the demands for a literate citizenry inherent in the new millennium. In all of these discussions, the focus comes around to teaching and learning. Teaching must be more effective so that students learn more. Some common approaches to improving teaching are:

◆ Setting high standards.
◆ Taking over schools based on test scores.
◆ Awarding extra pay to teachers/administrators when students perform well.
◆ Adopting packaged "comprehensive" programs.
◆ Introducing competition in the form of charter schools and/or vouchers.

Two "answers" related to student learning are mandatory retention and summer school. These solutions do not necessarily require professional development. Inevitably, however, the conversation comes back to teaching and the training of teachers. Why? Because teaching is fundamental to good education; it makes a difference.

Typically, professional development takes the form of training teachers to use instructional techniques, often in connection with specific (or "canned") programs. The training is usually short term and often of little interest to the teachers who receive it; it may not even be directly related to their classroom work. Typically, training consists of a presentation or two followed by some discussion. Even in so-called long-term efforts, in which school districts and states may invest a great deal of money, it is rare for teachers to attend more than ten sessions. And even these efforts tend to be piecemeal, not tied together in a coherent way nor integral to teachers' daily work with students. Teachers are "run through" a series of sessions that then stop abruptly, making little difference. They are left on their own to make what they can of the ideas on which the training is based. There is a difference between the surface learning that results from such short-term training plans and the deep learning that leads to sustained changes in behavior that a training design can provide.

Short-term efforts just aren't good enough. They represent the kind of search for a magic bullet that, in the long run, hampers educational reform. True change, with long-term positive outcomes, results when a number of different variables are addressed in a plan that is *designed*. In this book, we advocate a comprehensive approach that embeds professional development in the life of the school and within larger, long-term efforts. Our definition of "design" is a system of interconnected components that work together to accomplish a goal or purpose. The better individual components "work" and the better they work *together,* the more effective and efficient the system will be. Design offers a dramatic contrast to one-shot panaceas.

Professional development must be ongoing; the more systematically it is applied, the more likely success will be. Good teacher training programs are most effective when they are part of a larger design for ongoing improvement. Design is just as important for education as it is for airplanes or automobiles. Design makes it work.

Design refers to the way features of any human endeavor are constructed and coordinated to work together. Design includes components such as tools (machinery, texts, etc.); time; human resources; functions of staff and stakeholders; communication and education; and the concepts, philosophies, and attitudes of staff and stakeholders. A good design equals success; a bad design equals failure. As educators, we are not accustomed to thinking about design in this way.

Learning is a constructive process that takes place over time, constantly building on what is known. Learning is natural, integral, and essential to the work of teachers and the success of students. Many times teachers attend conferences and institutes and gain important knowledge; but more often, they learn little and there is no change in their work (although they may feel confirmation in what they are already doing). That shouldn't be surprising: it's very difficult, if not impossible, for an outside consultant to help teachers construct pedagogical knowledge in a one-time large-group session.

The professional development system we have described in this book is deeply rooted in the realities of teachers' ongoing work. It recognizes that teaching is not just a collection of skills but high-level intellectual work (Lieberman and Miller 1999). Implementing a professional development system is much more difficult than scheduling and providing a day or even a week of inservice for teachers. It requires providing ongoing, high-quality, varied support for teachers in their learning.

At the same time, implementing a professional development system requires paying attention to a range of contextual factors. These implementation factors are part of the design; they support the professional development system and make it work. Implementation, in fact, is the key to success, because it must work against the barriers to and meet the challenges of school change.

What Works?

There is no precise blueprint for designing a professional development system that works. The design must be intimately related to the goals, vision, and needs of individuals, groups, and organizations. People "own" such a design because it includes them and gives them a chance to grow, change, and contribute. You and your colleagues can, however, learn about the features of designs that work; there are definite, recognizable structures in which to encase the individual and group problem solving and decision making unique to your situation.

In *Teachers Transforming Their World and Their Work*, Lieberman and Miller (1999) describe teachers as the center of all efforts to improve schooling. Schools, they say, must be redesigned and teachers must be part of the process. They present three converging constructs that are related to "what works" in educational change. We have added a fourth construct, as shown in Figure 14–1. (A *construct* is a theory that integrates diverse ideas. A professional development design must integrate ideas that *seemingly compete*.)

Combine Content and Process

In designing professional development, you are always thinking about *content*. A number of chapters in this book define and describe a broad range of content areas related to implementing the language/literacy framework: guided reading, writing assessment, and writing workshop, to name a few. Your professional development system must offer a vision of what is to be accomplished as it pertains to both teachers and their students:

◆ What will it look like?
◆ What student behavior are we looking for as evidence of learning?

What works in designing professional development?[1]

Combine content and process.
Give attention to the content to be learned but also institute processes to build commitment and community.

Attend to the needs of both teachers and students.
Ensure student success but also give teachers the support they need to achieve their new goals.

Balance action and reflection.
Get right into action but also take a reflective stance.

Combine strong overall design with individual ownership.
Establish structures that support success and long-term development but also provide for individual growth, reward, and ownership.

[1]The first three factors are drawn from the work of Ann Lieberman and Lynne Miller, *Teachers Transforming Their World and Their Work*, Teachers College Press, New York, 1999.

Figure 14–1. *What Works?*

◆ What defines good reading or writing at each point in a student's learning?
◆ What do good classrooms look like?
◆ What do teachers do that is effective in teaching reading and writing?

Answering these questions means knowing how to observe, interact with students in powerful ways, and use instructional procedures effectively. Teachers are always hungry for more content.

At the same time, professional development design must accommodate *process*. Process refers to the ways people engage in learning so that they build commitment and ownership, form a community with shared meanings. Process provides for continuous learning about content, even after initial training is completed. Questions here include:

◆ What is the teacher's role as a learner?
◆ How do teachers take charge of their own learning?
◆ How do teachers support one another in their decision making?
◆ How does the group work together to build community and ownership?
◆ How do teachers build shared responsibility?

The processes you employ while teachers are learning content make it possible for them to go beyond that particular content. As they learn about themselves and others, they are learning "how to learn" as teachers. They create cognitive structures that enable them to learn from their teaching. Conversation within the learning group makes it happen.

Content without process is not dynamic; learners are not engaged, and they do not learn how to support one another. But process without content is empty; learning becomes a group exercise, and participants walk away hungry for specific information. That is why this book includes such detailed examples of teachers, staff developers, and coaches focusing on specific contexts for literacy learning. They need something to talk about, and they need challenges, not just shared opinions.

Attend to the Needs of Both Teachers and Students

The goal of professional development is student success. We all want to see tangible results of our teaching. Student learning is the primary force, always at the fore. A professional development system will incorporate rigorous application of instructional approaches, ways of looking for evidence of student learning, and close observation and monitoring of behavior. Every literacy lesson is directed toward maximum student learning, and the outcome must be measured systematically.

At the same time, the professional development system must attend to the learning and personal needs of teachers. Ideally, the design includes in-classroom support and coaching. The design also includes teachers' own perspectives and agendas. The basics are provided in terms of materials and support in organizing them. Time is provided for teachers to learn. The expectation is that there will be continuous engagement over time rather than a quick fix.

When all attention is focused on student learning with no attention given to supporting teachers, the system will not work. On the other hand, you can also design systems that support teachers but make no difference for students. We have all attended inservice sessions that make us "feel good" or entertain us but offer little substance, direction, or challenge.

Balance Action and Reflection

Learning is active; the only real way to establish a new approach is to try it for yourself. It is important that teachers actively engage in whatever procedures they are learning. A professional development system will include ways of engaging teachers as learners so that their interest is aroused and they begin to see how procedures work with their own students.

At the same time, it is important for learners to reflect on, analyze, and deepen their learning. In this way, they learn more about how to learn. Without reflection and analysis, a specific procedure becomes a mechanical action, applied the same way time and again. Instruction is not powerful because teachers do not understand the dynamic decision-making role they play in adjusting teaching to students; they lose interest.

Combine Strong Overall Design with Individual Ownership

A design has structure; that's what makes it work. A professional development system will have some built-in features that are essential: continuing over time, providing a balance between action

and reflection, and coaching, for example. You need to require long-term commitment and set schedules. Only you can decide what kind of structure is essential, but a system simply will not work if it changes all the time and has no expectations or organizational underpinnings.

At the same time, a good professional development system takes into account the individuals it serves and the context in which it is implemented. The design retains the essential features but adjusts others to fit the context. The people within the particular context have an important role in making decisions and solving problems.

In this book we mostly describe internal designs for ongoing professional development within schools and districts. We do not mean to imply that all designs must be internal; rather, a combination of external and internal programs often works well.

We recognize that well-designed and researched external providers of professional development can also offer a productive option. Teachers should be free to check out an external program and then choose whether to participate; often, an individual or team who participates in an external program develops expertise and enthusiasm that act as a catalyst for the entire staff's ongoing development. Well-established programs, such as Reading Recovery, for example, provide a proven change process that can overcome resistance to change because it shows results. Often, individual schools and/or districts have difficulty launching a program with the complexity and quality of Reading Recovery, but they can use it as part of their overall design.

Every individual brings different meaning to an experience. As teachers engage in the analytic process, they build one understanding upon another and each is unique. They value others' perspectives; as they interact, their own views are challenged and expanded. Individuals have the opportunity to have a role in the learning of others.

A good design has built-in mechanisms that ensure that the people involved become *invested*. They experience the satisfactions and personal rewards of learning. They achieve ownership of the design not because they can change it at will but because they have been brought together during the process of creating it.

Imposing structure without individual investment results in lack of commitment, even sabotage. People feel powerless. You are simply handing down edicts. Working for individual investment without structure, however, means you probably won't get much accomplished.

———————— ♦ ————————

Integrating these four constructs is a challenging balancing act, but unless you manage it, your professional development program will not achieve its goal:

> It is crucial to remember that the ultimate goal of change is to make schooling better for all children. Procedures are essential, but they are empty when they do not support basic principles and deeply held values about learning and teaching. Principles are important, but they lose their value when they do not have procedures to support them. The building blocks are not ends in themselves but a means to a richer and more engaging education for the young and a richer and more rewarding working and learning environment for the adults as well. (Lieberman and Miller 1999, p. 6)

The Challenge of Change

Learning means change, and the goal of professional development must be change; otherwise, why do it? While change can be exciting, it is also threatening and sometimes draining. Not every person will be enthusiastic about embarking on a new venture.

We have conducted interviews with a large number of stakeholders in educational environments—teachers, administrators, parents, school board members—and have identified ten barriers to school change (see Figure 14–2). These same factors appear in the research literature on educational change (Fullan and Hargraves 1991; Wilson and Daviss 1994; Goodlad 1984).

Unstable Environments
Schools and school districts are in constant upheaval. In one school we know, the following changes took place within one year:

◆ Thirty percent of the staff were new teachers.
◆ A specialist teacher resigned and no replacement was available.

Barriers to Change

1. *Unstable environments:* Changing administration, transient teachers, student mobility

2. *No clear vision:* Competing agendas among staff, administration.

3. *Isolationism:* Tradition of working individually and alone rather than as professional colleagues.

4. *Rigid organizational patterns:* Rules, regulations, traditions, and ways to manage time that are hard to change.

5. *Balkanized domains:* Separation of departments, grade levels, and other groups that compete.

6. *Fear of leading:* Fear of jealousy, negative attention for stepping out front.

7. *Paralyzing sameness:* A feeling of inertia, resulting in reluctance to expend extra energy that change requires.

8. *Fear of failure:* Lack of confidence that the change will "work" or that individuals can accomplish the goals.

9. *Oppressive power relationships:* Feelings of powerlessness because changes are imposed; lack of ownership.

10. *Desire for the quick fix:* Going too fast without time to reflect, build ownership, and improve the program.

Figure 14–2. *Barriers to Change*

◆ Student enrollment increased by 15 percent.
◆ The principal resigned midyear and was replaced by a new administrator whose educational philosophies were radically different from those of the teachers in the school.
◆ The book orders were insufficient and additionally took many months to fill.
◆ A staff developer was returned to the classroom full time, disrupting the professional development program.
◆ There were competing professional development programs, requiring "double time" from the staff.
◆ Substitutes were often unavailable, and students were regularly "farmed out" to other classrooms.

In a situation like this, professional development efforts will almost certainly fail.

School districts, too, are very unstable. It's been said that the average tenure for a superintendent is three years, and we believe it! Central office personnel are always changing; the "new guys" have new goals and new policies. Often they mandate new approaches and new materials. Many teachers have learned simply to wait out the administration—something new is always just around the bend.

Even if the administration is fairly stable, change efforts often falter because they are superficially attempted or not supported. There seems to be an insatiable desire to adopt one quick fix after another. Or the change is totally dependent on the charisma and skills of one individual who then leaves for another position.

No Clear Vision

Often there are competing philosophies and/or agendas. Few fields of endeavor are more divided than literacy education. Alternate views of how to teach children to read and write are often polar opposites. In recent years, there has been a movement toward comprehensive literacy frameworks such as the one described in this book; however, there are still many differences. Some are real differences; others have to do with superficial characteristics of instruction but are nevertheless important to individuals.

Creating common vision requires time and patience. People need to work together, with a focus on student learning. Divisiveness among staff can lead to an incoherent and inconsistent approach to curriculum. Barriers can be created over unimportant details. Holding a common vision can mobilize a group and bring people together.

Isolationism

Schools are full of people, yet they have been described as lonely places (Knoblock and Goldstein 1971; Sarason 1982). The tradition of closing your door and working alone with your students is strong in the elementary school. Short-term professional development is insufficient to open the classroom doors. Even long-term professional development will be ineffective if the tradition of isolationism cannot be overcome.

Rigid Organizational Patterns

Scheduling and using time are the result of tradition in many schools. Most organizational patterns are instituted for convenience rather than because they promote student learning. Consider:

◆ The traditional school calendar, which is based on letting children work on the farm during the summer. (Year-round school with "spaced" holidays would be more conducive to learning).

◆ Bells that ring regularly, disrupting learning (a holdover from the days when people did not have watches?).

◆ The assumption that the office may interrupt instruction at any time via the intercom or in some other way. (Every day this demonstrates that the time of office workers and outside personnel is more important than teaching and learning.)

◆ Scheduling special subjects (music and art, for example) without regard to blocks of time needed for reading. (This demonstrates a lack of balance in priorities.)

◆ Requiring all students to attend assemblies even when they have no educational value for some age groups.

◆ Discouraging before- and after-school programs and conferences because of building rules and regulations.

◆ Requiring particular topics and books at certain grade levels even when students cannot understand them or read them, thus wasting time that could be spent on intensive instruction that would move students forward in their ability to read.

◆ Locking buildings so that teachers are unable to meet with one another or work in their classroom after the students leave.

Some of the traditional organizational patterns are so ingrained that people don't even notice them or think they *can* be changed.

Balkanized Domains

The Balkans were famous for division and civil war. That's not unlike some schools. Think of all the ways people in schools are separated:

◆ Primary and intermediate teachers.
◆ All grade levels
◆ Specialist teachers and classroom teachers.
◆ Administrators and teachers.

- New teachers and experienced teachers.
- Teachers who hold different philosophies and opinions.

The notion that different teachers working at different grade levels are valued differently is revealed in this comment from a kindergarten teacher: "I was always made to feel like all I did was baby-sit the kids, I didn't really 'teach' anything. The real teaching was done in first grade. My friends in primary grades said that they were always treated differently from the immediate grade teachers who worked with the older students."

Fear of Leading

In the majority of schools, there is a hierarchical structure for managing and conducting business or for responding to mandates or constraints imposed by central administration. In and of itself, hierarchical organization is not a problem. It becomes one when hierarchical structures create differences in status and authority that squelch teachers' willingness to lead. Teachers do not want to design something for others or tell others what to do, because they fear they will do or say something wrong and suffer the consequences.

A fourth-grade teacher who was put in charge of designing an integrated literacy program for the intermediate grades got sick to her stomach every time she convened the curriculum committee. Several teachers resisted her attempts to organize their work on the new curriculum; and one teacher who had always been the leader was jealous because she had not been picked to organize and direct the curriculum committee. The work of the committee went nowhere because of hurt feelings and competing agendas.

Paralyzing Sameness

Change takes more energy and time than does staying the same. People involved in change must make extra efforts. Excitement carries many of us along so that we hardly notice we are working harder. The satisfaction is greater, but we do need to recognize the work involved. A staff developer who was completely committed to her work said: "The biggest obstacle is time management, dividing my time between classroom obligations, training class obligations and observations, and stocking and managing the literacy center."

The situation worsens when people are not committed to change, when it's someone else's idea. Then, the energy just may not be there. It's easier to do the same things you've always done:

- The lesson plans change only slightly from year to year.
- The same purchased wall decorations go up holiday after holiday.
- The books the students read are the same, so you do not have to read new ones.

Sitting in her classroom after school one day, a teacher said: "I've been teaching first grade in this same room for twenty-five years. I have nine boys who are repeaters. I no longer feel I'm making a difference." That statement is the essence of burnout. This paralyzing sameness drags people down.

Fear of Failure

Change is also risky; you might fail. Somehow, if you keep on doing the *same* thing, you are less likely to be evaluated by your peers or by the administration. A school may have low achievement but find dozens of reasons for it. When you strike out to do something new, suddenly you may become quite visible. Many teachers are not accustomed to risky situations, especially as their work is usually unobserved by other adults. Opening your classroom to analysis means that you might be criticized; leading a committee to do something new means you suddenly enter the spotlight and run the risk of failure.

Oppressive Power Relationships

Most educational change is simply handed down from on high. Sometimes entire programs, with materials and scripts, are delivered to the school and people are told to change. They are trained to use the new materials under the guise of professional development. Often, teachers feel helpless; they feel manipulated instead of respected as professionals.

Central and school administrations *do* play a dynamic role in the change process. But there must also be ownership at the school level: "High expectations yield high results with kids and staff alike," as one principal said. These expectations work in combination with collegiality, support, and respect.

Desire for the Quick Fix

Perhaps the greatest barrier to real improvement is the insatiable desire for the quick fix. Problems in education *seem* easy to fix. The search for quick solutions is fueled by complaints from policymakers and the public. Problems are exacerbated by the unstable environment; administrators want to make their mark and move up or on. Everyone wants something that will work dramatically and *instantly*. More and more, though, educators are realizing that real school improvement takes place steadily over time.

A principal asked to give advice to other principals commented: "Our best advice would be to go slow. We built our program over five or six years. Be sure to have positive leaders in the staff on board, have a good problem-solving process, build in the financial and administrative support in the beginning, be sure to give attention to parental concerns, and be patient but persistent."

———— ◆ ————

Not all ten of these conditions will exist in any one school or district, but these barriers are pervasive. Thus, it is important to recognize them and direct your efforts so that you have a good chance of overcoming them. A good design incorporates systems for breaking down and preventing the development of barriers. We agree with Allington and Walmsley (1995, p. 12) that:

◆ Change comes from within, not afar.
◆ Change will not necessarily cost more money.
◆ There are no quick fixes.
◆ There is no one best way.

Why Teachers Resist Change

Teachers make learning happen day after day in their classrooms. It is often said that teachers resist change; we believe that under certain circumstances everyone resists change. The most powerful source of resistance to change is *how change has taken place in the past*. Just about every teacher has some history with change, most of it bad.

When we began implementing Reading Recovery over sixteen years ago, we were puzzled why some very good educators, many of whom we had seen as leaders, refused to participate. After four or five years, these same people

came enthusiastically aboard. Here's what many of them said: "Every project we do here lasts only three years. I was waiting to see if it would still be around, because I'm tired of starting new things and then told to drop them."

When change is haphazardly applied or forced by a more powerful group on a less powerful one, it is natural to question and resist. When people do not have any stake in the change effort's success, it will surely dissipate. Ownership is essential, but you won't make it happen by fiat (Hargreaves 1994). If no one owns the vision, nothing will happen. If only a few own the vision, you will create warring camps. In *Change Forces*, M. G. Fullan (1993) describes "what gives change a bad name." In Figure 14–3, we list these conditions along with a few others we have encountered in our work in schools.

Stress and Burnout

There is much talk about teacher burnout, and many teachers do feel they are under stress. Attempts to relieve stress include counseling, reassignments, and the like, and these measures may be needed for individuals. But a staff developer's job is to create a learning environment that decreases bad stress and provides creative stress.

Stress and burnout are indicated by statements like these:

Why Teachers Resist Change

Change has involved:
◆ Adoption for opportunistic or symbolic reasons.
◆ No follow-through.
◆ Large-scale, visible projects that attempted too much and failed.
◆ Projects that were "in name only" and made no difference.
◆ Narrow prescriptive changes that constrained curriculum and teacher.
◆ School-based changes that lacked support and clear goals.
◆ Imposition of change from above.
◆ Short-term efforts that made no difference and changed with the administration or political climate.

Figure 14–3. *Why Teachers Are Reluctant to Change*

- ◆ I no longer feel I am making a difference.
- ◆ My job is the same day after day.
- ◆ I'm not learning anything new.
- ◆ The kids don't respond to my teaching.
- ◆ My results are terrible.
- ◆ I feel alone.
- ◆ No one will help me.
- ◆ I don't know what to do.

We've all heard these statements many times. A good staff development system will provide for better results and colleague support, thereby alleviating many causes of stress.

Do It Right the First Time

Only a few experiences with change that fails can cause teachers to lose heart. New ideas come up and an increasing number of teachers, all of whom care about their students, will say, "Been there, done that." They may have been there, but they didn't go the distance, because the design wasn't strong enough. The professional development system is part of a larger design; every facet is important. Of course, nothing is perfect. For every problem you anticipate, another will arise. The mistake is ignoring barriers to change and repeating the same kinds of initiatives over and over. It is always cheaper in the long run to opt for quality.

Embedding Professional Development Within a Larger Support System

A professional development system is most effective when it is embedded within a larger design for change—one that accounts for the barriers that are likely to arise. The success of professional development doesn't depend solely on the quality of the teaching and coaching; some seemingly unrelated factors can have a big impact. The more you can attend to and control these factors, the more likely it is that your professional development program will create lasting change. Support factors exist both within and outside the school. A wide network of support is extremely helpful (see Figure 14–4).

Inside the School

Factors within the school, taken together, create a climate for learning for both students and teachers. In a school where the highest priority is placed on learning, everything works together.

The supportive school is an inviting and attractive place. Student work is displayed everywhere. Likewise, the school reflects the engagement and ownership of the professional staff

---

Embedding Professional Development Within Larger Support Systems

Inside the school . . .	Outside the school . . .	Across a larger network . . .
◆ High priority for learning.	◆ High priority for learning.	◆ Collaborative networks for teachers by grade level and interest.
◆ Administrative support and leadership.	◆ Administrative support and leadership.	◆ Sources of new information.
◆ Climate of expectations for learning.	◆ Provision of adequate materials and supplies.	◆ Opportunities for specialized training.
◆ Workable schedules.	◆ Personnel resources to support professional development.	◆ Guidelines for quality implementation.
◆ Positive, welcoming atmosphere.	◆ Training and ongoing support for staff developers.	◆ Support for research.
◆ Available, attractive meeting places.	◆ Materials to support professional development.	◆ Training and ongoing support for staff developers.
◆ Professional reading/viewing materials.	◆ Resources to provide professional reading materials.	◆ Self-renewing system.
◆ Collaboration on materials and supplies.		
◆ Staff involvement in decision making on materials, schedules.		

Figure 14–4. *Embedding Professional Development Within Larger Support Systems*

(perhaps their writing or art work is on display, or brief biographies are posted). There is an attractive meeting area in which groups of teachers can work and plan together. There is a book room filled with sets of children's literature. There is also a good professional library and a collection of videotapes depicting exemplary teaching. There are ample materials and supplies in classrooms, and teachers decide what books to buy and what materials to acquire.

The Role of the Principal The principal is a key factor in supporting ongoing professional development. According to Barth (1990, p. 64):

◆ The principal is the key to a good school. The quality of the educational program depends on the school principal. ("Show me a good school, and I'll show you a good principal.")
◆ The principal is the most important reason why teachers grow—or are stifled—on the job.
◆ The principal is the most potent factor in determining school climate.

Probably the most effective support a principal can provide is her or his visible presence as a learner. Many principals participate in staff development sessions along with the teachers; in the process, they learn a great deal about the complexities of teaching and learning—helpful information, particularly when administrative certification does not include any coursework on teaching and learning literacy.

You may think teachers will be uncomfortable having the principal participate in sessions, and that may be the case in the beginning. Everything depends on the principal's attitude as a learner. In a community where a professional development system is working, there is a high level of trust and sharing. Collaborating with the principal is the best way to create this climate.

In addition to placing a high value on teachers' participation in ongoing professional development, the principal can:

◆ Control classroom interruption through policies about intercom use, scheduling of assemblies, etc.
◆ Create and work with a leadership team to plan schedules to maximize learning time.
◆ Make resources available for building a collection of professional materials.
◆ Designate a meeting place where teachers can keep materials and work together.
◆ Regularly evaluate the results of professional development, looking for evidence of learning on the part of teachers and indices of achievement on the part of students.

The Leadership Team Real change will not happen if it belongs only to one person or even a few. Even the principal and a staff developer working together are not sufficient. An effective way to guide and support the process is to convene a team of leaders. It's important that this group:

◆ Be real leaders—experienced teachers that others respect.
◆ Have real work to do and real decisions to make.

The leadership team represents broader ownership of the goals of the professional development program and can give valuable advice to staff developers. The team:

◆ Guides the assessment of student achievement and regularly examines and interprets assessment data.

School leadership teams and principal participation are keys to success.

- Works with the staff developer to create schedules and make arrangements for professional development.
- Works to build a common vision within the school.
- Solves problems as they occur.
- Provides visible leadership that sets the "norm" for learning.

It's not easy to create a learning climate within a school, and you can't wait to begin until everything is in place. We have seen leadership and a learning climate emerge *from* the staff development that takes place; we have also seen a leadership team begin to create a supportive setting *before* beginning a major professional development effort. Either way, the important thing is to attend to the school as the primary setting for professional development.

Factors Outside the School

The most important context for change is the school, but factors outside the school can support or impede positive change. The political climate within a district, for example, can inspire and support change or work against it. Community involvement too can make a difference. The factors below can impact the success of any professional development effort.

School District Administration A school exists within a larger context. The climate in the district, to some extent, shapes the schools, although we are all familiar with the exceptional school in a district where nothing much is happening otherwise. These exceptional schools are very vulnerable, however; losing a principal or having destructive policies imposed can disassemble a good program in a single year. School district administrators and board policy can support schools by actively encouraging change, insisting on quality, and allocating resources skillfully and strategically.

To make an impact, school reform must move beyond the walls of the exceptional schools. All children cannot be served by depending on the accidental combination of people with charisma and just the right skills. It takes district initiatives to promote widespread change, and that involves well-designed professional development. Typically, districts try to do too much and spread it too thin (again, the quick fix).

District personnel can contribute to the stability of the professional development system or they can destroy it. Encourage district personnel to avoid policies that get in the way of school improvement. Sometimes, teachers and a principal work hard over several years building strong programs and making connections with the parents and community only to have the principal summarily moved to "fix" another school. In fact many district administrators move principals regularly which works to increase their allegiance to central administration and decrease their ability to build neighborhood constituencies. Ambition and politics work to the detriment of children's learning.

At the district level, administrators and school boards can demonstrate high priority for learning and lend their support to long-term efforts. The extra personnel and other resources needed to initiate change are usually approved (or denied) at the district level. It helps if district personnel take the long view of professional development and school change.

Parents and Community Networks of parents and outside partners can provide strong support for professional development and educational improvement. Too often the work that goes on inside the school from day to day absorbs all our attention. For example, we may become so focused on helping children take tests that we forget our overarching goal of producing literate members of the community capable of contributing to its quality of life.

Part of every professional development design must be teaching teachers how to communicate with parents about what they are doing. When change is taking place in the school and parents hear about it only through their children or through vague or inaccurate rumors, distrust and suspicion are almost certain to arise. Clear communication with parents and strong outreach and involvement programs are essential.

State Policies and Allocation of Resources State policymakers can take a strong role in educational change by the way they supervise the allocation of resources. The approach they take can be positive—encouraging long-term professional development of high quality and providing the necessary resources, for example. It can also be negative—micromanaging resources and exercising too much control. For example, eliminating professional development proposals or programs to which teachers are committed simply because they are associated with words or references that have fallen out of favor is micromanagement. In contrast, in one state we know, choice of curriculum remains a professional decision by local teachers and administrators; and the results are excellent.

Federal Climate Education exists within a federal climate that controls and provides funding. This funding is especially important for districts and schools with large numbers of at-risk children.

Colleagues discussing children's records.

Many of the resources for professional development come from the national government. States and school districts (and even schools) have managed to find creative ways to acquire and use federal dollars to achieve their goals. It's important for school staff members to know how to use these funding sources for real school improvement and to meet goals that people in the school and community are committed to.

We want to emphasize that funding *can* make a difference—but it may not. In our professional careers, we have seen many millions of dollars spent with little result. It's how you use the money that counts. Here are some cautions:

◆ Much can be done with only a little funding and a lot of good will. Creativity is just as important as funding.

◆ If an innovation arises from and is solely dependent on outside funding, it will disappear when the funding disappears.

◆ Funding isn't worth it if it takes you away from your goals or the strings attached involve doing something that is wrong for students.

◆ Spend dollars where they make the most difference, and don't spend them until you have a strong design in place.

◆ Don't let the mere availability of some categorical funding lead you to adopt a crummy program; a poor something is *not* better than nothing.

It goes without saying that the federal agenda (tied to resources) influences the state and, so too, the district and building. A professional development design will consider this agenda.

Across a Larger Network

Within a building, a good professional development system opens classroom doors so that teachers become learning colleagues; so too, it can open the building doors, creating collegial relations across schools and districts. Establishing networks of teachers across schools and even across states and countries greatly benefits local professional development programs.

A regional or national network is a source of new information. It links teachers according to their common interests and goals. Such a network provides opportunities for specialized training, enables the group to identify professional standards that all can support, and provides a way of replicating research results. A network can provide constant stimulation and education for staff developers so that they, in turn, can do a better job in their work with teachers.

A network can be very helpful in solving the problems of change. Working across networks, in different contexts and with different problems, promotes "out of the box" thinking. You get different ideas by looking at things from different perspectives. Everyone involved in a network begins to see that he is not the only one who has problems, that she is not the only one who is experiencing success. Everyone sees that teacher development and educational change are ongoing. The system must be self-renewing.

Suggestions for Extending Your Skills as a Staff Developer

1. Form a small group of staff developers and identify a school that has implemented a collaborative literacy team made up of teachers, support staff, and administrators. Select a primary teacher, intermediate teacher, specialist teacher, and principal and ask them a number of questions from the list below:
   - What major obstacles did you face at the beginning of the collaborative venture and during the years you were a member of the literacy team?
   - How did you resolve each obstacle?
   - What role did you play in the collaborative team?
   - How committed were you to the collaborative venture?
   - How did your group decide who would be the leader?
   - How did group members share responsibility?
   - What advice would you give anyone who is thinking about starting a literacy collaborative?
   - How did you support one another during the collaborative process?
   - What impact did the team approach have on student achievement?
   - How did parents respond to a collaborative team approach to teaching their child to read and write?

   - Did you feel ownership in the group process while making decisions about curriculum, teaching techniques, and evaluation measures? Why or why not?
   - Did you feel others valued your ideas? How did you know they did or did not value your ideas?

   Analyze the responses looking for patterns of agreement and disagreement.

2. Determine if and how the four principles in Figure 14–1 are operating within the collaborative team your group identified above.
   - What kinds of barriers to change did respondents reveal?
   - How were the barriers resolved?

3. Select a school that your group feels is reluctant to change. Interview several teachers and the principal at this school. Ask the following questions:
   - How is your school managed and run?
   - What role do you have in making decisions about the curriculum or assessment practices?
   - How much support do you feel from your colleagues and principal?
   - Do you feel isolated? Why or why not?
   - What would you like to see changed?
   - What are your biggest obstacles?
   - What do you feel good about?

   Analyze the answers to the above questions and compare them with the ideas mentioned in Figure 14–3 about why teachers are reluctant to change.

4. Share the results of the interview data you and your colleagues have collected and develop a three-year literacy staff development plan using the guidelines presented in this chapter.

Chapter 15

Design, Professional Development, and Performance Standards

The standards set out realistic expectations for children who are taught well. They are demanding because nothing less will prepare children for their futures.
—LAUREN RESNICK
NEW STANDARDS: READING AND WRITING GRADE BY GRADE *(9)*

The previous chapter contrasts "quick fix" thinking, which focuses on one variable, with the concept of design. Having a design means you are able to handle multiple variables. The capability for design and the handling of multiple variables emerges through practice and professional development as teachers and staff developers gain expertise. Design does not mean doing everything at once; it does mean working over time to bring more variables into the design work.

Design as applied to professional development and educational change is a powerful idea.[1] Design encompasses some important concepts, including a vision of what is possible (standards), detailed plans to make that vision come true (a number of components working together), and continual renewal by way of analyzing success and failure (ongoing development).

Performance standards are currently at the heart of educational policy-making. Performance standards are created so that all stakeholders in education (parents, community, teachers, federal and state policymakers) will have a common vision for success—something to strive for. We believe that standards have value if all stakeholders participate in creating the vision they support.

If we are to achieve that vision, design is essential. Standards are not checklists imposed from above. You can use standards in very practical ways as part of an overall design to reach important goals. There are performance standards for students as well as performance standards for teachers; both are tied directly to a vision for change.

Standards are directly related to professional development. In fact, the only way to fulfill the vision (the achievement implied in standards) is by increasing the skills of teachers. The standards movement has led to the criticism of preservice teacher education and an unprecedented demand for good training. Darling-Hammond (1996, p. 196) reports that the National Commission on Teaching and America's Future has identified six goals to be achieved by 2006:

1. All children will be taught by teachers who have the knowledge, skills, and commitment to teach children well.
2. All teacher education programs will meet professional standards, or they will be closed.
3. All teachers will have access to high-quality professional development, and they will have regularly scheduled time for collegial work and planning.
4. Both teachers and principals will be hired and retained based on their ability to meet professional standards of practice.
5. Teachers' salaries will be based on their knowledge and skills.
6. High-quality teaching will be the central investment of schools. Most education dollars will be spent on classroom teaching.

Performance Standards

Standards have been around a long time but never have they been so specifically and actively applied. Standards are used to guide the designing of curriculum as well as the teaching of it. Assessment is tied to standards. Student attainment of standards is beginning to be used to adjust the salaries of administrators and teachers.

What Are Standards?

Standards can be defined in two ways (Noddings 1997):

◆ *Content* standards describe the curriculum. They define, for example, that students are supposed to learn a certain kind of content at a certain time. They define what teachers teach and what students are supposed to learn. An example of a content standard is: "Students will know the similarities and differences among groups in our diverse society."

◆ *Performance* standards specify what students should be able to *do*, the level of attainment that is expected at points in time. They define how students must perform on tasks that have been identified as critical evidence of learning. An example of a performance standard is: "Students will explain why individuals and groups respond differently to their social environments" or "Students will explain and give examples of how art and literature vary and contribute to the development and transmission of culture."

The performance standard requires the essential knowledge specified in the content standard.

Resnick (1999) and her colleagues have constructed literacy performance standards at both primary and intermediate levels, specifying performance at each grade level and even providing examples of students' reading and writing behavior. You can find examples of performance standards in every area of the curriculum, prepared by national professional associations like the National Council of Teachers of Mathematics, the National Council of Teachers of English (in collaboration with the International Reading Association), and the National Council for the Social Studies.

Existing standards may provide some helpful examples and good reference points. Real results, however, are achieved when standards arise from the design process rather than being imposed by external forces.

Are Standards Good or Bad?

Standards have big goals. They address the national interest in having a well-prepared citizenry. They also seem to guarantee that no child will be left behind; that is, they seek to reduce disparity by assuring high levels of learning for all (Gratz 2000). Most educators and policymakers agree that standards should not prescribe teaching methods but instead bring people together around common goals. Also, standards provide a way to compare all students with reachable criteria rather than simply having them compete with one another. We agree with Darling-Hammond and Falk's caution that

> much of the current discussion about standards and assessments places the onus for learning almost entirely on

the child. When policymakers urge that students be held accountable, they frequently call for grade retention and the withholding of diplomas as the primary responses to low achievement. They rarely say anything about major rethinking of schooling or teaching practices. . . . Few have examined how schools and teaching practices might need to change to enable students to succeed or how a closer look at student learning might trigger more effective responses. (1997, p. 191)

Standards can be positive if the following conditions exist:

1. Standards are clearly stated and understood by everyone.
2. Standards place responsibility for attainment on the educational system; that is, educators, policymakers, and politicians hold themselves to high standards.
3. People who use standards have been deeply engaged either in creating them or in making them come alive through analysis and application.
4. Attainment of standards is defined in terms of multiple measures rather than one high-stakes test.
5. Standards result in constant examination of students' opportunities for learning and for practicing skills.

Gratz (2000) has described standards as a "runaway train" that is moving too fast. While admitting that standards could have positive outcomes if well implemented, he states: "The vision for standards is far from the reality, the list of unintended consequences is growing longer, and new signs of the coming rebellion are appearing every day" (p. 687). We suggest that instead applying standards simplistically, we use them as part of the larger design process.

What Are Performance Standards for Teachers?

The standards for students are descriptions of what they should know and be able to do; these specifications lead to demands for professionals capable of teaching to achieve the standards. The assumption is that a widely accepted set of stan-

dards for teaching performance can ensure the consistency needed to meet this goal (Ambach 1996).

Wise and Leibbrand (2000) point to the polarized views of teacher preparation. Some educators and policymakers are calling for stronger preparation of teachers, ongoing training, and performance standards. Others, perhaps in response to the coming teacher shortage, consider content knowledge to be sufficient and are employing unlicensed teachers.

In the past, licenses to teach were earned by successfully completing college courses (many of them in pedagogy) and a number of weeks of practice teaching. Then, to retain his or her license, a teacher needed to complete higher-level courses or attend inservice programs.

The creation of performance standards rests on a different assumption—what can teachers demonstrate that they know and can do? Like performance standards for students, these standards are specific in terms of behavior. That does not mean they are simple, because standards for teachers' performance would always involve their ability to adjust instruction to meet learners' needs. Chapters 8, 9, and 10 explore using several scales designed to assess teachers' skill in providing lessons. These scales are based on complex and interrelated sets of behavior and illustrate the challenges involved in establishing performance standards for teaching.

Performance standards for teachers of literacy should reflect the spiral of learning. Like standards for students, they should:

1. Represent a clear picture of what teachers need to know and be able to demonstrate.
2. Place responsibility for attainment on teachers but also on the educational system. Teachers need high expectations for their performance, but they need to see it as a problem-solving learning process in which they have expert help.
3. Be used by people who understand the specified behavior deeply because they have taught and analyzed their teaching themselves.
4. Provide for multiple ways of assessing performance; assessment should take place over time and be related to professional development.

Informal discussions support ongoing professional development.

5. Result in an ongoing examination of the kinds of support systems teachers need as well as the quality and nature of the professional development they receive.

Exploring Design in Relation to Performance Standards

Let's begin by thinking about how design is applied in the field of engineering. Even though we aren't engineering experts, we expect the airplanes or cars we ride in to be *very* well designed—our lives depend on it. There is a narrow margin for dysfunction, and function depends on good design. In these complex machines, many components work together. Each component has its own design, which is carefully constructed both to work efficiently and effectively *and* to fit in with the larger design.

If we think of design in terms of education, we find even more complexity. Here our designs have to take a dynamic social environment into account. Our schools are made up of people; our outcomes consist of what people learn—what they know and can do. Human beings' knowledge, skills, interrelationships, and circumstances are always changing. That may be one reason we tend not to apply design concepts to education. Instead of building on what we know, separate pockets of people are always reinventing

approaches and techniques that may or may not be truly innovative.

In fact, of course, *every* kind of design depends on people and their strategies and skills. Designing an airplane fuselage takes people's skill, knowledge, and collaboration. Different people do different tasks; some have to teach others. Always, assessment is ongoing. So applying design to education is not so far afield:

◆ It gives us *direction*, keeps us moving along a line of vision rather than meandering this way and that.
◆ It requires the *cooperation* of people who need to fit complex processes together into a whole.
◆ It provides group support for individual thinking and *problem solving*.
◆ It allows us to combine our thinking so that the outcome is greater than we could accomplish alone (*synergy*).
◆ It allows us to *renew* our processes and build on what we know.

Design Versus Invention

Design is not the same thing as invention. Invention involves tinkering around trying to make something work, with no guarantee you will ever succeed. For example gas turbines were around for years; they compressed air and added and burned fuel, but they didn't operate with efficiency. It took fifty years of tinkering before scientists managed to invent the first jet engines; the accumulation of knowledge and skill contributed to the process.

When you've come up with the invention, the next stage is to design an effective and efficient way to use it. Design is a much more orderly procedure:

◆ You want to continue to refine the invention without going back to tinkering—to create a standard way to achieve current benchmark performance with rare surprises. You want to control uncertainties so that constant progress is possible.

◆ Having achieved that, you want to have some ongoing way of learning from your efforts.

In other words, you constantly improve your product and you learn from the process.

Every technology has to go through this transition and there are many mistakes in doing so. In education, we tend to go back to the tinkering stage all the time. Forward movement is not possible, because we haphazardly try one thing and then another. What we need is *design:* a process that learns from success and failures and builds on what we have learned. We need long-term efforts, with ongoing learning at every level, under the auspices of wider networks.

Prerequisites for Good Design

George Smith has identified two prerequisites for creating good technological designs (see Figure 15–1), which can be extrapolated to creating designs for educational change.

Identify Measurable Parameters

The first step in any design is to identify measurable parameters. A *parameter* is a constant with variable values. For example, distance traveled is a constant that can vary in terms of the number of miles. A parameter varies according to the circumstances of its application. Distance traveled varies with speed and time.

One parameter may be used to predict other parameters. For example speed and time may both be measured and used to predict distance traveled. Indeed, traveling by car can be viewed as a complex combination of related parameters. We constantly measure time and speed and calculate the distance we'll be able to travel, but other parameters (fuel consumption, for example) are involved as well. We may even bring more unpredictable parameters to bear, such as the extent to which we know the most direct route; we can make this parameter more predictable by getting good directions and a road map. The kind of car we have—four or eight cylinders—also makes a difference.

In the example above, we are talking about two kinds of parameters:

Prerequisites for Good Design

1. Identify measurable parameters:
   ◆ Performance parameters are ways of measuring what is going on—how the phenomenon is working.
   ◆ Correlating parameters let you predict performance based on factors that are within your control.

2. *Modularize the process.*
   ◆ You need to "modularize" or break down the process so that you can look at the components and work to refine them.

Figure 15–1. *Prerequisites for Creating Good Designs*

◆ A *performance parameter* is a variable that can be measured. Performance parameters refer to important factors and ways of measuring them that let you know what is going on. For example, speed can be measured in miles per hour and related to time and fuel consumption. If you drive fast, you get there sooner, but you may use more fuel per mile.

◆ A *correlating parameter* lets you predict performance. The value of the parameter varies with the circumstances of its application. You establish the performance parameters and then identify those that are related to one another. We can predict that increased speed reduces the time needed to travel a given distance, for example.

There are measurable parameters in fields other than engineering. For example, in the 1980s the economist Amartya Sen explored the famine in India. In his studies, he identified many measurable parameters. He looked at crops, food processing and delivery, employment, transportation, technical skills, birth rate, and so on. One parameter dominated every other factor related to famine—the level of education of women. If women are better educated, the birth rate goes down and more and better knowledge serves the family. The quality of life increases. In this case the process of design—the push to identify parameters and look for correlations—led to a discovery that has allowed groups to start addressing the heart of India's famine problem rather than its superficial aspects. India began a major initiative to increase women's education, and where that happened, famine decreased.

The parameters that are most important are not apparent in advance. You may have some theories, but you never know which parameters will be informative or have the highest correlation to other parameters. No one would have expected that studying the education of women in India would reveal something that would make the most difference overall.

Measurable Parameters in Literacy Education

In literacy education, there are many measurable parameters that may be correlated.

As in other fields, there are two kinds of measurable parameters:

◆ A *performance parameter* in education is something that can be measured. Here we can think about the amount of instruction (time spent) required for students' learning. We can think about the allocation of personnel. We can think about the number of words read. We can think about scores on tests and the quality of writing produced.

◆ A *correlating parameter* in education lets us predict performance based on its relationship to one or more other factors. We can find relationships between the time spent reading, the amount of quality instruction received, the number of books read, and test scores. By varying combinations, we may increase the probability that we will see a rise in test scores.

Ongoing efforts to define parameters in literacy have yielded a multitude of factors that can be correlated with student achievement. It is highly unlikely that any one of these factors *alone* produces achievement. Yet we are always looking for the magic bullet. Engaged time on task is a good example: it would seem that time spent on reading instruction will produce better reading scores, and some research has shown this to be the case (Rosenshine and Stephens 1984). The problem comes when we stop there, define the concept simplistically, and prescribe a solution. Plenty of teachers have spent great amounts of time on reading instruction, knocking out writing, art, language, and other topics, without producing a discernible rise in reading achievement. In reality it's a *combination* of factors, and we have to find the *right combination*.

By varying combinations, we can predict increased achievement.

Performance standards in education represent what students are expected to know and do. Performance standards for teachers represent what teachers must know and be able to do. They involve the creation of measurable outcomes. The performance standards you use can be part of the design process because they are a source of measurable perimeters.

Measurable Parameters as the Key to Design

The key to design is to use informative parameters. Designers try to identify parameters with strong correlations. They search for the uncertainties that are worth concentrating on, those that they can control and change.

For example, in literacy, a factor like time spent on reading instruction is one parameter, but others are the *appropriateness of the text* for helping the student expand her or his reading power and the *teacher's ability to introduce the book* strategically (a performance parameter that could be measured using an instrument similar to the guided reading analysis scale included in Chapter 10 and Appendix B). Still other parameters might involve writing or phonics lessons and their quality. All might be related to the speed with which the reader moves up the gradient of difficulty (see Chapter 4). The designer looks at the interrelationship of the important factors, controlling the quality of some and working to improve others so that the process works at maximum effectiveness.

We are not talking here about experimental research in which minute variations are tested one at a time. For example, you could give one group two books and the other one book and get no measurably different results because *something else entirely* (another parameter) contributed overwhelmingly to student progress. You would, in fact, have gone down the wrong path.

In the context of instruction, many variables work together and they change all the time. Holding parameters constant is just about impossible, because teachers vary so in their knowledge and interactions, but we can create more predictability by identifying and correlating parameters. The designer maintains a basic level of control and then improves what he is already doing.

Staff developers and teachers who are instituting a new program must recognize that the design is complex, that they need good measurable parameters, and that they should expect to examine those parameters (and add new ones) over time as they work on the design of a program for literacy improvement. The development of measurable parameters can be shared across a network of schools. Some of the parameters that affect learning are likely to be common to many teachers, schools, and students.

Modularize the Process

It's impossible to design anything unless you break it into components. When you're working on an original invention (e.g., the jet engine), you need to discover how the modules or components work; you isolate a component and discover how it feeds into the whole. The most elementary reason for doing this is to divide and conquer. You want to take a very complicated large problem and break it into several small problems. Then you are in a much better position to solve them.

Modularization also enables more people to work on the design. As long as you have an overall design, separate teams can work on each component (the compressor, the turbine, etc.). Each group has its own particular problems and designs its own component. Components that lend themselves to modularization can be designed largely in isolation from one another. There are performance and correlating parameters for that component. It is testable in isolation, making it less expensive and more manageable. Modularization is a process of gaining control—each component is more manageable than the whole.

Modularization in Literacy Education Professional development is one component of the larger design for educational change. But within professional development systems, there are components as well. The chapters of this book talk about course sessions, coaching, and different forms of extended learning. Each is a component to be designed, and they must all fit together into the whole.

Each of these components has subcomponents—ways to engage teachers, ways to reveal processes, ways to build learning over time. You can also identify measurable parameters for each of these subcomponents. For example, you can determine whether your course instruction in guided reading, in combination with coaching, is producing results by analyzing teachers' performance in classrooms, perhaps using a scale. Then you can measure another correlation by determining whether students are moving up the gradient of text difficulty.

Feedback is important throughout the process of identifying parameters and setting up appropriate modules. Here, expert assistance and/or workers with different perspectives can help each other "see" parameters that they might have ignored. The process of feedback can push the discovery process so that new relationships among components will appear.

Steps in the Design Process

After identifying informative parameters and setting up appropriate modules, you are ready to *begin* designing. What usually happens in education, however, is that the process *stops* here, a circumstance that must change. We need to design a system improving literacy education through in-depth work over time. There are seven steps in making systemic change a reality (see Figure 15–2). Throughout the process—at every step—feedback is, again, important. Without feedback, design will not work. In the discussion below we offer two running examples of the design process, one involving an individual teacher, the other, an entire school.

Establish a Vision

Decide your overall goal, your vision, of what you want to achieve. Think about what's possible rather than about your past experiences. Creating a vision is a much more important piece of the pie than people think, and little time is usually spent on it. The vision clarifies what you want your outcomes to be—what it will look like.

A Classroom Vision Kecia, a kindergarten teacher (described in some detail in the vignette at the end of this book), has the overall goal of helping her kindergarten students become better writers. First, she looks at where her instruction seems to be failing. She has been telling children about spacing for months, but when she looks at her students' writing, she doesn't see spaces between words.

Figure 15–2. *Steps in the Design Process*

She has identified a measurable parameter—children using spaces between words when they write. She wants to see written papers with good spacing and identifiable words. Her analysis is embedded in an overall knowledge of the progression of early writing, so she knows spacing will make an important difference in her students' learning. Her vision gives her a clear picture of what her young students can do and what they need to be able to do next.

Kecia then looks at her literacy curriculum. She identifies several instructional components as important in contributing to children's ability to use spacing—shared reading, independent writing (with a minilesson), and interactive writing. After considering these components in relation to one another, she decides that interactive writing is the one most likely to produce measurable outcomes, but she wants to be sure she reinforces this learning in other settings. Wanting her interactive writing lesson to be powerful and focused, Kecia evaluates what she's been doing in previous lessons. She sees she's been moving

through her lessons without a strong instructional focus. Using a scale, she identifies specific instructional moves she will make throughout the lesson (that is, in each subcomponent). Her analysis has led her to some measurable parameters of her own behavior that she hopes will correlate with children's learning.

A Schoolwide Vision A school leadership team has the goal of increasing student performance on a state proficiency test. They've noticed highly unpredictable performances by the students. Some scores are strong but others fall far below expectations.

They study the test to identify precisely what students have to be able to do. They create a number of measurable parameters, including making inferences, recognizing and using textual organizational features, writing summaries, and interpreting poetry. They identify ways to measure these parameters at several grade levels and assign groups to design related instruction at each grade level.

At the same time, Joan, the staff developer at the school, designs a professional development program that will parallel the needed instruction. Joan and several of her colleagues expand the vision to include what teachers need to know and be able to do as well as what students need to know and be able to do.

Create a Preliminary Design

The preliminary design involves creating a rough, overall view of the entire system that will achieve your goal. Sketch out what it would look like, given the requirements, goals, and constraints. Limit yourself to performance and considerations of principle concern. Go for the big picture and don't get bogged down in detail. Attach the requirements, goals, and constraints on the individual components. Tell each of the component groups: "This is what we want from you."

◆ Specify what you demand from each component.
◆ Identify the major obstacles that will occur.

As with every step, gathering feedback on the preliminary design is critical to its eventual success.

A Teacher's Preliminary Design Kecia sketches out her instructional plan in broad strokes, noting how she can draw students' attention to using spaces in each instructional component—interactive writing, shared reading, and independent writing. She thinks about the evidence of learning she will need to see within each component. Then she looks within the interactive lesson structure.

A Schoolwide Preliminary Design The school leadership team lays out the components they have chosen. Texts will offer opportunities for students to learn about and use text structures such as "compare and contrast" as well as offer opportunities to draw inferences, which they can discuss with others. Instructional designs will engage students at each grade level in performing the kinds of behavior required by the test; those parameters will be the evidence of learning. Professional development will enable teachers to employ instructional designs with skill and results.

Create the Detailed Design

In this step each component is designed separately. Teams take the preliminary design and depart from it as needed to meet the needs. Typically, a lot of people are involved. Factors that have been missed in the preliminary design become subjects for study in the detailed design. Concentration is required, and the design is highly specific. Designers' work is guided by the overall vision and requirements, and feedback is helpful.

A Detailed Design for Classroom Work Kecia plans her interactive writing lesson in detail. Up to now, her work has consisted simply of thinking about her teaching. Now she makes notes. Using the scales as a guide, she thinks about how she can emphasize spacing in every part of the interactive writing lesson. She jots down some clear language to use and identifies the students (those having the most difficulty) she wants to ask to come up and place their hands on the text to "hold" the space. She drafts her brief summary statement to the group, in which she will remind them of what they have learned and what they should try in their own writing.

A Schoolwide Detailed Design The various groups meet to work on their components. Grade-level teams, guided by the parameters and preliminary design, work on specific instructional plans they can apply across the year in guided reading and literature study, the two curriculum components they have decided are most related

to the parameters. The librarian and a team of teachers look at and analyze the available books, articles, and other reading materials. They identify additional others that can be purchased for the school collection. (Teachers, guided by this committee, will later choose from these alternatives.)

Joan assesses what teachers are already doing and identifies how they need to be supported, given the parameters and the preliminary design. She observes in classrooms and talks with teachers. She prepares a detailed plan for several professional development class sessions as well as for the coaching she will do. Her instruction will be differentiated: some teachers are already using these instructional techniques and getting good results, others will be using them for the first time.

Set Up a Systems Group

While the individual components are being designed, a systems group focuses on the project as a whole. They oversee the ongoing component design but keep thinking about how the components will be put together in the overall design. (For example, the staff developer and leadership team might ensure that the scheduling works for both primary and intermediate teachers or coordinate ordering new books with course meetings.) If you have defined the components well, there usually aren't too many system problems.

Systems Thinking at the Classroom Level Kecia continues to think about her literacy curriculum as a whole. She thinks that her detailed instruction will be effective but that she can increase its power by referring to spacing during shared reading and independent writing. She also plans her schedule to take a systematic look at every student's writing before and after the intensive instruction.

A Schoolwide Systems Group The school leadership team acts as the systems group. They look at the instructional designs to see how they match the parameters—what student behavior will result? They look at new parameters to see whether they measure something important in the whole scheme of things. They look across grade levels and subject areas. They examine the plans for professional development to determine whether they relate to teacher performance parameters.

Review the Design

At this point you ask a team of people not working on the design to come in and critique it. They probe into the details, catch mistakes, and make designers rethink things. This rethinking is quite valuable, because it is hard to recognize details when you are in the midst of the process. The reviewer should critique the design as harshly as possible.

Review of the Classroom Design Kecia seeks advice from her literacy coach, Tina, who acts as a sounding board for her design. In a preconference, Tina and Kecia look at what she wants to see as evidence of learning (the measurable parameters), at the components she has identified, and at her design. Tina asks questions and looks with Kecia at students' writing samples. She agrees that they need help on spacing; in general, she confirms Kecia's design, offering a few suggestions.

A Schoolwide Design Review The leadership team looks at the overall design, with components in place. Joan also asks a colleague with experience in designing such programs to take a look at their plan. The review shows that they have developed well-designed instruction and that the professional development program focuses on the right topics. They see, though, that insufficient professional development time has been allocated. The plan calls for two intensive days with no follow-up. The group rethinks the design and plans four half-day sessions, giving teachers time to try the ideas (with coaching by the staff developer) on the second and fourth half-days.

Build and Test the Prototype

Evaluate every design parameter as your instruction plays out in the classroom. Compare what you see to the predictions you made in the design process and the correlations you found. Be extremely critical of anything that went into the original design.

A Classroom Prototype Kecia teaches her class, noticing children's responses. She collects their written work for the day to reflect on later. She also meets with Tina to discuss the lesson.

A Schoolwide Prototype The leadership team and other teachers at the school put the plan into action over several months. Joan provides staff development, coaches, and collects data on students and teachers. Observing the teachers, she finds they are paying close attention to the strategies they are working to develop. Students are beginning to use informational text structures when they write and notice them when they read.

Analyze Failure

When something works, we never really know why. Failures tell us what we have been ignoring. Failure is anything short of your expectation. If your expectation is to have 100 percent of your students meet the criteria you've established to achieve your vision and only 80 percent do, that's partial failure. In this sense, the concept of failure is *not* negative; failure gives us valuable information. The question is why? What is causing the shortfall? It's the detective work that helps us improve the design. Most failure analyses investigate catastrophic failures. (For example, airplane crashes are subjected to intensive analysis that may take months or years.) But lesser failures can also be productively examined.

Failure analysis can identify crucial parameters. If even one critical parameter is not properly determined and its best value is not established, learning will diminish. Our study of Reading Recovery and other interventions, for example, indicated that even though the number of hours was similar, collapsing teacher training into an intensive two-week period resulted in greatly lowered student achievement as well as in lower assessments of the quality of teaching (see Pinnell et al. 1995).

We learn so little from success and so much from failure. Failure can never be attributed to just one factor. Pin down the uncertainties that may make a difference and weight them. Identify the ones you can do something about. Boil it down to the decisions that make a difference.

Analyzing Failures in Classroom Instruction Kecia identified her problem through a form of failure analysis in the first place. After the lesson, with Tina's assistance, she analyzes again. Together Tina and Kecia look at the students' work. They see substantial improvement, which they attribute to these factors:

◆ Kecia taught powerfully and intensively throughout the interactive writing lesson.
◆ She focused children's attention on spacing in very specific ways throughout the lesson.
◆ She summed up the learning and helped them apply it in other areas.

Teachers and literacy coach examining student data.

Thinking About Design

Design can take place at many levels. Design work in the classroom is ongoing and largely informal, but teachers do analyze their failures, establish a vision, and design and test instructional approaches. Their designs have to take into account logistics, individual students, and materials.

Even when we consider multiple variables and create long-term plans, we may only be approaching the concept of design. It's not simply a matter of sitting down and doing it. Design is a complex idea. In engineering, preliminary design is accomplished by a carefully selected small design team. They are *experts* in design. A school staff, district team, or university team may need assistance in identifying parameters and describing and developing components. But they will learn from the process as they analyze their failures and keep on adjusting their designs.

Kecia and Tina notice that while most of the children have improved, five students still are having trouble with spacing. Kecia hypothesizes that these students need more application time and probably have trouble learning in a whole-group setting. She redesigns her instruction to include a small-group minilesson for them. And she adds another parameter—can these children recognize and use spaces in reading?

A School Analyzes Failure The school leadership team looks at students' scores on the proficiency test, analyzing them by the parameters they have identified. They also compare the test scores with teachers' assessments of student behavior given the desired behavior. The staff developer analyzes teacher behavior related to the identified parameters.

The team finds overall improvement on the test, but about 15 percent of the students still fall below expectations. Teachers look closely at this group of students and finds that two thirds of them are in classrooms with new teachers. A closer look determines that while these teachers have attended the inservice sessions and borrowed books from the school collection, their own classrooms have inadequate collections of informational texts. In addition, Joan finds that these same teachers have not taken on the new instructional behavior as easily as others. They hypothesize that more coaching support, two special small-group meetings, and better book collections may make the difference. The design process continues.

Design can also improve the field of education as a whole. Wilson and Barsky (1998) call for widespread use of research and development in education. They say that while basic research has revealed some good information (although much more is needed), we are not connecting the achievements of teachers with these findings: "What is missing is an applied academic research discipline to provide institutionalized support for the emerging forms of R&D" (p. 234).

Parents, educators, and policymakers tend to think that one or two changes will make the difference, but we have learned over and over that what we need is an overall design for change. Teachers for years have closed their classroom doors and exercised their creativity, but now demands for accountability cause policymakers to go in different directions, to abandon the reforms of their predecessors and launch new ones. The whole process is uninformed by what has occurred in the past. What we need is a national process that seeks and analyzes educational reforms in light of an overall design for change.

The process is one of learning—in classrooms, schools, districts, regions, states, and as a nation:

> Learning holds the power to change a life from something small and weak to an ever-expanding, self-directed engine of development and opportunity; it alone offers the tools that will let us live together more smoothly, usefully, and harmoniously as citizens and workers. . . . Institutional changes that are both sweeping and positive don't endure and succeed by chance. In education or any field, lasting fundamental change grows out of, and is sustained by, a compelling vision. That vision is gripping enough to inspire people to commit themselves to work for its realization—to begin and sustain the arduous processes of change in pursuit of the goals that the vision holds out. (Wilson and Daviss 1994, p. 26)

As a staff developer, you have the opportunity to contribute to the learning of teachers and students. More than that, you can work with your colleagues to construct a vision that will sustain learning in the millennium to come.

Suggestions for Extending Your Skills as a Staff Developer

1. Select a familiar object whose design has changed over the years. Remember, the modern refrigerator began with a cache or root cellar. A few possibilities:
   - Kitchen appliances (mixers, blenders, refrigerators, microwave ovens, etc.).
   - Radios, record/tape players, and televisions.
   - Computers.
   - Telephones.
   - Cars, airplanes.
2. For the selected object, consider:
   - At what point was there an invention and what did it look like?
   - How was the design process used to improve the invention?
   - What characteristics were changed and what were the benefits?
   - How did failure analysis contribute to the process?
3. Now make a plan for using the design process in some aspect of your work or even your personal life. You can work in your own classroom, but be sure to involve a friend. Or work with colleagues at your school. If you want to work in some another arena, identify the area of concern.
4. Take one goal you and your partner or group want to achieve. Try something that is somewhat complex but can be accomplished within a short time. Examples are:
   - Teaching a group of teachers how to do guided reading.
   - Teaching a group of teachers how to select books.
   - Working with a group of students to improve their use of routines in reading workshop.
   - Working with a group of students to extend their reading to different genres.
5. Decide what you want to happen. As part of the process, identify measurable parameters and modularize the process. You will now have some descriptions of exactly what you want to look for, and you will have broken down the process.
6. Create a rough, overall design for reaching your goal.
7. Divide into teams (if applicable) to create detailed designs for each component; use the measurable parameters as a guide. Be sure to come together periodically to see how your components will fit together.
8. Invite someone not involved in your design process to look at what you have done and critique it.
9. Try out your design, gathering information related to the parameters.
10. Analyze the process—where you succeeded and where you failed.
11. Now reflect on your application of the design process.
    - What was easy? What was hard?
    - Did the detailed design cause changes in the preliminary design?
    - How did criticism help you?
    - How did failure analysis help you?
    - How could you apply the design process in other areas?

Endnote

1 Much of the information in this chapter was supplied by George Smith, Tufts University, engineer and professor. We are also grateful to Kenneth Wilson and Constance Barsky, professors of physics at The Ohio State University.

Chapter 16

Making the Most of What We Know

*Change is too important
to leave to the experts.*
—*MICHAEL FULLAN*
CHANGE FORCES *(39)*

Teacher education takes place every day in every school across the United States. Most of the time, teachers try to improve their own instruction and/or help one another do so. But there is a growing trend toward on-the-job teacher education, variously called training, coaching, professional development, and peer assistance, among other labels. At its heart, this trend recognizes that teaching is complex and challenging. Learning to teach takes time and support.

As part of this trend, the role of staff developer has emerged as central to the goal of improving schools, especially in literacy education. A large number of staff developers are at work in our schools. They support the thousands of new teachers who enter service every year, but they also work extensively with experienced teachers to help them refine their practice.

The role of the staff developer is critical in helping students become competent readers and writers who can use literacy as a tool for learning throughout their lives. Through these on-the-job teacher educators, instruction can be improved and changed. The task is not one of simply appointing good teachers to teach others. Teacher educators themselves need tools, understanding, and a complex range of skills; they also need settings and organizational arrangements that will allow them to use their knowledge and skills.

Ways to Provide Staff Development

There are many different ways to provide professional development in a school or district. They fall into four basic categories (see Figure 16–1):

◆ The staff developer who is based in one school and works solely with the teachers in that school.

◆ District staff development consultants who work in all the schools in the district.

◆ Hired consultants who work with schools and school districts.

◆ University professors, who teach preservice teacher education students, work with teachers in schools where their students practice teach, and teach graduate courses to inservice teachers.

School-Based Teacher Educators

School-based teacher educators are based in one school and provide professional development for the teachers and other staff in the school. When the professional development is devoted exclusively to literacy, they are sometimes called *literacy facilitators, literacy coordinators,* or *reading resource teachers.*

School-based teacher educators play a unique, relatively new role in literacy education. Previously, it was rare to have a staff developer stationed in a single school, but federal support for new literacy initiatives has allowed many schools to be able to allocate staff in this way. The school-based professional development provider is often a teacher on the staff who is appointed to the role and may receive special training. Professional development may make up anywhere between 50 and 100 percent of his or her job.

The school-based teacher educator has a variety of responsibilities, including:

◆ Providing ongoing training for teachers through

a series of sessions focusing on different aspects of literacy learning and teaching.

◆ Helping both new and experienced teachers improve their work by way of discussion and observation.

◆ Providing in-class coaching to teachers who are putting new approaches into practice.

◆ Working with the school staff over time toward a vision of literacy achievement.

◆ Measuring work against systematic assessment.

The most important advantage of having a school-based teacher educator is that she is able to work closely with administrators, staff, and students over time. A school-based person is available to support teachers as they work in their classroom. A key characteristic is ongoing, informal communication as the teacher educator helps teachers make decisions. Coaching can take place frequently, and progress is faster for both teachers and students.

When a highly trained literacy coordinator works effectively with a committed group of teachers over time, literacy achievement improves (Williams 1999; Williams and Scharer 2000). One example: one school trained a literacy coordinator during the 1995–96 school year. The school implemented the Literacy Collaborative framework in 1997–98 (not without the classic problems related to change). Scores on the Gates-MacGinitie Reading Test increased by 42.1 percent from fall 1995 to fall 1997 and an average of 11.2 percent from 1995 to

Independent reading.

Ways to Provide Professional Development for Literacy Teachers

Provider and Role	Advantages
School-Based Teacher Educator ◆ Works in one school over time. ◆ Continues to teach students in the school. ◆ Is released from the classroom to coach teachers. ◆ Provides ongoing training courses at the school. ◆ Works with administrators and leadership team. ◆ Gathers data and discusses results with staff. ◆ Meets with teachers to follow overall plan. ◆ May specialize in primary or intermediate.	◆ Knows staff, administration, students over time. ◆ Establishes credibility through demonstration. ◆ Can root training in the life and problems of the school. ◆ Can develop and implement a professional development system that is efficient and totally integrated with the vision of the school. ◆ Communicates with teachers daily—formally and informally. ◆ Is part of school community—parents, students. ◆ Is available for daily problem solving. ◆ Has a stake in school achievement. ◆ Provides regular coaching in classrooms. ◆ Sees progress over time in teachers' and students' work. ◆ Makes sure to follow through so that new skills build on previous skills. ◆ Builds a learning climate in the school. ◆ Makes connections between purchase of materials, instruction, and the vision of the school. ◆ Has extensive time to provide professional development of all kinds.
District-Based Teacher Educator ◆ Works at the district office but spends considerable time in schools. ◆ Provides professional development for teachers at a range of schools and across grade levels. ◆ Provides some districtwide institutes or conferences. ◆ Works with administrators and teachers at a range of schools. ◆ May specialize in grade level or area. ◆ May provide support for school-based teacher educators.	◆ Understands entire school system, including politics, community, past problems. ◆ Sees the big picture in the district. ◆ Has access to central office resources and to decision makers. ◆ Gets to know staff, administration, students in a variety of schools over time. ◆ Knows districtwide trends, patterns, initiatives. ◆ Can assist in getting resources. ◆ Develops broader expertise in providing professional development in many settings. ◆ Becomes specialist in professional development. ◆ Has more opportunities for ongoing training (conferences, etc.).
Private Consultant ◆ Works independently or is attached to a professional development company or publisher. ◆ Provides a wide range of professional development at conferences and in schools and school districts. ◆ Works on a "cost for service" basis. ◆ May specialize in grade level or area.	◆ Brings in fresh, new ideas from the outside. ◆ Is often knowledgeable about new research and instructional approaches. ◆ Has a wide range of contacts—knowledgeable about what is happening in many places. ◆ Often has access to fresh new materials. ◆ Develops a high level of expertise through constant work in many schools. ◆ Often develops sophisticated style that engages teachers' interest. ◆ Often has a wide network of other experts with whom they communicate.
University-Based Teacher Educator ◆ Works at university or college with whom the school/district has a relationship. ◆ Teaches undergraduate and graduate courses and/or works with field-based projects. ◆ Conducts field-based studies to inform education.	◆ Has expertise in developing new ideas. ◆ Can guide action research in schools and districts. ◆ Communicates with leaders in the district. ◆ Is knowledgeable about new research. ◆ Can assist in curriculum development. ◆ Can assist in development of new approaches. ◆ Evaluates and critiques new approaches.
Combination of Providers ◆ Involves a coordinated combination of professional development providers, each fulfilling different functions.	◆ Can work together to ensure in-school ongoing professional development in combination with access to the wider community, district-level involvement, and access to new research.

Figure 16–1. *Variety of Ways to Provide Professional Development for Elementary Teachers in Literacy*

1999. (See Appendix A for a more detailed discussion of the Literacy Collaborative.)

District-Level Teacher Educators

Districtwide teacher educators also play an important role in professional development. In the best model, a district-level teacher educator in the central office trains and works with building-level teacher educators throughout the district. These school-based teacher educators have outside support and experience ongoing renewal and at the same time are able to work closely with teachers in one school.

Teacher educators with a number of schools to support will want to look closely at Chapter 9, Assessing the Classroom Context. The more they get to know each school, the more effective they will be. They may also want to work with district officials to create a schedule that allows them to work closely with each school for a period of time, so that they can build momentum and provide some in-class coaching. District-level teacher educators often coach teachers or work with in-the-building coaches, and the chapters on coaching (Chapters 9 through 12) apply to that aspect of their role.

District-level teacher educators have the advantages of knowing the big picture in the school district and having access to an outside network. Chapter 14 discusses how to embed professional development within larger systems. District-level persons can be very helpful to the schools and the district in developing designs for effective professional development. They can provide conferences and institutes to get things started, but can also work toward a long-term commitment to networks of learning across the district.

Private Consultants

Much of the professional development work in school districts is provided by outside consultants, either through conferences and institutes or through longer-term programs. School district administrators employ consultants because:

◆ They are highly expert individuals who have a particular expertise not available among district personnel.
◆ Their services are usually discrete and do not require long-term commitment.
◆ They are provided by publishers as part of an agreement to purchase their materials.

Privately based professional developers have the advantage of a state or national outlook and usually have a network for gathering new information. They are often polished presenters and may bring fresh, new ideas into the district or school.

Privately based teacher educators working over time with teachers may want to examine closely some of the suggestions in Chapter 1 related to developing a community of learners. Even with short-term work, they can assess the context and form relationships with their adult learners. The suggestions on planning a course may also be helpful (see Chapter 6).

University-Based Teacher Educators

The roles of university-based teacher educators are somewhat dictated by their being part of an institution of higher learning. Universities have rules and organizational patterns different from schools and school districts. Nevertheless, schools of education and elementary schools are partners when it comes to improving literacy education and preparing the new generation of teachers.

University-based teacher educators have the advantages of access to new research and the opportunity to do research themselves. They are knowledgeable about state initiatives and issues related to licensing. Generally, they have access to a broad network of information through professional associations, and they can bring research-based approaches to the school or district.

The suggestions for developing effective courses in Chapter 6 can be applied by university-based teacher educators, as can the ideas on coaching in Chapters 9–12.

Increasing Effectiveness in a Variety of Roles

The suggestions and guidelines in this book can be used in a variety of ways by the whole range of professional development providers. Any teacher education program is more effective when the providers know the context, work with people over time, and provide follow-up coaching. Each type of provider has strengths to bring to the design for professional development. By working together, we can make learning happen.

You may not be able to work in depth with a school, but planning and implementing an effective course may lay the groundwork for the group to move on to in-class assistance as a next step. All teacher educators face the challenges outlined in Chapter 14—the barriers to change. All teacher educators can be part of creating effective designs for school change.

A Year of Learning

Chapter 2 discusses the idea of interrelated processes connected in a spiral of learning (see Figure 16–2). The spiral of learning represents sequences of learning in a variety of areas—not stages of learning for individuals. As teacher educators, the sequence guides us to take our teacher/learners from where they are to where

they want and need to go next. Let's revisit this learning spiral as it plays out over a year of staff development in an elementary school.

The School Context

The school is Franklin Elementary, located in an urban area. The month is August, and the teachers are beginning the work of the academic year. The community Franklin serves is widely diverse in terms of race, culture, and language groups; for the most part, the parents of students are working class. Between 65 and 70 percent of the children receive a free or reduced-price lunch. There are about six hundred children in the school, a hundred per grade (K–5), with four teachers per grade.

Figure 16–2. *The Spiral of Learning*

Impetus for Change Four years ago, the school staff and principal made a commitment to a long-term school improvement project that included ongoing professional development for all teachers in the school. An impetus for the change was low scores on standardized reading tests; teachers also expressed dissatisfaction with their ability to teach. Literacy was identified as a possible "lever" for change. If they could install a dynamic reading and writing program and increase achievement in that area, improvement overall would be possible.

The first step was to form a leadership team and prepare in-school teacher educators. In partnership with a nearby university, two teachers received a year of training to be literacy coordinators. During this year they implemented new approaches in their own classrooms and learned professional development skills.

Professional Development Lynda, the primary-grade literacy coordinator, works with teachers in grades K, 1, and 2. She teaches an initial course, which is offered after school—two sessions each month for nine months. In the course she introduces a wide range of research-based instructional approaches in literacy. She also provides regular in-class coaching. She works with teachers in her professional development role in the morning; in the afternoon, she teaches social studies, mathematics, and science to a class of first graders.

Steve is the intermediate-grade literacy coordinator. He teaches a professional development course for teachers in grades 3, 4, and 5, coaches teachers in the classroom, and works with his own class of fourth graders in the afternoon.

Together Lynda and Steve add up to one full-time staff development position for twenty-four teachers. They also work with learning disability teachers, extra reading teachers, a speech and language teacher, and special area teachers. They work collaboratively on some projects (such as developing the school book room, which includes volumes for grades K–5). For other projects, they assemble teams of teachers at their respective grade levels.

The Current Staff Last year, Lynda taught an initial course for six teachers; she'd worked with

four teachers the year before that. The school has four new primary teachers this year. Lynda has identified three different groups of primary teachers who will need her assistance:

1. Four teachers who are new to the instructional approaches as well as new to teaching. These teachers will need the full initial course and have agreed to participate as part of their employment.
2. Five teachers who have recently completed the initial course and need ongoing support sessions as well as in-class coaching, plus another teacher who has switched from teaching grade 2 to teaching kindergarten and needs some help getting started.
3. Two teachers who have been working with the approaches for at least two years and have become very expert in their work.

Steve has identified similar groups among the intermediate-grade teachers. His work at the intermediate level has been going on for only two years; however, he had full participation from the group the first year, and there were only two new teachers last year. This year, he is working with five teachers who either are new or are new to the literacy framework. Of the seven experienced teachers, two have moved from another school where they had participated in similar training as well as an action research project. Steve will provide an initial training course for the new teachers and continue to coach and work with the experienced teachers.

In our yearlong scenario below, we'll call the first group "new" teachers, even though some of them have quite a few years of experience. They are new to the instruction going on at Franklin school. We'll call the second and third groups "experienced" teachers, because they have been working with the framework for at least two years. These teachers represent a variety of experience and backgrounds. Three of them are highly expert and are engaged in action research. They do not attend the literacy coordinator's scheduled classes, but they do receive coaching in their classrooms.

Summer [August]

New Teachers Both Steve and Lynda meet for several days with the new teachers in their classes. They provide basic information about the school and investigate ways teachers can observe students' learning. Assessment techniques are covered, and participants practice them. Both Steve and Lynda spend time on schedules, classroom management, and organization. They also make sure that these teachers have the basic materials they need to work successfully with the instructional approaches they will be using. They show them the book room and other materials that will be needed. [PROVIDING THE BASICS]

Lynda introduces the literacy framework and provides demonstrations of guided reading lessons, interactive and shared writing lessons, and word study minilessons. Steve also introduces the literacy framework, asking participants to do their own reading and writing as they move through the procedures and processes of independent reading, independent writing, and poetry study. Based on these initial sessions, participants will be able to establish some specific routines in their classrooms during the first three weeks of school. [DEMONSTRATING THE PROCESS/ESTABLISHING THE RATIONALES/ENGAGING THE LEARNERS]

Experienced Teachers Lynda and Steve also meet for a day with the returning teachers to review results from the past year, revisit goals for the coming year, and communicate professional development opportunities. They identify some areas of need and plan their professional development sessions for the year with these needs in mind.

Whole Staff New teachers join the experienced teachers as everyone looks at what will happen this year. Schedules are shared and the schedule for professional development sessions (set the last week of school the previous June) is revisited. There will be four sessions for the entire staff over the year. In addition, Lynda will meet with the primary teachers once each month, Steve, with the intermediate teachers. These sessions will focus on special topics and

may include discussions at grade level and across grade levels. Staff members share some of their reflections over the summer, any learning experiences they've had, and what they hope to work on this year. [ASSESSING THE CONTEXT]

Staff committees check the book room and get it up and running. Last year, Lynda and Steve, along with a group of teachers, had analyzed the "gaps" in their collection of books for guided and independent reading and ordered a lot of new ones. A secretary has unpacked the books, but the teachers need to assign them to the appropriate levels. [PROVIDING THE BASICS]

Autumn

New Teachers As school starts, both Lynda and Steve continue their staff development classes for new teachers. They show videotaped lessons and talk about them. With Lynda's and Steve's guidance, the new teachers observe more experienced teachers, Through reflection and discussion, Lynda and Steve foster a beginning understanding of why the approaches they are introducing help students. [DEMONSTRATING THE PROCESS/ ESTABLISHING THE RATIONALES]

Teachers try out some specific procedures for themselves. Lynda focuses on guided reading, independent writing, interactive/shared writing, reading aloud, and word study (with application) at first. She continues to discuss classroom management. [TRYING IT OUT] She guides the teachers in reflection and evaluation—"how did it go"

Connecting reading and writing.

discussions. They also talk about students' responses, and Lynda's observations help them notice more. With Lynda's assistance, they concentrate on the procedures, refining them over several months, adjusting them to meet children's growing needs. [ESTABLISHING ROUTINES AND PROCEDURES]

Steve also asks teachers to try out approaches and provides demonstrations, examples, and in-class support. He continues to spend time on routines and management, especially within reading workshop and writing workshop. Teachers establish independent reading and independent writing, both of which begin with a minilesson and in which students read or write silently for one hour. Steve also works with them on holding community meetings with students. New intermediate teachers have the opportunity to observe experienced teachers and talk with them about how they create a learning community and provide efficient minilessons and read-alouds. [TRYING IT OUT/ESTABLISHING ROUTINES AND PROCEDURES]

Experienced Teachers Lynda and Steve also provide support for more experienced teachers. In one session for the entire staff, teachers examine the book collection. They look at text structures and genre from kindergarten through fifth grade and relate their analyses to their students' reading abilities. A major topic for discussion is how reading aloud can help students in grades K through 5 learn about genres. Three intermediate teachers begin a study of genre. [EXTENDING LEARNING]

In their monthly meetings, Lynda and her group of primary teachers work on refining their knowledge of word study, which they did not have time to do the previous year. They also examine and analyze guided reading lessons. They relate their observations and experience to the reading process. Teachers are interested in making their text selections and introductions more effective. [DEMONSTRATING THE PROCESS/ESTABLISHING THE RATIONALES]

In his work with intermediate teachers Steve focuses on implementing word study. The teachers are interested in challenging their students and making connections across the curriculum. The group also examines a large number of informational books and considers how to help their students learn to use structures like com-

pare/contrast, description, temporal sequence, and cause/effect. Several sessions are held on each topic, with teachers gathering information from their work with students and then sharing and analyzing it. [EXTENDING LEARNING]

Both Steve and Lynda spend time in the classrooms of experienced teachers. At this point, all teachers have established basic routines and can "do" the procedures. Steve and Lynda continue to help them refine procedures and push them toward analyzing the process themselves. They also help teachers analyze children's behavior as a way of thinking about their lessons. [COACHING FOR SHIFTS IN BEHAVIOR/COACHING FOR ANALYSIS AND REFLECTION]

Winter

New Teachers During the winter, Steve and Lynda continue their twice-a-month sessions with new teachers. Lynda has a particular problem. A teacher has to leave because of illness, and a new teacher replaces her. Lynda works with the new teacher one-on-one in her classroom for a week to help her establish routines and introduce some instructional approaches. Lynda's and Steve's observations in classrooms guide their work with new teachers. [ASSESSING THE CONTEXT]

In their staff development sessions, both groups continue to work on understanding more about how to interpret children's reading and writing behavior. They look at decision making related to various instructional techniques within the framework—interactive writing and guided reading for primary teachers and literature study for intermediate teachers. Both groups look at effective minilessons in word study and continue to work on matching books to readers. [DEMONSTRATING THE PROCESS/ESTABLISHING THE RATIONALES]

Steve and Lynda begin a period of intensive coaching with the new teachers. Sometimes they still work alongside them in classrooms to help establish routines, but by now the instruction is for the most part managed smoothly. They observe students' behavior closely to determine how to help the teachers adjust instruction in response to readers and writers. [ASSESSING THE CONTEXT]

Lynda and Steve work to help teachers make their teaching more powerful; they offer specific suggestions for change but an additional goal is to help the teachers reflect on and analyze their teaching for themselves. The focus is on meeting students' needs, not simply looking at techniques. [COACHING FOR SHIFTS IN BEHAVIOR/COACHING FOR ANALYSIS AND REFLECTION]

Experienced Teachers Steve and Lynda meet with the experienced teachers in monthly sessions. The primary teachers focus on shifts in reading behavior over time. Their goal is to understand better how children develop reading strategies. To do so, they look at running records of reading behavior taken over time. Because teachers in the school have been systematically collecting running records over a number of years, they are able to look at a small group of students from kindergarten through the end of second grade. Behavioral evidence, documented precisely, enables them to trace reading progress and expand their knowledge of the development of the reading process. [EXTENDING LEARNING]

This activity spurs individual teachers to look closely at how their own students have developed since the beginning of the year. Coaching in classrooms is closely aligned with the ongoing work in the staff development sessions. Although there is always room to explore a particular teacher's concerns, many coaching conversations focus on students' reading behavior and on the components of instruction. For example, the coaching conversations that surround guided reading help teachers think about book selection and introductions in relation to what they are learning about the reading development of their students. They look closely to find evidence of comprehension as shown in running records and ongoing observation during lessons. Lynda interjects new information into the conversations as necessary. [COACHING FOR ANALYSIS AND REFLECTION]

Steve's course meetings with more experienced intermediate teachers focus on reading strategies. Teachers are particularly interested in how to help students understand ideas "beyond the text." Using videotapes, they examine students' behavior during guided reading discussions of fiction and nonfiction texts, looking for evidence that students are able to make inferences and connections between their own lives as well as other texts. [EXTENDING LEARNING]

Members of the experienced group also notice the relationships between instructional moves and student understanding (as evidenced in behavior). They accompany this discussion with a continued look at informational texts. Teachers think about how to apply their learning in their own teaching. They make a personal commitment to learn with their teacher colleagues as part of the regular workflow and life of the school. Teachers initiate professional development themselves and are willing to contribute to the growth of their colleagues. The staff developer and principal reinforce teachers' expectations and support teachers' extended learning. [EXTENDING LEARNING]

The intermediate teachers have uncovered something that is difficult for many of their students as well as for them. When they introduced guided reading, they used mostly fiction. Now they are also using informational texts, but many students demonstrate that they don't understand these text structures; many also have difficulty using visual features such as graphs and illustrations. Working with informational tests is new learning, so the teachers shift back to earlier points in the spiral of learning; however, they make the shifts more quickly and more easily. In coaching sessions, Steve demonstrates

Teacher and students reading together.

how to discuss texts and also shows them some specific techniques for helping children understand diagrams and charts. [DEMONSTRATING THE PROCESS] Teachers then try out some of the techniques for themselves and evaluate their students' responses. [TRYING IT OUT/ESTABLISHING ROUTINES AND PROCEDURES] They refine their teaching as Steve continues to coach them. [COACHING FOR SHIFTS IN BEHAVIOR]

Whole Staff The entire staff meets together for one session. Steve and Lynda decide to focus the session on nonfiction texts, since that is something all the teachers are talking about. The principal attends and participates in this session, because reading and interpreting nonfiction is an area of the proficiency test that concerns her. She knows that giving students a few weeks of "test-taking skills" is not the answer. She is interested in building student and teacher awareness of and confidence with nonfiction over the grades.

As the session begins, teachers share some of their new learning. The three teachers involved in action research share their study of genre with the group. [EXTENDING LEARNING] In cross-grade-level teams, they look at a range of nonfiction texts that they have used with students in their classrooms. They arrange these texts along the gradient of difficulty and discuss the demands the texts make on readers. [COACHING FOR ANALYSIS AND REFLECTION]

The group looks at the range of texts and identifies critical structures they want to help their students understand. Then, they meet in grade-level teams to think about how these structures can be made a natural part of the curriculum throughout the grades. This process requires looking across the literacy framework. Difficult informational books would not support emergent and early readers who are trying to build a reading process. Reading aloud and interactive/shared writing are ideal ways to support reading and writing informational texts. [EXTENDING LEARNING]

There is a short discussion of the demands of the proficiency test and the kinds of informational reading and analysis that are required of fourth graders. In grade-level teams, teachers also quickly check midyear assessment data and identify areas that need more focused instruction. The established benchmarks in reading and writing are helpful here. [EXTENDING LEARNING]

Spring

New Teachers Lynda's work with the new teachers continues in staff development sessions. By now they have established the basic routines for each component of the literacy framework, but they are using them mainly as separate activities. In class sessions, they explore how to use reading and writing behavior (collected through assessment but also from their observation and records) to inform word study. Lynda demonstrates the interrelationship among components via videotaped lessons and by having them observe experienced teachers. [DEMONSTRATING THE PROCESS]

She encourages teachers to analyze their own lessons to see how they might get greater power by making connections (for example, linking interactive writing with word study minilessons or moving from guided reading into independent writing). They continue to look at records of student behavior to understand progress over time. They identify students who need more help, and Lynda demonstrates and works with teachers on ways to support them.

An engaged reader

[DEMONSTRATING THE PROCESS]

Lynda coaches the teachers to analyze how they use their time both overall and within individual procedures. She also helps them see how their teaching within procedures can be more powerful, especially in terms of making connections across the framework. [COACHING FOR SHIFTS IN BEHAVIOR] They are moving toward self-analysis.

Steve's work with new intermediate teachers focuses on helping them learn to use their assessment data effectively. He also wants them to begin to assess their own work in components of the framework. Teachers look at records of students' reading—letters in their reading response journals, lists of books read. They see how these analyses can help them understand more about their students' reading patterns. [ENGAGING THE LEARNERS/ESTABLISHING THE RATIONALES]

Steve demonstrates how to help students reflect on the range of books they are reading. He shows how to look for evidence over time that students are making inferences. [DEMONSTRATING THE PROCESS] Teachers try out these techniques with their students, along with techniques for helping students write higher-quality responses in their journals. Their goal is to help their students understand texts better. [TRYING IT OUT/ESTABLISHING ROUTINES AND PROCEDURES]

Experienced Teachers Lynda and Steve continue to meet with the experienced teachers as well. Lynda's group shifts their focus to literature study, an area they are having difficulty working into the schedule. All teachers are reading aloud to students regularly and following up with interactive, shared, and independent writing; but except for one classroom, children have done little independent study and discussion. Literature study is something everyone wants to develop.

First they look at their schedules and find ways to incorporate literature study. [ASSESSING THE CONTEXT] Then they find ways to be able to observe (with Lynda present) the teacher who is working strongly in literature study. [DEMONSTRATING THE PROCESS] In staff development meetings, they discuss their observations and relate students' responses to their previous discussions of the reading process. [ESTABLISHING THE RATIONALES]

They try out literature study in their classrooms, with Lynda's assistance in working out

routines. They work out ways of teaching students to talk with one another. [TRYING IT OUT/DEMONSTRATING THE PROCESS] As the routines are established, teachers begin to step back and observe children's responses; Lynda's coaching helps them reflect on what children are learning and on how text selection helps in the process. [COACHING FOR ANALYSIS AND REFLECTION]

Steve's experienced group continues its focus on teaching for reading strategies in relation to both fiction and nonfiction texts. They create minilessons that connect the books they read aloud with the writer's craft. The school buys some good informational picture books, and teachers used them to study memoir, biography, and informational texts.

Whole Staff At the end of the year, staff members meet together to look at assessment data on students and also to reflect on the year. The principal meets with the staff for the entire session. The action researchers share their work, and the rest of the staff offer comments. Some areas of focus for the following year are tentatively determined. [EXTENDING LEARNING]

Partners in Learning

The teachers in Franklin Elementary are working at different levels and focusing on different processes, but over the course of the year all of them have:

◆ Learned about and tried new approaches.
◆ Continually analyzed their work to make it more effective and efficient.
◆ Worked on the routines and refined their use of procedures.
◆ Supported one another as learners.
◆ Examined the results of their work by looking at student behavior as well as formal assessment data.
◆ Grew more analytical in their evaluation of texts.
◆ Became more strategic at meeting individual needs.
◆ Shared concerns and helped one another with specific problems.
◆ Grew in their understanding of students' progress over time, within grades as well as across the grades.

- Learned to identify one another's strengths and ask for help.
- Became more familiar with the range and diversity of books across the gradient.
- Thought about and critiqued the diversity of the book collection.
- Indicated when they wanted another set of eyes in the classroom.
- Asked for help from the literacy coordinators.
- Became more independent.
- Learned from their teaching.

These literacy coordinators and teachers are truly partners in learning. They are coming to think of the students not as "my class" but as "our children." The learning experienced by teachers in another school will not be the same, and next year's learning will not be the same as this year's. What teachers learn is inextricably tied to each day's work with that day's students.

> The pressures forcing the creation of a new educational vision are precisely the same ones forcing our economy to reinvent itself—pressures that value mind over muscle, process before product, and quality above quantity.
> —Wilson and Daviss (9)

It is our sincere hope that the ideas and guides to professional development that we present in this book will help our readers achieve these ideals.

A Day
of Learning

Kecia (left) and Tina (right) during preconference

We end this book with a story of learning in an elementary school. It's a February Tuesday in Kecia's kindergarten classroom. Her students' emerging literacy is very much on Kecia's mind—as it is every day as she reads them stories, encourages them to browse in the class library, and helps them compose stories in the writing center. Because Kecia and the other teachers in her school are part of a professional development program offered by the school district in partnership with a nearby university, Kecia is also learning—learning how to become a more effective professional educator who understands how best to support her students' literacy development. With the help of her colleague and literacy coach, Tina, Kecia is able to study and reflect on her teaching.

The kindergartners in Kecia's class are a diverse group. They began the year with different background experiences. Many of them did not know the letters of the alphabet, none of them could read, and writing was new for most of them. Now they can all write their names as well as simple messages. This morning before school Kecia looked at the messages Kaite, Tyler, Mackenzie, and Phillip had composed the day before:

This morning before school Kecia looked at the messages Kaite, Tyler, Mackenzie, and Phillip had composed the day before.

Examples of Kindergarten Writing—Day One

Clearly, they have learned a great deal about writing.

But Kecia notices that most of the children are not using word spacing, even though she has discussed this idea with them during group writing, shared reading, and individual conferences. Kecia decides that today she will focus on spacing in an interactive writing lesson. (In interactive writing, the teacher and students work together to decide what to write, and then the teacher and various students participate in writing various letters or words of the text on an easel for everyone to see. For a detailed discussion of interactive writing, see McCarrier, Pinnell, and Fountas 2000.)

Just before Kecia's teaching day begins Tina, her literacy coach, stops by and Kecia invites her to observe her lesson and help her think about her teaching. They examine the students' writing samples together, and Tina asks Kecia what she notices about her student's writing.

KECIA: They are able to identify and record sounds in words. They can say words slowly and hear beginning and ending sounds, especially on known words. They can hear dominate consonants.

TINA: What about these particular samples will help you with your lesson today?

KECIA: Most of the samples are one sentence. I can see that almost all of the children made a logical attempt at words. Next, I want to ask them to make their writing more readable by using spacing between words. I made a quick tally of those who use spaces and those who don't, and the majority of the class doesn't use them. In interactive writing, I make a big deal about it. We have to use spaces so we can read it. I tell them to do the same thing when they are writing for themselves. When we read, we need spaces.

TINA: So spacing will be the focus for your lesson. How can you emphasize it so that you really get students' attention?

KECIA: Interactive writing will let me be very explicit about it. I can talk about spacing before we begin and call their attention to it as we write the text.

TINA: You can only make a few teaching points during any lesson. Is there anything you'll have to let go?

KECIA: Yes. I have a tendency to deal with anything that comes up. This time, I'm going to let some teaching points go, such as the parts of words, and really emphasize spaces.

TINA: That sounds good; it may make your lesson more concise. You don't have to do everything in one lesson. Is there any other time in the day that you can also help children learn about spaces?

KECIA: I am going to weave it throughout the day. As they are doing independent writing in the center, I'll watch for spaces and praise the children when they use them. In writing workshop, I can make spacing the topic of my minilesson. The children will know that I expect spacing; it will be a consistent emphasis throughout the day.

TINA: How might you end this interactive writing lesson?

KECIA: Maybe come up with a summary statement that will help them make the transition to independent writing—something that will motivate them to check on their spacing themselves.

TINA: That's right. You'll be explaining what you expect but at the

> Interactive writing will let me be very explicit about it. I can talk about spacing before we begin and call their attention to it as we write the text.

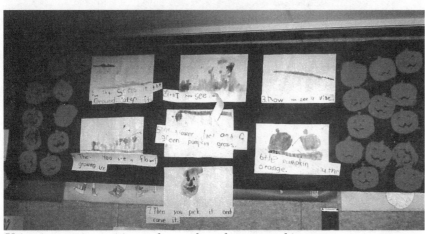

Using interactive writing to learn about how pumpkins grow.

> You'll be explaining what you expect but at the same time showing them how they can use what you have taught them in their own writing. I notice that you are always pushing them to become independent learners.

same time showing them how they can use what you have taught them in their own writing. I notice that you are always pushing them to become independent learners.

Then the bell rings. After the opening routines, Kecia begins the lesson.

KECIA: Every Tuesday, you have a chance to go to the library and choose a new book. If you bring your book back, what do you get to do?

KAITE: Get a new book.

KECIA: Raise your hand if you've brought your book back. [*About half the class raise their hand.*] All of you with your hand up will get to check out another book, won't you? [*The children nod.*] Those of you who forgot to bring your book back won't get to check out another one, but I know you are looking forward to going next week. You know, I was thinking. Something I do a lot of times to help me remember things is I write it down. For example, I wrote down today that we were going to read. Those library books are important, aren't they? What could we do to make sure the library books come back every Tuesday?

TIM: We could write a note at home on Monday.

KECIA: What might the note say?

MACKENZIE: "Please remember to bring your library book tomorrow."

KECIA: How could we make Mackenzie's message help us realize exactly when to bring the library books back?

JAMIE: "Please would you remember to bring your books back tomorrow."

KECIA: I think it's important to have the word *Tuesday* in our message.

PAULINA: "Please remember to bring your book back on Tuesday."

KECIA: Howard, does that make sense to you? If you read that note, would you know when to bring your library book back?

Kecia pointing out spaces between words.

Interactive writing lesson from the coaching session.

[*She repeats the message twice. Howard agrees that the message will work.*] I think that's a good message. Let's repeat it several times. [*They do.*] Why are we saying it over and over? Sammy?

SAMMY: So we can remember it.

KECIA: Yes, so we can remember it while we write it. What is the first word we are going to write?

EVERYONE: "Please."

KECIA: Is it on our word wall?

EVERYONE: No.

KECIA: Let's say the word together slowly. [*They do.*] Jake, why don't you come up to the easel and write the first letter. [*Jake writes the* p *and also the* l. *The rest of the children say the word and check Jake's work. They say the word again, and Jake hears and writes the* e.]

KAITE: Next I hear a *z*.

KECIA: It does sound like a *z*, and sometimes we write a *z* for that sound. This time it's an *s*, which can also stand for that sound. [*She writes the rest of the word* please, *and then has children read the first written word and repeat the rest of the message.*] Now there's something I want you be careful with. Everyone's eyes up here. We need to be sure to leave a space here. Matthew, can you come up and start *remember* but leave a big space here? [*Matthew goes to the easel, says the word* remember, *and writes* re.] Yes, that's just like whose name?

EVERYONE: Rebekah. [*Kecia writes* m, e, m, b, e *and Matthew writes the* r *at the end.*]

KECIA: Now check to see—did Matthew leave a space between words?

EVERYONE: Yes.

KECIA: He sure did, and that space will help us read our message much more easily. Because when we squish all our words together, it makes it harder to read.

KAITE: People will think that it's just one long word.

Now I'm going to ask you to check something when you go to the writing center today. Look carefully at your writing and say, "I made spaces between my words today."

KECIA: Exactly. So, Matthew, thank you very much for making sure that space got in there. That was a long word, wasn't it?
MACKENZIE: Three claps [*syllables*]!

[*Kecia and the children complete the message in this fashion, after which they read the text several times and check for spacing.*]

KECIA: Now I'm going to ask you to check something when you go to the writing center today. Look very carefully at your writing and say, *I made spaces between my words today.* Let's check our message again. Did we put spaces between our words?
CHILDREN: Yes.
KECIA: So today, in the writing center, check your spaces. Why is it important?
ALEXANDRA: So it won't look just like one big long word that people won't know how to read.
KECIA: That's right. We left good spaces in the message we wrote today, didn't we?

Later, during Kecia's free period, she and Tina discuss the lesson.

TINA: What did you want to accomplish in this lesson?
KECIA: I wanted to make the point that they needed to use conventional spacing. I also wanted to help them monitor their own use of spaces. We needed to remember to return library books, so that message was a natural choice for interactive writing. Even through returning books to the library has nothing to do with using spaces in writing, the reminder provided an authentic reason for them to use spacing.
TINA: That's right. The message gave them a real reason to write. You were also concerned about their ability to monitor spac-

Kecia talking to a kindergarten student during writing workshop.

ing themselves in their independent writing.

KECIA: Today I kept hitting that hard. Previously I just mentioned spacing along with other instructional points that came up. I wasn't focused on spacing; there were too many things I was trying to do. Today I intentionally limited my teaching points to emphasize spacing.

TINA: What were some important ways you think were effective in emphasizing spacing?

KECIA: During the lesson, Katie noted that if they didn't use spacing, "people will think that it's just one long word"; at the end of the lesson I revisited this idea. I asked them to check the words for spacing throughout the writing, and at the end I summed it up.

TINA: You really picked up on what they were saying, how they were showing you they understood. Do you think you were more explicit in the language you used than you have been before?

KECIA: It was hard to resist addressing everything that came up. I always want to teach too many things at once. But today I kept my emphasis on spacing so that it kept echoing throughout the lesson.

TINA: You selected what you wanted to bring to their attention and let other things go?

KECIA: Yes. Whatever the teaching point is, I try to keep my focus so it runs like a thread through the lesson and then throughout the day.

TINA: Your hope is that children will shift their behavior and you will see evidence in their independent writing. How will you know if that happens?

KECIA: I need to observe and notice whether they are using spacing in their independent writing. Then I'll know that it "took" and they can do it by themselves. That will mean it's a good lesson. If not, I'll have to revisit spacing tomorrow.

TINA: Let's look at the work Katie, Tyler, Mackenzie, and Philip did in the writing center today. [*See the examples provided.*]

Examples of Kindergarten Writing—Day Two

I think that you've become much clearer in your mind about how to emphasize certain things so that it becomes clearer in the children's minds as well.

KECIA: See, Katie has put spaces between *I, smell,* and *a.*

TINA: And Tyler has written his message in a single line with spaces between each word. And he's using some conventional spelling!

KECIA: And look how much Mackenzie has written. She's spaced between words before, but up till now she's only used words on our word wall, and her messages have been choppy. In her message to me today she's used large, clear spaces. The frequently encountered words are spelled conventionally, and she's attempted to spell the other words according to how they sound.

TINA: Philip has the least experience, but even he shows some improvement. It's easier to see that he's writing a message, and the concept of words seems to be emerging: he's attempted to use spaces.

KECIA: So all four of them are just a little better about using spacing. I'll certainly point that out tomorrow and celebrate it. I'll say, "I notice that a lot of people at the writing center checked and asked themselves, *Did I space?*"

TINA: What have you really taught them to do?

KECIA: I hope that they understand how to use spaces in a conventional way in their writing.

TINA: You have gone beyond teaching an activity; you are teaching your students a process about how to write sentences. And you are teaching them not only how to do the task but how to check on themselves. I think that you've become much clearer in your mind about how to emphasize certain things so that it becomes clearer in the children's minds as well. What would be the next step for them?

KECIA: Maybe I could get them to check on whether the writing everyone is doing has spaces.

TINA: How would that help them?

KECIA: They would get a lot of practice in checking on spaces. Also, they'd know that their friends will be looking for spaces, so they'll be more conscious of it when they are.

Kecia (left) *and Tina* (right) *during coaching.*

TINA: So you are always thinking of the connections you can make?

KECIA: It's much better to use something strategically.

TINA: You're hoping that during writer's workshop you'll get more evidence of the effectiveness of the lesson, and you can reinforce it with your minilesson and conferences. Will that help you plan for tomorrow?

KECIA: Incorporating a minilesson or interactive writing into writing workshop provides an immediacy; I'm right there and I can go around and work with the children who need extra help. At the end of workshop, we share as a whole group, so we can revisit the issues that come up in individual conferences.

TINA: If you find that many of the children have begun to use spaces, you could work with them in writing workshop and reserve your time to work specifically with children who really need you, one on one, providing close attention.

At the end of their conversation, Kecia writes down a couple of goals:

Today is not the first, last, or only day of learning for Kecia, Tina, and the children in this classroom. The school is alive with learning: learning is embedded at all levels and unfolds on many fronts. Children learn ever more about literacy. Kecia has many opportunities to learn as she meets with her colleagues, invites Tina into her classroom, assumes leadership and research roles in the school, and begins to help her less experienced colleagues. As a learner, she refines and extends her understanding of the craft of teaching. Tina is also a teacher and a learner.

Professional development requires listening carefully, observing closely, and asking pertinent questions. Listening, observing, questioning, and learning are the heart and soul of effective teaching and effective professional development and are what this book is all about.

> Listening, observing, questioning, and learning are the heart and soul of effective teaching and effective professional development.

Appendix A: Learning from Teachers and School-Based Teacher Educators

This background appendix describes research and development programs in which we have collaborated over the last fifteen years. We are grateful to our colleagues Diane E. DeFord and Andrea McCarrier for being our partners in these efforts.

Whatever the method, approach, or materials, *teaching* makes the difference. A recent large-scale study revealed that every additional dollar spent on raising teacher quality netted greater gains in student achievement than did any other use of school resources. Therefore, "if we can focus our energies on providing this generation of teachers with the kinds of knowledge and skills they need to help students succeed, we will have made an enormous contribution to America's future" (Darling-Hammond 1996, p. 194).

But *what* must teachers know and be able to do to ensure successful literacy for all students? The answer is complex and requires that we investigate all aspects of teaching and learning. The more we learn, the more we realize we need to know. One thing we do know is this: decision making is the foundation of effective teaching. Professional development takes many forms, but if it is to make a difference, it must ultimately help teachers become better decision makers.

Our work with teachers, children, and staff developers in three contexts—Reading Recovery, the Literacy Collaborative, and a two-year research project in Chicago—has helped us identify the concepts and skills related to teachers' learning described in this book.

Reading Recovery

Good education requires teaching *all* children. It means adjusting the level of support as needed so that everyone acquires the critical reading and writing skills needed to succeed in today's society. Some children, for a variety of reasons, require more support in learning to read and write. It is essential to catch students before they fall so far behind their classroom peers that they cannot profit from even excellent instruction (Allington 1991; Torgeson, Wagner, and Rashotte 1997a, 1997b).

What Is Reading Recovery?
Reading Recovery is a research-based early intervention program designed to ensure that initially struggling students build effective reading and writing processes (Askew et al. 1999; Pinnell 1987). For up to twenty weeks, the lowest-achieving first graders receive one-to-one tutoring from a specially trained teacher for thirty minutes each day in addition to their regular classroom literacy instruction.

The results have been remarkable: the great majority of students make accelerated progress and catch up with their grade-level peers within the twenty-week period. Research also shows that given good classroom teaching and no extraordinary circumstances, most of these students continue to make satisfactory progress with no extra help. This success may be attributed to a *combination* of characteristics:

- Early intervention—catching the child before the gap becomes too great.
- Accelerated learning—children don't just make progress but catch up to where they can profit from what is going on in the classroom.
- One-to-one tutoring, which builds precisely on what the child knows without wasting attention on what he already can do.
- Daily intensive lessons that combine reading and writing.
- Intensive professional development for teachers.

Professional Development Within Reading Recovery

Reading Recovery teachers are uniquely trained. They start working with children in one-to-one lessons immediately. After initial training in using assessment measures, they meet once a week (or every two weeks) in two- or two-and-a-half-hour training classes taught by a "teacher leader" who has had a year of in-residence training at a university. The teacher leader conducts class sessions, guides the implementation of Reading Recovery within the school (gathering data and selecting the children who will participate), and coaches teachers regularly.

Class sessions feature a one-way glass screen (see Figure 1). On the mirror side of the glass, one class member, in turn, works one-on-one with a child in a regular Reading Recovery lesson. The remaining members of the class observe the lesson *through* the glass; they can see and hear the lesson and talk among themselves about what is going on ("talking while observing"). Guided by the teacher leader, who directs and redirects the conversation, they look for evidence of learning, make inferences about the reasons for a child's behavior, and discuss teaching decisions and aspects of teaching such as pace and interaction. Gradually, they move from learning a repertoire of effective procedures and instructional approaches to deep discussion and analysis. A group observes two lessons during a class session.

After the lesson being observed is completed, the demonstrating teacher rejoins the group for a discussion. The goal is *not* to critique the lesson or make teaching suggestions. The lessons are a context in which the *observers* can learn more. As they talk with one another, they sharpen their observational and analytic skills. Over the course of their training, they see and discuss many lessons, building a repertoire of "case examples"; because they all see the same lessons, they are able to construct shared meaning. As they become more comfortable with one another, the discussion opens up. Errors simply provide the chance to learn.

After their initial year of training, Reading Recovery teachers participate in four, five, or six days of ongoing professional development every year for as long as they work within the program.

The teacher leader is key to Reading Recovery effectiveness. Teacher leaders enroll in a yearlong, full-time training program, during which they teach children daily in Reading Recovery lessons, attend classes on teaching and theory, and learn the role of the leader, including the teaching and coaching of adults (Lyons, Pinnell, and DeFord 1993). They also attend a yearly summer institute and participate in ongoing professional development. The entire Reading Recovery system is designed so that research informs practice; teacher leaders and teachers are expected to grow and change every year.

Reading Recovery has clear expectations for program implementation. Essential features of the program—one-on-one tutoring of all first graders who need it, training using a one-way glass, ongoing individual coaching from a trained teacher leader, and collecting data on every child—must be in place before the trademarked name can be used.[1] The data are sent to the National Data Evaluation Center, and the results of the program are published each year.

How Reading Recovery Informs This Book

Reading Recovery teachers become highly expert in as well as deeply committed to and enthusiastic about their work in a way that people often find surprising. They attend workshops and conferences, eager to delve more deeply into the processes. A very large majority of Reading Recovery teachers say they have never experienced such in-depth training, and they highly value their colleagues' contributions to their learning (Bussell 2000).

Figure 1. *National-Louis University trainer Sallie Forbes leads a conversation among teacher leaders in the class while observing a Reading Recovery lesson through a one-way glass. Observers from left to right: Sharon Gilpatrick of Madison, Wisconsin, Michelle Shurtz of Southern Illinois University, Linda Scott of Harlem, Sallie Forbes, Program Director of Illinois Reading Recovery. The teacher is Donna Wisniewski. The student is Samantha Orczykowski.*

In this book we focus on classroom teachers, not Reading Recovery teachers, but our own training in Reading Recovery and our study of the processes involved has taught us that:

◆ Learning and development for teachers is an ongoing process that takes time, support, and a variety of experiences.

◆ There must be an overall design to provide such training.

◆ Conscious attention must be paid to implementation.

◆ Observation, analysis, and reflection are critical for teachers' learning.

◆ The role of the leader is not only to tell and demonstrate but also to encourage and facilitate reflection and analysis so that the resulting knowledge is deep, not superficial.

◆ Learning with a peer group is essential— shared meaning and perspectives result in deeper understanding.

◆ Coaching teachers individually makes the difference in putting new practice into action and analyzing and reflecting on it.

◆ Although there must be milestones and celebrations, training is never "done," because learning is continuous and ongoing.

The Literacy Collaborative

Because Reading Recovery training proved so effective, we wanted to develop a dynamic professional development program for regular classroom teachers that incorporates its essential features. The Literacy Collaborative®,[2] a broad-based cooperative effort designed to improve reading, writing, and language instruction in elementary schools, is the result.[3] Classroom instruction in the Literacy Collaborative is by no means patterned on the individual tutoring of Reading Recovery, but the fundamental structure of professional development for teachers is similar. The Literacy Collaborative provides long-term professional development and systemic support for teachers as they take on new instructional approaches and expand their skills. The overall goal of the Literacy

Collaborative is to improve significantly literacy achievement in the elementary grades.

Our work at the primary level (kindergarten, first grade, and second grade) began in 1986, with a series of teacher study groups; formal training of literacy coordinators began in 1993. Work on the intermediate (grades 3 through 6) framework also began with teacher study groups, in 1995, but it built on earlier work by Irene Fountas at Lesley University. Formal training of intermediate literacy coordinators was established at Lesley University in 1999.

Literacy coordinators are school-based teacher educators who provide seminars and coaching for teachers. They receive an initial year of training (seven weeks over an academic year) followed by a field year of supported experience working with teachers. A two-year training program has been designed to prepare university- and district-level personnel to offer literacy coordinator training in their local area. Currently the Literacy Collaborative network includes over four hundred schools located across the United States.

What Does Membership in the Literacy Collaborative Entail?

The Literacy Collaborative is organized around a number of interrelated elements:

◆ Teachers use a comprehensive framework for literacy development that includes a wide range of reading and writing contexts (see Chapter 4).

◆ Professional development is available at the school and offered through a combination of class sessions, individual assistance, and coaching.

◆ A school leadership team is established to guide the process.

◆ A full-time staff developer called a literacy coordinator facilitates the professional development courses, provides in-class assistance, and teaches children daily.

◆ Teachers new to the school (or to the framework) initially receive intensive training.

◆ After the initial training, teachers participate in a variety of ongoing professional development opportunities, including regular meetings, coaching, study groups, and action research.

◆ A book room in the school houses a leveled collection of books organized according to a gradient of difficulty.

◆ Classrooms have extensive libraries, including leveled books, beautifully illustrated children's literature, informational books, poetry, series books, and references.

◆ Safety nets include one-to-one tutoring for first graders (Reading Recovery).

◆ There is a parent outreach program that includes books for students to take home and read.

Work in the Literacy Collaborative is long term; the school staff makes a commitment to at least five years of partnership with a university.

Hallmarks of Literacy Collaborative Instruction

Instruction in Literacy Collaborative schools includes a combination of direct teaching and independent application of important principles in reading and writing and is tailored to the learners. Instruction on topics already mastered is inefficient; instruction on concepts that are too difficult is ineffective. Teachers identify learners' strengths and needs through both systematic and informal assessment and use a combination of whole-group, small-group, individual, and independent work as appropriate for the particular skills and strategies being taught. Overall instructional goals are to:

◆ Ensure that students read and write for real purposes so that they understand the role of literacy in their lives.

◆ Teach basic principles that allow students to become independent, strategic readers, writers, and spellers.

◆ Help students develop a flexible range of comprehension strategies in reading and composition strategies in writing.

◆ Teach students how to manage their own reading and writing and thus extend their learning.

Instruction for younger students involves a combination of reading and writing experiences that help them learn the purposes of literacy (Booth 1999; Hundley and Powell 1999; McCarrier and Patacca 1994). The primary-level language and literacy framework (see Chapter 2; also see Fountas and Pinnell 1996) includes a range of:

- Reading instruction: reading to children, shared reading, guided reading, and independent reading.
- Writing instruction: shared writing, interactive writing, guided writing, and independent writing.
- Word study: phonics and spelling.

Early emphasis is placed on knowing frequently encountered words while at the same time learning important principles about letter-sound relationships and how words "work." (Adams 1990; Bradley and Bryant 1983; Bryant et al. 1990; Ceprano 1980; Ehri 1991).

The alphabet is the tool of the reader and writer; all words in our system are based on this limited set of graphic signals. To identify letters, a basic skill, young children must learn to notice the features (many involving very small differences) that distinguish one letter from another (Lyons 1999). The Literacy Collaborative curriculum emphasizes learning to hear the sounds in words (phonemic awareness) as well as learning to look at letters and words and acquiring critical concepts about how print works (Clay 1991; Snow, Burns, and Griffin 1998; Vellutino and Scanlon 1987). Children learn letter-sound relationships in several different ways, including structured minilessons, interactive word walls and charts, and hands-on work in ABC or word study centers (Chall 1989; Henry 1999). In each classroom, systematic word study helps students examine phonics and spelling principles. Children are taught to apply what they know while reading and writing.

Reading instruction ensures that students comprehend written text as well as learn to use phonics skills while reading for meaning (Pearson and Fielding 1991, Pressley 1998; Snow, Burns, and Griffin 1998). Instruction in writing assures that students learn to spell conventionally while writing to communicate (Henderson 1990). Writing, in fact, contributes substantially to children's learning to read words (Ehri and Wilce 1985).

Instruction in grades 3 through 6 continues to involve students in a wide range of reading and writing contexts (see Fountas and Pinnell 2000). The three-block framework for the intermediate grades includes language and word study, reading workshop, and writing workshop.

The teacher introduces reading workshop with a minilesson. Then students read independently and silently while the teacher confers with individuals, brings students together for small-group instruction in guided reading, and meets with literature discussion groups. Writing workshop also includes minilessons, guided writing, and independent writing. Content area reading and writing, including sustained investigations or research projects, are emphasized. Students make strong connections between reading and writing and explore a range of genres, including nonfiction, fiction, and poetry. They read and write continuous text every day.

The Literacy Collaborative's Textual Base

Literacy Collaborative schools invest in several kinds of books on which to base students' reading, writing, and word study:

1. There is a school "book room" of leveled texts shared across grade levels K through 6. Teachers talk with one another about the supports and demands texts make on readers. Benchmarks are established for every level on the gradient of difficulty, so that systematic assessment is built into the process and teachers can follow students' progress over the years as they expand their strategies to deal with more complex texts.

2. In addition to a good school library, there are good book collections in each classroom. Classroom collections include a range of leveled books, excellent children's literature (for students to read silently and for teachers to read aloud), and informational books to support research. Collections include a wide variety of genres.

3. The school supports home reading. In all grades students take home and return the books they read in guided and independent reading. Children in kindergarten through grade 2 have KEEP BOOKS®[4] (very short paperbacks sporting colorful covers and containing interesting stories) as part of the family outreach program. KEEP BOOKS are designed to support the development of early reading strategies. Because these little books are so inexpensive (25 cents each), children can take them home and keep

them. It costs about $25 to give a child a book a week from kindergarten through about midway through grade 2.

Professional Development Within the Literacy Collaborative

The key to implementing a Literacy Collaborative program is the initial yearlong training of a literacy coordinator. Literacy coordinators:

1. Complete seven weeks of intensive training at a university (scheduled at intervals over a period of a year).
2. Implement and reflect on all aspects of the literacy framework as they work with students daily in a classroom.
3. Participate in regularly scheduled study groups.
4. Videotape and analyze their teaching.
5. Gather observational data on children and complete case studies.

Once trained, literacy coordinators spend at least half the school day providing staff development. They also continue to participate in ongoing professional development via their association with a university in the Literacy Collaborative network.

At present, universities prepare literacy coordinators for both primary and intermediate levels, in separate training programs. Schools may elect to join the Literacy Collaborative program at the primary level, the intermediate level, or both. Schools who join at both levels have two half-time literacy coordinators who work closely together and coordinate their efforts.

Teachers in Literacy Collaborative schools agree to:

1. Implement the language and literacy framework in their classrooms.
2. Collect assessment data on student progress.
3. Participate in an initial course that involves forty hours of classes, usually held outside the school day and scheduled over one or two years.
4. Continue to participate in ongoing professional development and other study opportunities after the initial training.
5. Allow the literacy coordinator to coach them in their classroom.
6. Talk with the literacy coordinator and their colleagues about their teaching.

7. Videotape and analyze their teaching as they become more familiar with the approach.
8. Engage in ongoing individual learning as need and opportunity arise.

Reflection is a key assessment tool that strengthens instruction. Through coaching and conversations with their colleagues, teachers continually reflect on the effectiveness of their teaching (Joyce and Showers 1980, 1982).

How the Literacy Collaborative Informs This Book

Through our association with the Literacy Collaborative we have worked directly with children, observed in hundreds of classrooms, analyzed countless hours of teaching, and, most important, analyzed a myriad of coaching sessions. Quite simply, we have learned how to implement comprehensive school improvement via professional development; at the same time, we have learned how difficult change really is and how long it is likely to take.

Your own situation may be quite different from that of a literacy coordinator, who works in only one school. You may be working at the district level and be responsible for several schools. You may be teaching at a university or working with preservice teachers. Nevertheless, we have found that the principles that underlie literacy coordinators' work are fundamental to just about every kind of teacher education. If you are involved in any kind of extended professional development for elementary teachers, the work that literacy coordinators do is informative.

An In-Depth Study of Teaching and Coaching

In conjunction with the University of Chicago Center for School Improvement, we designed a study to examine how literacy coordinators develop knowledge and skill in three domains: pedagogical knowledge; analytic and inferential skills; and coaching and mentoring.[5] We wanted to identify the understanding teacher educators need as well as how they use this knowledge to help teachers develop *their* knowledge and skills, in terms of both specific techniques and more complex conceptual understanding. To that end we observed and interviewed teachers and literacy coordinators who were part of a two-year study of teacher decision making and pedagogical reasoning. Our goal was to uncover information that would be useful in designing ongoing professional development programs.

The following questions guided our research.

◆ What characteristics of instruction are related to higher achievement in reading and writing?
◆ How is teachers' knowledge related to higher achievement for students?
◆ How can literacy coaches make a positive impact on the work of teachers?

Developing Scales for Analysis

Each of ten teachers was observed and videotaped over a two-year period. Our ongoing analysis of these lessons was the foundation for the three scales presented in Chapters 9 and 10:

◆ Aspects of Teaching.
◆ Guided Reading.
◆ Interactive Writing.

A process for creating and using such scales also emerged. The scales were tested and refined throughout the two-year period. In the final stage of the study, a team of experts analyzed a total of thirty-six interactive writing lessons and forty-two guided reading lessons using the scales.

Creating a Composite Measure of Reading Ability

At the same time, we analyzed achievement data relative to the students taught by the participants in the study. The primary assessments we employed were the Observation of Early Literacy Achievement (Clay 1993a) and the Degrees of Reading Power (DRP), a standardized reading comprehension test for first and second graders.

The Observation Survey is administered individually (it takes approximately forty-five minutes per child). The components of this assessment provide detailed information about the development of early literacy skills: familiarity with the alphabet, sound-letter correspondence, and reading small books of increasing difficulty. Such a detailed, individually administered assessment is necessary to acquire a reliable portrait of young children's reading ability. In addi-

tion, the Observation Survey provides an authentic assessment of learning that is closely related to the instructional approach the Center for School Improvement is attempting to promote at the primary grades. Students are asked to read and interact with texts drawn from trade books and children's literature.[6]

The DRP uses a cloze format—paragraphs or short passages that have had key words deleted. The student is asked to select the word that makes the most sense in the context of the passage. Thus the assessment has a holistic quality that measures how well students understand the overall meaning of the text. This assessment provides an appropriate complement to the text reading portions of the Observation Survey. The Observation Survey measures the most difficult text the student can read with accuracy; the DPR measures the most difficult text the student can read with comprehension.

Using item response theory in connection with a Rasch model,[7] we constructed a composite measure of reading ability. The composite scale provides a reliable measure of overall reading ability that efficiently uses information from each component of the different assessments. In addition, it creates a common metric for all students from kindergarten through second grade and helps solve difficult floor/ceiling problems that arise when one focuses on individual components. Having an internally reliable measure is essential when examining gains over time. The composite scale maintains a consistent measure of growth in student ability and allows comparisons between students across grade levels.

What the Study Showed

The teachers who were ranked highest on all three scales were also those whose students demonstrated the highest achievement. Therefore, scales like these, which help us analyze the complexities of literacy lessons, are promising tools for helping staff developers become much more specific in their dealings with individual teachers.[8] These instruments help the staff developer improve his or her analytic capabilities as a foundation for coaching. They are not intended for use in classrooms or as a basis for the evaluation of teachers. Instead, they should be used to map student learning of critical reading and writing processes in relation to the instruction going on in classrooms. The scales help pinpoint productive areas for discussion.

Not surprisingly the results of the study also confirmed that the tasks performed by teachers and teacher educators are detailed and complex. At any given time, teachers are required to:

◆ Observe as much of children's behavior as possible.
◆ Connect an individual child's behavior to information already gathered on that student.
◆ Organize knowledge about individuals into a collective concept that encompasses first the small group being taught and then the entire class.
◆ Create and continually revise a profile of class progress.
◆ Continually sample individual behavior across the group in order to revise the class profile.
◆ Recall behavior that they recognize from past experience as indicating students are processing and understanding text.
◆ Form and continually re-form a tentative theory about how text is processed (the reading process) or how text is constructed (the writing process).
◆ Monitor behavior for orderly conformation to an underlying sense of organization and management.
◆ Monitor their and their students' behavior in relation to an underlying sense of time and pacing.
◆ Predict student responses to the particular text being written or read.
◆ Collect ongoing data to confirm or disprove hypotheses.

The above list of tasks implies a competency exhibited over and over in the brief (fifteen- or twenty-minute) literacy lessons that make up a good curriculum. To be effective even when working with beginning readers and writers, teachers have to know the demands that using language will place on them. Knowing how to select a text for their students to read and how to help their students compose text when they write is critical to every other action teachers take.

Teachers must also know what the students know and be able to decide what they need to know next—and doing this successfully implies a deep understanding of the reading and writing processes and their interrelated components *combined with* the ability to observe and analyze behavior.

Our results support the argument that teacher education, at least for teachers of literacy, cannot be accomplished in a few courses or even a few years. Teacher education must be deeply rooted in the work of teaching. And teachers need considerable on-the-job support in order to learn from their own teaching. It is no wonder that many administrators, policymakers, and publishers seek "scripts" for teaching rather than investing in long-term, demanding, difficult, and often frustrating development of teachers as professionals.

The teacher educator or literacy coach must not only have all the skills that teachers need but also be able to step back from the process to observe and analyze two levels of learning—students and teachers. The literacy coordinator is not required to have an in-depth knowledge for any given group of children and relies on the teacher to be the "expert" about the students in his class; however, the ability to observe quickly, analyze records, and remember details is essential for building credibility and giving good advice. In other words, the literacy coordinator has to know enough about student behavior in general and about the particular students in the class to give good feedback, select good examples, and hold credibility as an expert. The goal is to promote *teachers' learning*.

The literacy coordinator's primary role is to analyze the teacher's current understanding, observe instructional interactions, and select examples to expand the teacher's craft and her understanding of theory. The literacy coordinator is required to:

◆ Analyze classroom records and student achievement data over time.
◆ Observe and interpret student and teacher behavior during lessons.
◆ Recognize evidence of teacher learning.
◆ Connect student behavior to a tentative theory built from many observations in many classrooms.
◆ Make hypotheses about a teacher's current level of understanding and skill, based on observation over time.

- Observe instructional interactions, looking for examples (both positive and negative) that can help a teacher expand his knowledge and skill.
- Evaluate instructional interactions in light of specific procedures and techniques.
- Interpret instructional interactions in light of a repertoire of potential teaching techniques.
- Identify salient characteristics of ongoing instruction.
- Assess instruction by noting characteristic patterns and matching them with the characteristics of effective teaching—organization, management, pace, timing, positive interactions, and the like.
- Select examples for discussion that will support a teacher's reflection and learning.
- Search for appropriate ways to engage teachers in conversation about their teaching.
- Think in advance about specific goals for a wide variety of teachers.
- Search for a balance between demonstrating, telling, and promoting self-analysis on the part of the teacher.
- Support a teacher in making specific plans and setting goals.
- Provide specific and understandable suggestions.
- Be sensitive to the level of trust and credibility that has been created within the relationship with a teacher.

In other words, the literacy coordinator must be a master at sizing up the situation, connecting it to a broad, deep knowledge base, and then making very quick decisions about what will help a teacher most at a particular moment. These decisions will be affected by whether a teacher:

- Is new or experienced.
- Has difficulty with management and organization.
- Lacks confidence and needs much encouragement and demonstration.
- Is highly expert in some areas but a beginner in others.
- Is locked into previously learned patterns of teaching and has difficulty contemplating change.
- Has read a great deal.
- Is eager for theoretical explanations.

- Sees observation as evaluation and approaches it with apprehension.
- Can learn with just a few demonstrations.

How the Research Project Informs This Book

This research project strengthened our resolve to help teacher educators put theory into action in support of teachers of reading and writing in the elementary school. It provided some very specific ways of analyzing literacy lessons and sharpening the analytic skills of staff developers. It also provided useful insights into coaching.

Teachers are individuals and must be treated as learners. Nevertheless, their needs may not take precedence over student learning. In this very human environment, the school-based teacher educator walks a fine line. Only with intensive, in-the-classroom help can real change, depth of learning, and expansion of power take place. Coaching supports the classroom teacher as she applies knowledge, develops skills, polishes technique, and deepens her understanding.

Coaching is the most difficult part of a teacher educator's job, and the most difficult part of coaching is deciding what points to make. Teacher educators like to demonstrate teaching procedures, and teachers ask them to: but the goal is to help teachers become independent learners who can continue their own development. So it is important for individuals to try the approaches themselves. Analyzing lessons helps teachers reach their goals.

When looking for evidence of learning, it is important to apply a flexible gradient of progress. (The spiral of learning is described in Chapters 2 and 8.) Teachers need to see, hear about, and try out techniques before they can be expected to reflect on them and analyze their reactions to them. Learning does not stop after an approach or technique is established in the classroom; rather, that is where learning *begins*.

As they work and reflect on their teaching, teachers are always constructing tentative theories of how students learn. They refine their work until the process "comes together" into an organized foundation of understanding. At this level the teacher acts and interacts without having to pay conscious attention to routines and procedures, giving full attention to student responses. The learning spiral is repeated time and again for new procedures, materials, and techniques. Teacher educators become experts at analyzing the process.

It takes time, reflection, and conversation with others to make real shifts in teachers' thinking, learning, and practice. This kind of ongoing, close-to-practice professional development is a radical change from "one shot" inservice currently offered in most school districts. Teacher development is effective when:

◆ Complex ideas are experienced, analyzed, and discussed across a variety of learning contexts.

◆ Professional development is grounded in the practice of teaching students.

◆ Professional development involves conversations surrounding the act of teaching.

◆ Teacher learning is supported by a learning community that shares a language in which to communicate complex ideas.

◆ The demonstration of specific teaching approaches is balanced by reflection and analysis.

Putting Learning into Action

Our learning in the three contexts we've discussed in this appendix has helped us consider the interrelationship of *implementation* (training, scheduling, team leadership), *professional development*, *coaching*, and *collaboration*. At times, we need to focus on the fine details of teaching. At other times, we need to look for progress benchmarks across the grades. At still other times, we need to look at the commitment and allocation of resources to support change. Educational change, particularly as it pertains to developing students' critical literacy skills, cannot be halfway or halfhearted. We need comprehensive efforts; we need long-term support pro-

vided through specific, clear, understandable professional development; we need constructive problem solving; we need standards for student achievement, for teacher performance, and for implementation.

Endnotes

[1] Reading Recovery® is a trademark of The Ohio State University and Marie M. Clay. Right to use the trademark is granted royalty free to sites that meet standards for program implementation.

[2] The Literacy Collaborative® is a trademark of The Ohio State University. Designated sites may use the trademark royalty free.

[3] We are indebted to Andrea McCarrier for her vision, her dedication, and her tireless devotion to the education of teachers and literacy coordinators in the Literacy Collaborative.

[4] KEEP BOOKS® are distributed (not for profit) by The Ohio State University. More information is available at *keepbooks.org*.

[5] We are indebted to our University of Chicago colleagues Anthony Bryk, Sharon Greenberg, David Kerbow, Carmen Manning, Virginia Watson, and Linda Wold for their support of and active collaboration in this research as part of the work of the Center for School Improvement.

[6] The Observation Survey also reliably predicts how students in the early grades will perform on other standardized tests, such as the Iowa Test of Basic Skills (ITBS). The Observation Survey and the ITBS reading test are correlated at .72 for first and second grade—a strong general relationship. The correlation between the ITBS reading test and the Illinois Goals Assessment Program is .73 for third grade. By using the Observation Survey with students from kindergarten to second grade, we are able to gain a clear sense of their progress toward third-grade state and district standards.

[7] Rasch analysis is a latent-trait model that produces instrument-free individual student measures of ability and person-free measures of test item difficulty on the same interval scale. The scale units are linear and thus appropriate for calculations and statistics. The measure of reading ability constructed from the Observation Survey components and the DRP had an internal consistency reliability of .98.

[8] We realize that many other classroom and school factors contribute to student scores, so we cannot attribute these results to teachers' implementation of particular teaching approaches. These scales should be more rigorously tested with a larger sample of teachers to determine whether the factors measured here are related to student achievement. These results do provide evidence that such additional testing is warranted, however.

Appendix B: Detailed Guided Reading and Interactive Writing Scales

Guided Reading: A Scale for Analysis

The following scale is designed to be used by teacher educators in analyzing guided reading lessons. The scale is organized into four functions, all of which are developed throughout guided reading lessons. The scale is further divided into columns, each of which refers to a different element of guided reading. Two kinds of knowledge are presented and defined: (1) item knowledge; and (2) process knowledge. Finally, a rating scale (from 0 to 5) is defined.

Functions

1. **Readers construct and extend the meaning of texts.** The teacher helps children construct meaning by bringing their personal, world, and literary knowledge to the understanding of the text. The teacher also helps children go beyond the text to make inferences and connect meaning.

2. **Readers monitor and correct their own reading.** Readers use sources of information, including meaning, language structure, letter-sound information, and visual patterns in words, to check on themselves as readers, search for more information, and correct themselves when needed.

3. **Readers maintain fluency and phrasing while reading continuous text.** Readers connect the text with language and know how good reading sounds. They read at a good rate, slowing down and speeding up as appropriate. They read in phrase units and notice and use punctuation to help them in their expressive reading.

4. **Readers problem-solve words on the run while reading continuous text.** Readers slow down to problem-solve words and use a variety of strategies in a flexible way; then they speed up again. This problem solving takes place against a backdrop of accurate reading and does not destroy the momentum of the reading or the comprehension of the reader.

Columns

1. **Text:** The new book or other piece of written language that the children read.
2. **Introduction:** The teacher and children talk about the book before children read it.
3. **Reading the text:** Each child in the group reads the book/story softly or silently to him/herself.

4. **After reading:** The teacher and children revisit the text for discussion and specific teaching points.
5. **Extending the text (optional):** Experiences are designed to help students extend their understanding of the text (for example, writing, sketching, using graphic organizers, or other extensions).
6. **Word Work (optional):** Children work with magnet letters or whiteboards to explore word solving.

Knowledge

1. **Item knowledge** refers to specific units of language such as letters, sounds, words, parts of words, punctuation, and rules. This category refers only to children's *knowledge of items,* not to their use of knowledge in writing and reading.
2. **Process knowledge** refers to "in the head" strategies that can be applied in many reading and writing contexts. It includes references to the way readers/writers use various kinds of information as they write and read.

Rating Scale

0 = no evidence of learning and/or supportive teaching

1 = very minimal evidence of learning and/or supportive teaching

2 = some evidence of learning and/or supportive teaching

3 = moderate evidence of learning and/or supportive teaching

4 = high level of evidence of learning and/or supportive teaching

5 = demonstrates a model for excellence in teaching that results in a high level of student learning

1. Meaning

1. Readers construct and extend the meaning of texts. The teacher helps children construct meaning by bringing their personal, world, and literary knowledge to the understanding of the text. The teacher also helps children go beyond the text to make inferences and connect meanings.

Text	Introducing the Text	Reading the Text	After Reading the Text	Extending the Text
◆ Contains concepts and ideas that are meaningful to children or are available through teacher support. ◆ Contains words that readers understand. ◆ Contains words that readers recognize. ◆ Contains new words that can be solved.	*The teacher helps students:* ◆ Activate prior knowledge. ◆ Understand unfamiliar ideas and concepts. ◆ Understand the meaning of the whole text. ◆ Use illustrations to support meaning. ◆ Raise questions. ◆ Anticipate the language and events of the text. ◆ Develop interest.	*The teacher helps students to (prompts them to):* ◆ Think about the meaning of the text while reading. ◆ Think about the meaning of words. ◆ Connect words by their meaning. ◆ Recall details while reading. ◆ Confirm or reject predictions.	*The teacher helps students:* ◆ Address and answer questions. ◆ Summarize the text. ◆ Analyze the text. ◆ Connect this text to others they have read. ◆ Connect this text to prior experience or knowledge. ◆ Expand meaning of known words. ◆ Learn meaning of new words.	*The teacher helps students:* ◆ Extend meaning of the text through inference or interpretation. ◆ Use tools (e.g., graphic organizers) to analyze text. ◆ Create new texts through writing. ◆ Connect text to the arts. ◆ Use the text as a basis for writing. ◆ Compare text to others.
0 1 2 3 4 5	0 1 2 3 4 5	0 1 2 3 4 5	0 1 2 3 4 5	0 1 2 3 4 5

Overall Rating for Meaning	Did the teacher help children develop item knowledge?	Did the teacher help children develop processing strategies?
0 1 2 3 4 5	0 1 2 3 4 5	0 1 2 3 4 5

2. Monitoring and Self-Correction

2. Readers monitor and correct their own reading. Readers use sources of information, including meaning, language structure, letter-sound information, and visual patterns in words, to check on themselves as readers, search for more information, and correct themselves when needed.

Text	Introducing the Text	Reading the Text	After Reading the Text	Extending the Text

◆ Includes language structure that children can say with some support.
◆ Contains many words known to these readers, so problem solving takes place against a backdrop of accurate reading.
◆ Contains words that can be solved with current skills.
◆ Contains words that can be solved with teacher support.
◆ Is appropriate in length and layout so that readers can use language, meaning, and visual information to monitor.
	The teacher helps students:
	◆ Predict and derive the overall meaning of the text and use this information to monitor and self-correct.
	◆ Use knowledge of language patterns (syntactic structures) to monitor and self-correct.
	◆ Think about how to problem-solve words while reading continuous text.
	◆ Rehearse difficult language patterns and realize that they will meet those patterns in the text as they read.
		The teacher helps students to (prompts them to):
		◆ Use multiple sources of information to monitor and self-correct.
		◆ Use meaning to check on whether the text makes sense.
		◆ Cross-reference one source of information with other sources.
		◆ Use visual information to monitor and self-correct reading.
		◆ Use many kinds of information in an orchestrated way.
		◆ Be flexible in accessing and using information systems to monitor and self-correct reading.
			The teacher helps students:
			◆ Attend to examples of processing that illustrate strategies, for example:
			  ◆ Self-correcting.
			  ◆ Rereading to search for meaning or syntactic support.
			  ◆ Anticipating meaning.
			  ◆ Monitoring for meaning.
			  ◆ Using visual information.
			◆ Understand from the teacher's explicit demonstrations that they should use effective strategies in their future reading.
				The teacher helps students:
				◆ Notice aspects of text that will be useful in monitoring and self-correcting reading in the future, for example:
				  ◆ Plot structure.
				  ◆ Text structure.
				  ◆ Aspects of character.
				  ◆ Language styles.
				  ◆ Language features.
				  ◆ Details in illustrations.

0 1 2 3 4 5	0 1 2 3 4 5	0 1 2 3 4 5	0 1 2 3 4 5	0 1 2 3 4 5

Overall Rating for Monitoring and Self-Correcting	Did the teacher help children develop item knowledge?	Did the teacher help children develop processing strategies?
0 1 2 3 4 5	0 1 2 3 4 5	0 1 2 3 4 5

3. Fluency and Phrasing

3. Readers maintain fluency and phrasing while reading continuous text. Readers connect the text with language and know how good reading sounds. They read at a good rate, slowing down and speeding up as appropriate. They read in phrase units and notice and use punctuation to help them in their expressive reading.

Text	Introducing the Text	Reading the Text	After Reading the Text	Extending the Text
◆ Contains features that support phrasing and fluency. ◆ Is engaging and interesting. ◆ Contains known words or words these readers can solve with help. ◆ Contains mostly words that do *not* require problem solving, making fluency possible. ◆ Provides for problem solving against a backdrop of accurate reading.	*The teacher helps students:* ◆ Gain and use the meaning of the whole text. ◆ Become aware of language structures and phrase units. ◆ Become aware of features of print such as layout to assist them in reading fluently. ◆ Attend to and use punctuation and its relation to phrasing or tone of voice. ◆ Raise their awareness of how reading is supposed to sound.	*The teacher helps students to (prompts them to):* ◆ Be aware of how their reading sounds. ◆ Use phrase units. ◆ Notice and use punctuation. ◆ Use expression to show interpretation of the author's meaning. ◆ Recognize known words quickly, using the information needed. ◆ Read at a good rate.	*The teacher helps students:* ◆ Revisit the text to notice features such as dialogue, layout, and punctuation. ◆ Appreciate fluent, phrased reading and how it contributes to good reading. ◆ Gain an internal definition of phrased fluent reading by hearing it. ◆ Practice reading with phrasing and fluency. ◆ Connect phrasing and fluency with the meaning of the text.	*The teacher helps students:* ◆ Practice fluency and phrasing through oral interpretation. ◆ Think about characters and how they would sound while extending the text through art or drama.
0 1 2 3 4 5	0 1 2 3 4 5	0 1 2 3 4 5	0 1 2 3 4 5	0 1 2 3 4 5

Overall Rating for Fluency and Phrasing	Did the teacher help children develop item knowledge?	Did the teacher help children develop processing strategies?
0 1 2 3 4 5	0 1 2 3 4 5	0 1 2 3 4 5

4. Word Solving

4. Readers problem-solve words on the run while reading continuous text. Readers slow down to problem-solve words and use a variety of strategies in a flexible way. Then, they speed up again. This problem solving takes place against a backdrop of accurate reading and does not destroy the momentum of the reading or the comprehension of the reader.

Text	Introducing the Text	Reading the Text	After Reading the Text	Extending the Text
◆ Contains words that are almost all known by children. ◆ Contains words that are almost all in the spoken vocabulary of children. ◆ Contains new vocabulary words that can be made available through a brief introduction. ◆ Contains new words that offer opportunities for problem solving using the strategies readers control. ◆ Contains new words that offer the opportunity for children to learn how words work and develop word-solving strategies.	*The teacher helps students:* ◆ Think about the meaning of words in the text that they will read. ◆ Say some of the words that will offer problem-solving opportunities because they are new. ◆ Become aware of or remember word-solving strategies that they can use to analyze new words. ◆ Focus on a few words as good examples rather than a large number of words. ◆ Attend to words, letters, and word parts that will assist them in solving words in many texts.	*The teacher helps students to (prompts them to):* ◆ Use word-solving strategies, including: 　◆ Letter/letter clusters. 　◆ Sound/letter relationships. 　◆ Beginnings and endings of words. 　◆ Word parts. 　◆ Known words. 　◆ Onset and rime. 　◆ Analogy. ◆ Check accuracy of words using multiple sources of information. ◆ Solve words using multiple sources of information.	*The teacher helps students:* ◆ Notice and be aware of word-solving strategies though clear, explicit examples. ◆ Notice aspects of words that are tricky or interesting. ◆ Develop vocabulary by revisiting new words in the text. ◆ Revisit word structure through visual analysis and connect with syntactic structure. ◆ Realize through examples from their own reading how to use word-solving strategies.	*The teacher helps students:* ◆ Use new words in other contexts for reading and writing. ◆ Extend their knowledge of words through studying their meaning or structure. ◆ Make collections of words in categories such as homonyms. ◆ Use sketching or other kinds of activities to illustrate words.
0 1 2 3 4 5	0 1 2 3 4 5	0 1 2 3 4 5	0 1 2 3 4 5	0 1 2 3 4 5

Overall Rating for Word Solving	Did the teacher help children develop item knowledge?	Did the teacher help children develop processing strategies?
0 1 2 3 4 5	0 1 2 3 4 5	0 1 2 3 4 5

Interactive Writing: A Scale for Analysis

The following scale is designed to be used by literacy coordinators in analyzing interactive writing lessons. The same rating rubric that was established for the guided reading analysis scale applies.

I. Composition: Planning

A planning function operates throughout the process of writing. Planning includes establishing a purpose for writing. Beyond purpose, planning involves using knowledge gained from past experience to shape the content, form, and function of the piece. Planning is activated during the experiences that precede and surround writing. It involves the ongoing learning experiences that help students establish purpose and be aware of the audience for the writing. Interactive writing to report results of a science experiment, for example, stimulates children from their observations of phenomena, from note taking, from discussion and synthesis of knowledge gained over time, and from exposure to appropriate reporting formats. For interactive writing, planning may involve a combination of direct experiences, literature sharing and discussion, and inquiry. Typically, a series of related experiences are involved. The planning function occurs throughout the lesson as teachers and students continually refer to the reason for writing, to the audience, to the information that should be included, and to the appropriate format for the piece.

Text	Preparing to Write	Composing the Text	Writing [Encoding] the Text	Extending the Text
The interactive writing text: ◆ Grows out of meaningful experiences. ◆ Involves ideas and topics students understand. ◆ Fulfills a real purpose.	**The teacher helps students:** ◆ Understand the purpose for the writing. ◆ Think about form in relation to purpose, genre, format. ◆ Remember what they've learned through experience, reading, and talk. ◆ Develop foundational knowledge to assist in composing the piece. ◆ Develop listening/speaking vocabulary related to content and purpose. ◆ Develop foundational knowledge of structure, organization, genre of text to be selected and used. ◆ Notice aspects of literary texts and informational texts that will form a foundation for composition.	**The teacher helps students:** ◆ Remember the content and larger purpose of writing. ◆ Keep audience and purpose in mind. ◆ Evaluate the composition in terms of purpose/audience. ◆ Think about aspects of text such as coherence, cohesion, clarity, and voice.	**The teacher helps students:** ◆ Remember the content, audience, and purpose while writing the text. ◆ Constantly evaluate the text in terms of overall purpose and audience. ◆ Revise while writing if needed for consistency with audience/purpose.	**The teacher helps students:** ◆ Reflect on the audience and purpose while rereading. ◆ Extend the text in light of the larger purpose. ◆ Evaluate the text in the light of the planning process. ◆ Think about overall content, purpose, and audience when planning extension.
0 1 2 3 4 5	0 1 2 3 4 5	0 1 2 3 4 5	0 1 2 3 4 5	0 1 2 3 4 5
Overall Rating for Composition: Planning 0 1 2 3 4 5	**Did the teacher help children develop item knowledge?** 0 1 2 3 4 5	**Did the teacher help children develop item knowledge?** 0 1 2 3 4 5	**Did the teacher help children develop processing strategies?** 0 1 2 3 4 5	**Did the teacher help children develop processing strategies?** 0 1 2 3 4 5

2. Composition: Deciding the Precise Text

Building on concrete and literacy experiences (composition: planning), the teacher engages children in conversation designed to compose a precise text that they will then write. There may be negotiation and discussion but it is specific to the type of text, the precise words, the layout of text, and the suitability of words, phrases, and sentences relative to the purpose for the writing. During composition, children will be referring back to the overall foundation of knowledge that is described in the planning function; however, the focus is on the particular words to use in *this* text.

Text	Preparing to Write	Composing the Text	Writing [Encoding] the Text	Extending the Text
The interactive writing text: ◆ Is one that the children can say. ◆ Is one that the children can remember. ◆ Is related to the content, purpose, and audience established during planning. ◆ Has potential for helping children learn about the writing process at text level.	*The teacher helps students:* ◆ Generate possible language from which they can draw during composition. ◆ Foreshadows the composition of the whole text through examples.	*The teacher helps students:* ◆ Recognize language that could be used in the text (through modeling). ◆ Generate alternative sentences and/or organizational structures and select from among them. ◆ Negotiate specific words, phrases, and sentences. ◆ Say the message several times to assist the memory. ◆ Make connections between this text and other texts they know. ◆ Connect text and illustrations (existing or planned). ◆ Think about how to start, events to use in sequence, and how to end. ◆ Monitor the length and characteristics of the text so children can write and read it.	*The teacher helps students:* ◆ Remember the composed text while writing it word by word. ◆ Return to the whole text while writing word by word. ◆ Evaluate layout of print as appropriate to purpose, audience, and the precise message.	*The teacher helps students:* ◆ Revisit the text to notice and evaluate choice of words, layout, and organization. ◆ Revise the text as needed to reflect the intent of the composition.
0 1 2 3 4 5	0 1 2 3 4 5	0 1 2 3 4 5	0 1 2 3 4 5	0 1 2 3 4 5

Overall Rating for Composition: Deciding What to Write	Did the teacher help children develop knowledge?	Did the teacher help children develop item	Did the teacher help children develop processing strategies?
0 1 2 3 4 5	0 1 2 3 4 5	0 1 2 3 4 5	0 1 2 3 4 5

3. Construction: How Print Works

Constructing a text refers to the actions that the teacher and children take to inscribe a composed message or story. Text construction includes writing the actual words, letter by letter; arranging words in space on the page; and using conventions such as space, capitalization, and punctuation to make the text readable. Constructing the text involves continuous conversation, within which children learn a specific vocabulary to talk about writing. For this analysis, think about the selection of format (appropriate to purpose), arrangement of print on the page, connection between print and illustrations, and print conventions. Children are learning to use the printer's code while at the same time keeping meaning and purpose in mind.

Text	Preparing to Write	Composing the Text	Writing [Encoding] the Text	Extending the Text
The interactive writing text: ◆ Is one that the children can say and remember while attending to layout and conventions. ◆ Is possible for the group of children to write or contribute to the writing. ◆ Presents opportunities for problem solving all aspects of written text. ◆ If there are pictures, has integrated illustrations and print.	**The teacher helps students:** ◆ Notice print layout and other aspects of text in those they hear read aloud. ◆ Talk about the kinds of texts (genres) that could be used for different purposes and the layout or structure related to each. ◆ Engage in shared reading of texts during which they notice print conventions (punctuation, spacing, etc.).	**The teacher helps students:** ◆ Compose a text that requires attention to print conventions (e.g., dialogue or question marks). ◆ While composing, think about the layout of print. ◆ Compose a text that requires problem solving about all aspects of text, including layout, punctuation, and connections to illustrations. ◆ Make decisions about layout/conventions appropriate to genre.	**The teacher helps students:** ◆ Make decisions about text layout. ◆ Shift from thinking about the message to considering conventions such as layout and punctuation and then shift back to message. ◆ Think about and make decisions about punctuation.	**The teacher helps students:** ◆ Revisit the text to remember the processes involved in constructing it (deciding on layout, use of punctuation, etc.). ◆ Reread the text to notice the way conventions were used, such as punctuation and words. ◆ Apply principles of construction (how print works) to their own writing.
0 1 2 3 4 5	0 1 2 3 4 5	0 1 2 3 4 5	0 1 2 3 4 5	0 1 2 3 4 5

Overall Rating for Construction: How Print Works	Did the teacher help children develop item knowledge?	Did the teacher help children develop processing strategies?
0 1 2 3 4 5	0 1 2 3 4 5	0 1 2 3 4 5

4. Construction: Word Solving

Constructing a text refers to the actions the teacher and students take to inscribe a composed message or story. Text construction includes writing the actual words, letter by letter; arranging words in space on the page; and using print conventions. For this analysis, think about children's learning the structure of words. Within interactive writing, children have the opportunity to participate in the construction of words that they do not yet know. Word solving takes place within the process of writing continuous text. It involves drawing students' attention to spelling principles so that they can learn how words work. It may involve teaching students to say words slowly and hear the sounds, notice visual feature of letters, notice letter clusters and patterns, link letters and sounds, connect words, think about relationships between meaning and spelling of words, and use references and resources.

Text	Preparing to Write	Composing the Text	Writing [Encoding] the Text	Extending the Text
The interactive writing text: ♦ Contains words that children can write or partially write with present strategies *and* teaching. ♦ Contains words that are used in conversation by the teacher or students. ♦ Offers opportunity to learn new words in a meaningful context. ♦ Contains words with patterns that illustrate principles. ♦ Contains word-solving challenges. ♦ Offers opportunity to make links with word walls, word charts, and other print in the classroom. ♦ Contains words students know and high frequency encountered/used words.	*The teacher helps students:* ♦ Use in conversation the range of words that will be useful. ♦ Notice words that are used in conversation by the teacher or students. ♦ Notice the words in books that are read aloud. ♦ Notice the structure of words in shared reading. ♦ Notice the structure of words while writing. ♦ Use life experience to broaden vocabulary. ♦ Use literary experience to broaden vocabulary. ♦ Use words in specific ways related to content or theme.	*The teacher helps students:* ♦ Compose a text that requires problem solving at the word level. ♦ Put words together in a sentence or longer text to express precise meaning. ♦ Within a sentence, generate alternative words and select from among them. ♦ Say the message several times to remember specific word construction. ♦ Make connections between the words they are using in the composition and words they have learned or studied (for example, word wall words). ♦ Where appropriate, link words they are using in the composition to words in other texts they know.	*The teacher helps students:* ♦ Shift from text level down to word level and back to text level without losing meaning. ♦ Say words slowly and connect sounds to letters and letter clusters within words. ♦ Attend to visual features of words, including word parts and spelling patterns. ♦ Make connections between words they know and new words they want to write. ♦ Solve words by analogy. ♦ Solve words using letters and sounds. ♦ Solve words using knowledge of visual patterns. ♦ Find words in other contexts (use references and resources) such as on the word wall. ♦ Solve words while remembering the whole text or a part of it.	*The teacher helps students:* ♦ Revisit the text to locate familiar words. ♦ Revisit the text to make connections between words. ♦ Revisit the text to notice letter-sound relationships. ♦ Revisit the text to notice visual (spelling) patterns. ♦ Revisit the text as a resource for words to use in other writing. ♦ Revisit the text to locate words that illustrate principles. ♦ Use words from the text in word study activities.
0 1 2 3 4 5	0 1 2 3 4 5	0 1 2 3 4 5	0 1 2 3 4 5	0 1 2 3 4 5

Overall Rating for Construction: Word Solving	Did the teacher help children develop item knowledge?	Did the teacher help children develop item knowledge?	Did the teacher help children develop processing strategies?
0 1 2 3 4 5	0 1 2 3 4 5	0 1 2 3 4 5	0 1 2 3 4 5

5. Reading/Writing Connections

Interactive writing provides a context for connecting reading and writing. The text that the children compose and write, with teacher assistance, is intended to be read. Interactive writing is used to build up a large collection of readable texts that children can refer to and use as resources throughout the school year. While composing the text, children think about reading it. Children reread the text *while* constructing it, *after* writing it, and on an ongoing basis. Reading/writing connections are made at the word level and at the text level. In general, the interactive writing text that children can read after construction and shared reading is a more difficult text than children would be expected to read on their own in books. The interactive writing text is a more complex narrative or expository text than children can read alone.

Text	Preparing to Write	Composing the Text	Writing [Encoding] the Text	Extending the Text
The interactive writing text: ♦ Is readable with the high support of text reading. ♦ Has syntactic patterns that the children can say independently or with teacher support. ♦ Has words that are in children's speaking/listening vocabulary. ♦ Is meaningful to children. ♦ Is based on children's ideas and contributions.	**The teacher helps students:** ♦ Build experience and vocabulary that will be needed to read the text. ♦ Bring understanding of content, ideas, texts, or events to the composition of the text. ♦ Realize that the text they produce must be readable for themselves and for others. ♦ Talk about experiences in a way that will help them bring meaning to the rereading of the text.	**The teacher helps students:** ♦ Compose a text that will be readable. ♦ Think about the text they compose from the point of view of a reader. ♦ Use books as models when appropriate. ♦ Connect to other books they have heard read aloud. ♦ Connect to books they have read. ♦ Connect to other pieces of interactive writing that they have produced and reread many times.	**The teacher helps students:** ♦ Reread while writing to recapture the meaning and language structure of the composed message. ♦ Use reading strategies during rereading that will assist writing. ♦ Use early reading behavior such as word-by-word matching, rereading to search using meaning, structure, and visual cues. ♦ Engage in the reading process while rereading text.	**The teacher helps students:** ♦ Reread the text through shared reading. ♦ Be conscious of and demonstrate fluent, phrased reading (expressiveness). ♦ Reread the text in different formats (chart, pocket chart). ♦ Use the text for independent reading ("reading around the room," duplicated versions of the text, sentence strips, etc.). ♦ Compare and contrast this piece to other interactive writing pieces or other texts they have read or heard read. ♦ Analyze the text to think about how it provides meaning. ♦ Apply understandings about the text they have written and are reading to other reading and writing tasks.
0 1 2 3 4 5	0 1 2 3 4 5	0 1 2 3 4 5	0 1 2 3 4 5	0 1 2 3 4 5
0 1 2 3 4 5	**Did the teacher help children develop item knowledge?** 0 1 2 3 4 5	**Did the teacher help children develop item knowledge?** 0 1 2 3 4 5	0 1 2 3 4 5	**Did the teacher help children develop processing strategies?** 0 1 2 3 4 5

Overall Rating for Reading/Writing Connections

0 1 2 3 4 5

Observation of Guided Reading

Observer: _____   Teacher: _____   Date: _____

Grade: _____   Number of Children in Group: _____

Preparation	Independent Activities
Text selected: Level: Notes:	Number: Engagement¹: **1 2 3 4** Types represented:

Introduction of Text	Engagement: **1 2 3 4**	Start: End:
Teacher's Language	*Children's Language*	*Other Observations*

Reading the Text	Engagement: **1 2 3 4**	Start: End:
Teacher's Language	*Children's Language*	*Other Observations*

After Reading the Text	Engagement: **1 2 3 4**	Start: End:
Teacher's Language	*Children's Language*	*Other Observations*
Word Work:		
Extension/Assignment:		

¹RUBRIC FOR ENGAGEMENT: 1 = Only a few children are on task and attending to intruction. There are many distractions, including noise and movement. Instruction is severely undermined. 2 = About half of the children are on task and attending to the instruction, but there are many distractions, including noise and movement. Instruction is undermined. 3 = Most of the children are on task and attending to the instruction. There are occasional distractions and some children are moving about. Instruction, in general, is being provided most of the time. 4 = Almost all children are on task and attending to the instruction. Instruction is being provided most of the time. There are only a few distractions.

General Aspects of Teaching

Lesson: _____

Teacher: _____ **Grade Level:** _____ **Date of Lesson:** _____

Observer: _____ **Scale¹** _____

	Rating	Notes
Materials The teacher has materials well organized and available for use in an efficient way during the lesson.	0 1 2 3	
Organization The teacher is prepared, and the lesson flows efficiently from one activity to another.	0 1 2 3	
Time The teacher uses sufficient time appropriate for each component of the lesson.	0 1 2 3	
Pace The teacher makes maximum use of time by keeping the lesson moving; there is limited "down time."	0 1 2 3	
Intensity The teacher is actively teaching on some important aspect of learning throughout the lesson and teaches in a persistent and intensive way.	0 1 2 3	
Feedback/Praise The teacher provides specific feedback of a positive nature; negative feedback is constructive and specific.	0 1 2 3	
Interaction The teacher actively encourages the children to interact, respond, participate, ask questions, and volunteer comments.	0 1 2 3	
Engagement The teacher involves the children in the designated task(s), holding their interest and attention throughout the lesson.	0 1 2 3	
Enthusiasm Through verbal and nonverbal actions, the teacher conveys interest in and enthusiasm for the activity.	0 1 2 3	
Rapport Through verbal and nonverbal actions, the teacher conveys a warm, affectionate, and positive attitude toward children.	0 1 2 3	

¹Scale: 0 = Not at all true—needs demonstration, teaching and support to achieve basic level; 1 = True sometimes—needs improvement; 2 = True most of the time—needs some refining; 3 = Consistently true throughout the lesson—an excellent model for this aspect of teaching.

Reflection Prior to Classroom Visit
A Guide for Thinking About Coaching

Observer: _____   **Date:** _____

Teacher: _____   **Grade:** _____

Think about:
- What kinds of questions does the teacher ask you?
- What are some of the confusions the teacher expresses?
- Are there differences between the way the teacher talks and what you observe in the classroom?
- What kinds of behavior provide evidence of teachers' strengths and skills in classroom work?
- What does the teacher say about children? To what degree does he/she describe children's behavior as evidence of learning?

The goal is to create a context in which "good dissonance" can take place. Criticism is offered in a constructive and positive way through nonthreatening conversations.

Make notes in response to the questions below:

1. What are your perceptions of the teacher's strengths?	
2. What do you think the teacher needs to learn **next** (conceptually) to reach another level of understanding?	
3. What are the teacher's **own** perceptions of his/her strengths and needs?	

Notes from preconference:

Observation of Lessons

Teacher/Grade: _____   Focus of Instruction: _____

Observer: _____   Date: _____   Time: _____

Teacher	Student(s)	Notes/Questions

Potential topics for discussion:

Use of Time, Engagement, Routines

Observer: _____

Date: _____

Classroom/Teacher: _____

Grade: _____

School: _____

Number students: _____

Instructions. Note exact time an instructional activity starts. Change to new instructional activity any time the teacher changes focus, moves to a new area with different materials, moves the students, or signals in some way that the instructional activity is changing. For example, when a teacher at the easel changes from reading aloud to interactive writing, this requires a new line. For a "transition" (for example, when students are moving from one area to another, sharpening pencils, getting materials, etc.), use a line, write *transition* as the instructional activity, and note the time started.

The STARTING TIME for each new instructional activity noted is also the ENDING TIME for the previous instructional activity. This form accounts for every minute of class time, with no gaps between the instructional activities noted on the lines. A guided reading or interactive writing lesson should be noted in this guide, with the time started. Then, switch to the form for that activity. This form should reflect the appropriate box and time for guided reading and interactive writing. The INSTRUCTIONAL ACTIVITY describes whatever the teacher and students are doing—individually or as a group. ESTABLISHED ROUTINES are those activities that you note as being routines of instruction or procedures for student behavior.

Rubric for engagement:
1 = Only a few students are on task and attending to the instruction. There are many distractions, including noise and movement. Instruction is severely undermined.
2 = About half of the students are on task and attending to the instruction, but there are many distractions, including noise and movement. Instruction is undermined.
3 = Most of the students are on task and attending to the instruction. There are occasional distractions, and some students are moving about. Instruction, in general, is being provided most of the time.
4 = Almost all students are on task and attending to the instruction. Instruction is being provided almost all of the time. There are only a few distractions.

Time Started	Engagement	Instructional Activity	Note Established Routines
	1 2 3 4		
	1 2 3 4		
	1 2 3 4		
	1 2 3 4		
	1 2 3 4		

Time Started	Engagement	Instructional Activity	Note Established Routines
	1 2 3 4		
	1 2 3 4		
	1 2 3 4		
	1 2 3 4		
	1 2 3 4		
	1 2 3 4		
	1 2 3 4		
	1 2 3 4		
	1 2 3 4		

Name: _____   **Date:** _____

Notes: **Lesson:**

Action Plan

_____

_____

_____

_____

_____

_____

Observer: _____

Name: _____   **Date:** _____

Notes: **Lesson:**

Action Plan

_____

_____

_____

_____

_____

_____

Observer: _____

Block Form

Adams, M. J. 1990. *Beginning to Read: Thinking and Learning About Print*. Cambridge: MIT Press.

Allington, R. L. 1991. "Children Who Find Learning to Read Difficult: School Responses to Diversity." In *Literacy for a Diverse Society*, edited by E. H. Hiebert. New York: Teachers College Press.

Allington, R. L., and P. M. Cunningham. 1996. *Schools That Work: Where All Children Read and Write*. New York: HarperCollins.

Allington, R. L., and S. A. Walmsley. 1995. *No Quick Fix: Rethinking Literacy Programs in America's Elementary Schools*. New York: Teachers College Press; Newark, DE: International Reading Association.

Ambach, G. 1996. "Standards for Teachers: Potential for Improving Practice." *Phi Delta Kappan* 78: 207–10.

Anderson, R. C., P. T. Wilson, and L. C. Fielding. 1988. "Growth in Reading and How Children Spend Their Time Outside of School." *Reading Research Quarterly* 23 (summer): 285–303.

Askew, B. J., I. C. Fountas, C. A. Lyons, G. S. Pinnell, and M. C. Schmitt. 1999. *Reading Recovery Review: Understandings, Outcomes, and Implications*. Columbus, OH: Reading Recovery Council of North America.

Askew, B. J., and Gaffney, J. S. 1999. "Reading Recovery: Waves of Influence on Literacy Education." In *Stirring the Waters: The Influence of Marie Clay*, edited by J. S. Gaffney and B. J. Askew, 75–98. Portsmouth, NH: Heinemann.

Atwell, N. 1998. *In the Middle: New Understandings About Writing, Reading, and Learning*. 2d ed. Portsmouth, NH: Heinemann.

Barth, R. S. 1990. *Improving Schools from Within*. San Francisco: Jossey-Bass.

Booth, D. 1999. "Language Delights and Word Play: The Foundation for Literacy Learning." In *Voices on Word Matters: Learning About Phonics and Spelling in the Literacy Classroom*, edited by I. C. Fountas and G. S. Pinnell, 91–102. Portsmouth, NH: Heinemann.

Bradley, L., and P. E. Bryant. 1983. "Categorizing Sounds and Learning to Read: A Casual Connection." *Nature* 301: 419–21.

Brown, J. S., A. Collins, and P. Duguid. 1989. "Situated Cognition and the Culture of   Learning. *Educational Researcher* 18: 32–42.

Bruner, J. S. 1973a. *Beyond the Information Given: Studies in the Psychology of Knowing*. Ontario, CA: Penguin.

———. 1973b. "Organization of Early Skilled Action." *Child Development* 44 (2): 1–11.

———. 1990. *Acts of Meaning*. Cambridge: Harvard University Press.

Bryant, P. E., M. MacLean, L. Bradley, and J. Crossland. 1990. "Rhyme and Alliteration, Phoneme Detection, and Learning to Read." *Developmental Psychology* 26 (3): 429–38.

Bussell, J. 2000. "A Study of the Role of Teacher Leaders as Key Personnel in Scaling Up Reading Recovery as an Educational Innovation." Ph.D. dissertation. Columbus: The Ohio State University.

Ceprano, M. A. 1980. "A Review of Selected Research on Methods of Teaching Sight Words. *The Reading Teacher* 35: 314–22.

Chall, J. S. 1989. "Learning to Read: The Great Debate Twenty Years Later." *Phi Delta Kappan* 70: 521–38.

Christopher, M. 1992. *Challenge at Second Base*. New York: Little Brown.

Clay, M. M. 1975. *What Did I Write?* Portsmouth, NH: Heinemann.

———. 1991. *Becoming Literate: The Construction of Inner Control*. Portsmouth, NH: Heinemann.

———. 1993a. *An Observation Survey of Early Literacy Achivement*. Portsmouth, NH: Heinemann.

———. 1993b. *Reading Recovery: A Guidebook for Teachers in Training*. Portsmouth, NH: Heinemann.

———. 1998. *By Different Paths to Common Outcomes*. York, ME: Stenhouse.

Cochran-Smith, M. 1984. *The Making of a Reader*. Norwood, NJ: Ablex.

Coerr, E. 1993. *Meiko and the Fifth Treasure*. New York: Bantam Doubleday Dell.

———. 1993. *Sadako and the Thousand Paper Clowns*. New York: Bantam Doubleday Dell.

Costa, A. L., and R. J. Garmston. 1994. *Cognitive Coaching*. Norwood, MA: Christopher-Gordon.

Darling-Hammond, L. 1996. "What Matters Most: A Competent Teacher for Every Child." *Phi Beta Kappan* 78 (3): 193–200.

———. 1997. *The Right to Learn: A Blueprint for Creating Schools That Work*. San Francisco: Jossey-Bass.

Darling-Hammond, L., and B. Falk. 1997. "Using Standards and Assessments to Support Student Learning." *Phi Beta Kappan* 79 (3): 190–201.

Darling-Hammond, L., and M. W. McLaughlin. 1996. "Policies That Support Professional Development in an Era of Reform." In *Teacher Learning: New Policies, New Practices*, edited by M. McLaughlin and I. Oberman, 202–18. New York: Teachers College Press.

Dewey, J. J. 1904. "Significance of the School of Education." *The Elementary School Teacher* 4: 441–53.

———. 1916. *Democracy and Education*. New York: MacMillan.

———. 1938. *Experience and Education*. New York: MacMillan.

Duckworth, E. 1996. *The Having of Wonderful Ideas and Other Essays on Teaching and Learning*. New York: Teachers College Press.

Ehri, L. C. 1991. "Development of the Ability to Read Words." In *Handbook of Reading Research*, vol. 1, edited by R. Barr, M. Kamil, P. Mosenthal, and P. D. Pearson, 383–417. New York: Longman.

Ehri, L. C., and L. S. Wilce. 1985. "Does Learning to Spell Help Beginners Learn to Read Words?" *Reading Research Quarterly* 22: 47–65.

Fountas, I. C., and G. S. Pinnell. 1996. *Guided Reading: Good First Teaching for All Children*. Portsmouth, NH: Heinemann.

———. 1998. *Matching Books to Readers: Using Leveled Books in Guided Reading K–3*. Portsmouth, NH: Heinemann.

———. 2000. *Guiding Readers and Writers Grades 3–6: Teaching Comprehension, Genre, and Content Literacy*. Portsmouth, NH: Heinemann.

Freeman, E. B., and D. G. Person. 1998. *Connecting*

Informational Children's Books with Content Area Learning. Needham Heights, MA: Allyn and Bacon.

Friend, M., and L. Cook. 2000. *Interactions: Collaboration Skills for School Professionals.* New York: Longman.

Frost, R. 1993. *The Road Not Taken, and Other Poems.* New York: Dover.

Fullan, M. G. 1985. "Change Processes and Strategies at the Local Level." *The Elementary School Journal* 84 (3): 391–420.

———. 1993. *Change Forces.* New York: Falmer Press.

Fullan, M. G., and A. Hargraves. 1991. *What's Worth Fighting for in Your School?* Toronto, Ontario: Ontario Public Schools Teachers Federation; Andover, MA: The Network.

Garmston, R., and B. Wellman. 1999. *The Adaptive School: A Source for Developing Collaborative Groups.* Norwood, MA: Christopher-Gordon.

Goodlad, J. 1984. *A Place Called School: Prospects for the Future.* New York: McGraw-Hill.

Gratz, D. B. 2000. "High Standards for Whom?" *Phi Delta Kappan* 81: 681–87.

Halliday, M. A. K. 1975. *Learning How to Mean: Explorations in the Development of Language.* London: Edward Arnold.

Hargreaves, A. 1994. "Restructuring Restructuring: Postmodernity and the Prospects for Educational Change." In *Teacher Development and the Struggle for Authenticity,* edited by P. Grimmett and J. Neufeld, 52–82. New York: Teachers College Press.

Hartley, S., and S. Armstrong. 1997. *Animal Homes.* New York: Scholastic.

Harwayne, S. 1999. *Going Public: Priorities & Practice at the Manhattan New School.* Portsmouth, NH: Heinemann.

Henderson, E. H. 1990. *Teaching Spelling.* 2d ed. Boston: Houghton Mifflin.

Henry, J. 1999. "Becoming a Writer: Learning Through Interactive Writing." In *Voices on Word Matters: Learning About Phonics and Spelling in the Literacy Classroom,* edited by I. C. Fountas and G. S. Pinnell, 37–44. Portsmouth, NH: Heinemann.

Howe, J. 1999. *Pinky and Rex and the Spelling Bee.* New York: Simon and Schuster.

Hundley, S., and D. Powell. 1999. "Investigating Letters and Words Through Shared Reading." In *Voices on Word Matters: Learning About Phonics and Spelling in the Literacy Classroom,* edited by I. C. Fountas and G. S. Pinnell, 155–69. Portsmouth, NH: Heinemann.

Johnston, P. 1997. *Knowing Literacy: Constructive Literacy Assessment.* York, ME: Stenhouse.

Joyce, B., and B. Showers. 1980. "Improving Inservice Training: The Message of Research." *Educational Leadership* 37 (5): 379–85.

———. 1982. "The Coaching of Teaching." *Educational Leadership* 40 (1): 4–16.

———. 1995. *Student Achievement Through Staff Development.* White Plains, NY: Longman.

Kagan, R. 1982. *The Evolving Self: Problems and Process in Human Development.* Cambridge: Harvard University Press.

Knoblock, P., and A. P. Goldstein. 1971. *The Lonely Teacher.* Boston: Allyn and Bacon.

Lambert, L., D. Walker, D. P. Zimmerman, J. E. Cooper, M. D. Lambert, M. E. Gardner, and P. J. Ford-Slack. 1995.

The Constructivist Leader. New York: Teachers College Press.

Lampert, M. 1999. "How Do Teachers Manage to Teach? Perspectives on Problems in Practice." In *The Complex World of Teaching: Perspectives from Theory and Practice,* edited by E. Mintz and J. T. Yun, 255–72. Cambridge, MA: Harvard Educational Review.

Lieberman, A. 1996. "Practices That Support Teacher Development: Transforming Conceptions of Professional Development." In *Teacher Learning: New Policies, New Practices,* edited by M. W. McLaughlin and I. Oberman, 185–201. New York: Teachers College Press.

Lieberman, A., and L. Miller. 1999. *Teachers Transforming Their World and Their Work.* New York: Teachers College Press.

Lindfors, J. 1999. *Children's Inquiry: Using Language to Make Sense of the World.* New York: Teachers College Press; Urbana, IL: National Council of Teachers of English.

Lyons, C. A. 1999. "Letter Learning in the Early Literacy Classroom." In *Voices on Word Matters: Learning About Phonics and Spelling in the Literacy Classroom,* edited by I. C. Fountas and G. S. Pinnell, 57–66. Portsmouth, NH: Heinemann.

———. 2000. "Developing Collaborative Literacy Teams." In *Collaboration for Diverse Learners: Viewpoints and Practices,* edited by V. Risko and K. Bromley, 168–87. Newark, DE: International Reading Association.

Lyons, C. A., and G. S. Pinnell. 1999. "Teacher Development: The Best Investiment in Literacy Education." In *Stirring the Waters: The Influence of Marie Clay,* edited by J. Gaffney and B. Askew, 302–31. Portsmouth, NH: Heinemann..

Lyons, C. A., G. S. Pinnell, and D. E. DeFord. 1993. *Partners in Learning: Teachers and Children in Reading Recovery.* New York: Teachers College Press.

McCarrier, A. M., and I. Patacca. 1994. "Children's Literature: The Focal Point of an Early Literacy Learning Program." In *Extending Charlotte's Web,* edited by B. Cullinan and J. Hickman, 189–206. Norwood, MA: Christopher-Gordon.

McCarrier, A. M., G. S. Pinnell, and I. C. Fountas. 2000. *Interactive Writing: How Language and Literacy Come Together, K–2.* Portsmouth, NH: Heinemann.

McGovern, A. 1999. *Secret Soldier: The Story of Deborah Sampson.* New York: Scholastic.

McLaughlin, M. W., and I. Oberman, eds. 1996. *Teacher Learning: New Policies, New Practices.* New York: Teachers College Press.

Moll, L. 1990. *Vygotsky and Education.* New York: Cambridge University Press.

Noddings, N. 1997. "Thinking About Standards." *Phi Delpa Kappan* 79 (3): 184–89.

Paulson, G. 1989. *The Winter Room.* New York: Bantam Doubleday Dell.

Pavlov I. P. 1941. "Lectures on Conditioned Reflexes." In *Conditional Reflexes and Psychiatry,* vol. 2, translated by W. H. Gantt. New York: International.

Pearson, P. D., and L. Fielding. 1991. "Comprehension Instruction." In *Handbook of Reading Research,* vol. 2, edited by R. Barr, M. Kamil, P. Mosenthal, and P. D. Pearson, 815–60. New York: Longman.

Piaget, J. 1955. *The Child's Construction of Reality.* London: Routledge and Kegan Paul.

———. 1959. *The Language and Thought of the Child.* London: Routledge and Kegan Paul.

Pinnell, G. S., and I. C. Fountas. 1998. *Word Matters: Teaching Phonics and Spelling in the Reading/Writing Classroom.* Portsmouth, NH: Heinemann.

———. 1999. *Matching Books to Readers: Using Leveled Books in Guided Reading, K–3.* Portsmouth, NH: Heinemann.

Pinnell, G. S., and C. A. Lyons. 1999. "Literacy Coordinator as Instructional Leader: The Development of Technical Knowledge and Skill." Paper presented at the American Education Research Association, Toronto, CA.

Pinnell, G. S., J. J. Pikulski, K. K. Wixson, J. R. Campbell, P. B. Gough, and A. S. Beatty. 1995. "Listening to Children Read Aloud: Data from NAEP's Integrated Reading Performance Record (IRPR) at Grade 4." Report No. 23-FR-04, prepared by the Educational Testing Service. Washington, DC: Office of Educational Research and Improvement, U.S. Department of Education.

Pressley, M. 1998. *Reading Instruction That Works: The Case for Balanced Teaching.* New York: Guilford Press.

Resnick, L. B. 1989. *Knowing, Learning, and Instruction.* Manwah, NJ: Lawrence Erlbaum.

———. 1999. *New Standards: Reading and Writing Grade by Grade.* Washington, DC: National Center on Education and the Economy.

Risko, V., and K. Bromley, eds. 2000. *Collaboration for Diverse Learners: Viewpoints and Practices.* Newark DE: International Reading Association.

Rosenshine, B. and R. Stevens. 1984. "Classroom Instruction in Reading." In *Handbook of Reading Research,* vol. 2, edited by R. Barr, M. Kamil, P. Mosenthal, and P. D. Pearson, 745–98. New York: Longman.

Rowe, K. J. 1995. "Factors Affecting Students' Progress in Reading: Key Findings from a Longitudinal Study." *Literacy, Teaching, and Learning: An International Journal of Early Literacy* 1: 57–110.

Sarason, S. B. 1982. *The Culture of the School and the Problem of Change.* 2d ed. Boston: Allyn and Bacon.

———. 1990. *The Predictable Failure of Educational Reform: Can We Change Course Before It's Too Late?* San Francisco: Jossey-Bass.

Schon, D. 1983. *The Reflective Practitioner.* New York: Basic Books.

Senge, P. 1990. *The Fifth Discipline: The Art and Practice of the Learning Organization.* New York: Doubleday.

Senge, P., Cambron-McCabe, N., Lucas, T., Smith, B., Dutton, J., and A. Kleiner. 2000. *Schools That Learn: A Fifth Discipline Fieldbook for Educators, Parents, and Everyone Who Cares About Education.* New York: Doubleday.

Sizer, T. 1992. *Horace's School: Redesigning the American High School.* Boston, MA: Houghton Mifflin.

Skinner, B. F. 1953. *Science and Human Behavior.* New York: MacMillan.

Snow, C. E., M. Burns, and S. Griffin, eds. 1998. *Preventing Reading Difficulties in Young Children.* Washington, DC: Committee on the Prevention of Reading Difficulties in Young Children, Commission on Behavioral and Social Sciences.

Steffe, L., and J. Gale. 1995. *Constructivism in Education.* Manwah, NJ: Lawrence Erlbaum.

Tello, J. 1994. *Amalia and the Grasshopper.* New York: Scholastic.

Thorndike, E. L. 1913. *Educational Psychology.* New York: Columbia University Teachers College.

Torgeson, J. K., R. K. Wagner, and C. A. Rashotte. 1997a. "Approaches to the Prevention and Remediation of Phonologically Based Reading Disabilities." In *Foundations of Reading Acquisition and Dyslexia: Implications for Early Intervention,* edited by B. Blachman, 287–304. Mahwah, NJ: Lawrence Erlbaum.

———. 1997b. "Prevention and Remediation of Severe Reading Disabilities: Keeping the End in Mind." *Scientific Studies of Reading* 1: 217–34.

Vellutino, F. R., and D. B. Scanlon. 1987. "Phonological Coding, Phonological Awareness, and Reading Ability: Evidence from a Longitudinal and Experimental Study." *Merrill Palmer Quarterly* 33: 321–63.

Vygotsky, L. S. 1978. *Mind in Society.* Cambridge: Harvard University Press.

Williams, E. J. 1999. *Literacy Collaborative 1999 Research Report.* Columbus, OH: The Ohio State University.

Williams, E. J., and P. Scharer. 2000. *Literacy Collaborative 2000 Research Report.* Columbus, OH: The Ohio State University.

Wilson, K. G., and C. K. Barsky. 1998. "Applied Research and Development: Support for Continuing Improvement in Education." *Daedelus: Journal of the American Academy of Arts and Sciences* 127 (4): 233–58.

Wilson, K., and B. Daviss. 1994. *Redesigning Education.* New York: Henry Holt.

Wise, A. E., and J. A. Leibbrand. 2000. "Standards and Teacher Quality: Entering the New Millennium." *Phi Delta Kappan* 81: 612–21.

Index